Grocery E-Commerce

Consumer Behaviour and Business Strategies

Edited by

Niels Kornum
Copenhagen Business School, Denmark

Mogens Bjerre
Copenhagen Business School, Denmark

Edward Elgar
Cheltenham, UK • Northampton, MA, USA

Published by
Edward Elgar Publishing Limited
Glensanda House
Montpellier Parade
Cheltenham
Glos GL50 1UA
UK

Edward Elgar Publishing, Inc.
136 West Street
Suite 202
Northampton
Massachusetts 01060
USA

A catalogue record for this book
is available from the British Library

Library of Congress Cataloguing in Publication Data

Grocery e-commerce : consumer behaviour and business strategies / edited by
    Niels Kornum, Mogens Bjerre.
        p. cm.
    Includes index.
    ISBN 1-84542-298-8
    1. Selling–Groceries. 2. Electronic commerce 3. Grocery shopping. I.
    Kornum, Niels, 1955- II. Bjerre, Mogens, 1959-

HF5439.G75G76 2005
381'.41–dc22   2005046190

ISBN 1 84542 298 8

Printed and bound in Great Britain by MPG Books Ltd, Bodmin, Cornwall

Contents

List of Figures	*vii*
List of Tables	*ix*
List of Contributors	*xi*
Preface	*xiv*

1. Grocery E-Commerce – Consumer Behaviour and Business Strategies: An Introduction
   Niels Kornum and Mogens Bjerre — *1*

2. Competing for the Online Grocery Customer: The UK Experience
   Muriel Wilson-Jeanselme and Jonathan Reynolds — *7*

3. To Pay or Not to Pay, That is the Question. Conceptual Model and Empirical Results on Consumers' View on Home Delivery
   Herbert Kotzab and Christoph Teller — *36*

4. Household Desires on Home Delivery: An Empirical Study on Attended Reception of Convenience Goods
   Bengt Nordén — *58*

5. A Comparison of In-Store vs. Online Grocery Customers
   Andrea M. Prud'homme and Kenneth K. Boyer — *79*

6. Understanding Consumer Adoption of Online Grocery Shopping: Results from Denmark and Sweden
   Torben Hansen and Suzanne C. Beckmann — *97*

7. Behind the Values: Understanding Consumer Behaviour and E-Grocery Business from a Dialectic Culture Perspective
   Christine Sestoft — *122*

8. Effective E-Grocery Logistics
   Hannu Yrjölä and Kari Tanskanen — *160*

9. Cost Drivers and Profitability of DC Based Grocery Home Delivery Systems
   Niels Kornum and Mads Vangkilde — *183*

10. A Reality Check on E-Grocery Delivery Options – The Swedish Case
    Elisabeth Karlsson — *204*

11. Packaging Trends for E-Commerce Shipments in the United
States: A Focus on Perishables!   *230*
S. Paul Singh

12. First-Movers in the E-Grocery Sector – A Framework for
Analysis   *241*
Mads Vangkilde

13. Innovative Opportunities and Strategies for Online
Transactions   *276*
Peder Inge Furseth

14. The Future of Grocery E-Commerce – Will Business be Able
to Meet Customer Needs and How?   *294*
Niels Kornum and Mogens Bjerre

Index   *320*

Figures

2.1	Indexed growth in e-commerce sales, US-UK 2000-2004	*8*
2.2	Internet advertising per capita, US/UK	*8*
2.3	Choice task example	*16*
2.4	The preference of offline and online shoppers	*20*
2.5	Ordering time utility curve for online grocery shoppers	*22*
2.6	Latent classes for online shoppers	*24*
2.7	'As I ordered it' segment	*25*
2.8	Latent classes for offline shoppers	*26*
2.9	Time conscious segment for offline shoppers	*27*
3.1	Dimensions of consumer logistics	*38*
3.2	Home delivery model	*41*
3.3	Shopping frequency	*45*
3.4	Use of means of transport	*47*
3.5	Estimated transportation costs	*49*
3.6	Willingness to pay	*50*
6.1	Diagrammatic representation of the obtained results	*116*
7.1	Model of political consumption discourse	*133*
7.2	The specific state-form and life-mode consumption theory	*134*
7.3	Model of new business from a behind the values perspective	*148*
8.1	The costs of the local distribution centre	*171*
8.2	Home delivery cost structure	*174*
8.3	The EGS downstream cost structure	*177*
9.1	Model of analysis	*188*
9.2	Impact of order size on profitability	*189*
9.3	Break-even of e-grocers	*197*
9.4	E-grocers' cost categories	*198*
9.5	Delivery fee size to break-even	*199*
10.1	The development of e-grocery in Sweden	*206*
10.2	E-grocery delivery options	*209*
10.3	Delivery cost per order	*217*
12.1	First-mover disadvantages	*252*
12.2	The conceptual framework	*260*
12.3	The analytical framework	*260*
13.1	The two phases of multi-channel retailing	*278*

13.2   The number of online orders among the companies in 2003
       compared with 2004   *287*
13.3   Conversion rate among the companies in 2003 compared with
       2004   *288*
13.4   Comparison of amounts of consumer purchases for online
       retailing and travel in Norwegian kroner   *290*
13.5   Customer satisfaction when buying online: a comparison of
       three industries   *291*

Tables

2.1	Attributes and level of attributes used for the main survey	*14*
2.2	Utilities for offline grocery shoppers	*17*
2.3	Calculation of the weighting of each attribute for offline grocery shoppers	*18*
2.4	The preference structure given by the weighting of each attribute for the offline grocery shoppers group	*18*
2.5	The preference structure given by the weighting of each attribute for online grocery shoppers	*19*
2.6	The data used to test the hypothesis	*21*
2.7	Choosing the right number of segments	*23*
2.8	Order-winning and -qualifying criteria	*25*
2.9	Preferences of offline shopper segments	*27*
2.10	Reference contrasts between on- and offline shoppers	*28*
3.1	Specific differences between the examined retail formats for consumer logistics	*43*
3.2	Research design	*44*
3.3	Spatial and temporal distance	*46*
3.4	Results of hypotheses testing	*51*
3.5	Multi-regression model	*53*
4.1	Household characteristics and shopping behavior	*69*
4.2	Household attitudes towards delivery methods	*70*
4.3	Share of households not wanting to receive goods on a certain day of the week	*72*
4.4	Share of households preferring to receive goods during a certain time period	*72*
4.5	Share of households that would use home delivery if there was no charge when shopping amount exceeds 500 SEK	*73*
4.6	Share of households that would use home delivery if the charge was 60 SEK	*74*
5.1	Descriptions of participating grocers	*86*
5.2	Descriptions of data collection methods	*88*
5.3	Selection criteria	*89*
5.4	Service quality	*90*
5.5	Product quality	*91*

5.6	Behaviors	*92*
6.1	Confirmatory factor model results	*108*
6.2	Discriminant validity of constructs	*109*
6.3	Construct means and standard deviations	*110*
6.4	Classification results	*111*
6.5	Summary of multiple discriminant results	*112*
6.6	Respondent characteristics	*114*
7.1	Respondents characteristics	*139*
8.1	Delivery concepts of some existing e-grocers	*163*
8.2	Summary of the major characteristics of the alternative models	*170*
8.3	Different service models analysed	*173*
8.4	The implications of customer order-based operation for the middle and upstream operations of the supply chain	*176*
9.1	Price of transportation per order	*190*
9.2	Price of picking and packing per order	*191*
9.3	Percentage of total sales of other warehouse handling costs	*192*
9.4	Correlation between sales revenue and square meters	*193*
9.5	Percentage of total sales of warehouse facility costs	*194*
9.6	Percentage of total sales of warehouse investment depreciation	*194*
9.7	Percentage of total sales of administrative costs	*195*
9.8	Percentage of total sales of other administrative costs	*196*
9.9	Percentage of total administrative costs of sales revenue	*196*
10.1	Evaluated delivery options	*212*
10.2	Parameter values	*213*
10.3	Scenarios for evaluated delivery options	*214*
10.4	Synopsis of evaluation results	*215*
10.5	Descriptive statistics of the participant and respondent profile	*219*
10.6	Customers' valuation of different delivery options	*222*
10.7	Customers' attitudes towards different ways of financing reception boxes	*224*
12.1	Assessing perceived value of resources	*258*
13.1	Strategy suggestions based on the innovative opportunities	*286*

Contributors

Dr. Suzanne C. Beckmann is Professor in the Department of Intercultural Communication and Management, Copenhagen Business School. Her research interests are in integrated communication management, strategic planning and market orientation, consumption studies and consumer behaviour in (post)modern consumer society, methodological developments in marketing research, and corporate social responsibility.

Mogens Bjerre is associate professor in the Department of Marketing, Centre for Retail Studies, Copenhagen Business School. Retail business formats and the organization of retail concepts have been a focal point of his research over the past 10 years, as have the marketing activities of manufacturers vis-à-vis retailers.

Kenneth K. Boyer is an associate professor of supply chain management in the Department of Marketing and Supply Chain Management and director of the Last Mile Supply Chain Center at Michigan State University. He is the co-author of the book *Extending the Supply Chain*.

Dr. Peder Inge Furseth is associate professor in the Department of Innovation and Economic Organisation, Norwegian School of Management BI. The topics of innovation and competition in the distributive and service sectors have been central to his research. Furseth currently researches on multichannel retailing and banking sponsored by a dozen Scandinavian companies.

Torben Hansen is associate professor in the Department of Marketing, Consumer Research Group, Copenhagen Business School. His main fields of research are consumer behaviour and marketing research methods. He has conducted research and published books for both practitioner and academic audiences and has contributed to various journals.

Elisabeth Karlsson is a PhD student in the Department of Business Administration, Logistics and Transport Research Group, School of Economics and Commercial Law, Göteborg University. Her PhD research focuses on efficiency in logistics systems for groceries, with a particular focus on the impact of e-commerce.

Niels Kornum is associate professor in the Department of Marketing, Centre for Retail Studies, Copenhagen Business School. The topic of grocery e-commerce has been a focal point of his research for nearly a decade, including several projects in collaboration with the grocery and e-grocery business.

Herbert Kotzab is a professor in the Department of Operations Management at the Copenhagen Business School. His main research focus comprises Supply Chain Management of retailing companies and interorganizational business processes in hypercompetitive industries.

Bengt Nordén is a senior lecturer in the Department of Business Administration, School of Economics and Commercial Law at Göteborg University, Sweden. His main research field is consumer aspects on logistics delivery systems and the promotion of e-commerce to consumers.

Andrea M. Prud'homme is a PhD candidate in the Department of Marketing and Supply Chain Management at Michigan State University. Her research interests include international business, quality management, customer satisfaction, and 'last mile' logistics.

Jonathan Reynolds is Director of the Oxford Institute of Retail Management, a Fellow of Templeton College and University Lecturer at the Said Business School, University of Oxford. He has been actively involved in e-commerce research for over twenty years, specialising in the marketing and strategy aspects of the topic, and has published widely.

Christine Sestoft is an ethnologist and a doctoral student in the Department of Marketing, Consumer Research Group, Copenhagen Business School. The topic of her PhD project is society and new (political) modes of consumer behaviour based on a case-study within grocery e-commerce. Focal research themes are culture, politics and consumption in consumerist societies.

S. Paul Singh is a Professor at Michigan State University. He has researched on-line shopping and the impact of packaging in making this business segment successful. He has been engaged in several industry sponsored projects since 1998 and examined packaging and order fulfillment challenges for a range of products including perishables.

Kari Tanskanen is a professor in the Department of Industrial Engineering and Management, Helsinki University of Technology. During last 15 years he has led several big research projects in the area of logistics and supply chain management. He was the leader of the ECOMLOG research programme that focused on the logistical challenges of e-commerce, especially in the grocery sector.

Christoph Teller is assistant professor in the Department of Retailing and Marketing, Vienna University of Economics and Business Administration. His main research focus comprises consumers' role within distribution channels seen from a logistical and a behavioural point of view.

Mads Vangkilde is a PhD student in the Department of Marketing, Centre for Retail Studies, Copenhagen Business School. Coming from a position at IBM as a Project Manager, Mads is researching, teaching and now publishing within the area of (grocery) e-business. Finishing his PhD in the first quarter 2006, his contributions allow an early look at things to come.

Muriel Wilson-Jeanselme is a doctoral student in the Said Business School and a member of Templeton College. Her research on consumer attitudes towards grocery e-commerce adoption is part of a wider study addressing marketing strategy effectiveness among a range of e-commerce product and service providers.

Hannu Yrjölä is executive director of the BIT Research Centre at Helsinki University of Technology. E-grocery has been the most important of his personal research interests since 1997. It combines Information Technology and Logistics, his main competence areas.

Preface

E-commerce in general has obtained much attention in textbooks and other academic literature. *Grocery e-commerce,* on the other hand has only been one out of many other perspectives when e-commerce in general has been examined. This is only natural, since e-commerce covers a wide range of topics. Still, grocery e-commerce differs from other types of consumer goods in a number of aspects for example low margin business, low value density of products and high frequency purchases. Thus, these specific characteristics have to be accounted for, in order to understand what this business is all about and why grocery home delivery is so difficult to implement.

In order to address this lack of focus on the specific conditions for the e-grocery business, a workshop entitled the *First international workshop on consumer behaviour and distribution in the e-grocery sector* was held 24 and 25 May 2004 at Copenhagen Business School. The objective of the workshop was to gather researchers from countries with extensive business experience in implementing grocery home delivery systems. Selected papers presented at this workshop are the backbone of this book and represent empirical research from the USA, the UK, the Nordic countries and Austria. We want to thank Copenhagen Business School and Department of Marketing for their support to implement this workshop and the contributing authors, Tina Hindsbo and Daniel B. Stuhr for their commitment to advance this book without delay.

The main ideas behind arranging this workshop originated from a research and innovation programme called Ebizz Oresund. This programme endured from 2001 to 2004 and examined the barriers and prospects for grocery e-commerce in a cross-country collaboration between firms and researchers in Sweden and Denmark (http://ebizzoresund.teknologisk.dk Danish only). The programme was co-founded by the Swedish government agency Vinnova and the Danish Ministry of Science, Technology and Innovation. We wish to thank these authorities, and the partnering firms, for their support to the research that enabled the workshop and further on also this book to materialise.

Last, but not least, we want to thank our families for their encouragement and support in the process of creating this book.

Copenhagen, June 2005

1. Grocery E-Commerce – Consumer Behaviour and Business Strategies: An Introduction

Niels Kornum and Mogens Bjerre

The pioneering e-grocers have learned some harsh initial lessons trying to become profitable. Webvan, as one of the more extreme examples, failed for rather obvious reasons. They invested more than 800 million[1] dollars in infrastructure, despite having relatively few customers. But many others with far more modest investment rates also have ceased operations, for example Streamline (US), Rema Hem til Dig[2] (Norway), Matomera[3] (Sweden), ISO Telekøb[4] and Super Best (Denmark). However, with the appearant success of Tesco.com, it would *not* be fair to suggest that the e-grocery business will never be profitable at all. A more reasonable question is: Under what conditions will this business model be profitable?

Even today, a very small proportion of the total grocery turnover is from online sales. Thus, online grocers are confronted with a number of challenges, but two of these seem to be crucial to the industry: 1) The online industry, like the offline industry, needs efficient handling and volume to reach break-even, because the two industries face the same conditions of relatively low margins and a low value- and logistically demanding assortment. This, however, does not necessarily correspond to the behaviour and needs expressed by the consumers, for example, are they willing to pay a delivery fee? 2) Do consumers find the offline shops more attractive than online shops and which parameters do they consider important? To what extent does their viewpoint impede the online grocery industry's possibilities for growth?

The e-grocer needs efficient operations and thus, in principle, she/he wants to offer as narrow an assortment as possible, sell groceries in as large order sizes as possible, and collect delivery fees to cover some of the costs. From the outset, the interests of consumers are opposed to the interest of the online grocery providers. They want as large an assortment as possible and free delivery of small and fresh portions as often as possible.

What then are the prospects for the e-grocery business to meet customers' needs? The *first theme* of this book addresses consumer behaviour issues. Questions as to how the consumers assess the advantages/disadvantages of the offline versus the online store are relevant. Do consumers evaluate the offline shop as advantageous in so many areas that this seriously impedes the prospects of the e-grocery business? One of the potential disadvantages of grocery e-commerce is often reported to be that the customers pay a delivery fee for home delivery. Still, to what extent do consumers think that delivery fees are fair and are they willing to pay these fees?

The *second theme* in this book focuses on business strategies related to e-grocers. From a firm internal perspective, both efficiency and cost considerations, for example simulation and ABC costing studies, are important. Studies of the network surrounding the e-grocer include studies of the competitive environment of the firm, as this can create value and barriers for the future development of the e-grocer.

From this background, the research in this book will focus on BTC e-commerce or home shopping or home delivery in the grocery sector. This includes ordinary grocery shopping, provided that this shopping channel is compared with online grocery shopping. The studies presented in the book include two overarching themes.

THEME 1: CONSUMER DECISION PROCESSES AND SOCIO-CULTURAL CONTEXTS

The decision and adaptation process involved in consumers' online shopping concerns the steps from initial awareness to potential online sales. The result of the adaptation process as experienced by the consumer and the perceived post-purchase advantages/disadvantages will influence whether for example the online consumer will make repeat purchases online. The decision process of the grocery online consumer is embedded in a social and cultural context that influences both the content of decisions and the processes as such. Lifestyles, work habits, family and friendship networks and the like all on impact the perception and behaviour related to on- and offline grocery shopping.

The company and country where grocery e-commerce has had its greatest successes is Tesco.com, in the UK. *Chapter 2,* contains a study where the *UK experience* addresses the question: Which online offering will be most attractive for acquiring customers and then retaining them? Here the authors *Wilson-Jeanselme and Reynolds* present a choice-based conjoint analysis of both online and offline grocery shoppers in the southeast of the UK.

Consumer preferences are compared to and contrasted between off- and online shoppers and the customer's preference for selected online grocery offerings is identified.

The success of e-grocers in other markets has been modest to non-existent. Why is that? Unfortunately no direct scientifically based comparisons between the UK and other countries are available in order to answer this question once and for all. The authors of Chapter 1 point anecdotally to increasing difficulties of accessibility and 'over-crowded British High Streets' in larger cities as two factors motivating consumers to use the online alternative. Whatever the reason for the differences between the UK and other countries in this respect may be Tesco.com seems to be successful in convincing the customers that a delivery fee is necessary, and as it turns out the delivery fee seems to make up the difference between profit and deficit. The e-grocers in other countries seem to have had less luck convincing consumers to pay the fee.

In line with this, *Kotzab and Teller* in *Chapter 3* ask why consumers apparently prefer offline to online shopping and why or why not consumers are willing to *pay a delivery fee*? They present the results from face-to-face interviews with customers visiting two Austrian outlets: a do-it-yourself category killer and a grocery supermarket. How do these consumers evaluate the benefits and sacrifices when their existing shopping in physical shops is compared to a presented online shopping system with specific characteristics? The willingness to pay a delivery fee is also an issue raised by Kornum and Bjerre in *Chapter 14* and *Nordén* in *Chapter 4*. The results that Nordén presents are based on a questionnaire sent to households in four residential areas in a city in Sweden.

Besides analysing the delivery fee issue, Nordén also investigates the consumers' preferences related to *delivery method* (home delivery, delivery at work or traditional shopping) and the timing of delivery. To the pioneers of grocery e-commerce, these issues were more or less a trial-and-error process, whereas recent initiatives can be informed by research.

Karlsson in *Chapter 10* also addresses issues related to delivery method, specifically customers' demands and preferences regarding the service characteristics of delivery options for e-grocery, based on a focus group study and a web survey. The focus group study was based on customers from two e-grocers and the web survey was based on three e-grocers operating in two Swedish cities.

Besides the delivery method, home delivery may also differ from shopping in an ordinary physical shop with regard to other aspects. Thus, customers who use an online channel may have differing perceptions of service and product quality from their in-store counterparts. From this background, *Prud'homme and Boyer* in Chapter 5 intend to determine if and how these two customer segments differ. The examined customers origin from three grocers who provide both online services and in-store shopping in physical shops.

In *Chapter 6* the perspective widens from the customers of selected firms to consumers in general. Thus, in a web survey *Hansen and Beckmann* here examine the *determinants of Danish and Swedish consumers' online grocery adoption processes*. The authors focus on whether adopters of online grocery shopping adopters associate higher compatibility, higher relative advantage, lower risk, and lower complexity with Internet grocery shopping as compared with (a) consumers who have never bought anything on the Internet and *also* when compared to (b) consumers who have purchased goods/services on the Internet, but not groceries.

Whereas Chapter 6 examines the purchasing process, *Chapter 7* focuses on how the grocery online consumer is embedded in a social and cultural context that influences both the content of decisions and the processes as such. Specifically, *Sestoft* suggests that it is fruitful to examine the values of the grocery online consumers from a cultural perspective. In applying this perspective, Sestoft wishes to answer the question of whether the present configuration of online grocery businesses has a future – and if not, why? And could it be made more attractive to contemporary consumers? The study is based on 10 in-depth interviews with Danish respondents who are experienced online grocery consumers.

THEME 2: BUSINESS STRATEGY AND DISTRIBUTION

One of the main problems of e-commerce in the grocery sector is that only very few firms have been able to make a profit. Thus, it is important to identify the main cost drivers of the business and address the question of how to balance the needs expressed by consumers and the resources used by the firm as a consequence of these generated needs. Another aspect of being a pioneering firm in relation to e-commerce is whether these firms can maintain their position in the long-term. As already mentioned, the online groceries have had substantial problems making a profit from their e-commerce business. A crucial element in this effort is to reduce costs to a level that is balanced with the turnover. The reason for this is clearly that both the off- and online business is very labour intensive with regard to shops/call centres, warehousing and transport operations. How could these operations be made more efficient, and which distribution and packaging strategies should these firms apply?

According to *Yrjölä and Tanskanen* in *Chapter 8,* logistics is an important reason for poor profitability in the e-grocery sector. Significant problems in managing both information and material flows have been identified, thus leading to extreme logistics costs and low value to customers. The chapter describes recent international developments in the e-grocery business and summarizes the findings of the Finnish Ecomlog project. Research results are presented that evaluate the prospects of shop-versus DC-based systems and the implications for supply and distribution from a wider supply chain perspective. Furthermore, the findings from a cost analysis comparing attended and unattended home delivery are presented, along with calculations of distribution centre costs in a home delivery system. Both transport (home delivery) and distribution centre costs seem to be crucial parameters when assessing the prospects of the e-grocery sector being or becoming profitable. In line with this, *Kornum and Vangkilde* in *Chapter 9* identify the cost drivers and model the profitability of a DC-based grocery home delivery system founded on both Danish industry data and secondary international sources. They model a system with free delivery, average order sizes that equal sizes experienced by the existing industry, and unattended delivery without delivery boxes or the like, which has been proven to work by a Danish e-grocer. Based on this, the authors reveal under which conditions such a system will break-even or be profitable. In *Chapter 10, Karlsson* examines typical cases of delivery options and the cost per order by means of a routing and scheduling tool. The study is based on real order data from the customer database of a major e-grocer and cost data from one of the leading distribution companies in Sweden with experience of e-grocery home delivery. The delivery method studied was attended home delivery and the two options were two versus three time windows for deliveries between 1 and 9 pm on weekdays. An integrated part of delivery is packaging and in *Chapter 11, Singh* describes the packaging trends for US e-commerce shipments and presents the parameters that are critical in the development of optimum packaging for fresh produce to be sold by e-commerce directly to the consumer. Packaging considerations are crucial because fresh produce requires careful protection from the physical and climatic changes in the shipping environment.

Cost structures and profitability considerations related to distribution and delivery are important short-term issues for the e-grocers. But what are the longer-term strategic considerations? One crucial question is to what extent the pioneering e-grocers incur a first-mover advantage. In *Chapter 12, Vangkilde* addresses this issue from a conceptual perspective. He outlines the concept by reviewing the theory of the Resource-Based View of the firm (RBV) and Resource Dependency Theory (RDT), and incorporates these theories into a model that outlines the interrelatedness of a focal online first-mover with off- and online competitors and customers. The author plans to apply the model to the e-grocery sector in Denmark.

In *Chapter 13, Furseth* examines the strategies implemented by 11 selected e-commerce companies in Norway, including five traditional retailers and grocery items. The author identifies the strategies the managers used and why they chose them. In addition, customers of these companies were interviewed in order to identify their preferences, online shopping rate and conversion rate. The study includes different business categories and e-commerce formats retailers, banks or transactional websites (ticket sales) and examines to what extent customer preferences vary accordingly.

CONCLUSION, FUTURE PROSPECTS AND RESEARCH

In *Chapter 14*, the editors summarise findings and evidence primarily from this book. What are the preferences of the customers/consumers and what strategic and operational initiative is recommended for businesses to implement? Also, variances in conditions between pure players versus bricks & clicks as one dimension, and the online grocery supermarket versus the specialty e-grocer as another dimension are reported. Finally, future research prospects are outlined.

NOTES

1. *Chicago Tribune* 18 July, 2001, 'What killed Webvan was bricks, not clicks', by Jorge Rufat Latre.
2. 'Rema Home to You' if directly translated
3. 'Food and Extras' if directly translated
4. 'ISO Tele Shopping' if directly translated

2. Competing for the Online Grocery Customer: The UK Experience

Muriel Wilson-Jeanselme and Jonathan Reynolds

UNDERSTANDING THE GROWTH OF ONLINE RETAILING IN THE UK

Over the last two years, the UK has become something of a showcase for online retailing: plaudits for having the world's largest online grocer in the form of Tesco.com; surprise at the growth of online retail sales compared to those in the USA, (Figure 2.1), including those of a number of existing retail businesses; and enthusiasm that the amount of Internet advertising is growing as fast, if not faster, than in the USA. In fact, 3.2% of all advertising spending in the UK is now online (Interactive Advertising Bureau, 2004) (Figure 2.2).

Why has e-commerce grown at a faster rate in the UK than even in the USA? We suggest that there are three reasons (Reynolds, 2003). First, UK consumers' expenditure as a whole has been particularly buoyant over the past five years, growing at an average annual rate of 3.5% per annum (National Statistics, 2004). A number of product categories have benefited from this growth, including sales of computing, electrical and electronic goods. This stands in stark contrast to the other large European economies and the variable performance in the USA. Secondly, we detect a degree of dissatisfaction with the conventional offline offer in the UK. This is not so much in terms of choice or price, which have become more competitive – especially in a period of low inflation but in terms of the increasingly poor accessibility of conventional retail space, particularly at peak shopping periods, such as Christmas. Finally, selectively strong domestic web site growth combined with US online business targeting the UK market first means that UK consumers benefit from a 'double investment' by web businesses (Reuters, 2004).

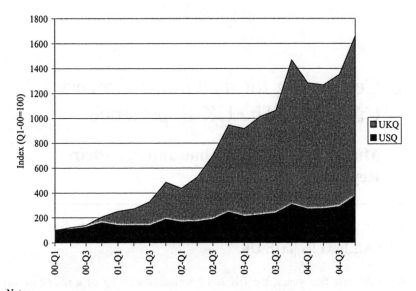

Notes:
Both series are by value and were re-based and re-indexed in US$ at £1=$1.85. In Q4/04, total
retail sales were: $987bn (USA) $130 billion (UK) (13%). Total online sales were: $21.4 billion
(USA) $7.6 billion (UK) (35%). Online sales as a % total sales were 2.2% (USA) 5.8% (UK).

Sources: IMRG (UK); US Department of Commerce.

Figure 2.1 Indexed growth in e-commerce sales, USA-UK 2000-2004

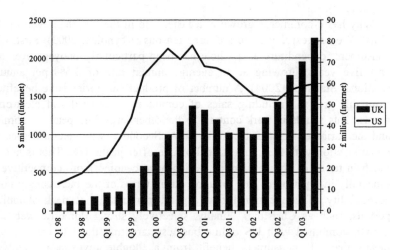

Sources: Interactive Advertising Bureau, the Advertising Association.

Figure 2.2 Internet advertising per capita, USA/UK

THE INDIRECT EFFECT OF E-COMMERCE ON CONSUMER BEHAVIOUR

Faster growth, however, also means that UK retailers need to understand the ways in which the Internet affects the perceptions of the consumer much more rapidly than in other markets. And these effects are not always directly apparent. We know, for example, that many so-called high involvement goods, such as brown or white goods or cars, tend to prompt substantial information search activity by consumers before purchase (Reynolds, 2002; Keen et al., 2004). Conventionally, this has been undertaken through word-of-mouth, the reading of hard copy reviews and showroom visits, as consumers build up a set of choices. The Internet of course adds a new dimension to this process by substantially enriching consumers' product and price awareness.

The consequences for retail buying behaviour are complex. For example, do consumers 'reward' particularly informative retailer web sites by making a purchase? Not always, particularly when price comparison is an issue. US research suggests that some 71% of 'informed consumers' browsed online 'sometimes or often' before subsequently buying in a store (UCLA, 2003). (Conversely, around 10% of US online consumers used stores as showrooms, before buying online.) In the UK, according to Forrester Research, 50% more consumers indicated that they undertook product research regularly than those who made purchases online. And the halo effect of such behaviour is substantial. Forrester estimated the value of European offline sales (sales made to online browsers subsequently in offline stores) to be worth €83 billion across Europe at the end of 2002. One of the strategies that multi-channel retailers must therefore learn is that of online conversion, or of subsequent conversion in the store. UK catalogue shop retailer Argos' Click and Collect service does just this by allowing customers to reserve products online at their local store until the end of the following working day (www.argos.co.uk).

The Indirect Effect on Prices

There has been a spirited debate about the effects of the Internet on price levels (Sinha, 2000; Baker et al., 2001). Early commentators saw the Internet as a final opportunity to prove the so-called 'law of one price': that identical goods should sell for the same price throughout the world if trade were free and frictionless. The consequences for marketers, they argued, would be 'fierce price competition, dwindling product differentiation, and vanishing brand loyalty' (Kuttner, 1998). These were strong claims and the implications for marketers were significant. But does the evidence of five or more years of serious e-commerce activity bear out the claims? The early evidence was unclear. Many researchers did see on average lower prices online than offline for identical goods, notably books and CDs. (Brynjolfsson and Smith, 2000) But they also noted similar price ranges (dispersion between the highest and lowest prices) to those prevailing offline, contrary to what the law of one price might suggest. They blamed this dispersion on two main factors. First, consumers were too lazy, impatient, or poorly informed to search beyond the first two or three sites. Secondly, consumers showed a lack of trust in new online retail brands offering the same products at lower prices. And this effect has persisted. Price dispersion in 2000 for both retail and e-tail markets was shown to be comparable to that observed in 1976 (Brynjolfsson and Smith, 2000).

More recent work has suggested that it is marketers themselves who have helped this process, by creating the obfuscation necessary to prevent a levelling down of prices, through line extension; re-packaging and re-launches of products (Reynolds, 2003). Simply put, consumers find it difficult to find and compare like with like in many situations and it is not in most retailers' interest for this situation to change.

So should retail marketers relax? We argue not. Whilst price dispersion online may well persist, online consumers are becoming more confident. Work by the Interactive Media in Retail Group shows that the online sales of electrical consumer goods were up 38% in July 2004 on the previous year, for example (Interactive Media in Retail Group, 2004c). VISA Europe observed: 'people are becoming as comfortable online as they are in the High Street' (Bottellier, 2004). Hand in hand with growing confidence comes greater price awareness perhaps not in specific like-for-like comparative terms, but in more general terms. Online consumers become more aware of the upper and lower price limits for particular kinds of goods. Whilst they may not be willing or able to make painstakingly detailed comparisons, they will inevitably become more sensitive to issues of price and more alert to the merits or otherwise of pricing claims made by retailers both on- and offline. We already know that many consumers are inclined to believe that the selling price of a product is substantially higher than its 'fair' price would be. The debate takes on an extra dimension in the context of a low inflationary or even deflationary environment, where for some categories of goods it is already difficult to raise prices because of the greater visibility of the increase.

The Indirect Effect on Brands

Such increased awareness puts pressure on retail brands. Whilst some consumers' confidence in online buying has increased, what has also become clear from recent research is that online consumers still use brand as a proxy for retailer credibility in areas ranging from shipping reliability to after-sales service (Burt and Sparks, 2003; Reynolds, 2002, 2003). Indeed, brands like Amazon, Barnes and Noble and Borders appear to be able to support an online price premium among consumers, even when the price differences are made explicit by price comparison engines. If premiums can be supported here, then it suggests that greater premiums are sustainable in product categories that are more heterogeneous.

But retail brands appear to have to work increasingly hard to convince consumers of the justification for whatever price premium they seek to command. In the case of those established retail brands that have historically relied upon store atmosphere and image to reinforce the claims they make, the Internet offers a much 'thinner' medium for the retail theatre that characterises the offer in certain kinds of business. The web as a medium is more rational and less emotional than retail marketers might like. It is no accident that the upscale UK department store sector, for example, is relatively poorly and generally ineffectively represented among retail sites. Further, the choice criteria that consumers use to make selections online are different from those employed offline (Keen et al., 2004; Lee and Tan, 2003; Szymanski and Hise, 2000). There may be new brand variables to be considered – speed and reliability of delivery, for example; as well as factors that do not make the cut – such as location, or level of personal service. As a result the retail brand on the web may be able to draw upon fewer cues than the store channel to reliably communicate brand values – or be unable to rely upon consumers' in-store experience. A conventional retailer seeking a complementary web site presence may also find that presenting itself consistently will cause problems. Those companies making claims never to be 'undersold', or beaten on price (such as the UK John Lewis Partnership, for example) have found such claims difficult to extend to their web sites.

THE DEVELOPMENT OF TESCO.COM

Not all traditional UK retailers have participated in the growth described above. Just seven companies are understood to have accounted for 50% of the annual investment of £100million made in 2003 by the top 100 UK retailers (Interactive Media in Retail Group, 2004b). One of these is Tesco.com, which achieved UK sales of £719 million in 2004–05 and delivered 150,000 customer orders per week. It is the biggest grocery online retailer in the world, with activities in the US, Ireland and South Korea. This is a fast growing and profitable business with sales up 24% in the last year and which generated £36 million profit in 2004–05, up from £28m the previous year. Tesco.com offers over 40,000 grocery products, as well as electrical, entertainment and baby products. Tesco.com claims to be profitable in its main grocery category. For the parent business, Tesco.com contributes some 2.5% of UK sales – £2 million per day.

According to Tesco, Tesco.com has around 1 million customers who place an average of 21,000 orders a day. According to Nielsen NetRatings, almost 55% of Tesco.com shoppers are men and over 80% of Tesco.com shoppers are aged between 25 and 49 years of age. The operation continues to grow. Online traffic monitor, Hitwise, reported in 2004 that Tesco.com's online traffic increased by 27% in the eight months to August (Retail Bulletin, 2004)

Tesco.com infiltrates the existing store network, maximising capacity utilisation and benefiting from the sunk costs of an established infrastructure. Orders are picked at local stores, using a paperless picking system, which has enabled Tesco to reach over 90% of the UK population. Deliveries are made in two-hour time windows chosen by the customer between 10 a.m. and 10 p.m., for a variable fee dependent upon delivery time.

As part of their focus on customer loyalty across all channels, the same loyalty card is used in both Tesco and Tesco.com, allowing customer points to be accrued regardless of the channel chosen. Head Office also logs all customer feedback and interviews 1,000 Tesco.com shoppers every three months.

> The success of our Internet shopping service is reflected by the results of our most recent customer surveys, in which 98% of customers stated that they would re-use the service. Now we have to collect and analyse information online, and that is imperative in continuing to serve the customer effectively in the future. (Carolyn Fowler, Customer Relationship Manager, Tesco.com)

The Tesco brand acts as the unifying feature of the Tesco service irrespective of channel and the Tesco Clubcard provides a seamless information flow from shoppers: assisting in the identification and development of detailed customer segments, which may well be multi-channel. By definition, common buying and merchandising functions service both physical and virtual channels. From this established base, the brand has been extended into a series of virtual warehouses for categories of product that are not available (and for which there is no space) in store.

Analysts estimate that the existing store network has the capacity to allow online sales to grow to between £1.4–1.5 billion before more radical solutions are required. Tesco.com has had a first-mover advantage within the UK grocery marketspace, but there is a growing amount of competition for this revenue from both traditional and non-traditional sources. It remains to be seen how its online market share (some 45% of the UK online grocery market) will withstand the growth of competitive offers from Sainsbury, Asda and Waitrose.

UK CONSUMER REACTIONS TO THE OFFERINGS OF ONLINE GROCERY RETAILERS

Which online offering will prompt consumers to choose one supermarket's web site over another when making the final choice to buy groceries online? In the light of rapid e-commerce growth in the UK and the particular success of Tesco.com, it is this question that occupies the remainder of this chapter. To investigate this question, we have examined consumers' preferences using a range of techniques (Hair et al., 1998). The first step we performed was to calculate a set of consumer utility values of Internet capabilities for online shoppers and offline shoppers using choice-based conjoint techniques (http://www.sawtoothsoftware.com). These consumer utility values were then used in formal testing of customer acquisition and retention based hypotheses. The second step was to perform a latent class analysis in order to identify consumers with similar in-group preferences. Finally simulations were performed and share of preference for the Tesco online offering was analysed between online (retention) and offline shoppers (acquisition).

Calculating Consumer Utility Values

Qualitative interviews were conducted first in order to identify which attributes are important for consumers before quantitative field work was performed. Ten in-home 45-minute qualitative interviews were conducted with a random sample of consumers from an independent school chosen as representative of the research population. Ten attributes were selected to include in the choice-based survey based on the theoretical background and primary qualitative data. Each attribute was divided into two or three levels to refine their meanings. Table 2.1 presents these attributes and their levels.

The choice-based conjoint study also used respondents drawn from the parents of independent school pupils.[1] Respondents were primarily women. This population was chosen because they potentially represented high net worth families who may be time constrained but technologically aware. In addition they were likely to be a homogeneous group along the axis of similar life cycle stage, social activities, and in terms of attractiveness to grocery retailers. Their income profiles would suggest that they buy a higher proportion of high margin products and services. Following a paper-based pilot study of one independent school, which yielded a 19.8% response rate, the main survey focused on parents in four further independent schools and was administered electronically. The schools were located in Surrey and South West London and were independent schools to ensure a homogeneous sample, where house prices, income profiles and cultural preferences of participating parents would be similar.

Table 2.1 Attributes and level of attributes used for the main survey

	Level 1	Level 2	Level 3
1. Special offer section	Has a special offer section	No new special offer section	
2. New product section	Has a new products section	No new products section	
3. Help line number	Help line no	No help line number	
4. Delivery time	Delivered in 6 hours	Delivered in 24 hours	Delivered in 48 hours
5. Delivery cost	No delivery cost	£5 delivery cost	
6. Delivery time reliability	Delivery at agreed time	Delivery an hour early or late	
7. Quality	No items below quality	5 items below quality	
8. Ordering time	20 minutes to place an order	35 minutes to place an order	1 hour to place an order
9. Substitutes	No substitutes	5 substitutes	
10. Discount on Internet prices	0% discount on Internet prices	10% discount on Internet prices	

For reasons of efficiency and to generate a higher response rate it was decided to carry out the main survey via the Internet using Sawtooth software.

The questionnaire was in two parts. The first section had questions on loyalty behaviours and demography (value of their house, dual or single income, how many times they shopped online in a year, etc.). The respondents were women from 27 to over 50 years old, comprising a mixture of working and non-working mothers who had between 1 and 3 children. A number of modifications were carried out following the pilot to increase the internal consistency of the questionnaire and its structure.

In the main survey, four other independent schools were chosen. Deliberate random sampling was not undertaken as each family in this homogeneous population (defined as all four schools) was equally accessible and had an equal probability of being selected.[2] In total the main survey achieved 261 completed questionnaires. The actual number of questionnaires returned was much higher but some were considered incomplete if one screen or one question was not completed. The useable response rate was 12.7%, but this could have been increased by reducing the number of choice tasks. The choice tasks were displayed in the form of fourteen screens and a number of respondents stopped at ten screens. These responses were considered to be unusable and 12% of returned questionnaires were rejected for this reason. The gross response rate was in the order of 25%. Using a priori estimates of standard errors for attribute levels with 258 respondents and total choice tasks of 3096 shows that the efficiency of any attribute level ranges from 0.9991 to 0.9998. This test of design efficiency shows that the realised useable response rate poses limited scope for design threats to validity. Hair et al., (1998) suggest that design validity problems only begin to emerge at a response level of less than 130 for designs with average numbers of choice tasks, attributes and levels. Conjoint designs are generally more robust than other multivariate techniques in terms of sample size effects on validity (Hair et al., 1998).

For validation purposes, two fixed holdout tasks were included (Hair et al., 1998). These were the only two choice tasks constant across all respondents as the other tasks were randomised. There was a 99% fit between the holdout samples and the main survey data. Figure 2.3 shows an example of one of the 12 choice task screens.

If the fundamental issue with regard to acquiring consumers is the ability to understand their perceived value of the online transaction, this prompts the question: 'What will persuade offline shoppers to choose a certain online supermarket over another one when making the final decision to shop online for groceries?' The criterion or criteria that prompt consumers to make their decision is what Hill (2000) calls order winning criteria. Once these have been identified, managers will need to provide the best possible performance against them to secure the consumer's business. Hill (2000) has also identified what he terms order-qualifying criteria. These are criteria against which the company will need to provide an adequate, but not necessarily the best service, in order to be considered as a viable service provider. To identify order-winning criteria of offline shoppers, Logit analysis was used (see Appendix 1). This analysed the choice results of consumers, estimating a utility for each level of each attribute. Only main effects were included.

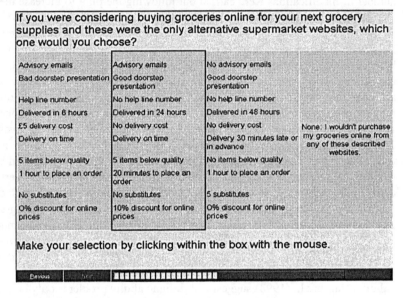

Figure 2.3 Choice task example

Table 2.2 summarises the utility for each level of each attribute for the offline grocery shoppers group. The utilities sum to 0 within each attribute (zero-centred).

This table shows the utility for each attribute level, where a utility is a measure of relative desirability. When computing utilities using Logit analysis, every attribute level is assigned a utility also referred to as a part-worth (Hair, et al., 1998). The higher the utility, the more desirable is the attribute level. For example the level '20 minutes to place an order' has a utility of 0.52. This high utility level means it has a large positive impact on influencing respondents, that is, potential consumers, to choose this online offering as compared to a low utility level such as '35 minutes to place an order'. It is therefore useful to compare utility levels within attributes to find out which level has the greatest impact on influencing consumers. However at this stage it is not possible to apply this comparison between attributes.[3]

Table 2.2 Utilities for offline grocery shoppers

	Attribute level	Utility
1.	Has a special offer section	0.10
1.	No special offer section	−0.10
2.	Has a new product section	0.00
2.	No new product section	−0.00
3.	Help line number	0.01
3.	No help line number	−0.01
4.	Delivered in 6 hours	0.40
4.	Delivered in 24 hours	0.00
4.	Delivered in 48 hours	−0.40
5.	No delivery cost	0.29
5.	£5 delivery cost	−0.29
6.	Delivery at agreed time	0.22
6.	Delivery an hour early or late	−0.22
7.	No items below quality	0.58
7.	5 items below quality	−0.58
8.	20 minutes to place an order	0.52
8.	35 minutes to place an order	0.15
8.	1 hour to place an order	−0.67
9.	No substitutes	0.30
9.	5 substitutes	−0.30
10.	0% discount	−0.24
10.	10% discount	0.24

The next step is to determine the weighting of each level of each attribute. The objective is to determine the relative importance of each attribute and to quantify it. Each attribute's absolute utility level difference is expressed as a proportion of the total of the 10 attributes' absolute differences. The results are shown in tables 2.3 and 2.4.

Table 2.4 clearly shows the preference structure of offline shoppers. The two order-winning criteria are ordering time followed by quality. The gap between 'ordering time' and the strongest order-qualifying criterion, namely 'delivery time', is 9.61%. It therefore seems safe for a company to strategically position itself against the two strong order-winning criteria to acquire consumers and thereby increase online market share. To ensure that this is the right decision, market simulation could show by how much the company's share of consumer preference will drop if it does not provide the best service in delivery time.

Table 2.3 Calculation of the weighting of each attribute for offline grocery shoppers

Attribute	Highest utility level	Lowest utility level	Difference	Proportion
Special offer section	0.10	−0.10	0.20	3.56
New product section	0.00	0.00	0.00	0.00
Help line number	0.01	−0.01	0.02	0.36
Delivery time	0.40	−0.40	0.80	14.23
Delivery cost	0.29	−0.29	0.58	10.32
Delivery reliability	0.22	−0.22	0.44	7.83
Quality	0.58	−0.58	1.16	20.64
Ordering time	0.67	−0.67	1.34	23.84
Substitutes	0.30	−0.30	0.60	10.68
Discount	0.24	−0.24	0.48	8.54
Total			**5.62**	**100.00**

Table 2.4 The preference structure given by the weighting of each attribute for the offline grocery shoppers group

Attributes	Offline shoppers %
Ordering time	23.84
Quality	20.64
Delivery time	14.23
Substitutes	10.68
Delivery cost	10.32
Discount	8.54
Delivery time reliability	7.83
Special offer section	3.56
Help line number	0.36
New product section	0

To investigate the preference structure of the online shoppers group, Logit analysis was used. Their preference structure is shown in Table 2.5.

Table 2.5 The preference structure given by the weighting of each attribute for online grocery shoppers

Attributes	Shoppers %
Ordering time	20.77
Quality	18.08
Delivery time	14.23
Delivery time reliability	12.31
Discount	9.23
Substitutes	8.85
Delivery cost	8.46
Help line number	3.85
Special offer section	3.46
New product section	0.77

Ordering time and quality are – as for the offline shoppers group – the two main order-winning criteria, but with lower weighting. For example, the difference in weighting between offline and online shoppers for ordering time is just above 3%. The two next strong order-qualifying criteria are delivery time and delivery time reliability. The spacing between these last two is small, which implies that the company may need to consider both as important when developing an online marketing strategy. Delivery time reliability is the attribute that differs the most in terms of preferences between the two groups under investigation. Delivery time reliability could represent more of an abstract concept for offline shoppers, as they have not experienced late or early delivery when waiting for their groceries at home. In contrast this attribute gains in importance when shoppers have experienced a delivery that is not on time and therefore disturbs their timetable. Time seems therefore to be an important factor for this particular group. As a result, online shoppers seem to be time poor and are seeking to shop efficiently without compromising quality. Substitutes surprisingly do not seem to be a major issue as long as quality is present, as opposed to findings for the offline shoppers group.

The chart in Figure 2.4 compares and contrasts the preferences of both groups – offline and online shoppers. For both groups the three most important criteria by rank order – namely, ordering time, quality and delivery time – are identical. The weighting is however different for ordering time and quality. For these criteria the weighting for the offline group is 3.07% higher for ordering time and 2.56% higher for quality. This could be related to a fear of spending too much time placing an order when not being familiar with the web site and a fear of not getting such good quality as when items are picked up by the respondent. Subsequent attributes are however different when comparing offline shoppers with online shoppers. For example delivery time is followed by reliability (another dimension of time) for online shoppers, while offline shoppers are still anxious about the content of their shopping basket. Would the substitutes be ones they would have chosen themselves? Delivery time reliability only comes into consideration once the consumer has experienced a delivery that is too late or too early. A customer acquisition strategy needs to differ from a retention strategy as consumers' needs and fears seem to be different.

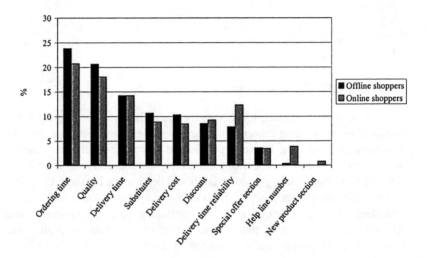

Figure 2.4 The preference of offline and online shoppers

Some preferences appear to change over time. For example, the more a consumer shops online, the more the fear of having the wrong substitutes will decrease. Another example is that the offline shoppers group may also become more time sensitive, so delivery time reliability may also gain in weighting.

With regard to the price attribute, an online customer-acquiring strategy will need to offer free delivery to consumers, while an online customer-retaining strategy will need to discount prices on the Internet as opposed to in their physical stores. Online shoppers are therefore price sensitive in a different way. The £5 delivery charge is not a concern compared with an online discount as they increase their volume purchase. As a result discounts could have higher weighting for an acquiring strategy than for a retention strategy.

However, only looking at the relative weighting of each attribute may not be sufficient to increase acquisition and retention and better position the company in its industry. For example this analysis of the weighting of each attribute shows that ordering time is the number one order-winning criterion, but it does not show if one level (e.g., 20 minutes to place an order) is statistically more significant than another level of the same attribute (e.g., 35 minutes to place an order). This is tested below.

Significant differences in utility values are tested using the following hypothesis:

Ho: There is no significant difference in utility values between the levels of ordering time.
Ha: There is a significant difference in utility values between the levels of ordering time.

Decision rule: If $t_{obt} > t_{crit}$ at $p = .05$ then reject the null hypothesis.

Table 2.6 shows the values used to calculate a two-tailed value of t_{obt}

Table 2.6 The data used to test the hypothesis

Description of level	Utility value	Standard error	t_{obt}	df	t_{crit}
20 minutes to place an order	0.50	0.04	112.2	128	1.96
35 minutes to place an order	0.46	0.05			

Result: As $t_{obt} > t_{crit}$ at $p = .05$ the null hypothesis is rejected and the alternate accepted. There is a significant difference at the 5% probability level in customer utility values between placing an online order within 20 minutes and placing one within 35 minutes.

If the ordering time utility curve is drawn, its relatively steep slope confirms that small changes in ordering time performance will produce large changes in customer utility values (see Figure 2.5).

The operational customer acquisition and retention implications of this are obvious. Given the top ranking accorded to ordering time for both offline shoppers and online shoppers and the shape of the utility curve for ordering time, improving the efficiency of ordering time should be a key competitive priority. The same significance tests were carried out on the remaining attributes that were found to be significant at $p = .05$.

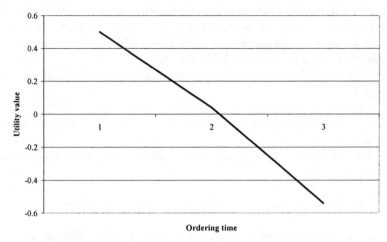

Figure 2.5 Ordering time utility curve for online grocery shoppers

As expected, the top three attributes of ordering time, quality and delivery time had the steepest utility curves. The utilities were further analysed by shopping frequency. An example of this is given below, which suggests that offline shoppers undervalue the importance of ordering time until they use a web site to order groceries, at which point this utility value increases across all categories of frequency. Clearly, a best in class web site ordering time is a strong factor in retaining customers.

Latent Class Analysis

Now that the major differences have been noted between online and offline shoppers when buying groceries, it will be helpful to look in more depth at these differences by segmenting the two groups into subgroups using latent class analysis. Latent class can be defined as an attempt to find groups of respondents who share similar preferences and utilities, and it will show whether or not, among one group, preferences differ to an extent that makes differentiated marketing approaches worthwhile. If this is the case then an aggregate model will not be appropriate because various segments will highlight different preferences. From an applied managerial perspective, developing clusters of consumers' preferences is useful in terms of prospective acquisition and retention strategies.

Segmenting Online Shoppers – Customer Retention

The first step in latent class analysis is to choose the right number of segments to study, as it this forms part of a marketing strategy to define the markets in which the company will decide to compete. This requires comparing solutions with different numbers of groups. To that effect, five groups have been analysed by examining the PctCert statistic, CAIC and chi square. The results are shown in Table 2.7 below.

Table 2.7 Choosing the right number of segments

	PctCert	CAIC	Chi square	Change between groups in chi-square
1 group	18.8	3594.0	806.5	
2 groups	25.4	3426.9	1090.4	283.9
3 groups	28.7	3401.1	1233.0	142.6
4 groups	31.7	3390.0	1361.0	128.0
5 groups	34.9	3369.4	1498.4	137.4

From Table 2.7 the following observations can be drawn:

- The objective is to establish the optimal number of latent classes to be calculated. This is found when the difference in chi-square between one group and the next has become small. For example there is a large chi-square difference going from one group to two (283.9). With four groups the difference is minimal (128), suggesting that four might be the right number to study.
- The CAIC decreases dramatically from one group to two groups and then continue to decrease until four groups. The difference between two CAIC is at its minimum for four groups. It then increases slightly again for larger numbers of groups. Four segments seem therefore to be the right number to look at, as then the CAIC becomes nearly flat for a larger number of groups.

However when looking at four market segments, only two group solutions are well defined in terms of their preferences and would not provide an opportunity for a company to strategically position itself against dominant order-winning and qualifying criteria against all four groups. In this regard a five-group solution (i.e., segmenting the population into five latent classes) provides a better understanding of the order-winning and qualifying criteria of each group. Figure 2.6 shows the proportion of online shoppers when divided into five groups or segments. The question to answer is if there is a significant difference in the preference structure between these classes of online shoppers, which will allow the development of a more focused retention strategy.

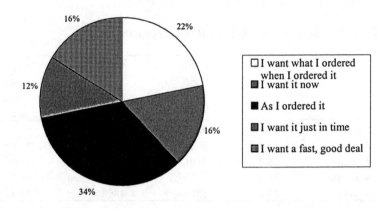

Figure 2.6 Latent classes for online shoppers

The pie chart in Figure 2.6 shows that the 'As I ordered it' segment (refer to Table 2.8 for the dimensions of this segment) represents the most important segment in terms of size (34%) while the 'I want it just in time' segment represents only 12% of the online shoppers. Within each latent class, order winning and order qualifying were identified. Figure 2.7 shows an example of the preference structure for the 'As I ordered it' segment.

Shoppers belonging to the 'As I ordered it' segment appear to value quality above other services. Quality is therefore the order-winning criterion. Substitutes and delivery cost follow and are defined as order-qualifying criteria. It seems that the content of the shopping basket is important for this segment, which implies that the company will increase performance if it delivers the best service with regard to quality and substitutes.

One interesting outcome of Table 2.8 is that price is not part of the order-winning criteria list in any of the latent classes. Indeed, it does not seem to be a critical aspect of the choice-making process in the mind of the consumer when selecting an online grocery store. The absence of price as an order-winning criterion could be accounted for by the high-income profile of the population under investigation. Even if price is not a determinant attribute it could however become critical if most competitors provide certain consumers with high performance quality and ordering time (for example, as in the case of the 'I want a quick good deal' segment who represent 16% of the online shoppers).

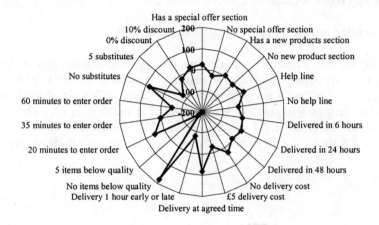

Figure 2.7 'As I ordered it' segment

Table 2.8 recaps the order-winning and qualifying criteria for each latent class of the online shoppers group.

Table 2.8 Order-winning and -qualifying criteria

Latent class	Order winning criteria	Order qualifying criteria
I want what I ordered when I ordered it	Quality	Delivery time Ordering time
I want it now	Ordering time	Delivery time
As I ordered it	Quality	Delivery cost Substitutes
I want it just in time	Delivery time reliability	–
I want a fast, good deal	Ordering time	10% discount

From Table 2.8, it seems that to increase customer retention rate well above the average for the industry, a company needs to provide the best service on the order-winning criteria (i.e., quality, ordering time and delivery time reliability) depending on the segment whilst not neglecting the order-qualifying criteria – this is particularly the case when the gap between the utility weights is not too large.

In addition, once the consumers' preferences have been understood, the company needs to look at the implications for its own internal processes. For example, an order-winning criterion of delivery time alongside delivery time reliability requires flexible logistics processes.

Segmenting offline shoppers - customer acquisition

For comparability purposes with the online shoppers group, this section will also use a five-group solution. The research question to answer is whether the group of offline grocery shoppers under study differs significantly in terms of their preferences. The total number of respondents is 127, which is similar in size to the online shoppers group (129 respondents). The chart in Figure 2.8 shows the proportion of each segment for the offline shoppers group.

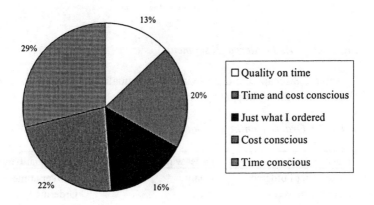

Figure 2.8 Latent classes for offline shoppers

Figure 2.8 shows that the 'Time conscious' segment (refer to Table 2.9 for the dimensions of this segment) is the largest (29%) in terms of size while the 'Quality on time' segment is the smallest (13%) of the offline shoppers' group. Figure 2.9 shows an example of the preference structure of the 'Time conscious' segment. For this particular latent class, ordering time is the strongest order-winning criterion, followed by delivery time. We have called this segment 'Time conscious'. As a result a company will only maximise online market share by providing the best service with regard to these attributes.

Figure 2.9 Time conscious segment for offline shoppers

Table 2.9 summarises the determinant preferences of consumers for each segment of offline shoppers if they were to make the decision to shop online for groceries.

Table 2.9 Preferences of offline shopper segments

	Order-winning criterion	Order-qualifying criteria
Quality on time	Quality	Delivery time reliability
		Substitutes
Time and cost conscious	Ordering time	Delivery cost
		Quality
Just what I ordered	Quality	Substitutes
Cost conscious	Delivery cost	10% discount
Time conscious	Ordering time	Delivery time

Similarly, compared with the online shoppers group, the majority of segments for the offline shoppers include quality and ordering time as a strong order-winning criterion. However the 'Cost conscious' segment is unique in the sense that the preference is on price only. In contrast the 'Just what I ordered' segment focuses on the content of the shopping basket. This shows that an aggregate model is less reliable in developing an acquisition strategy based on consumers' preferences.

Table 2.10 Reference contrasts between on- and offline shoppers

Top order-winning criterion	Online shoppers %*	Offline shoppers %*
Ordering time	32	49
Quality	56	29
Delivery time reliability	12	
Delivery cost		22
Total	100	100

Notes: Total share of preference across all latent classes

Table 2.10 compares and contrasts order-winning criteria between on- and offline shoppers. From this table, three differences can be observed. The first is that offline consumers are mainly concerned with the ordering time aspect, while online consumers are also concerned with the reliability of the delivery and not just the time taken to place to order. This could be due to the fact that offline shoppers are unfamiliar with supermarkets' web sites and ordering processes. For a retention strategy two dimensions of time need to be considered while for an acquisition strategy providing the best service on ordering time alone seems sufficient. Secondly, it seems that consumers who have already experienced online shopping have a greater concern over quality than offline shoppers. Online shoppers will consequently prefer an online supermarket that will ensure that no item of poor quality will be found in the shopping basket. As a result it is essential to perform above the industry average with regard to this strong order-winning criterion in order to improve the customer retention rate.

Finally, offline shoppers are concerned by the price component – both the delivery cost and the 10% discount. Lower price seems to be an incentive to attract some offline shoppers, but once they have shopped online their main concerns are the content of the shopping basket and time.

CONCLUSION

This chapter has demonstrated and sought to account for the rapid growth of e-commerce within the UK. Much of this growth comes from a small number of conventional retailers that have invested in electronic channels to sell their goods as a source of market share growth. Amongst these, Tesco.com appears to provide a profitable business model within the fiercely competitive grocery-retailing sector. Image research seems to suggest that Tesco.com is meeting the needs of its users – but the service has had little competition until recently, and consumers did not have the ability to choose an alternative service provider. The main part of this chapter reports on research exploring preference differences between online and offline grocery shoppers. We conclude that even if ordering time and quality come first for both groups, the weighting of these factors is different between the two groups. The weighting of ordering time and quality is higher for offline shoppers than for online shoppers, consequently by advertising and ensuring that the purchase process will be quick and easy for a first time buyer, companies could increase customer acquisition. This customer acquisition rate could also be improved by ensuring that internal resources also able to provide 'best in industry' quality items to consumers. Nevertheless, subsequent attributes prove to be more different between these two groups. For example delivery time reliability remains a concern for online shoppers while offline shoppers are still focusing on the content of their shopping basket with regard to the importance of substitutes.

In addition significant differences were revealed when looking at segments with similar preferences within a group using latent class analysis. An implication for managers in terms of their customer acquisition and retention strategies is to segment consumers with similar preferences in order to target the chosen group(s). For example if Tesco wishes to increase customer retention, it could be more efficient to select one or two latent classes within the online shoppers and focus resources on their most important preferences rather than looking at the whole online shoppers' group.

This study also shows that looking at different combinations of attributes, as opposed to only looking at the relative importance of each attribute, would greatly improve Tesco's share of preference.

NOTES

1. Independent schools in the UK are schools in the private sector, unsupported by state funds and which therefore charge fees for attendance (sometimes, paradoxically, called 'public schools').
2. The four schools, which participated in the survey, are considered to be the 'population' of interest. We did not take a sample of parents because they were all contactable and each was theoretically equally likely to reply. The major risk to validity lies in the non-respondents. We undertook follow up work with the non-respondents to establish any possible causes of response bias. Because contacting the whole population of interest is so rare the assumption is

made that some form of sampling is always necessary. The new approach we are demonstrating to understanding Internet user preferences could of course be expanded to a much larger population using classic random sampling techniques. For example, if we wanted to generalise for parents of all independent schools in Surrey we could have taken a random sample of the Surrey schools first and then a random sample of a consolidated list of all parents in the selected schools. (These parents may be proxies for high net worth, high consumption grocery customers, which in turn could be the real business target) This approach could have also been applied to the whole of the UK. There are of course numerous difficulties in these approaches - not least The reluctance of independent schools to participate if there is no connection with them.

3. We should also note, however, that the number of levels specified for an attribute may have an impact on the range of part-worths for that attribute, and hence influence the estimated size of the importance weight.

APPENDIX 1: NOTES ON STATISTICAL METHODS USED

(Some of this appendix draws on material provided by kind permission of Sawtooth Software, 2002, http://www.sawtoothsoftware.com/)

What is Choice–Based Conjoint Analysis (CBC)?

The main characteristic distinguishing choice-based conjoint analysis from other types of conjoint analysis is that the respondent expresses preferences by choosing concepts (products) from a set, rather than by rating or ranking them.

In CBC experiments, respondents choose from a number of products described by varying levels of attributes, which is a natural procedure as it mimics the actual buying process. By observing how respondents choose products in response to changes in the underlying attribute levels, we can estimate the impact (utility) each attribute level has upon overall product preference. Once we learn respondents' preferences for the various attribute levels, we can predict how buyers might respond to any potential combination of levels in our study, whether or not that actual product was ever displayed during the interview.

The Role of CBC

Choice-based conjoint analysis has attracted much recent interest in the market research field and there are several reasons for its increasing popularity (Moore, 2004; Cohen and Orme, 2004; Deal, 2002). Some researchers favour it because the task of choosing a preferred concept is similar to what buyers actually do in the marketplace. Choosing a preferred product from a group of products is a simple and natural task that anyone can understand.

Choice-based conjoint analysis lets the researcher include a 'None' option for respondents, such as 'I wouldn't choose any of these'. By selecting that option, respondents who do not like any of the options can express their lack of interest. Comparing 'None' usage across groups of respondents can reveal segments that are relatively more or less likely to purchase product concepts.

Most conjoint analysis studies use 'main effects only' assumptions. Choice-based conjoint analysis can be easily performed at an aggregate level rather than for respondents individually, making it feasible to quantify interactions. This capability is enhanced by the random designs used by the Sawtooth CBC System, which, given a large enough sample, permits the study of all interactions, rather than just those expected to be of interest when the study was designed.

It is possible in choice-based conjoint analysis to have 'product-specific' (alternative-specific) attributes. For example, in studying transportation we might consider walking shoes and bicycles. The attributes describing shoes are different from those describing bicycles, and yet one might want to learn how much improvement in walking shoes would be required to switch a respondent from cycling to walking. (We should note that product-specific attributes are also feasible with other types of conjoint analysis, though not often used.) Sawtooth's CBC Advanced Design Module permits alternative-specific designs.

Choice-based conjoint analysis does have a disadvantage, however: it is an inefficient way to elicit preferences. Each concept is typically described on all the attributes being considered in the study, and each choice set contains several concepts. Therefore, the respondent has to do a lot of reading and process a lot of information before giving each answer. For that reason, choice-based conjoint studies have traditionally not been used to estimate the values that individual respondents attach to attribute levels, as is generally done with traditional conjoint methods. Instead, data from groups of respondents are typically aggregated for analysis. This can be done either by combining all respondents or by studying subsets defined by specific market segments. 'Utility values' can be produced for each group of respondents that summarise the choices made by those individuals. And, as in other conjoint methods, the utility values can be used to simulate and predict respondent reactions to product concepts that may not have actually appeared in the choice tasks (questions).

Aggregating respondents in CBC analysis assumes respondent homogeneity, which may not always be appropriate or desirable. New developments in the technique have recognised segment-based or even respondent-by-respondent differences. Latent class analysis can simultaneously delineate homogeneous segments and estimate their preference functions. Most recently, computationally intensive Bayesian estimation has permitted estimating individual-level utilities from choice data. These methods have proven to give a better understanding of market structure and generally to lead to more accurate predictions.

Estimating Utilities with Logit

What are utilities?

A utility is a measure of relative desirability or worth. When computing utilities using logit, every attribute level in a conjoint project is assigned a utility (also referred to as a part-worth). The higher the utility, the more desirable the attribute level. Levels that have high utilities have a large positive impact on influencing respondents to choose products. When using logit, latent class or hierarchical Bayes (HB), the raw utilities are zero-centred within each attribute. For example:

Level	Utility
$300	−0.6
$200	0.1
$100	0.5

This example shows respondents preferring lower price levels to higher ones.

Choosing Effects for Logit

By default, CBC estimates utilities for all 'main-effects'. Main-effects reflect the impact of each attribute on product choice measured independently of the other attributes. Main-effect models are the simplest ones, resulting in a single utility value associated with each attribute level in the study.

Additional terms can be added to the model to account for two-way attribute interactions. For example, if the combination of 'Red' with 'Mazda

Miata' results in greater preference than the main-effect utilities would suggest, an interaction term can capture and reflect that synergy. Interaction terms can also reflect differences in price sensitivity for different brands. It is suggested that only interaction terms that result in a significant improvement in the overall fit of the model should be added. Including too many terms in a model can lead to overfitting, which has the potential for modelling a good deal of noise along with true effects.

When using aggregate logit, it is important to investigate whether including interaction terms can significantly improve the fit of the model. With methods that recognise respondent differences (latent class and HB), many complex effects (including, but not limited to, interactions) can be reflected in market simulations using only main-effects. It is our experience that including interaction terms in logit models can often significantly improve predictability of the model, but that those same terms added to latent class are not as valuable and can even, in some cases, be detrimental. Thus, with little effort, one can achieve excellent results with latent class or HB using CBC's default main-effects.

Logit Analysis

Logit analysis is an iterative procedure to find the maximum likelihood solution for fitting a multinomial logit model to the data. When only main-effects are estimated, a value is produced for each attribute level, which can be interpreted as an average utility value for the respondents analysed.

The computation starts with estimates of zero for all effects (utilities), and determines a gradient vector indicating how those estimates should be modified for greatest improvement. A step is made in the indicated direction, with a step size of 1.0. In Sawtooth, the user can modify the step size; a smaller step size will probably produce a slower computation, but perhaps more precise estimates. Further steps are taken until the solution stops improving.

For each iteration the log-likelihood is reported, together with a value of 'RLH'. RLH is short for 'root likelihood' and is an intuitive measure of how well the solution fits the data. The best possible value is 1.0, and the worst possible is the reciprocal of the number of choices available in the average task. For these data, where each task presented four concepts plus a 'None' option, the minimum possible value of RLH is 0.2.

Iterations continue until the maximum number of iterations is reached (default 20) or the log-likelihood increases by too little (less than 1 in the fifth decimal place); hence the gradient is too small (every element is less than 1 in the fifth decimal place).

REFERENCES

Baker, W.L., Lin, E., Marn, M.V. and Zawada, C.C., (2001), 'Getting Prices Right on the Web', *The McKinsey Quarterly*, 2 (2), Special Edition, 54–63.

Bottellier, H. (2004) quoted in IMRG (2004a).

Brynjolfsson, E. and Smith, M.D., (April 2000), 'Frictionless Commerce? A Comparison of Internet and Conventional Retailers', *Management Science*, 46 (4), 563–585.

Burt, S., and Sparks, L., (2003), 'E-commerce and the Retail Process: a Review', *Journal of Retailing and Consumer Services*, 10(5), 275.

Cohen, S. and Orme, B., (2004), 'What's Your Preference?', *Marketing Research*, Summer, (16)2, 32.

Deal, K. (2002), 'Get Your Conjoint Online, in Several Flavors', *Marketing Research*, Winter, 14(4), 44.

Hair, J.F., Tatham, R., Anderson, R. and Black, W., (1998), *Multivariate Data Analysis*, Prentice Hall.

Hill, T. (2000), *Manufacturing Strategy: Texts and Cases*, Basingstoke: Palgrave Macmillan.

Interactive Advertising Bureau (2004), 'Online Advertising Leaps 76%', Press Release, 11 October, www.iabuk.net.

Interactive Media in Retail Group (2004a), *The IMRG e-Christmas 2003 Online Shopping Review*, www.imrg.org.

Interactive Media in Retail Group (2004b) '*My High Street at Home*', www.imrg.org.

Interactive Media in Retail Group (2004c), *IMRG E-Retail Sales Data Index*, www.imrg.org.

Keen, C., Wetzels, M., De Ruyter, K. and Feinberg, R., (2004), 'E-Tailers versus Retailers: Which Factors Determine Consumer Preferences', *Journal of Business Research*, 57(7), 685.

Kuttner, R. (1998), 'The Net: A Market Too Perfect for Profits', *Business Week*, 11 May.

Lee, K.S. and Tan, S.J., (2003), 'E-retailing versus Physical Retailing: A Theoretical Model and Empirical Test of Consumer Choice', *Journal of Business Research*, 56(11), 877.

Moore, W.L., (2004), 'A Cross-validity Comparison of Rating-based and Choice-based Conjoint Analysis Models', *International Journal of Research in Marketing*, 21(3, Sep), 299.

National Statistics (2004), *United Kingdom National Accounts (Blue Book)*, London: The Stationery Office.

Retail Bulletin (2004), 'Tesco Building Online Share', *Retail Bulletin*, 247, www.theretailbulletin.com.

Reuters (2004) 'Google Launches UK Froogle Shopping Site', 12 October, http://www.reuters.co.uk/newsArticle.jhtml?type=internetNewsandstoryID=6479 094andsection=news.

Reynolds, J. (2002), 'E-Tailing', in P.J. McGoldrick (ed.), *Retail Marketing*, 3rd Edition, London: McGraw-Hill, pp. 585–638.

Reynolds, J. (2003), 'Prospects for Electronic Commerce', in J. Reynolds and C. Cuthbertson (eds), *Retail Strategy: The View from the Bridge*, London: Butterworth-Heinemann, pp. 119–136.

Sawtooth Software (2002), http://www.sawtoothsoftware.com/.

Sinha, I. (Mar-Apr 2000), 'Cost Transparency: The Net's Real Threat to Prices and Brands', *Harvard Business Review*, 78(2), 43–48.

Szymanski, D.M. and Hise, R.T., (2000), 'E-Satisfaction: An Initial Examination', *Journal of Retailing*, 76(3), 309–322.

UCLA (2003), *The UCLA Internet Report Year Three*, UCLA Center for Communication Policy.

3. To Pay or Not to Pay, That is the Question. Conceptual Model and Empirical Results on Consumers' View on Home Delivery

Herbert Kotzab and Christoph Teller

STARTING POINTS OF CONSIDERATIONS

The well-known 'theory' of the wheel of retailing (e.g. by Hollander, 1960; McNair, 1931) explains what institutional changes can take place when an innovator enters a retail arena. Typically such 'revolutions' refer to the introduction of new retail formats, for example, the first supermarkets in the 1920s, the first convenience store in the 1940s, the first Wal-Mart, Target and K-Mart stores in the 1960s, the first category killers and club stores at the beginning of 1980s, the first superstores at the end of the 1980s and the first Internet book store in 1995 (Retail Center, 2003).

Although grocery shopping especially has undergone a lot of changes in the last 100 years, all these changes more or less relate to the store dimension of retailing meaning the way retailers offer their goods to prospective consumers while the logistics dimension has become more and more visible as a result of the upcoming significance of a new form of distance retailing using the new information technology, better known as Internet retailing and e-tailing or e-grocery, respectively. The benchmark for such forms of retailing is amazon.com, an Internet book retailer, which showed the competition that it is not enough just to create a 'fancy' website; you must also have strong logistics support.

But what about Internet-based grocery retailing? In 1998, the Consumer Direct Cooperative introduced the concept of 'consumer direct services', which includes all online services for food and grocery items where end users could place their orders via electronic means (e.g. computers, fax machines, mobile phones) (Corbae and Balchandani, 2001; Pflaum et al. 2000; ECRE, 2002). The finalized orders were afterwards shipped directly to the consumer's home. The market for such services was expected to grow immensely as experts assessed the European consumer direct market volume at EUR 100 billion by the year 2010 (Corbae and Balchandani, 2001).

The main difference between Internet retailing, especially the consumer direct services, and traditional grocery retailing can be seen in the adoption of logistical functions/activities when delivering the goods to the consumers' home. Corbae and Balchandani (2001) refer to over 900 million deliveries that should be delivered to more than 35 million single households. Academics and/or practitioners have discussed this problem as a 'last-mile-problem' and presented several mainly technical solutions ranging from pick up points to delivery boxes installed in a household (e.g. ECRE, 2002; Pflaum and Wilhelm, 2002; Prockl and Wilhelm, 2002; Kopczak, 2001; Doukidis and Pramataris, 2001; Lee and Whang, 2001; Punikavi et al., 2001; Punikavi and Tanskanen, 2002; Tanskanen et al., 2002).

However, from an academic retail marketing perspective, we may consider this discussion as a renaissance of the concept of home delivery that can be seen either as a specific function of any form of retailing or a hybrid form of distance-based and store-based retailing (Schnedlitz et al., 1997). In this particular case, home delivery is a specific function of retailing. In a traditional grocery setting, a retailer typically 'outsources' home delivery to the consumers, and an Internet retailer 'reintegrates' this type of logistics from the consumers back to the firm.

Nevertheless there is overall agreement between the consumer direct and Internet retailing discussions that consumers are willing to pay for this extraservice (Anonymous, 2002), because consumers who use such services perceive store shopping as an annoying activity and appreciate consumer direct services as a handy/convenient way to shop for groceries: 'Customers want convenience and they want service that will make their lives easier' (Reda, 2003). The main notion behind this is that the costs for all necessary logistics services are to be borne by the consumers.

We are not sure about this assumption, as we are missing the voice of the consumer throughout the discussion. The convenience hypothesis is taken for granted in all contributions, which we consider to be an expression of consumer direct myopia. Therefore we wanted to investigate this assumption from a consumer's point of view. Consequently, we have chosen to look first at which processes consumers typically perform when it comes to individual purchases from a point-of-sale to a point-of-consumption. Thereby we have developed a model of consumer logistics that shows different characteristics, dependent on the underlying retailing model, and discusses the consequences for in- and outsourcing of logistical services from a consumer's point of view. This leads to the generation of a set of hypotheses, which we tested in different retail settings in order to enhance our understanding of the phenomena and to identify possible contingencies based on the retail sector. Here we will present the results of our investigation in a grocery – supermarket and in a Do-It-Yourself (DIY) – category killer environment. We selected these two 'cases' because of the heterogeneous nature of consumers' demands, in order to identify potential differences. This heterogeneity merely stems from the type of products sold there and the location of the stores; thus leading to different outcomes for shoppers' convenience; that is, home delivery will be more or less attractive for consumers.

CONSUMERS' ROLE WITHIN DISTRIBUTION – STATIONARY VS. DISTANCE RETAILING

Distribution normally refers to all processes that help to connect a point of origin with a point of consumption (e.g. Kotzab and Bjerre, 2004). Retail logistics, however, typically looks at the processes that are necessary to connect the point of origin with a point of sale (POS), which in a traditional setting is a store. Home delivery refers to all possibilities that connect a point of sale with a point of consumption (POC). In that sense, home delivery can be found in any form of retailing no matter whether store-based or distance retailing (e.g. e-grocery) (see also Figure 3.1).

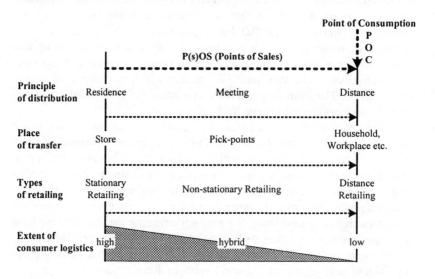

Figure 3.1 Dimensions of consumer logistics (Teller and Kotzab, 2004)

This distinction between different dimensions in our model refers to the typology of retail formats by Hansen (1990). She uses the place of transfer of goods and the place of contact between consumer and retailer as one of the central distinguishing criteria to build up this typology. The left hand side describes stationary retailing whereas the place of transfer is the premises of the retailer, that is, the residence or store. Here the consumer must leave the point of consumption – usually the household – to get the goods needed. This procedure requires the largest effort of consumer logistics endeavours, including planning, transport to/from the store, picking, packing, and so on. The other extreme is distance retailing, such as mail order, where goods are transferred and a personal contact is made at the POC. All these consumer logistics endeavours are carried out by the retailer and will therefore only be seen from the end-customer's point of view. In between, there are hybrid types of retailing where the transfer takes place in a 'neutral' place within the continuum. Examples could be stands in street markets or pick-points for home delivery. In that context the term 'ambulant retailing' describes the non-permanent premises of retailers who choose their location according to the location of the end-customer.

From that point of view, any home delivery service from distance retailers contributes to the increase in convenience from a consumer's point of view (see e.g. Eastlick and Feinberg, 1999). But why, when Internet adoption is very high in many industrialized countries (GfK, 2004), do we not see a significant rise in the market share of e-grocers? The main argument here is that logistics costs are higher than in a traditional setting. In promising to revolutionize the supermarket industry, Webvan.com spent USD 830 million mainly on logistics (USA Today, 2001). But how can this happen when the accepted notion is that consumers are willing to pay for the extra services (= convenience)? This leads us to the assumption that consumers are either not conscious of all the logistical services they perform when shopping in stores or they do not consider them to be important.

Consequences of In- or Outsourcing Logistical Services from a Consumer's Point of View

Since consumers have the choice of selecting either store-based or distance retailers from which to procure their goods, they can decide to in- or outsource their logistical shopping efforts. We define this form of logistics as 'consumer logistics' (Granzin and Bahn, 1989), which we consider as the efficient management (= planning, organizing, controlling, implementation) of the total flow of final products and related information from a POS to a POC carried out by an end-consumer (Teller and Kotzab, 2004). Taking the total cost principle of logistics into account, consumer logistics costs cover the total costs of shopping and of consumer logistics such as planning, transportation, picking, packing, time and opportunity costs. But these costs have so far received little attention in the literature (Bell et al. 1998). In most cases publications apply a more fragmented view to such phenomena when investigating the influence of a single or a few cost factors on consumer behaviour.

The consequence for retail clients when carrying out consumer logistics is that they cover all costs. In contrast to that, consumers using a distance-retailing channel can avoid those costs, but may be charged a delivery fee. In the consumer direct literature we find the assumption that distance retailing services, such as the undertaking of consumer logistics, generate higher convenience to the consumer. Barth et al. (2002) also note that consumers are conscious of their shopping efforts, including consumer logistics. However, they are not able to convert those perceived efforts into costs since this is too difficult and time consuming (Bart et al. 2002, p. 107).

This raises the question of how a service will increase convenience if the inconvenience is not perceived or seen to be relevant by most end-customers. We might phrase it as follows: what is the impact of consumer logistics efforts on the willingness to pay for home delivery services from the customers' point of view? Here home delivery services are understood as all activities provided by a third party to process orders placed by a customer to receive products they need without leaving the POC.

Our question contains two central variables: an independent variable consumer logistics efforts and a dependent variable – consumer logistics' influence on the willingness to pay. We operationalize the independent variable with following measures:

- shopping frequency, in order to get an idea of how often consumers complete logistical activities;
- distance between POS and POC, in order to determine the extent to which consumers overcome spatial and temporal distances for their shopping needs;
- size of the shopping basket (= amount payable at the checkout), to determine the amount of goods to be picked and moved to the POS;
- estimated transportation costs, to indicate the perception of consumer-specific transportation efforts.

The willingness to pay for someone else to deliver the purchased items to the individual POC serves as an indicator for:

- Measuring the affinity to outsource consumer logistics to the retailer or any other party; and

- Evaluating the extent to which consumer logistics is seen to be monetarily relevant for end-customers.

To answer the research question, we have listed four hypotheses that scrutinize the role of consumer logistics for home delivery services. Since we cannot draw on comparable findings in the field of consumer research, we will formulate our hypotheses in a more open way. The reason for this is to investigate fundamental structures upon which more precise assumptions and/or hypotheses can be established. However, we assume a positive relationship between the consumer logistics variables and the willingness to pay for home delivery.

- *Habituation Hypothesis* (H_H) The shopping frequency influences the willingness to pay for home delivery services.

Shopping frequency serves as a measure for the extent to which a person undertakes the procurement of goods using a particular stationary retail format. In fact, this variable can also be seen as a measure for the degree of experience and habituation with shopping in stores. For the sake of simplicity, we differentiate between frequent and infrequent shoppers depending on the type of goods bought.

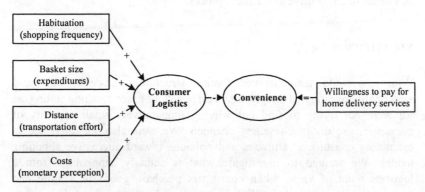

Figure 3.2 Home delivery model

- *Shopping Basket Hypothesis* (H_B) The size of the shopping basket influences the willingness to pay for home delivery services.

In this hypothesis we focus on the logistical object to be selected, moved and stored. Although physical measures would best characterize the shopping basket from a logistical point of view, for survey reasons only we feel that the monetary value of all the goods bought is the best measure available to represent the shopping basket regarding size, weight and value. The value and therefore the size of the shopping basket may be seen as an indicator for the extent to which distribution efforts are being conducted by the end-customers.

- *Distance Hypothesis* (H_D) The spatial and temporal distance influences the willingness to pay for home delivery services.

The distance in terms of time and space covered by the end-customers to buy goods operationalizes the extent to which logistical tasks are undertaken. From a convenience point of view, a home delivery service should become more attractive the longer the distance is between the POS and the POC. This hypothesis focuses on the transportation efforts of end-customers in the process of buying or procuring goods.

- *Cost Hypothesis* (H_C) The perceived transportation costs influence the willingness to pay for home delivery services.

The ability to convert transportation efforts into costs operationalizes the perception of the most obvious logistical activities when buying goods. The awareness of the hidden costs of purchasing may trigger willingness to pay as a result of a cognitive assessment process.

METHODOLOGY

With respect to the observed market structure, we deliberately and empirically investigated the phenomenon in a store-based retailing setting, as we were not trying to find out why a comparatively small minority of consumers use distance-retailing channels. We were also not interested in examining consumers' attitudes and opinions toward alternative shopping modes. We wanted to investigate what is actually happening, from a logistics point of view, when consumers purchase goods in a store and connect the POS with their POC. In other words, we did not only want to know what consumers think about home delivery in general, but we also wanted to know how our respondents perceive what they do when they handle home delivery themselves for their households or themselves, respectively.

As part of the survey, we conducted face-to-face interviews in the stores. Thereby, we set our respondents in a quasi-biotic interview situation. The respondents had to evaluate their logistical efforts, and by doing so, we made their hidden contribution to the distribution of goods to their households obvious to them. This served as a basis for confronting them with the opportunity to have all their shopping efforts undertaken by someone else. This approach made it possible to maximize the internal validity of our results, although it has to be said that we focused on those end-users who did their shopping while they were being interviewed. We adopted our research design in two different shopping settings. On the one hand, we investigated shopping behaviour in a grocery setting, and on the other hand, in a Do-It-Yourself setting.

These two settings were chosen deliberately because the extent of consumer logistics carried out differs considerably between them. The main reason for this is the retail location and the distance to the end-customers. Table 3.1 shows the major differences between the two settings.

Table 3.1 Specific differences between the examined retail formats for consumer logistics

Place of transfer	Store	
Retail format	Supermarket (SM)	DIY-Category killer (CK)
Floor space	800 m^2	>10,000 m^2
Assortment	Convenience goods	Shopping goods
Advisory service	None (self-service)	Partly (standby service)
Principle of distribution	**Residence**	
Location	Central (city centre)	Dislocated (outskirts)
Reachability	By foot, car, public transport	Almost only by car
Extent of consumer logistics	**High**	
Assumed extent of total consumer logistics per trip – from a consumer's perspective	Low	High
Assumed convenience level for home delivery	Medium	High

Because of the location of the stores, we expected consumer logistics efforts to be different. We assumed that home delivery would be seen to be more attractive in the dislocated DIY-store, as it takes longer for consumers to get to the store than to the supermarket. Table 3.2 provides an overview of the details of the research approach.

All respondents were selected randomly. Every half hour after passing a defined point in the store – in most cases the entrance or the checkout – a potential respondent was asked to participate in the survey. If that person refused, the next one passing the selection point was asked. A critical discussion of this particular approach for gathering primary data can be found in Sudman (1980).

Table 3.2 Research design

Cases / Characterization	Study I (Supermarket)	Study II (Category killer)
Research topic	Evaluation of the shopping process	
	After the purchase of goods	Before and after the purchase of products
Research method	Face-to-face interview	
Research instrument	Standardized questionnaire including 27 (SM) and 33 (CK) closed and open-ended questions	
Interview situation	Semi-biotic	
Interview location/retail formats	Entrance/checkout area	
	Two supermarkets in the central city area	One DIY outlet in outskirts area
Respondents	People choosing those outlets to shop	
Interviewers	Students of the Department of Retailing and Marketing (Vienna University of Economics and Business Administration)	
Population	All customers of the selected outlets	
Sample size	308	611
Sampling method	Random sample base on time	
Duration of data collection	December 2002	December 2003
Analysis software	SPSS 12.0	

The following empirical results should be interpreted as focusing on how consumers in a specific retail setting perceive the inconveniences of shopping, which, in turn, are then expected to trigger the switch to home delivery service providers. The description of the results starts with a short characterization of the two samples followed by some descriptive result regarding the selected variables, after which we move on to the testing of the hypotheses. In the next sections we discriminate between the supermarket (SM) and the category killer (CK) sample. We have to admit that this research approach resulted in an over-representation of those end-consumers who like to carry out their own shopping and excluded all those who refuse to do their own shopping or have someone else to do it for them. We see these self-shoppers as the actual shopping professionals and thus as the main target group for retailing – regardless of industry – rather than those who influence the shopping process without carrying it out themselves. This professional shopper may be seen as the 'gate keeper' when it comes to deciding which channel or retail format to choose.

CHARACTERIZATION OF CONSUMER LOGISTICS CARRIED OUT BY END-CUSTOMERS

Shopping Frequency

Figure 3.3 shows how often respondents usually shop in the examined outlets. Groceries and other fast moving consumer goods sold were bought by almost all respondents (92.2%; valid cases (n) = 308) at least once a week. DIY goods were bought less frequently as the majority of our DIY customers (65.6%; valid cases (n) = 610) came to the selected store only a few times a month or less.

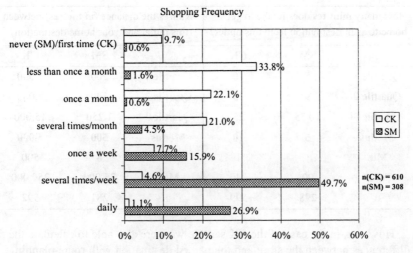

Figure 3.3 Shopping frequency

It seems obvious that different consumption patterns and the durability of the goods sold in the two different retail formats correspond to a different reason for buying them, and so the shopping frequency is high for groceries in a supermarket and low for products like paint in a DIY category killer.

Consumer logistics can therefore be seen as being conducted more often in a grocery setting, at least when we look at shopping frequency.

Spatial and Temporal Distances between POS and POC

The measure 'distance between a household (= POC) and an outlet (= POS)' can serve as an objective indicator to describe the transportation efforts in connection with bringing an individual shopping basket to an individual home. We also consider the distance, as perceived by the end-consumer, to be important. While in the case of the supermarket study we only assessed the subjective indicator, we could evaluate the category killer study on both measures. Looking at the central tendency, we found remarkable values. Whereas the supermarket seemed to be just around the corner for most of our respondents (Time: Median: 9 minutes, valid n = 298; Space: Median: 500 metres) it takes a long time to go from the category killer to the destinations of the respondents (Time: Median: 15 minutes, valid n = 599; Space: Median: 15,000 metres).

Table 3.3 Spatial and temporal distance

How many **minutes** does it take to get home/to your destination from this outlet?			What is the distance (in **metres**) between this outlet and your home/destination?		
	SM	CK		SM	CK
Quartile 1	5	10	Quartile 1	200	5,000
Quartile 2	9	15	Quartile 2	500	8,000
Quartile 3	10.75	25	Quartile 3	1,250	15,000
Modus	**5**	**10**	**Modus**	**500**	**5,000**
Min	1	1	Min	8	500
Max	90	240	Max	35,000	350,000
n	298	599	n	281	592

However, in the case of the CK sample we were also able to calculate the differences between the store and the named destination with route-planning software. Thereby we found out that the respondents overestimated the temporal distance (Wilcoxon-Test; $p < 0.01$) although it has to be said that the software does ignore problems such as traffic-jams on the trips. The overestimations, however, might also be due to the different use of transportation means (see also Figure 3.4).

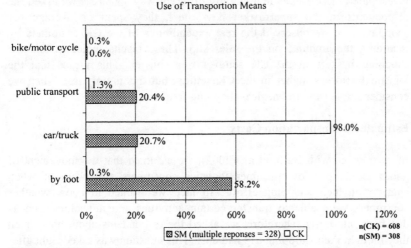

Figure 3.4 Use of means of transport

Most supermarket end-consumers (58.2%; n = 308) walked, while almost all the category killer customers used a car or a truck (98%, n = 608) to get to the stores. One reason for this could be different outlet locations, that is, central locations for the SM and peripheral location for the CK. When inspecting the zip codes of the homes of our respondents, we saw that the SM appealed to a far more local market than the CK. This made us think that the transportation efforts would be more challenging in a CK setting, as consumers need vehicles to travel the distance to and from the store and the products might be more bulky. This also means (besides the fixed costs of owning a vehicle) variable costs such as fuel, and fixed costs such as insurance or depreciation, being incurred by the consumer.

As well as getting more insight into possible differences in logistical efforts between procuring goods from supermarkets and from category killers, we were very surprised to find that our respondents were able to operationalize these efforts.

Shopping Expenditures

The expenditures per shopping trip serve as indicators to describe the shopping basket that has to be carried to the POC. We found out that the average expenditures in the supermarkets (Mean: EUR 25; Stdev: 21.2; n = 305) were half the amount of those in the category killer (Mean: EUR 53.7; Stdev: 196.6; n = 449), which might also be due to the products sold there and the number of shopping trips. We should, however, mention that we investigated these values in a slightly different way. Whereas we asked the respondents in the supermarket how much they spent on average per shopping trip, we observed the real expenditures of the CK customers by recording the amounts on the sales slip. These results indicated that the shopping baskets in the CK settings were bigger. This means that the logistical effort is higher in the CK setting, but this is only true when we consider single trips and neglect shopping frequency.

Estimated Transportation Costs

In accordance with Barth et al. (2002), we assumed that the movement of goods is the part of consumer logistics consumers are aware of when considering their shopping efforts. In fact, we wanted to know whether consumers were able to transfer certain activities and indicators such as distances into costs. Therefore, we asked the respondents about how much they thought their shopping trip had cost. This question was asked right after the respondents were asked to assess the spatial and temporal distances between the store and their destination. The results show that most supermarket customers were unable to assess the cost situation. They did not think that the delivery of their shopping basket to their home incurred any costs for them (Modus: EUR 0; n = 249). In contrast, most of the respondents in the CK store stated that an average shopping trip would be calculated at EUR 2 (Modus; n = 525) (see Figure 3.5).

In both settings we identified significant dependencies between the estimated transportation costs and the subjective distance measures but the strength of the correlations can only be considered as low (correlation analyses; $r < 0.3$; $p < 0.001$).

The results may lead to the assumption that our respondents were either unable or unwilling to convert their transportation efforts into cost. Another assumption could be that consumer logistics activities are not considered to be part of the shopping trip at all. This would support the view that consumer logistics is the hidden part of shopping for customers of stationary retailing formats.

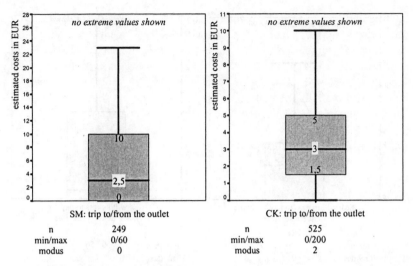

Figure 3.5 Estimated transportation costs

Willingness to Pay

After confronting the respondents with the logistical efforts necessary to complete a shopping trip, we proposed that the interviewer could carry out the picking of the goods bought instead. We also offered to pick and move the goods to the respondent's home or another destination. Immediately after describing our service we asked the respondents how much they would be willing to pay us. The box plots in Figure 3.6 give an overview of the results.

It surprised us that in both settings, most of the consumers were not willing to pay for such a service (Modus: 0; n(SM) = 281; n(CK) = 451). The share of unwilling respondents in the supermarket setting (25.3%; n = 281) was almost half of that of the category-killer setting (CK: 49.4%; n = 451).

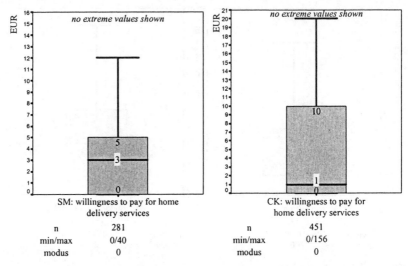

Figure 3.6 Willingness to pay

TESTING AND DISCUSSION OF HYPOTHESES

Concerning our dependent variable, it should be mentioned that we excluded all respondents who were not willing to pay for home delivery services, so it can be assumed beforehand that none of our dependent variables have any influence on the willingness to pay. Keeping that in mind, we first applied bivariate analysis methods and then developed a multi-regression model to compare the different influences in the willingness to pay between our dependent variables. The application of nonparametric tests was necessary because some samples showed no normal distribution.

Habituation Hypothesis (H_H)

To test the influence of the shopping experience and/or habituation on willingness to pay for home delivery services, we divided the samples into the two categories of frequent buyers and infrequent buyers. As shown in Figure 3.3, the values in those samples were different because of the special features of the different stores, therefore we applied different split criteria. In the supermarket setting we equated frequent buyers to those respondents who shop several times a week or daily; whereas frequent buyers in the category killer setting were equated to those shoppers who shop several times a month or more often.

We applied a Mann-Whitney U-Test to find out whether or not there were significant differences between the splits in the two samples. As far as the supermarket is concerned, there were indeed differences. Frequent buyers showed significantly less willingness to pay for home delivery services than all the other respondents (Mann-Whitney U-Test; $p = 0.01$). We found the same tendency for the CK sample, but in contrast to previous results, the values did not differ significantly between frequent and infrequent buyers (Mann-Whitney U-Test; $p = 0.69$). Based on these findings we conclude that the buying frequency (positively) influences the willingness to pay for grocery customers, although that is not the case when it comes to DIY customers.

Shopping Basket Hypothesis (H_B)

For the influence of expenditure as a measure of the distance that travels between the shopping basket being assembled at the POS and moved to the POC, we identified a dependency with the willingness to pay. Table 3.4 shows the results of a correlation analysis. There we can see that the dependency in both samples is significant ($p < 0.05$), but the strength of correlation is rather low in the supermarket setting. At least in the category-killer setting we can identify a weak correlation. Based on those results, we accept our shopping-basket hypothesis.

Table 3.4 Results of hypotheses testing

Supermarket					
Hyp.	Variable 1	Variable 2	r^*	p	n
H_B	Average Expenditures (EUR)		0.146	**0.034**	209
H_C	Estimated Costs (EUR)	Willingness to pay (EUR)	**0.41**	**0.001**	176
H_{Ds}	Spatial Distance (m)		0.062	0.391	192
H_{Dt}	Temporal Distance (min)		0.043	0.542	204
Category Killer					
Hyp.	Variable 1	Variable 2	r^*	p	n
H_B	Observed Expenditures (EUR)		**0.325**	**0.001**	228
H_C	Estimated Costs (EUR)	Willingness to pay (EUR)	0.275	**0.001**	196
H_{Ds}	Spatial Distance (m)		0.231	**0.001**	223
H_{Dt}	Temporal Distance (min)		0.139	**0.041**	218

*Spearman's rho

Cost Hypothesis (H_C)

The results concerning the influence of perceived transportation costs on the willingness to pay for home delivery services tend to be similar to those of the previous hypothesis (see also Table 3.4). Again we see significant dependencies in both samples. In the case of our supermarket sample we even see a medium correlation, but there is a very weak correlation in the CK sample. This is surprising, as category killer consumers estimated their transportation costs more precisely than those supermarket consumers. We conclude that estimated costs do have an impact on the willingness to pay, and therefore accept the cost hypothesis.

Distance Hypothesis (H_D)

As far as the supermarket sample is concerned, we could not identify any dependency at all (see also Table 3.4). This might of course be due to the comparatively small distances between POS and POC. In contrast to this we identified significant dependencies together with rather low correlations in the category killer sample. However, these results are surprising because we considered transportation efforts to be the key variable for the inconvenience perceived in the context of the picking goods from the investigated stores. Therefore, the distance hypothesis can only be accepted in the case of the category killer sample.

Comparable Influence of all Dependent Variables

In order to compare the influence of all our independent variables on the willingness to pay, we developed a multi-regression model (see also Table 3.5). In order to estimate the regression model we had to make minor changes to the variables 'shopping frequency' and 'spatial and temporal distance'. We converted the scale level of the variable 'shopping frequency' from an ordinal to a nominal one. In doing so, we made a distinction between frequent and infrequent shoppers. In the supermarket sample we considered end-consumers who bought groceries several times a week or on a daily basis to be frequent shoppers. Those shopping less than once a week were defined as infrequent shoppers. In contrast, the category killer respondents were considered to be frequent shoppers when buying DIY goods several times a month or more often. After this conversion we included the dummy-variable 'frequent shopping' in our model. Since we identified a fairly strong correlation between the variables spatial and temporal distance, we used the variable 'speed', which is space divided by time. This conversion makes sense because each variable alone does not explain the perception of distance to a satisfactory degree. In building the quotient using both variables we enriched the meaning of 'speed' with 'reachability'.

In both cases, it has to be said that none of the variables that could possibly characterize the logistical efforts of consumers shopping in stores explain the willingness to pay to any large degree ($r^2 < 0.2$). Both regressions can be considered to be significant (see F-Values; $p < 0.001$). In both cases the 'frequent shopping' variable has no influence on the willingness to pay (see t-values; $p > 0.05$). This is also true for the 'perceived distance' variable in the supermarket sample.

Table 3.5 Multi-regression model

Dependent variable: willingness to pay	Supermarket				Category Killer			
Independent Variables	Estimate	t-value	p	beta	Estimate	t-value	p	beta
Intercept	3.62	4.01	0.001		3.07	1.04	0.3	
Frequent shopping (Dummy)	- 0.12	- 0.15	0.88	- 0.01	0.67	0.26	0.8	0.02
Expentitures (EUR)	0.03	1.78	0.08	0.14	0.04	2.08	0.04	0.15
Estimated costs (EUR)	**0.19**	5.02	0.001	**0.39**	**0.25**	3.14	0.002	**0.22**
Perceived distance (m/min)	0	- 0.28	0.78	- 0.02	9.12	2.52	0.01	0.18
F-value (p)	9.81 (<0.001)				6.358 (<0.001)			
r^2	**0.199**				**0.119**			
Standard error of regression	4.013				17.053			
n	163				193			

The comparable impact of all variables on the dependent variable can be seen from the beta-coefficients. In both models we identify estimated costs to have the highest influence on willingness to pay. This simple attempt to include all variables that ought to operationalize the logistical efforts of a shopping trip into a multi-regression model failed. The reason for this is that our explanatory variables – except the estimated transportation cost – are not suitable for conversion into willingness to pay for home delivery services. These results from the multi-regression model support all the other results from our testing of hypotheses, and we conclude that customers are not willing to pay for home delivery services. Furthermore those who are willing to pay are not driven by the extent to which they carry out logistics efforts in the process of shopping.

Synopsis of Findings

When surveying the literature regarding home delivery of groceries or other fast moving consumer goods we identified two major directions: on the one hand, those publications predicting a quick and extensive shift in preferences towards consumer direct services and, on the other hand, contributions that concentrate on consumer behaviour and preferences in niche markets where home delivery has become successful, but is irrelevant from a market share perspective. As we have shown, home delivery plays a role in any retail setting, but a more important question is that of who will handle home delivery - the consumer or the retailer? Recently home delivery has been used as a kind of synonym for e-tailing.

We took a different approach, as we assumed that logistical efforts involved in buying might be perceived by end-users as inconvenient. We tested the consumers' readiness to outsource shopping to a third party and their willing to pay for such a service. The willingness to pay was used as an indicator for the convenience of a home delivery situation. Our results showed that most of the logistical efforts consumers were aware of during their home delivery process have an influence on their willingness to pay. However, this influence turned out to be of minor importance. We concluded that after-shopping processes are not seen to be inconvenient from a logistical point of view. Since we regarded all other influencing variables in connection with the perceived convenience of shopping, such as the assortment, prices, personnel, atmosphere, shopping involvement and shopping situation, and so on, as constant in our model, we were unable to determine which variable made consumer direct service or distance retailing really preferable to shopping in stores. We can, however, conclude that in our study, logistics although consciously perceived in the specific shopping situation is not a deciding factor in the end-consumer's mind, despite the fact that some research has assumed this to be the case when it comes to home delivery, for example in e-grocery. Why pay for something if it is not perceived to be important in a real shopping situation? However, it has to be taken into account that other influencing variables on the perceived attractiveness, such as personnel, atmosphere, involvement or prices, have been excluded in our approach. From a marketing perspective one could argue that the need for home delivery is still latent and it is retail marketing's mission to make this need explicit. For example, it seems that Tesco.com offers an interesting home delivery solution that satisfies its consumers

(McCue, 2004). Finally, it should be mentioned that our empirical results only account for the given retail environment in question, which is the inner city and the suburbs of Vienna/Austria. Our theoretical notions and empirical findings should be taken to be at an exploratory stage. Based on the shortcomings of our research work we envision the following implications for further research:

- Investigation of the influence of country specific retail environments, i.e. store density, market concentration, rural vs. urban markets etc., on the perception of consumer logistics in store-based retailing.
- Identification of the latent construct 'consumer logistics' as a particular influencing factor on consumers' choice of store and channel in different retail industries.

REFERENCES

Anonymous (2002), 'Dossier Globale Handelsstrukturen'. *LP-International*, **11**, 10 13.

Barth, Klaus, Hartmann, Michaela and Schröder, Hendrik (2002), *Betriebswirtschaftslehre des Handels*, Wiesbaden: Gabler.

Bell, David R., Ho, Teck-Hua and Tang, Christopher S. (1998) 'Determining where to shop: Fixed and variable costs of shopping'. *Journal of Marketing Research*, **35** (3), 352 369.

Corbae, Gerald and Balchandani, Anita (2001), 'Consumer Direct Europe (CDE) – Erfolg durch Zusammenarbeit', in D. Ahlert, J. Becker, P. Kenning and R. Schütte (eds), *Internet & Co. im Handel. Strategien, Geschäftsmodelle, Erfahrungen,* 2nd edition, Berlin: Springer, pp. 63 78.

Doukidis, Georgios and Pramataris, Katherine (2001), 'Business models for grocery e-tailers'. *ECR-Journal*, **1** (1), 44 59.

Eastlick, Mary Ann and Feinberg, Richard A. (1999), 'Shopping motives for mail catalog shopping'. *Journal of Business Research*, **45** (3), 281 290.

Efficient Consumer Response Europe (ECRE) (2002), *Consumer Direct Logistics*, Hamburg: German Press.

GfK (2004), *GfK Online Monitor*. Online: http://www.gfk.at/research_data/free_download/files/PRESS/Medien%20adhoc_GfK%20Online%20Monitor%20 2_2004.pdf, Accessed 30.08.04.

Granzin, Kent L. and Bahn, Kenneth D. (1989), 'Consumer logistics: conceptualization, pertinent issues and a proposed program for research'. *Academy of Marketing Science*, **17** (1), 91 101.

Hansen, Ursula (1990), *Absatz- und Beschaffungsmarketing des Einzelhandels*, 2nd edition, Göttingen: Vandenhoeck & Ruprecht.

Hollander, Stanley C. (1960), 'The wheel of retailing'. *Journal of Marketing*, **25** (1), 37 42.

Kopczak, Laura (2001), 'Designing supply chains for the "click-and-mortar" economy'. *Supply Chain Management Review*, **5** (1), 60 66.

Kotzab, Herbert and Bjerre, Mogens (2004), *Retailing in a Supply Chain Perspective*, Copenhagen: CBS-Press.

Lee, Hau and Whang, Seungjin (2001), 'Winning the last mile of e-commerce'. *Sloan Management Review*, **42** (4), 54 62.

McCue, Andy (2004), *Online Sales Boost Tesco*, Online: http://silicon.com, Accessed 22.09.04.

McNair, Malcom P. (1931), 'Trends in Large Scale Retailing'. *Harvard Business Review*, **10** (1), 30 39.

Pflaum, Alexander and Wilhelm, Mirko (2002), 'Home replenishment – adoption of an ECR principle to the last mile of consumer good distribution?', in O. Solem (ed.), *Promoting Logistics Competence in Industry and Research. Proceedings of the 14th Annual Conference for Nordic Researchers in Logistics*, Trondheim: NTNU, pp. 97 114.

Pflaum, Alexander, Kille, Christian, Willhelm, Mirko and Prockl, Günter (2000), *Consumer Direct - The Last Mile: Heimlieferdienste für Lebensmittel und Konsumgüter des täglichen Bedarfs im Internet - die letzte Meile zum Kunden aus der logistischen Perspektive*. Working Paper, Nürnberg: Frauenhofer Institut.

Prockl, Günter and Wilhelm, Mirko (2002), 'Smart practices in consumer direct logistics – new labels for old principles?', in O. Solem (ed), *Promoting Logistics Competence in Industry and Research. Proceedings of the 14th Annual Conference for Nordic Researchers in Logistics*, Trondheim: NTNU, pp. 79 96.

Punakivi, Mikko and Tanskanen, Kari (2002), 'Increasing the cost efficiency of e-fulfilment using shared reception boxes'. *International Journal of Retail & Distribution Management*, **30** (10), 498 507.

Punakivi, Mikko, Yrjölä, Hannu and Holmström, Jan (2001), 'Solving the last mile issue: reception box or delivery box?' *International Journal of Physical Distribution & Logistics Management*, **31** (6), 427 439.

Reda, Susan (2003), *Supermarkets Flex On-line Muscle*, Online: http://www.stores.org/archives/feb03cover.html. Accessed 03.08.04.

Schnedlitz, Peter, Cordula, Cordula and Kotzab, Herbert (1997), Direkt und Strukturvertrieb. Eine kritische Bestandsaufnahme, in P. Schnedlitz (ed.), *Schriftenreihe Handel und Marketing*, 13, Vienna: Department of Marketing and Retailing.

Sudman, Seymour (1980), 'Improving the quality of shopping center sampling'. *Journal of Marketing Research*, **17** (4), 423 431.

Tanskanen, Kari, Yrjölä, Hannu and Holmström, Jan (2002), 'The way to profitable Internet grocery retailing - six lessons learned'. *International Journal of Retail & Distribution Management*, **30** (4), 169 178.

Teller, Christoph and Kotzab, Herbert (2004), 'Proposing a model of consumer logistics', in E. Sweeney, J. Mee, B. Fynes, P. Enangelista, and B. Huber (eds), *Logistics Research Network 2004 Conference Proceedings - Enhancing Competitive Advantage through Supply Chain Innovation*, Dublin.

The Center for Education and Research in Retailing at Indiana University (Retail Center) (2003), *A Century Time Line of Retailing - Milestones of Influence, E-Commerce & Concurrent Events*. Online: http://www.bus.indiana.edu/retail /timeline/printable.htm, Accessed 30.09.2004.

USA Today (2001), *Tech Investor This Week*. Online: http://www.usatoday.com/ tech/news/2001-07-13-week.htm, Accessed 30.08.04.

4. Household Desires on Home Delivery: An Empirical Study on Attended Reception of Convenience Goods

Bengt Nordén

BACKGROUND AND PURPOSE

Background

At the beginning of 2000, a positive development of sales and marketing of goods and services in e-commerce was predicted, with a small but steady increase of sales for the next three years. E-commerce would then continue to grow and stabilize at a relatively high level (Tuunainen, 1999). For goods and services that could be delivered digitally via the Internet, a more positive development was predicted. For goods demanding physical delivery and, therefore, logistics activities, no complete logistics solutions were available. However, there were many actors willing to tackle the logistics challenge.

According to available statistics, the development in e-commerce for certain types of goods has not been as promising as expected, but it is still positive. For convenience/grocery goods, development has been less positive for many reasons. An exception is Tesco's home delivery service (www.tesco.com), which was reported to be profitable in 2002 (Child, 2002). There are, however, several examples of well functioning home delivery services in the grocery business; for example Net-extra (www.netextra.se), a Swedish company in Stockholm, and Peapod (www.peapod.com) based in the USA. A general reflection is that most actors in the e-commerce business have been dazzled by technological possibilities, but have forgotten to ask consumers how they want to live their lives in general and especially how they want to do their shopping. In 2003, only 11% of the Swedish retailing companies were selling goods to consumers on the Internet. However, 80% use the Internet in their marketing of goods (Hedlund, 2003). Sales, through ordering via the Internet amounted, in 2002, to about 6.5 billion SEK or 1.7% (3rd quarter, 2002) of total Swedish retail sales. Services are not included.

A basic advantage of e-commerce is that all actors – including customers – have immediate and easy access to actual information about other actors, products and offers. For B2C e-commerce to function efficiently, information search, ordering and logistics must operate to increase consumer benefits. Further, consumers must change their behavior and accept e-commerce in sufficient numbers to cover its costs. To increase volumes and logistics efficiency, e-tailers[1] from all lines of business must coordinate their logistics activities. The desired volumes can then create revenue and profits, so motivating actors to continue to operate and develop e-commerce.

Hannu Yrjölä (2001) quotes an investigation by Anderson Consulting (no references) where data compiled from Smart Store indicate that a typical supermarket has a net profit of 1% and Streamline's hybrid concept for home delivery has a net profit of 6%. The writer's conclusion is that this calculation must build on full volume and not actual volume.

E-commerce has certain prerequisites qualifications but offers new opportunities to consumers. Consumers must, among other things, have access to a computer and an Internet connection, have knowledge of products, and know how to interpret information and the way transactions and logistics activities should be performed.

As pointed out by many researchers, logistics services to customers are vital in most marketing and commercial relations. They add value to customers by delivering the product in the right form and quantity when requested. The degree of perceived logistics service quality is often decisive with regard to customers' willingness to become loyal customers in the future. The mission of logistics is, according to Ballou (1999), to move the right goods or services to the right place, at the right time, and in the desired condition, while at the same time making the maximum contribution to the firm.

The choice of service dimensions and the degree of these dimensions to offer are important strategic issues in all types of service delivery. Logistics services should if possible be treated in the context of the desired product and core service that the customers are asking for. In deciding what and how much to offer in terms of logistics services, key customer groups' desires and expectations are important. Accordingly, it is important to identify segments of customers asking for similar or varying logistics services on important dimensions (Gilmour et al., 1994; Mentzer et al., 2001).

Logistics service to consumers B2C logistics is an old topic, of which the mail order business is an example. The current interest in coordination of logistics activities has focused on the improved opportunities to coordinate activities by means of computer systems, the Internet and mobile communication. Logistics services to consumers are important in e-commerce, because in B2C e-commerce, stores are often replaced by a distribution center and retailer organized home delivery. In developing home delivery to consumers, many areas of knowledge are of interest especially lines of business serving consumers. Of special interest is how mail order companies handle deliveries to consumers. Classic mail order and e-commerce, however, differ to a certain extent when it comes to extended information on the Internet to customers before, during and after the transaction. Logistics services to consumers are, in many aspects, similar to logistics services to business customers, but consumers' qualifications and their evaluation of logistics services is in many respects specific. A critical element in home delivery is when and where the reception of goods takes place. How important are the reception issues to consumers? IT offers, however, possibilities to develop and adapt the type and level of delivery, reception and other services to consumer desires.

The high cost in logistics activities in e-commerce and home delivery is also a serious problem. Most customers ask for more and higher quality in service, but they do not want to pay the full price for extended service. The cost savings in transaction activities and some logistics activities have not been able to fully compensate for the increased costs in other logistics activities, and have for that reason not led to increased price competition in the retailing business. Hence, e-tailers now talk less about low prices and more about extended service to consumers and have been forced to put a specific price on home delivery. The past two years' development in sales volume and profit does not indicate that grocery e-tailers have solved their logistics and profitability problems.

A few conceptual studies on home delivery and related subjects have been made. Lardner (1998), points out that attended reception is a problem for the e-grocer, because it requires offering a short delivery window and response time. This leads to a situation where both delivery and picking timetables become more inflexible. Waller et al. (1999), on the same subject, say: From the customers' point of view a fixed delivery frequency is not enough if additional groceries are needed quickly. Furthermore, some customers require personal service. Punakivi and Saranen (2001), in a 'theoretical study with worked example', discuss success factors in e-commerce grocery home delivery. Parasuraman and Zinkhan (2002), in an overview of marketing to and serving customers through the Internet, looked at 'evaluation of service delivery' without mentioning home delivery and the logistics challenge. Other studies (e.g. Kwak et al., 2002) have investigated products it is possible to sell successfully via the Internet from a marketing/seller perspective.

Research Purpose

The purpose of this study is to explore Swedish consumers' desires regarding e-commerce shopping and reception methods, timing of attended goods reception, point of goods reception, and consumers' intentions to use home delivery when buying convenience goods.

THEORIES AND RESEARCH RELATED TO HOME DELIVERY

La Londe and Zinszer (1976) state that a successful approach to analyzing customer service and formulating customer service standards[2] would be to look at key elements of customer service and group them into three categories: pre-transaction, transaction and post-transaction elements. This seems to be a useful approach when studying consumer desires for home delivery and e-commerce. In addition, general logistics services are built on three main customer requirements, according to Bowersox and Closs (1996): *Availability* is the capacity to promptly fulfill customers' requirements for a variety of goods and services. Operational *performance* concerns how to implement delivery promises in an environment impossible to fully control, that is precision and consistency in delivery time, flexibility and recovery. *Reliability* is the capability and desire to provide accurate customer information regarding logistics operations and order status.

There are many definitions concerning how logistics creates value, but just a few concerning customers' desire for and appreciation of logistics services. Most traditional definitions of logistics services are based on the attributes of the creation of time and place utility in the logistics process and have a service delivery perspective. Perreault and Russ (1974), however, discuss these attributes by describing a number of elements of logistics services and a 15-element model. They comment on the customers' perspective and point out that customers are not really interested in these underlying activities; they are interested in results. Particularly, customers are concerned with the duration of the order cycle and its consistency, the effort required to place an order, and the time and energy spent in seeking progress reports when the order cycle time is uncertain.

The determination of logistics services should be based on customers' needs. So what do the customers need that logistics can provide? Simply stated, it is the availability (at the right time and place) of required products. For a manufacturer to produce and sell them, a wholesaler or retailer to resell them, and the ultimate consumer to use them, the necessary products must be available. Availability is uncertain when there is a risk of delivery of the 'wrong' product or of delivery at the 'wrong' time. As the business environment has changed, the attribute-based definitions of logistics services have evolved. The basic concept of utility creation became inadequate to express fully the value created by logistics. The idea of value has been broadened to include numerous value-added tasks: packaging, third-party inventory management, bar coding, information, and so on (Ackerman, 1989; Witt, 1991; Mentzer, 1993.) The value-added concept has expanded the traditional time and place utilities to include form utility, such as final assembly of bulky products at the market (Ackerman, 1989), but is still an attribute-based concept. In the literature, customer logistics services are often defined as a component of, or used as a substitute for, logistics value (Langley and Holcomb, 1991). However, customer service has been just as difficult to define as the value of service and the value of *logistics* service, and the meaning of customer service varies from one company to the next (Stock and Lambert, 2001).

Regarding customer service in a logistics services context, Mentzer et al. (1989) argue that there are two elements in service delivery: marketing customer service (MCS) and physical distribution service (PDS). The authors recognize the complementary nature of the two elements necessary to satisfy the customer and propose an integrative framework of customer service. This view is shared by others (Rinehart et al., 1989) and is thought of as an intellectual base for integrating marketing and logistics activities. Explaining PDS dimensions and integrating them into an overall customer service evaluation are necessary in order to meet customers' expectations and needs (Mentzer et al., 1989). This view is consistent with the concepts of service response logistics which position logistics capabilities as the core competency of the firm in achieving customer value and satisfaction (Davis and Manrodt, 1991, 1994).

Foggin (1991) applies total quality management (TQM) statistical tools to quantify and close the gaps between customer desires and delivery performance, discussing how TQM measures could help managers to define, benchmark, redesign, control and monitor the results of a company's customer service programs. All these methods consider satisfying the customer through the delivery of relevant attributes to be the cornerstone of successful logistics strategies. The concept of 'delighting' the customer is moving into mainstream logistics (Global Logistics Research Team, 1995). These techniques attempt to define accurately the value of logistics service attributes and measure the impact on the customer and the firm. Companies are moving beyond the simple concepts of utility and logistics as a cost centre (Novack et al., 1995). Note, however, that all these expanded definitions are still based on what the company provides, hence they are still attribute-based (an operational definition of customer value). Little concern has been shown for defining customer value from the perspective of what the customers value, that is a customer-based definition of customer value.

The service quality or gaps model (Parasuraman et al., 1985) is an attempt to understand customer satisfaction from the perspective of what customer value and require, not just in terms of the attributes that the company delivers. The model provides concepts to study the differences between customer perceptions and actual customer service on various attributes and to reduce those attributes to dimensions of value defined by the customer. Despite some limitations of the model, logistics researchers have begun to investigate whether it could be used to measure the value of logistics services. The original model was modified by developing logistics attributes that fit into the previously customer-defined value dimensions and by identifying additional gaps that could be applied to the logistics services context (Lambert et al., 1990). These views of services and logistics provided the cornerstones to create a customer-based foundation for better definition and measurement of the value of logistics.

The use of customer-based definitions of satisfaction as a part of logistics value brings physical distribution research, which traditionally focused on physically observable attributes of the phenomena, more in line with marketing, which has advanced further in understanding such an unobservable thing as customers" perceived value. Therefore, logistics practitioners are beginning to recognize the desire for a method to better understand the needs of their customers beyond a set of readily measurable service attributes.

Most empirical studies regarding logistics services deal with business customers. The terms 'service' and 'quality', though, often assuming service to consumers, are discussed and are, accordingly, focusing on consumer behavior.

No empirical studies on consumer/household desires regarding *time and timing of home delivery* have been made. In addition to the conceptual studies by Lardner (1998) and Waller et al. (1999) quoted earlier, only a few theoretical/conceptual studies on home delivery and related subjects seem to have been made. Kämäräinen et al. (2001) have, in a 'theoretical study with application in practice', studied reception boxes as an alternative to attended reception in the e-grocery business. They conclude:

Home delivery is not yet a very popular service among consumers. One reason for the slow progress has been the time-consuming and expensive order process. Internet-based solutions have solved most of the problems related to the order transaction process – making ordering simpler, cheaper and faster. However, there are still a lot of unsolved problems in the e-grocery business. One of the biggest obstacles is inefficient home delivery.

Their major conclusion is that the way e-grocery consumers receive the goods has a major impact on the grocery supply chain. Actually, inefficient home delivery has to do with picking problems, because an efficient supply chain cannot be created if picking and reception do not match demand. Consumer desires regarding the reception of goods are briefly mentioned.

RESEARCH QUESTIONS

The research questions to follow in this study have been influenced by research on logistics services (Mentzer et al., 1989; Mentzer, 1999; Mentzer et al., 2001; Sterling et al. 1989; Stock and Lambert, 1992) and service quality (Parasuraman et al., 1985; Parasuraman and Zinkhan, 2002).

Efficient home delivery, routing of transports and the reception of goods are a challenge to households as well as to home delivery providers. To increase sales volume and revenue, reasonable prices and quality in desired logistics services are important, as well as households' evaluation of extended logistics services. The providers' costs must, at the same time, be under control. Households' desires and requirements regarding the timing of home delivery call for better organization and planning in most logistics activities, such as picking, packing, transportation and delivery of goods. Households' desires and requirements for home delivery will also influence route frequencies, time scheduling of routes, size of route areas, and so on.

Most e-commerce concepts are concerned with reducing households' time, physical and mental efforts in store visits and in traveling, and with simplifying information search activities. Households' activities in *traditional shopping* involve, to a great extent, goods selection, ordering, handling, storing and transportation, and the resources needed are time, knowledge and physical capabilities. The household resource needed in *e-commerce and home delivery* is time for ordering and reception (checking, confirming goods received and payment). Home delivery offers households the chance to reallocate and save time spent on physical shopping activities. E-commerce offers households possibilities for finding information, using and processing this information, and of ordering 24 hours seven days a week. In discussing home delivery and the reception of physical goods, however, receivers are pressed for time and logistics services providers' promises and their implementation of these promises on reception are important for the future success of e-commerce. Households' desires regarding home delivery are influenced by previous experiences of home delivery, traditional shopping, access to stores and resources.

The receiver's sensitivity to the timing of delivery has many reasons: lack of time, necessity of checking and confirming the goods received, and necessity of taking care of the goods. There are at least four alternatives to households for reception of goods (Kämäräinen et al., 2001): Pick-up of goods in store, a shared reception box, a separate reception box[3] and attended home reception. In attended home reception, no investment in reception equipment is required. Besides, most households want to check the goods received, which can be done in attended home reception. *Household views on shopping methods and place for attended reception* are related to retailers' promises of point of time for delivery and their ability to fulfill given promises. The most convenient place for attended reception depends, to a great extent, on what is most important at the moment to the receiver and on the type of goods in question. Besides attended reception in the store, there are at least two options regarding the place for attended reception: at home or at work. In developing home delivery, it is valuable to know more about these attended reception methods: home delivery, traditional shopping and delivery at work.

Research Question A

What views do households have on three shopping methods for convenience goods: traditional shopping, home delivery and delivery at work? Are there segments of households having different views on shopping methods?

Household desires on specific days of the week and points of time for reception are important in scheduling routes and home delivery. If not all households' desires on timing can be fulfilled, it is, of course, valuable to know their preferences for certain days of the week and on what days they do not want to receive goods. A route does not necessarily involve exactly the same households every time, but covers households in an area with possibilities of coordination of routes. Delivery on request is very expensive and difficult. However, scheduled delivery offers possibilities of consolidating goods and the coordination of transport and picking. In attended reception, it is important to find out more about household desires regarding the length and precise points of time for reception (windows). In a system with home delivery, it is hardly economically defensible to offer the same level of service all days of the week. Is it possible to identify certain weekdays when would be feasible to offer limited or no home delivery service? (This type of information can solve practical problems in routing of transport, workforce and time planning, and avoid the negative image of home delivery.)

Research Question B

What days of the week do households definitely <u>not</u> want to receive goods? What preferences do household have regarding day of the week for delivery? What preferences do households have on points of time for reception? *What intentions do households have of using home delivery under certain conditions?* To what extent and under what conditions are households willing to change behavior and utilize home delivery? Are households willing to pay for home delivery? How much? Knowledge of these matters is important in designing logistics and in pricing home delivery.

In introducing a new shopping concept, e-tailers have opportunities to influence household attitudes and behavior by informing and promoting the advantages of home delivery. To influence and change household behavior, however, takes time and resources and should start from knowledge of household attitudes and behavior.

Research Question C

What intentions do households have of using home delivery based on certain delivery fees and conditions? Is it possible to identify households with different intentions of using home delivery?

METHOD

Conceptual Issues

The choice of items regarding household attitudes on shopping methods, and household desires on and intention to use home delivery was influenced by earlier studies in logistics and IT adoption. In order to find information on patterns in households' views on shopping methods and intention to use home delivery, a questionnaire was designed. Designing questions is not just a matter of language, structure and logic. To achieve concepts that are equivalent and are understood by most respondents is difficult. The questions were tested by 10 households, and adjustments in the wording of items were made from the test results and interviews.

It is a challenge to make the consumer understand that his/her service choice is a question of priority, cost and price. When asking households about their desires and requirements regarding home delivery, it is difficult to get an absolute and honest answer if home delivery offers are not conditioned by households' costs or sacrifices. This is because households do not *perceive* the cost and value of home delivery until they have to pay for it. In order to analyze what factors influence household desires and to have information about groups of households, data on household characteristics and on households' varying degrees of computer, Internet and e-commerce experience were collected.

Choice of Households

To study the effects of access to stores, households from four areas were chosen:

- The Färgelanda area contains two small villages, each with only one small service store in the neighborhood, but with three standard sized stores at a distance of 4 km. All stores are located close to each other. The number of households in each village is about 300.
- The Trollhättan area is a part of the city of Trollhättan (around 50,000 inhabitants) and consists mainly of privately owned houses in this medium sized city and there are several stores and supermarkets of varying sizes, locations and distances.
- The Guldheden area is situated in Gothenburg (around 450,000 inhabitants) and consists mainly of apartment houses with quite a few small stores close by and it has an above average share of elderly people.
- The Västra Frölunda area is situated in Gothenburg (around 450,000 inhabitants) and consists to a large extent of privately owned houses with several big stores close by.

Guldheden and Västra Frölunda also have several supermarkets at a distance of about 5,000 m.

Data Collection

In April 2000, a questionnaire and an introductory letter were mailed to 1399,[4] randomly selected households in four areas in southwestern Sweden. All households were asked to answer the same questions. Reminder letters were sent in April and May and reminder telephone calls were made in June 2000. The persons responsible for shopping were asked to answer questions on shopping methods, desires regarding timing of home delivery and intention to use home delivery. By the end of June 2000, 790 (56.5%) answers had been received. The quality of answers, however, declined with response time (April to June). The response rate for each question in this study was, therefore, between 423 and 768 responses.

Data Analysis

Some methodological requirements were also incorporated in the questionnaire. The data were analyzed using simple frequencies and cross tabulations. For comments on problems in data analysis, interpretations and conclusions of conceptual and methodological models, please see the presentation of results.

RESULTS

Description of Households

The gender structure in Table 4.1 is based on the sex of the owner of the telephone subscription. All housing areas have inhabitants with ages from 24 to 94 years, but Guldheden has a polarized age structure, that is many households with very old members and many households with very young members. Roughly 70% of the respondents shopping at least once a week on the way home from work had a store close to the road. In Färgelanda (a rural area), 61% of the respondents, and in the three urban areas, 43–47% of the respondents, said it was possible to coordinate shopping and other tasks.

The number of households with access to the Internet is as high as 73–77%. This was perhaps surprisingly high in 2000, but should be even higher today (2004).

Table 4.1 Household characteristics and shopping behavior

Housing area Household Characteristics	Färgelanda	Trollhättan	Guldheden	Västra Frölunda
Number of respondents	179	177	201	216
Respond. age	47.7	43.7	46.1	39.8
Gender fem/m	38.5%/61.5%	34.5%/65.5%	52.2%/47.8%	27.3%/72.7%
Number of household members	2.6	2.6	1.6	2.5
Members in employment	1.4	1.4	0.9	1.4
Shopping trips per week	3.4	2.3	3.3	3.1
Driving to visit stores (share)	75%	80%	20%	60%
Walking to visit stores (share)	20%	15%	60%	30%
Distance to store (in meters)	4000	2800	800	1300
Shopping min. once a week on way from work	46%	37%	42%	32%
Access to the Internet	73%	77%	78%	73%

Household Attitudes towards Shopping and Delivery Methods

Attitudes towards three delivery methods for convenience goods were studied: a) Home delivery (HD), b) Delivery at work (DAW), c) Traditional shopping (TS).

Table 4.2 Household attitudes towards delivery methods

Attitude	HD	DAW	TS
Very bad 1	22.3%	61.0%	1.0%
2	9.6%	14.5%	1.5%
3	10.9%	9.0%	1.3%
4	13.4%	9.0%	11.6%
5	10.8%	2.5%	8.8%
6	9.8%	1.0%	18.7%
Very good 7	23.2%	2.9%	57.0%
Median value	4	1	7
Mean value	4.03	1.92	6.10

The differences between means on attitudes towards home delivery, delivery at work and traditional shopping in Table 4.2 were tested for significance using paired sample t-test. All differences on attitudes are statistically significant ($p < .005$).

Home delivery is a very good or a good idea for 33% of the households, having a median value at 4 (mean 4.03), which might be an estimate of the market potential for home delivery.

Delivery at work is a very good or a good idea for 3.9% of the households. The result is not very encouraging. This delivery method is rejected or not known or understood by most households!

Traditional shopping is a very good or a good idea (mean 6.10) for 75.7% of the households. These results are in line with the results of a study on consumer attitudes towards e-commerce and traditional shopping (Nordén, 2004).

When analyzing the results in Table 4.2 by household characteristics and by households with varying access to stores, the following aspects should be taken into account.

Household Attitude towards Home Delivery (HD)

- Households within a distance of 1000 m (about half a mile) to stores have a slightly more positive attitude towards HD than others.
- Households with four or more members have a slightly more positive attitude towards HD than small households.
- Households with three or more members in employment have a more positive attitude towards HD than others.

- Households with any type of experience of the Internet have a more positive attitude towards HD than households with no access to the Internet.

Household Attitude towards Traditional Shopping (TS)

- Households within a distance of 1000 m (about half a mile) to stores have a slightly more positive attitude towards TS than others.
- Households with four or more members have a more positive attitude towards TS than others.
- Households with no experience of the Internet have a more positive attitude towards TS than others.
- Household attitude towards TS did not change according to number of members in employment.

Household Attitude towards Delivery at Work (DAW)

- Households experienced on the Internet through work have a slightly more positive attitude towards DAW than others. Other types of experience of the Internet or no experience of the Internet had no significance.
- No differences were found in households' attitudes towards DAW depending on the size of household, number of members in employment and distance to stores.

Comments on Shopping and Delivery Methods

Most households prefer to shop for convenience goods in a traditional way and have difficulties perceiving other shopping and reception options. However, *home delivery* is an alternative to *traditional shopping* and almost one out of four households perceive *home delivery* as an excellent idea. *Delivery at work* is not at all appreciated by most households and only a few households think it is a good idea.

Household Preferences on Point of Time for Reception

The issue of preferences was divided into two questions:

a) (Table 4.3) What days of the week do you absolutely *not* want to receive goods?
b) (Table 4.4) What is the best time period to receive goods?

Table 4.3 Share of households __not__ wanting to receive goods on a certain day of the week

Monday	Tuesday	Wednesday	Thursday	Friday	Saturday	Sunday
13%	8%	7%	5%	13%	34%	44%

Some households would not receive goods on weekends but would accept them midweek. When analyzing the results in Table 4.3 by household characteristics and varying access to stores, the following aspects should be taken into account:

- Households with three or fewer members in employment are more negative towards receiving goods on Saturday and Sunday than others.
- Household members' age and distance to stores have almost no influence on preference for receiving goods on certain days of the week.

Table 4.4 Share of households preferring to receive goods during a certain time period

Time period	9–noon	noon–4 pm	4–7 pm	7–10 pm
Share (%)	17.5	9	32	24

Most households prefer to receive goods late in the afternoon and in the evening, but preference varies with age and number of household members in employment, which seems logical. When analyzing the results in Table 4.4 by household characteristics and varying distance to stores, the following aspects should be taken into account:

- For households with all members unemployed, 51.5% prefer to receive goods in the morning.
- For households with two or more members in employment, 38% prefer to receive goods at 4–7 pm, and 30% prefer to receive goods at 7–10 pm.
- In households with members aged 65 or over, 50% prefer to receive goods in the morning.

Comments on Preferences for Receiving Goods Certain Days and Hours of the Week

Most households accept midweek reception but reception on weekends is not quite as popular. Preferences for shopping at weekends move to some extent to midweek, which will decrease crowding in stores and on roads on Friday afternoons and evenings and on Saturdays.

The preferences for certain days for reception should be considered when scheduling logistics activities. The strong preferences for home delivery in the evening are, however, an obstacle to effective transport and will limit the use of vehicles and other fixed utilities. Household preferences for a certain hour vary slightly with distance to stores. Factors like age, household size and number of members in employment, though, have a stronger influence on preferences for certain hours.

Household Intention to Use Home Delivery

This issue was divided into two conditions for questions:

a)   How often would you use home delivery if there was no charge when shopping amount exceeds 500 SEK?

b)   How often would your household use home delivery if the charge would be 60 SEK?

Table 4.5 Share of households that would use home delivery if there was no charge when shopping amount exceeds 500 SEK

Frequency	Twice a week or more often	Once a week approx.	Twice a month approx.	Once a month approx.	Would not use it
Share (%)	2.7	22.4	13.6	19.2	42.1

More than 50% of the households express an intention to use home delivery to some degree. However, the answers do not tell us if they intend to use it regularly or not. It is also obvious that as many as 42.1% of all households will not use home delivery even under these generous terms.

When analyzing the results in Table 4.5 by household characteristics and varying access to stores, the following aspects should be taken into account:

• Households with two or more members express an intention to use home delivery more frequently than others.

- Almost no differences in intention to use home delivery were found to depend on number of household members in employment or households with varying access to stores.
- Households with members aged 25–49 years express intention to use home delivery more frequently than others.

Table 4.6 Share of households that would use home delivery if the charge was 60 SEK

Frequency	Eleven times or more per year	Six to ten times per year	One to five times per year	Would not use it
Share (%)	6.8	8.6	19.6	65.0

The reply alternatives in Table 4.6 were changed compared with the alternatives in Table 4.5. It is, however, easy to compare the answers and conclude that the intention to use home delivery is considerably stronger if there is no charge when the amount spent on shopping exceeds 500 SEK, compared with a situation where the charge would be 60 SEK.

When analyzing the results in Table 4.6 by household characteristics and varying access to stores, the following aspects should be taken into account:

- Households where two members are in employment intend to use home delivery slightly more frequently than others.
- Household size and varying distance to stores have little influence on intentions to use home delivery.
- Households with members in the 25–49 year bracket intend to use home delivery slightly more frequently than others.

Comments on Household Intentions to Use Home Delivery

The results concerning household intentions to use home delivery are encouraging. However, it is not easy to make predictions on future behavior based on people's intentions. The differences regarding household intentions to use home delivery if there is a fee and if there is no fee respectively are obvious and must be analyzed further.

CONCLUSIONS AND RECOMMENDATIONS

It is easier for households at normal or short distances from stores to accept new store formats. Households at long distances from stores are very anxious to keep these stores. They regard home delivery as a threat to traditional stores and are suspicious of 'newfangled' ideas. The saying 'better the devil you know than the devil you don't know' seems to be relevant in the choice of shopping method. So, in order to convince households to utilize home delivery on a regular basis, it is important to inform households as to how home delivery works and, if possible, implement a home delivery system functioning parallel to a system with traditional stores.

Launching and marketing of B2C e-commerce should focus on consumer groups with a positive attitude towards e-commerce and home delivery.

The study found that households showing the most positive attitude also have relatively strong resources in some aspects, but these households' situation, in general, is pressed to the limit. Households with a positive attitude towards home delivery, accordingly, are pressed for time, have many members in employment, and so on. These households' acceptance of home delivery could be valuable in launching home delivery.

Almost no actor in the retail business could object to a development where sales concentration at weekends decreases, since this would create a better use of distribution systems, stores and staff. To convince more households to accept odd reception hours is a challenge. Low charges and other tempting offers can lead to better utilization of the home delivery systems' capacity over the days of the week and the hours of the day.

Home delivery in e-commerce is logistics from 'store to door'. More than one out of two households intends to use home delivery in the future. It is very likely, however, that households will use home delivery from time to time but not on a regular basis. If this is true, a flexible logistics system for home delivery should be designed.

Pricing of extended logistics services, for example home delivery, is sensitive to households' intentions to use home delivery. For some households, it is easier to accept costs included in the price. It is possible that the willingness to pay for home delivery is more of an attitude than the effect of a rational decision. Nevertheless, it is very important to consider aspects of delivery terms when pricing a variety of home delivery services to households and to remember the attitudinal aspect. These aspects are obvious to many mail-order companies.

B2C e-commerce results in more complex consumer behavior than e-commerce actors think and, in many respects, additional consumer resources are needed. Among other things, the consumer must have a computer, access to the Internet and knowledge of products, and must know how to navigate a web-page. As mentioned earlier, it is difficult to make predictions on future behavior based on people's intentions. Behavior can change due to new situations and new circumstances.

Households today have access to the Internet to a varying degree, which affects their future shopping behavior and intention to test and to use new shopping and delivery methods. The success of e-commerce, however, also depends on the development of delivery systems and reception methods. Very few consumers will in the future accept several attended receptions per week from separate distributors.

NOTES

1. E-tailer is an abbreviation of e-commerce retailer.
2. Key elements of customer service were identified in a study sponsored by the National Council of Logistics Management.
3. In some countries, especially in large cities, many apartment houses today have a caretaker.
4. The plan was to send questionnaires to 360 respondents in each of the four areas but 41 addresses were excluded, because they were not correct.

REFERENCES

Ackerman, K. (1989), 'Value-added warehousing cuts inventory costs', *Transportation & Distribution*, July.

Ballou, R.H. (1999), *Business Logistics Management*, 4th ed., New Jersey: Prentice Hall.

Bowersox, D.J. and Closs, D.J. (1996), *Logistics Management: The integrated supply chain process*, New York: McGraw-Hill.

Child, P. N. (2002), 'Taking Tesco Global', *The McKinsey Quarterly Review*, 3, p 135–144.

Davis, F.V. Jr and Manrodt, K.B. (1991), 'Principles of service response logistics', Proceedings, Council of Logistic Management, Chicago.

Davis, F.V. Jr and Manrodt, K.B. (1994), 'Service logistics: An introduction', *International Journal of Physical Distribution & Logistics Management*, 24 (4), 59.

Foggin, J.H. (1991), 'Closing the gaps in service marketing: Designing to satisfy customer expectations', in, M.J. Stahl, M.J. and G.M. Bounds (eds), *Competing Globally through Customer Value*, Westport, CT: Quorum Books.

Gilmour, P., Borg, G., Duffy, P. and Johnston N.D. (1994), 'Customer service: Differentiating by market segment', *International Journal of Physical Distribution and Logistics Management*, 24 (4), 18

Global Logistics Research Team (1995), *World Class Logistics: The Challenge of Managing Continuous Change*, Oak Brook: Council of Logistics Management.

Hedlund, A. (2003), 'När dammet lagt sig – Internet och e-handeln en del av svensk detaljhandel', Research Paper from Handelns utredningsinstitut (HUI), Stockholm.

Kämäräinen, V., Saranen, J. and Holmström, J. (2001), 'The reception box impact on home delivery efficiency in the e-grocery business', *International Journal of Physical Distribution & Logistics Management, 31 (*6), 414.

Kwak, H., Fox, R.J. and Zinkhan, G.M. (2002), 'What products can be successfully promoted and sold via the Internet?', *Journal of Advertising Research; New York*; Jan/Feb, 42 (1), 23.

LaLonde, B.J. and Zinszer, P.H. (1976), *Customer Service: Meaning and measurement*, Chicago: National Council of Physical Distribution Management,, 156–159.

Lambert, D.M., Stock, J.R. and Sterling, J.U. (1990), 'An analysis of buying indicators', Proceedings, Chicago, IL: AMA.

Langley, C.J. Jr and Holcomb, M.C. (1991), 'Achieving customer value through logistic management', in, M.J. Stahl and G.M. Bounds (eds), *Competing Globally through Customer Value*, Westport, CT: Quorum Books.

Lardner, J. (1998), 'Please don't squeeze the tomatoes online', *US News and World Report, 125 (6), 40.*

Mentzer, T., Gomes, R. and Krapfel, R.E. Jr (1989), 'Physical distribution service: A fundamental marketing concept', *Journal of the Academy of Marketing Science*, 17 (1).

Mentzer, T. (1993), 'Managing channel relations in the 21st century', *Journal of Business Logistics, 14 (1), 27.*

Mentzer, T., Flint, D. and Kent J.L. (1999) 'Developing a Logistics Service Quality Scale', *Journal of Business Logistics*, 20 (1), 9.

Mentzer, T., Flint, D. and Hult, G.T.M. (2001), 'Logistics services quality as a segment-customized process', *Journal of Marketing, Chicago*, Oct., 65 (4), 82.

Nordén B. (2004) 'Consumer Attitudes towards E-Commerce and Convenience Goods -The importance of environmental arguments in marketing E-Commerce', Not published; School of Business, Economics and Law, Göteborg University

Novack, R.A., Langley, C.J. and Rinehart, L.M. (1995), *Creating Logistics Value: Themes for the Future*, Oak Brook, IL: Council of Logistics Management.

Parsuraman, A., Zeithaml, V.A. and Berry, L.L. (1985), 'A conceptual model of service quality and its implications for future research', *Journal of Marketing* 49 (4).

Parasuraman, A. and Zinkhan, G. M. (2002), 'Marketing to and serving customers through the Internet: An overview and research agenda', *Journal of the Academy of Marketing Science 30* (4), 286.

Perreault, W.D. and Russ, F. (1974), 'Physical distribution service: A neglected aspect of marketing management', MSU *Business Topics*, 22, 3 (Summer), 37.

Punakivi, M. and Saranen, J. (2001), 'Identifying the success factors in e-grocery home delivery', *International Journal of Retail & Distribution Management*, 29 (4/5), 156.

Rinehart, L.M., Cooper, M.B. and Wagenheim, G.D. (1989), 'Furthering the integration of marketing and logistics through customer service in the channel', *Journal of The Academy of Marketing Science*, 17 (1), 63.

Sterling, J.U. and Lambert, D.M. (1989), 'Customer service research: Past, present and future', *International Journal of Physical Distribution and Materials Management, 19 (2), 3-23.*

Stock, J.R. and Lambert, D. M. (1992), 'Becoming a "World Class" company with logistics service quality', *International Journal of Logistics Management*, 3 (1), 73

Stock, J.R. and Lambert, D.M. (2001), *Strategic Logistic Management* 4th ed. Homewood IL: Irwin Publishing.

Tuunainen, V.K. (1999), 'Different models of electronic commerce', doct. dissertation, Helsinki School of Economics and Business Administration.

Waller, M., Johnson, E. M. and Davies, T. (1999), 'Vendor-managed inventory in the retail supply chain', *Journal of Business Logistics* 20, 1.

Witt, C.E. (1991), 'Adding value accuracy equals quality', *Material Engineering*, April.

Yrjölä, H. (2001), 'Physical distribution considerations for electronic grocery shopping', *International Journal of Physical Distribution & Logistics Management*, 31 (10), 746–761.

5. A Comparison of In-Store vs. Online Grocery Customers[1]

Andrea M. Prud'homme and Kenneth K. Boyer

INTRODUCTION

Groceries are a ubiquitous commodity for consumers and a highly competitive industry for grocery providers. While the need to buy groceries is virtually universal, it is a chore that many people may not look forward to doing, or may have difficulty performing because of physical or transportation limitations. The most common method for acquiring groceries requires consumers to physically go to the store, walk up and down the aisles gathering the items needed and proceeding to the checkout line. The use of the Internet for online grocery ordering has introduced another option for consumers that will eliminate the need to push a cart through the store, and if home delivery is used, will eliminate the trip to the store as well. However, the first generation of online grocers has overcome numerous challenges, including extending the supply chain from existing stores to customer homes and changing customer behavior to embrace a new form of shopping.

The Internet is increasingly becoming a medium that is utilized by a wide range of service providers in an attempt to increase efficiency and reduce costs while also maintaining a high level of quality in their customer facing operations (Boyer et al., 2002; Boyer and Olson, 2002; Hill et al., 2002; Froehle and Roth, 2004). Firms can properly leverage assets to ensure efficient operations and the 'right' kind of customer experience if they have a clear understanding of the needs and priorities of their customer base, which includes why customers use the online ordering channel (Kunkel, 2003) and the customers' satisfaction with the goods and service they receive. Ultimately, the ability of an online retailer to fulfill customer needs will affect the amount of the consumers' shopping dollars or 'wallet' that will be spent with a given supplier (Wolfinbarger and Gilly, 2001).

The grocery industry operates in an environment that is especially challenging with exceptionally low profit margins of 1 to 2% (Morganosky,

1997), thousands of items per retail outlet (Ring and Tigert, 2001), and intense price competition. This challenging environment puts grocers under extreme pressure to capture more market share, especially of those customers who will be more loyal to a single grocer. This is particularly true for grocers who offer online ordering where the cost to acquire a new online customer may be 5 to 20 times the gross margins achieved per order placed (Tanskanen et al., 2002). This means that online grocers need to capture customers and then keep them satisfied so that they will purchase enough goods to allow the grocer to recoup their recruitment costs, which will usually require multiple customer orders. Given the high cost of recruiting a new online customer compared to the gross profit margin per order, it is imperative that grocers serving this market niche have a good understanding of what drives online customer satisfaction so that customers who try this service will continue to use it, and eventually spend more using this channel.

It is quite possible that customers who use the online channel will have differing perceptions of service and product quality than their in-store shopping counterparts. Using customers from three grocers who provide *both*online services as well as selling through traditional brick and mortar stores, the purpose of this study is to determine if and how these two customer segments differ, in order to provide insight for online grocery providers to better meet the needs of their customer segments.

LITERATURE REVIEW AND HYPOTHESES

This section reviews existing literature on the grocery industry in general and Internet ordering of groceries specifically. We examine three primary aspects of this service: customers' selection criteria used in choosing a grocer, as well as their perceptions of the quality of the service and the quality of the products they receive. We then examine the behavioral intentions of customers to continue to purchase from their preferred grocer, along with the percentage of their grocery wallet that is spent with that grocer. Customer responses to a series of questions representing these areas will be compared for the two methods of service: traditional in-store grocery shopping compared to online ordering of groceries.

Summary of the Grocery Industry

A grocery provider supplies customers with a mix of tangible products and intangible services that enables them to gather a large variety of foodstuffs (and often other goods) from a single retail location. The equally important mix of intangibles and tangibles requires studying not only the traditional service dimensions as described by Parasuraman, et al. (1985) but also customer perceptions as they relate to the tangible aspects of product quality. There are numerous factors that affect customers' choice of a store for buying groceries, but the classic definition of strategy suggests that the two fundamental methods companies can use to capture customers are offering a low price or differentiating their products and services (Porter, 1980).

Although grocers may have options when determining which strategy to pursue in an effort to capture market share, the prevailing strategy in the industry has been low prices. The low price strategy has manifested in several distinct ways. One approach is through warehouse clubs that compete by offering prices that can be up to 26% lower than conventional supermarkets (Food Marketing Institute, 1992), but that requires customers to purchase in much larger than traditional quantities. Another low cost alternative for consumers is the 'superstore' that combines a grocery store and a large full-line discount store (Humphries, 1995) into a single facility. However, for customers who already do not enjoy trips through the store to get the goods they want, bigger is not always a better alternative (Consumer Reports, 2000). An alternative to the low price strategy emerged in the late 1990s with the advent of e-commerce, which allowed grocers to take advantage of a new technology that provided easy ordering of groceries for customers, via the Internet. This allows grocers to utilize an alternative to the low cost strategy by pursuing a *differentiation strategy* that competes on convenience for the customer by eliminating the need for the customer to physically move through the store selecting their desired items.

However, Internet grocery sales represent an especially challenging form of e-commerce (Baker, 2000; Palmer et al., 2000), for several reasons: 1) groceries are tangibles that prevent the entire business transaction from occurring electronically; 2) groceries are perishable so customers frequently wish to examine and select the products themselves, especially items such as meats or produce; and 3) because of the tangible and perishable nature of the goods, the grocery supplier will most often be local, which may limit market size. Fortunately, despite these substantial barriers, some customers appear to have a strong desire for online ordering. Because grocery shopping is perceived by many to be an unpleasant, inconvenient or physically challenging chore, it provides the opportunity for grocers to create customer value by providing customers with greater convenience (Lee, 2003).

Selection Criteria

The primary benefit of online grocery shopping is the ability to avoid entering the physical store, and if home delivery is being used the trip to the store can also be avoided. Over 70% of respondents in a recent study of US consumers who purchase groceries online reported convenience and time saving as the primary reasons for online buying. Other reasons were physical constraints that make in-store shopping difficult, hatred of grocery shopping and grocery stores, and a dislike of standing in line (Morganosky and Cude, 2000; Weir, 2001). Another recent study in Finland supports the idea that dramatic time saving is possible with online grocery shopping as compared to the time spent on traditional in-store shopping. Traditional in-store shopping takes an average of 48 to 58 minutes per trip, with 57% of the total trip time spent on travel to and from the store, and an average customer making several trips per week (Tanskanen et al., 2002). Since many customers have little spare time and don't enjoy pushing a cart up and down aisles (Weir, 2001; Lee, 2003), time saving and convenience are a significant advantage of online over in-store shopping. Internet ordering has often been profiled as one potential method of saving time, since customers can order any time, from anywhere and dressed in any way they wish.

In general online shoppers can be categorized as being goal-oriented and more focused on a quick and distraction free transaction than on the shopping experience (Wolfinbarger and Gilly, 2001; Zeithaml et al., 2002). Approximately 200 items account for 90% of a typical consumer's repetitive 'grocery list' (Tanskanen et al., 2002) but each time a shopper goes to the grocery store they must physically travel throughout the store to gather each item, needing to choose from an available selection of 30,000+ items to get the relatively few of these they actually need. In contrast, online shopping may allow customers to create a grocery list that allows for a 'one click' selection of the items they frequently purchase, or even an automatic delivery schedule (Consumer Reports, 2000; Lee, 2003).

A recent study by Pricewaterhouse found that 42% of current online grocery shoppers were 'always looking for ways to spend less time grocery shopping', although only 11% would be willing to pay more for the service (Bubny, 2000). Interestingly, many online shoppers already pay slightly higher prices, which could also be in addition to delivery fees charged (Consumer Reports, 2000; Ring and Tigert, 2001; Lee, 2003).

Zeithaml et al. (2002) suggest that service quality delivery through the Internet can be more important to customers than low price. Given the goal-orientation of online shoppers who often are willing to pay a premium for the service, we will test the following two-part hypothesis regarding the role of price and convenience for in-store versus online grocery shoppers:

H1a: The importance of *price* in selecting a grocer will be greater for in-store customers than it will be for online customers.

H1b: The importance of *convenience* in selecting a grocer will be greater for online customers than it will be for in-store customers.

Service Quality

Service quality has long been considered an essential component of almost any service business and has been shown to be a strong predictor of customer perceptions and loyalty (Woodside et al., 1989; Boulding et al., 1993; Zeithaml et al., 1996; Cronin et al., 2000; Metters et al., 2002). Because of the relatively little direct personal contact customers generally have with grocery employees, the grocery industry provides an interesting test of the importance of service quality. Fifty years ago US grocers tended to be smaller neighborhood retailers and employees generally knew their customers by name and provided highly personalized service (Terbeek, 1999; Palmer et al., 2000), however the prevailing trend over the past five decades has been an increase in the size and the de-personalization of grocery stores. If companies want to encourage repeat purchases and to build customer loyalty, they may need to shift their focus for e-business from a purely transaction one to a service focus (all the cues and encounters that occur before, during, and after the transaction) (Zeithaml et al., 2002). It appears to be intuitive that customers who experience better service quality will be more loyal and therefore more likely to continue purchasing from a given company. However, this relationship is likely to be moderated in an e-commerce setting in which the buying process is dis-intermediated or de-personalized, and the importance of the service quality can be expected to change (Kaynama and Black, 2000; Meuter et al., 2000).

Grocery shopping in the US generally entails little interaction between customers and the employees of the grocery provider, which would normally occur only at the checkout point. With the recent introduction of self-service checkouts, even this service encounter can be eliminated so that an individual could very easily shop without ever interacting with a grocery employee, further depersonalizing the experience. Most consumers use the Web for its shopping facilitations and do not expect the personal interaction and warmth that they would from traditional service firms (Zeithaml, 2002). It would intuitively seem that customers who place orders online would also have little interaction with grocery employees upon which to base perceptions of service quality; however, the nature of the encounters tend to be more intimate given the delivery method, which is often directly to the customer's front door or when the customer goes to the store to pick up the order and the grocery employee helps to load the groceries into the customer's car. We posit that online grocers can manage this 'moment of truth' carefully (Gadrey and Gallouj, 1998; Peters, 1999) to create a more personalized interaction with customers that differentiates their service from the large box stores typical of major chains. Thus we test the following hypothesis:

 H2: Perceptions of *service quality* will be greater for online
       than for in-store customers.

Product Quality

The very nature of groceries makes them as much a tangible good as a service, which introduces the additional element of product quality, and could change the importance and nature of service quality to overall customer satisfaction (Boulding et al., 1993; Meuter et al., 2000). It may be possible for customers to evaluate quality purely via information available online for intangible products and services such as travel arrangements, computer software or music, but tangible products often require physical handling and evaluation for selection by the consumer. For many individuals, it can be difficult to forgo the ability to 'try' and select the product for themselves. This is especially true for items that are rather personal and that consumers use subjective criteria to select. For example, is the 'perfect' pear hard because it won't be eaten for a few days or soft and juicy because it is needed for dessert tonight? In fact, for consumers who are not interested in online grocery shopping, the most frequently given reason, from 75% of the respondents, was the lack of ability to see and touch what they were purchasing (Bubny, 2000). Thus customers new to Internet grocery retailing face a hurdle in terms of becoming comfortable with a new way of purchasing a very personal item. The varying subjective nature of perceptions of product quality between individuals, or even when individuals make selections based upon specific but changing uses, makes this a difficult issue for online grocery providers to overcome (Tanskanen et al., 2002; Ellis, 2003). Thus we test the following hypothesis:

H3: Perceptions of *product quality* for product received will
     be higher for in-store than online customers.

Behaviors

The grocery business is extremely competitive and customers have become less loyal over the past decades. Retaining customers and getting them to do a greater proportion of their shopping with a given grocer can have a huge impact on profits. Given that typical net profit margins are in the 1 to 2%

range and that gross margins are in the 30% range, increasing the number of customers shopping with a specific grocer by even a small amount can have a large impact on profits. In the highly competitive grocery business, creating customer loyalty is key (Lee, 2003). Widely available groceries that are largely commodity items has created a market with extreme competition and a primary emphasis on price (Morganosky, 1997). Customer loyalty would appear to be even more critical for online grocers where customer acquisition is expensive. Furthermore, it has been found that online customers may need to place several orders to learn the ordering process well enough to experience significant time savings and to have a higher level of satisfaction (Boyer and Olson, 2002).

The impact of product and service quality on behaviors at the individual customer level has been a focus of research for some time and there is general acceptance that there is a strong link between customers' perceptions of service quality, loyalty and their behavioral intentions (Woodside et al., 1989; Boulding et al., 1993; Zeithaml et al., 1996; Cronin et al., 2000). These are connected in such a way that increasing customer satisfaction creates stronger customer loyalty to the firm, which leads customers to favor purchasing from the firm (Rust et al., 1995). Of those who currently shop online for groceries, only 7% are able to do so from their preferred or primary grocery store, although 43% would 'strongly agree' that they would rather use their own grocery store if it provided an online service (Bubny, 2000). Thus we examine the following two hypotheses:

H4a: On-line customers are more *loyal* to their grocery provider than in-store customers.

H4b: On-line customers *spend a larger portion* of their grocery wallet with their grocery provider than in-store customers.

METHODS

Samples

The samples consist of customers of three US grocers who provide both online ordering and serve customers through traditional 'bricks and mortar' retail stores. Data were collected from both traditional in-store shoppers and online customers of the three grocers. Although all three firms were generous in allowing access to their customers and provided assistance throughout the survey process, they prefer not to be identified by name, and are therefore assigned the fictional names of Grocers 1, 2 and 3. Because of the competitive nature of the industry, financial information on the firms can only be discussed in aggregate. The three firms have annual combined sales of over US$40 million from online/home delivery in six US states and traditional grocery sales of over US$50 billion from stores in 30 US states. These three grocers were selected because they have been serving the in-store and online markets for some time and are large enough in both channels to provide an adequate customer base to survey. The size, geographic dispersion and length of time the grocers have been serving their online markets makes them good choices for this survey and allows for generalization to the grocery industry as a whole. A summary of the grocers included in the study is detailed in Table 5.1.

Table 5.1 Descriptions of participating grocers

	Grocer 1	Grocer 2	Grocer 3
Locations	5 states in the southeastern US	1 state in the southeastern US	27 states, mostly in the western US
Annual sales	$15+ billion	Unavailable	$20+ billion
Traditional stores	800	100	1,550
Delivery markets	1 area	31 areas	6 areas

Data Collection

A summary of the data collection techniques can be found in Table 5.2, including the number of customers contacted the number of responses and the response rate. All customers included in the online category had purchased groceries online from the grocer at least once in the previous year. Collection of in-store only customer data was conducted in person over the course of several hours spent in the stores by asking randomly selected customers to participate in the survey in an opt-in process, until approximately 80 to 100 responses were collected for each grocer, using a method similar to Wakefield and Baker (1998). Only in-store customers who had not placed online orders are included in this sample. Customers from all groups were asked identical core questions that are used as the basis of this study.

Online customers with a range of experience with online grocery ordering (as determined by the number of orders placed) for Grocers 1 and 2 were sent e-mails and asked to complete the web-based survey. Grocer 3 posted a message on the order checkout web page inviting customers to participate in the web-based survey using an opt-in approach as the customer was concluding their grocery order. This resulted in a convenience opt-in sample of customers of Grocer 3, however a question was added to the survey for this grocer asking customers to indicate the number of online orders they had placed so that it was possible post hoc to ensure that the sample included an adequate number of individuals from an appropriate range of experience levels. Having customers across a range of experience levels was necessary to reduce potential sources of bias. The high number of customers contacted for Grocer 3 represents the total number of customers who logged on to the web site during the two-week period. Basic guidelines were used for survey research and data collection including customer contact with follow-up reminders as needed, a token incentive for survey completion and a promise of anonymity (Dillman, 1978).

Grocers 1 and 2 considered it important to compensate their online customers for their time and effort in providing this important feedback. The incentives offered varied slightly, but were valued at less than $10 per customer. Grocer 3 did not provide an incentive to their customers for participation in the survey. The immediate 'on the spot' opt-in process for the in-store customers negated the need for follow-up letters, as did the open invitation posted on Grocer 3's website. However, both Grocers 1 and 2 did utilize follow-up invitations for online customers.

As shown in Table 5.2, the overall response rate for online customers who received a direct invitation (Grocers 1 and 2) is quite high, with 869 responses from the 3,237 customers contacted, or 26.9%. Grocer 3 has a low response rate of only 8.6% due to the opt-in request to the survey rather than a special invitation, lack of incentive and no follow-up process. Overall the response results compare favorably to similar studies (Duray et al., 2000; Papke-Shields et al., 2002).

Differing data collection methods (e-mail invitations, in-person opt-in, and electronic opt-in) could result in potential sample bias. Several tests across the groups suggested that bias did not exist, which is consistent with research which indicates that surveys can be administered using a variety of media to contact the customers with little cause for concern as long as the research design is solid and the questionnaire used is consistent across sample groups (Couper, 2000; Couper, 2000; Klassen and Jacobs, 2001).

Table 5.2 Descriptions of data collection methods

	Grocer 1		Grocer 2		Grocer 3	
	In-store	Online	In-store	Online	In-store	Online
Sample selection	Random	Stratified	Random	Stratified	Random	Random
Invitation to customer	In-person opt-in	e-mail invitation	In-person opt-in	e-mail invitation	In-person opt-in	Website Opt-in
Incentive	No	Yes	No	Yes	No	No
Survey method	Written	Web	Written	Web	Written	Web
Customers contacted	NA	2,078	NA	1,159	NA	10,418
Responses	101	475	108	394	80	896
Response rate	NA	22.90%	NA	34%	NA	8.60%

SURVEY QUESTIONS AND RESPONSES

For each of the areas regarding selection criteria, service quality, product quality and behavior, customers were asked to respond to the questions on a seven point Likert scale ranging from 1 = strongly disagree to 7 = strongly agree. The individual grocer's name was inserted wherever 'Grocer_X' appears (see table 5.3). For each question, the response mean and (standard deviation) are reported for online and in-store customers, with items in *italic* indicating responses that are statistically significantly different at * $p < 0.05$ and ** $p < 0.01$.

Selection Criteria

There are very clear differences in why customers choose specific grocers. The data in Table 5.3 clearly support the first two hypotheses, H1a and H1b. Price is significantly more important to in-store customers and convenience is significantly more important to online customers. In strategic terms, online customers have communicated their competitive priorities/order winners clearly (Hayes and Wheelwright, 1984; Hill, 1994), and it is now up to online grocery providers to find better ways to meet the convenience needs of this channel.

Table 5.3 Selection criteria

	In-Store	Online	p
Price of products is important in selecting Grocer_X	5.92 (1.34)	5.10 (1.59)	**
Convenience is important in selecting Grocer_X	6.13 (1.34)	6.73 (0.68)	**

1 = strongly disagree to 7 = strongly agree   Mean (std. dev)   * $p < 0.05$ and ** $p < 0.01$

Service Quality

Measurement of *service quality* has been the subject of study and debate for the past two decades (Parasuraman et al., 1985; Cronin and Taylor, 1992; Teas, 1994; Llosa et al., 1998; Clerfeuille and Poubanne, 2003), although study of this area of service through websites is in its early stages (Zeithaml, 2002). The goal is to better understand the gap between customer expectations and customer experiences in order to close the gap to create more customer loyalty (Zeithaml et al., 1996; Mitchell and Kiral, 1998). A set of 10 questions based upon the original dimensions of service quality proposed by Parasuraman et al. (1985) was created to capture customer perceptions of tangibles, reliability, responsiveness, assurance and empathy. The intention was to ask a broad range of questions while also keeping the total number of questions asked to a manageable level. Table 5.4 indicates that where there are significant differences between in-store and online customers, the online customers have higher perceptions of service quality on seven of the ten questions, providing support for H2.

The only individual items that do not have significant differences are SQ4, SQ7 and SQ10. Items of particular interest include SQ3 (employees are responsive), SQ5 (I feel secure in service encounters), SQ6 (employees are courteous) and SQ9 (Grocer_X has good credibility). Each of these items has a significantly higher mean for online than for in-store customers. This indicates that online grocers are managing the 'moment of truth' at the customer's car or front door by being responsive, non-threatening (secure), courteous, and generally establishing good credibility. This is essential for making this business model work since customers may initially be wary of this new method of grocery shopping.

Grocery E-Commerce

Table 5.4 Service quality

	In-Store	Online	p
SQ1. Grocer_X employees are reliable in providing the service I expect	5.97 (1.12)	*6.14 (1.09)*	*
SQ2. Grocer_X employees are understanding of my service needs	5.87 (1.09)	*6.05 (1.12)*	*
SQ3. Grocer_X employees are responsive to my service requests	5.96 (1.12)	*6.12 (1.15)*	*
SQ4. Grocer_X employees are competent in providing the expected service	6.02 (1.10)	6.09 (1.13)	
SQ5. I feel secure in service encounters with Grocer_X employees	6.09 (1.03)	*6.28 (1.02)*	**
SQ6. Grocer_X employees are courteous in providing me service	6.20 (1.04)	*6.51 (0.93)*	**
SQ7. Grocer_X employees are available to answer my service-related questions	5.95 (1.12)	6.04 (1.25)	
SQ8. The tangible (appearance of trucks, staff, products) aspects of Grocer_X service are excellent	6.02 (1.13)	*6.29 (1.04)*	**
SQ9. Grocer_X has good credibility in providing the service I need	6.08 (1.01)	*6.28 (1.04)*	**
SQ10. I have access to communicate with Grocer_X regarding my service needs	5.96 (1.15)	6.10 (1.25)	

1 = strongly disagree to 7 = strongly agree   Mean (std. dev) $*p < 0.05$ and $**p < 0.01$

Product Quality

Product quality was of special interest to the grocery managers at the stores included in this study and was cited as a key challenge for the companies to execute well from an operational perspective. Other research has found that product quality is also an issue for online customers (Bubny, 2000; Consumer Reports, 2000; Wolfinbarger and Gilly, 2003). The product quality questions were created specifically to compare customer perceptions of differences between in-store and online product quality as they relate to the physical quality of the products they receive. The mean for all three of the product quality questions is substantially higher for in-store customers than for online customers and all are significant at the $p < 0.01$ level. This provides support for H3 that in-store customers do have higher perceptions of product quality than online customers.

One of the disadvantages of online ordering is that the customer sacrifices the ability to select their own products. This is not a big problem for packaged goods (i.e. cereal, canned soup, cookies, etc.) because these items are commodity goods that are protected by their packages and have a high degree of consistency. However, produce, meats, fruits and dairy products are much more variable and customers may be concerned about giving up the ability to select their own goods according to their preferences for ripeness, color, expiration date, and so on.

Table 5.5 Product quality

	In-Store	Online	p
PQ1. Grocer_X has prestigious products	*5.84 (1.09)*	5.57 (1.24)	**
PQ2. Grocer_X has an excellent assortment of products	*5.97 (1.06)*	5.40 (1.32)	**
PQ3. Grocer_X products are among the best	*5.76 (1.17)*	5.43 (1.24)	**

1 = strongly disagree to 7 = strongly agree   Mean (std. dev) $* p < 0.05$ and $** p < 0.01$

Behaviors

Zeithaml, Berry, and Parasuraman (1996) suggest that positive behaviors are reflected in the service provider's ability to get its customers to: (a & b) remain loyal to them, (c) pay price premiums and (d) communicate concerns to the company. While the operational dimensions are clearly important, the most important thing is tangible results. We turn now to an examination of customer loyalty and intentions. As shown in Table 5.6, there are very few significant differences for *behaviors*, with in-store and online customers providing nearly identical ratings on all but three individual items. In-store customers rate item BI3 (I would continue to do business ... even if I had to pay more) significantly higher than online customers. This is interesting for a couple of reasons. First, grocers tend to generically compete on price, yet it would appear that in-store customers would be willing to pay slightly higher prices without switching grocers. This is important because of the very low profit margins grocers earn. Secondly, online shopping is very convenience oriented, customers rate price as less important, and they often pay a service fee or slightly higher prices when orders are placed online. It is important to note that the mean response on this question for online customers of 3.99 is nearly identical to the 4.0 midpoint (neutral) value for the response scale of 1 = strongly disagree to 7 = strongly agree on this item. This suggests that the grocers have the home delivery service well priced for customers who are not upset that the prices are too high, but who are not willing to pay more for the service either.

There is a significant difference for the question regarding the percentage of grocery shopping done with Grocer_X. Online customers report they do more of their shopping (81.43%) than in-store customers (76.26%) with the specific grocer. This is a very significant finding since it implies a type of halo effect: online customers may like the service and increase the percentage of all their grocery shopping they do with a particular grocer.

Given the very low profit margins experienced by grocers in general, and the recruiting costs incurred by online grocers to attract new customers, this is a significant finding.

Table 5.6 Behaviors

	In-Store	Online	p
BI1. I would classify myself as a loyal customer of Grocer_X	5.97 (1.25)	6.05 (1.23)	
BI2. I do not expect to switch to another (online) grocer to get better service in the future	5.72 (1.43)	5.90 (1.48)	
BI3. I would continue to do business with Grocer_X even if I had to pay more	*4.37 (1.93)*	3.99 (1.80)	**
BI4. I would complain to Grocer_X employees if I experienced a problem with their service	5.73 (1.40)	*5.96 (1.28)*	**
BI1. I would classify myself as a loyal customer of Grocer_X	5.97 (1.25)	6.05 (1.23)	
PS1. What percent of your grocery shopping do you do with Grocer_X?	76.26(26.28)	*81.43(23.40)*	**

1 = strongly disagree to 7 = strongly agree   Mean (std. dev) $* p < 0.05$ and $** p < 0.01$

DISCUSSION AND CONCLUSIONS

The advent of an alternative method of grocery shopping via online ordering with home delivery or customer pick-up allows grocers to pursue an alternative to the current commonly used low price strategy. Over the past 50 years, grocers have increasingly refined their operations to pursue a strategy based on low prices, and while this approach has benefited customers tremendously, it has also reached a point of diminishing or non-existent, marginal returns for grocery providers. The difference in prices for identical items between any two grocers in the same community is typically minimal. Prices have been pushed down to the level where it is difficult, if not impossible, to develop a sustainable competitive advantage in this area.

Following the accepted model of operations strategy, the next question would be whether the alternative methods of providing groceries can support these priorities with clear operational decisions. As shown in Table 5.4, customers of online grocers clearly perceive a substantially higher level of service quality, although service has not been a differentiating factor for grocery providers in the past few decades. In fact, the increasing size and accompanying de-personalization of grocery retailers has decreased the importance of service and customer and employee interactions. However, online customers view all aspects of service quality as better handled with home deliveries or customer pick-up than with traditional in-store shopping.

In contrast, in-store customers rate product quality higher than online customers. Given the personal nature of selecting groceries, the varying definitions different customers may have regarding the quality of products such as produce, and the additional complication of individual customers varying their needs depending on the timing and usage of specific products, it is interesting to note that there is not an even more significant difference between the perceptions of in-store and online customers regarding product quality. It would appear that online grocers are handling this important aspect moderately well, but that there is still some room for improvement.

The end goal of most businesses is to retain customers and make profits. As shown in Table 5.6, online grocers receive comparable ratings for customer behaviors, and actually capture a higher percentage of overall grocery purchases. Despite the challenges of refining a new operating model, the data suggest that online grocers are able to develop a high degree of customer loyalty. There is good potential for improvements with respect to product quality that may allow home delivery grocers to capture a wider customer base. However, it is unlikely that online grocers will be able to capture 100% of a customer's grocery wallet, since this would require customers to perfectly plan their grocery needs ahead of time and completely eliminate the need for quick stops at the grocer to pick up forgotten or unanticipated items.

The data from this study illustrate that online ordering allows grocers to change the strategic focus of their operations in a way that is supportable through operations and allows online grocers to develop comparable, or even higher, levels of customer loyalty. This is important in that it supports the idea of 'equifinality' – that there is more than one strategic approach within an industry that is capable of capturing and retaining customers (Porter, 1980). This is particularly important in the grocery industry, where relentless competition and a few leading players control large portions of the market, and smaller grocers are seeking ways to differentiate themselves.

NOTES

1.   This research was conducted with Grant SES 0216839 from the US National Science Foundation.
2.   We appreciate the cooperation and assistance of the three grocers in the US.

REFERENCES

Baker, M. (2000). 'Online grocery shopping - time for a stock-taking'. *ICSC Research Quarterly* 7(1): 1.

Boulding, W., A. Kalra, R. Staelin and V. A. Zeithaml (1993). 'A dynamic process model of service quality: From expectations to behavioral intentions'. *Journal of Marketing Research* 30(1): 7.

Boyer, K. K., R. Hallowell and A. V. Roth (2002). 'E-services: Operating strategy - A case study and a method for analyzing operational benefits'. *Journal of Operations Management* 20(2): 175.

Boyer, K. K. and J. R. Olson (2002). 'Drivers of Internet purchasing success'. *Production and Operations Management* 11(4): 480.

Bubny, P. (2000). 'Not yet clicking'. *Supermarket Business* 55(7): 65.

Clerfeuille, F. and Y. Poubanne (2003). 'Differences in the contributions of elements of service to satisfaction, commitment and consumers' share of purchase: A study from the tetraclass model'. *Journal of Targeting, Measurement and Analysis for Marketing* 12(1): 66.

Consumer Reports (2000). 'Food fight'. *Consumer Reports* 65(9): 11.

Couper, M. P. (2000). 'Usability evaluation of computer-assisted survey instruments'. *Social Science Computer Review* 18(4): 384.

Couper, M. P. (2000). 'Web surveys: A review of issues and approaches'. *Public Opinion Quarterly* 64(4): 464.

Cronin, J. J., M. K. Brady and G. T. M. Hult (2000). 'Assessing the effects of quality, value, and customer satisfaction on consumer behavioral intentions in service environments'. *Journal of Retailing* 76(2): 193.

Cronin, J. J., Jr. and S. A. Taylor (1992). 'Measuring Service Quality: A Reexamination and Extension'. *Journal of Marketing* 56(3): 55.

Dillman, D. A. (1978). Mail and Telephone Surveys: The Total Design Method. New York, NY: Wiley.

Duray, R., P. T. Ward, G. W. Milligan and W. L. Berry (2000). 'Approaches to mass customization: Configurations and empirical validation'. *Journal of Operations Management* 18(6): 605.

Ellis, C. (2003). 'Lessons from online groceries'. *MIT Sloan Management Review* 44(2): 8.

Food Marketing Institute (1992). Alternative Store Formats: Competing in the Nineties. Washington DC, Food Marketing Institute.

Froehle, C. M. and A. V. Roth (2004). 'New measurement scales for evaluating perceptions of the technology-mediated customer service experience'. *Journal of Operations Management* 22(1): 1.

Gadrey, J. and F. Gallouj (1998). 'The provider - customer interface in business and professional services'. *The Service Industries Journal* 18(2): 1.

Hayes, R. H. and S. C. Wheelwright (1984). Restoring Our Competitive Edge: Competing Through Manufacturing. New York: Wiley.

Hill, A. V., D. A. Collier, C. M. Froehle, J. C. Goodale, R. D. Metters and R. Verma (2002). 'Research opportunities in service process design'. *Journal of Operations Management* 20(2): 189.

Hill, T. J. (1994). Manufacturing Strategy: Text and Cases. Burr Ridge: Irwin.

Humphries, G. (1995). Prospects for Food Discounters and Warehouse Clubs. London, Pearson Professional Ltd.: 78.

Kaynama, S. A. and C. L. Black (2000). 'A Proposal to Assess the Service Quality of Online Travel Agencies: An Exploratory Study'. *Journal of Professional Services Marketing* 21(1): 63.

Klassen, R. D. and J. Jacobs (2001). 'Experimental comparison of Web, electronic and mail survey technologies in operations management'. *Journal of Operations Management* 19(6): 713.

Kunkel, J. (2003). 'Reducing risk, maximizing return in online retailing'. *Chain Store Age* 79(9): S3.

Lee, L. (2003). 'Online grocers: Finally delivering the lettuce. Brick-and-mortar chains are finding profits in cyberspace'. *Business Week*(3830): 67.

Llosa, S., J.-L. Chandon and C. Orsingher (1998). 'An empirical study of SERVQUAL's dimensionality'. *The Service Industries Journal* 18(2): 16.

Metters, R. D., K. H. King-Metters and M. Pullman (2002). Successful Service Operations Management. New York: South-Western College.

Meuter, M. L., A. L. Ostrom, R. I. Roundtree and M. J. Bitner (2000). 'Self-service technologies: Understanding customer satisfaction with technology-based service encounters'. *Journal of Marketing* 64(3): 50.

Mitchell, V. W. and R. H. Kiral (1998). 'Primary and secondary store-loyal customer perceptions of grocery retailers'. *British Food Journal* 100(7): 312.

Morganosky, M. A. (1997). 'Format change in US grocery retailing'. *International Journal of Retail & Distribution Management* 25(6): 211.

Morganosky, M. A. and B. J. Cude (2000). 'Consumer response to online grocery shopping'. *International Journal of Retail & Distribution Management* 28(1): 17.

Palmer, J. W., K. Kallio, T. Saarinen, M. Tinnila, V. K. Tuunainen and E. van Heck (2000). 'Online grocery shopping around the world: Examples of key business models'. Association of Information Systems. July 10, 2004. (cais.aisnet.org)

Papke-Shields, K. E., M. K. Malhotra and V. Grover (2002). 'Strategic manufacturing planning systems and their linkage to planning system success'. *Decision Sciences* 33(1): 1.

Parasuraman, A., V. A. Zeithaml and L. L. Berry (1985). 'A conceptual model of service quality and its implications for future research'. *Journal of Marketing* 49(4): 41.

Peters, V. J. (1999). 'Total service quality management'. *Managing Service Quality* 9(1): 6.

Porter, M. (1980). Competitive Strategy. New York: The Free Press.

Ring, L. J. and D. J. Tigert (2001). 'Viewpoint: The decline and fall of Internet grocery retailers'. *International Journal of Retail & Distribution Management* 29(6/7): 266.

Rust, R., A. Zahoric and T. Keiningham (1995). 'Return on quality (ROQ): Making service quality financially accountable'. *Journal of Marketing* 59(4): 58.

Tanskanen, K., H. Yrjola and J. Holmstrom (2002). 'The way to profitable Internet grocery retailing, six lessons learned'. *International Journal of Retail & Distribution Management* 30(4): 169.

Teas, R. K. (1994). 'Expectations as a comparison standard in measuring service quality: An assessment of a reassessment'. *Journal of Marketing* 58(1): 132.

Terbeek, G. A. (1999). Agentry Agenda: Selling Food in a Frictionless Marketplace. New York: Breakaway Strategies, Inc.

Wakefield, K. L. and J. Baker (1998). 'Excitement at the mall: Determinants and effects on shopping response'. *Journal of Retailing* 74(4): 515.

Weir, T. (2001). 'Staying stuck on the Web'. *Supermarket Business* 56(2): 15.

Wolfinbarger, M. and M. C. Gilly (2001). 'Shopping online for freedom, control, and fun'. *California Management Review* 43(2): 34.

Wolfinbarger, M. and M. C. Gilly (2003). 'eTailQ: Dimensionalizing, measuring and predicting etail quality'. *Journal of Retailing* 79(3): 183.

Woodside, A. G., L. L. Frey and R. T. Daly (1989). 'Linking Service Quality, Customer Satisfaction, And Behavior'. *Journal of Health Care Marketing* 9(4): 5.

Zeithaml, V. A. (2002). 'Service excellence in electronic channels'. *Managing Service Quality* 12(3): 135.

Zeithaml, V. A., L. L. Berry and A. Parasuraman (1996). 'The behavioral consequences of service quality'. *Journal of Marketing* 60(2): 31.

Zeithaml, V. A., A. Parasuraman and A. Malhotra (2002). 'Service quality delivery through Web sites: A critical review of extant knowledge'. *Academy of Marketing Science. Journal* 30(4): 362.

6. Understanding Consumer Adoption of Online Grocery Shopping: Results from Denmark and Sweden

Torben Hansen and Suzanne C. Beckmann

INTRODUCTION

Like many other innovations (Frambach et al., 1998), Internet grocery shopping has faced serious difficulties in spreading to consumers (Ring and Tigert, 2001; Geuens et al., 2003). Research has attempted to explain the low consumer adoption by referring to the presence of transaction obstacles, including problems with slow load times, an inability to locate items, incomplete information, lack of human interaction, and missed or late deliveries (Kaufman-Scarborough and Lindquist, 2002), ease of use, that is, difficulties with site navigation and complex procedures, and security (Elliot and Fowell, 2000). In spite of such obstacles and problems a number of consumers have, however, carried out online grocery shopping. According to models of consumer adoption of innovations (e.g., Black et al., 2001), such consumers may simply be more innovative than others.

Findings of a number of studies (e.g., Lockett and Littler, 1997) suggest that innovative consumers share certain characteristics such as being better educated and having higher incomes. While such personal characteristics of innovators may be significant predictors of consumer adoption of online grocery buying, perceived characteristics of the innovation itself may also serve as predictors (Black et al., 2001; Verhoef and Langerak, 2001). Such characteristics may include, among others, perceived compatibility, perceived relative advantage, and perceived complexity (Rogers, 1983, 1995).

Much research (e.g., Verhoef and Langerak, 2001) concerning consumer adoption of online grocery shopping has studied consumers' intentions to carry out an online grocery purchase at some point in the future. Very few studies have been concerned with studying consumers who already have purchased groceries via the Internet. This is unfortunate since it is well documented that intention–behaviour inconsistencies often occur (see Shim et al., 2001). Reasons for such inconsistencies may include developments and changes in, for instance, Internet characteristics, consumer characteristics, product attributes, search conditions, or situational factors. Also, the future commercial success of online grocery buying depends, to a large extent, on understanding how already established online grocery consumers perceive characteristics of the online grocery channel. A retailer can hardly make a long-term living on just attracting new customers. Thus online grocery retailers have a high interest in gaining insights on what discriminates consumers who have adopted online grocery shopping from other consumers. Such insights may also help online grocery retailers to determine what online benefits to emphasize when seeking to attract consumers who have not yet bought groceries via the Internet.

Based on the above considerations this chapter sets out to empirically investigate whether consumers who *have* adopted online grocery buying perceive this innovation differently from other consumers. In addition, we examine the extent to which consumers' perception of certain online grocery shopping characteristics will discriminate between three segments of online consumers: (1) consumers who have never bought anything on the Internet yet; (2) consumers who have bought something on the Internet but not groceries; and (3) consumers who have bought something on the Internet including groceries. Finally, we investigate whether a number of well-known general innovator characteristics discriminate between these three segments.

ONLINE GROCERY BUYING AS AN INNOVATION

Robertson (1967) defined three types of innovation based on the degree to which they represent technological advances and changes in consumer behaviour: (1) Discontinuous innovation, which presents a major technological advance leading to new behavioural patterns among consumers adopting the product, (2) dynamically continuous innovation, which deals with a new product representing major technological advantages that do not basically change existing consumer behaviour, and (3) continuous innovation, which is a minor technological advance requiring no changes in existing consumer behaviour. In this sense, online buying represents a discontinuous innovation, since it covers technological advances as well as changes in consumer behaviour. In order to understand the diffusion of such innovations it is necessary to think of an adoption as the first step in the diffusion process. The adoption of an innovation depends on various factors, which are related to the innovation itself and to the consumer. Rogers (1983) suggests five factors that increase the rate of acceptance and diffusion of innovations. First, *communicability* is the ease with which the innovation can be observed or communicated among potential adopters. Second, *triability* or divisibility refers to the possibility of trying the innovation without huge investments. People already established with access to the Internet may not take this aspect into account unless a hardware replacement is considered. Third, *complexity*, which refers to the potential adopter's perception of the complexity of the innovation or of using the innovation. Fourth, *compatibility* is the degree to which the innovation is consistent with existing values and past behaviour. No doubt many consumers will perceive online buying as a very alternative way of purchasing. For example, information processing is very different online compared to shopping in a physical shop. Fifth, *relative advantage* is the degree to which consumers perceive the innovation as superior to existing alternatives. People in favour of online buying often point to the fact that this way of purchasing saves time and offers quality products at lower prices as compared to traditional shopping outlets.

In the next section, we discuss these factors in relation to consumer adoption of the Internet as an online grocery-shopping channel and propose seven research questions. Also, we argue that the construct of *perceived Internet (grocery) risk* (McKnight et al., 2002) should complement the five factors proposed by Rogers. For the purpose of investigating the ability of these factors to discriminate between various types of consumer adoption behaviour, we consider three online consumer segments:

- *Segment 1*: Internet users who have not purchased anything over the Internet yet (non-adopters of online shopping).
- *Segment 2*: Internet users who have purchased goods/services over the Internet but not groceries (online shopping adopters).
- *Segment 3*: Internet users who have purchased goods/services over the Internet, including groceries (online shopping adopters and online grocery-shopping adopters).

Segmenting consumers in relation to the study of adoption behavior is well known in the research literature (e.g., Martinez and Flavián, 1998; Lockett and Litter, 1997) and is also beneficial to the present study. An understanding of possible discriminating factors between the three segments is highly relevant for online retailers seeking either to attract new online customers or to keep existing online customers. For example, if segment 3 consumers view certain factors more positively than segment 2 (and/or segment 1) consumers, such a result may provide guidance to online retailers on which features to emphasize in order to attract new online grocery customers. On the other hand, if no discrimination is found between segments this may suggest that other factors (e.g., differences in consumers' personal characteristics) should be taken into account when seeking to understand consumer adoption of online grocery shopping.

RESEARCH QUESTIONS

Most people in the Western world now have online access either at home or at work, and several studies (Forsythe and Shi, 2003; Odekerken-Schröder and Wetzels, 2003) confirm consumer acceptance of the Internet as an information and shopping channel. Consequently, acceptance of the Internet as an innovation has already taken place to a large extent. We therefore choose not to include the concept of perceived triability, since this study concerns only already established Internet users. Instead, research questions are proposed concerning the concepts of perceived communicability, perceived complexity, perceived compatibility, perceived relative advantage, and perceived Internet grocery risk.

RQ 1: General Discrimination Between Segments 1, 2, and 3

Following the objective of this study, we first explore the question of whether the five constructs, perceived communicability, perceived complexity, perceived compatibility, perceived relative advantage, and perceived Internet grocery risk, together discriminate between segments 1, 2, and 3. A discrimination on the overall level is a prerequisite for investigating the discriminating effect of each of the individual constructs (i.e., the remaining research questions):

> *RQ 1*: To what extent will perceived communicability (which we conceptualize by 'perceived social norm', see below), perceived complexity, perceived compatibility, perceived relative advantage, and perceived Internet risk of online grocery shopping discriminate between segments 1, 2, and 3?

RQ 2: Perceived Social Norm (Communicability)

According to the theory of adoption of innovations (Rogers, 1983), innovations that can be observed by or communicated to other consumers are more likely to spread. Like any other fashion, online buying is obviously given much attention in the media and among many people interested in IT. Also, communication concerning the Internet as a grocery-shopping channel may take place among consumers via the Internet (e.g., in chat-rooms, newsgroups). On the general level, this notion receives support from Giese (1996: 51), who states: while it might have been overlooked early on, the Internet cannot now be ignored as a cultural phenomenon.

Communicability addresses how easily a product can be observed and communicated to others via formal and informal networks (Weich and Walchli, 2002). However, communicability can also be thought of as the degree of 'social acceptance' that is communicated to a consumer from other consumers (Blackwell et al., 2001). Based on such notions, and since online grocery shopping is not visible to other consumers unless the particular shopping event is communicated to others, we find it most useful to investigate the importance a consumer may attach to the perceived opinion of other consumers.

Additionally, previous research (e.g., Van den Poel and Leunis, 1999) indicates that consumers' perceived risk when considering buying online is larger than when considering buying offline. For the purpose of lowering perceived risk a consumer may seek to obtain normative guidance from other consumers. As it is generally believed that innovators and early adopters are less risk adverse than other consumers, general innovators and early adopters can be expected to pay less attention to social normative guidance (i.e., subjective norms, Fishbein and Ajzen, 1975) when considering carrying out online grocery buying. Based on such considerations, we investigate whether the subjective norm a consumer may attach to online grocery shopping will discriminate between segments 1, 2, and 3:

> *RQ 2*: To what extent will perceived social norm of online grocery shopping discriminate between segments 1, 2 and 3?

RQ 3: Perceived Complexity

Ring and Tigert (2001) propose that many of the Internet grocers' sites are simply difficult to shop from and to navigate. In a study of online grocery consumers, Raijas (2002) found that 'easiness to order groceries' might positively influence consumers' intent to choose an online grocery store. If consumers find what they are looking for, but are unable to complete the transaction process, they will most likely cancel the purchase (Odekerken-Schröder and Wetzels, 2003). Similarly, Elliot and Fowell (2000) found that major consumer concerns leading to unsatisfactory online experiences include difficulties with site navigation and complex procedures. Hence, consumers may hesitate to order groceries via the Internet because they consider completing the transaction process too complex. Also, consumers may find it too difficult to obtain relevant online information concerning groceries before buying the products on the Internet (e.g., Geuens et al., 2003). We therefore find it relevant to examine as follows:

> *RQ 3*: To what extent will perceived complexity of online grocery shopping discriminate between segments 1, 2 and 3?

RQ 4: Perceived Compatibility

If online shopping is not compatible with consumers' existing practices or habits, a usage barrier may occur. Online shopping is in many ways very different from shopping in physical stores. Online shopping provides less sensory stimulation (through smell, touch, music, in-store decorations, and the like) than offline shopping. Consumers' interpersonal interaction is lacking or at least reduced as well. A consumer who attaches high importance to such shopping aspects may not find online grocery shopping compatible with his/her existing shopping practices and may thus avoid making an online purchase. When deciding among shopping channels, it can be assumed that consumers make tradeoffs (Odekerken-Schröder and Wetzels, 2003) between the channels and that they are likely to choose the channel that is most compatible with existing needs and wants. We therefore expect perceived compatibility to influence consumers' online grocery buying behaviour:

> *RQ 4*: To what extent will perceived compatibility of online grocery shopping discriminate between segments 1, 2 and 3?

RQ 5: Perceived Relative Advantage

Perceived relative advantage refers to the degree to which an innovation is perceived by potential adopters as being better than the idea, product or service it supersedes (see Black et al., 2001). It has been empirically indicated that consumers' perception of relative advantages may influence their intention to adopt electronic grocery shopping (e.g., Verhoef and Langerak, 2001). Previous research suggests that the main relative advantages of carrying out Internet shopping include higher transaction speed (time advantage), the possibility of price reduction because of a reduction in operational costs and the opportunity for economic advantage through manufacturers internalizing activities traditionally performed by retailers (e.g., Anckar et al., 2002; Kaufman-Scarborugh and Lindquist,

2002; Keh and Shieh, 2001; Raijas, 2002). Indeed, based on numerous large-scale research tracking studies in the supermarket industry, Ring and Tigert (2001) note that (in general) low prices is always the first or second most important determinant of store choice in grocery shopping (p. 268). Anckar et al. (2002) also claim that as consumers generally dislike shopping for groceries, they have a desire to accomplish the task as fast as possible (p. 215). Thus it is highly relevant to investigate to what extent segment 1, 2, and 3 consumers will differ in their perception of the relative advantages of online grocery shopping:

> *RQ 5*: To what extent will perceived relative advantage of online grocery shopping discriminate between segments 1, 2 and 3?

RQ 6: Perceived Internet Grocery Risk

Perceived risk is a multidimensional construct as it may involve aspects such as perceived financial risk (Cheung and Lee, 2000; Roselius, 1971), perceived performance risk (Gemünden, 1985; Van den Poel and Leunis, 1999), perceived social risk (Korgaonkar, 1982), perceived time-loss risk (McCorkle, 1990), and perceived privacy risk (Jarvenpaa and Todd, 1996). Previous research (e.g., Van den Poel and Leunis 1999; Miyazaki and Fernandez, 2001) suggests that consumers' perceived risk when considering buying online is frequently larger than when considering buying offline and that perceived risk is a useful construct to explain barriers to online shopping (Cho, 2004; Forsythe and Shi, 2003). Since we seek to investigate the Internet as a potential grocery-shopping channel, we focus on perceived Internet grocery risk of carrying out online buying rather than risk related to the specific online retailer. Perceived Internet grocery risk is conceptualized as the extent to which a user believes it is unsafe to use the web for grocery shopping or that negative consequences are possible. Results by McKnight et al. (2002) suggest that perceived Internet risk negatively affects consumer intentions to transact with a web-based vendor. Other researchers have shown that perceived web security (Shih, 2004) and concerns over delivery (Cho, 2004) might influence consumer online behaviour. In an investigation of key dimensions of B2C web sites, Ranganathan and Ganapathy (2002) found that concerns about security had the greatest effect on the purchase intent of consumers. We therefore explore as follows:

> *RQ 6*: To what extent will perceived Internet grocery risk discriminate between segments 1, 2 and 3?

RQ 7: Innovator Characteristics of Respondents in Segments 1, 2, and 3

If the results obtained from RQs 1–6 indicate that consumers who *have* carried out online grocery buying perceive characteristics of the online grocery channel differently from other online consumers, this would suggest that online grocery shoppers, at least to some extent, are domain-specific innovators (Goldsmith and Hofacker, 1991). It is therefore also important to investigate whether consumers across segments 1–3 differ on their level of general innovativeness (Joseph and Vyas, 1984). However, as noted by Black et al. (2001), measuring general innovativeness is problematic since observed innovativeness cannot necessarily be considered as equivalent to innate innovativeness. Thus we investigate instead a number of demographic variables (age, educational level, and income) that have proven to discriminate innovators and early adopters from other consumers in several studies (e.g., Gatignon and Robertson, 1985; LaBay and Kinnear, 1981; Martinez et al., 1998). To obtain an impression of the extent to which consumers' level of general innovativeness discriminates between segments 1–3 we therefore formulate as follows:

> *RQ* 7: To what extent will demographic innovator
> variables discriminate between segments 1, 2 and 3?

METHODOLOGY

Data Collection

The data presented in this paper were collected from an online (web-based) survey of Danish and Swedish consumers using self-administered questionnaires. A total sample of 2,270 Danish/Swedish consumers was collected in August/September 2002. Although a few profitable exceptions exist (e.g., the Danish online grocery store 'Årstiderne'), in general online grocery retailers in both countries have faced serious difficulties making their business profitable. It is thus highly relevant to investigate which factors may facilitate Danish and Swedish consumers' adoption of online grocery shopping. The questionnaires were distributed to households by the use of an Internetpanel administered by a market research firm. In a comparison of print surveys with online surveys, Boyer et al. (2002) found that online surveys are generally comparable to print surveys in most respects (both methods had statistically similar response rates, scale/construct means and inter-item reliabilities), but differ in other respects (online surveys are likely to produce fewer missing responses). However, the authors recommend that researchers should carefully consider their goals and objectives. In the present study, we investigate consumer online grocery-shopping behaviour and not offline grocery-shopping behaviour. Hence, by conducting online surveys we make sure that the chosen households are qualified for the study purpose (households with access to the Internet either at home or at work/educational institution were included as respondents).

One should also be aware that the contact sample might influence the outcomes of the study, for example one may argue that consumers participating in an online panel may be more involved in the Internet per se as compared to non-panel consumers. To reduce problems related to the type of contact sample, the applied consumer panel has the following characteristics: (1) the panel consists of 5,000+ consumers who are representative of consumers with access to the Internet and is updated daily with at least 50 respondents, (2) participants are selected by chance via an automatically generated telephone number. During a telephone interview all consumers agreed to take part in studies via the Internet and 90% of the consumers who agreed to participate in the web-based survey completed the online questionnaire. Checks against unit non-response bias (Bosnjak and Tuten, 2001) were performed by comparing respondent demographics to those of the original set of respondents who agreed to participate in the survey and no significant differences were detected. The data used in the present research consist of sub-samples of the main panels. When a household consisted of more than one person, the respondent chosen was the household-member most often responsible for carrying out the grocery shopping. This resulted in a majority of women participating in the studies – a commonly detected tendency in studies of household grocery-shopping behaviour (see Raijas, 2002). Each respondent was assigned to one of the three segments depending on whether they had not purchased anything over the Internet yet (segment 1); had purchased goods/services over the Internet but not groceries (segment 2); or had purchased goods/services over the Internet, including groceries (segment 3).

Respondents

Many respondents may be uncertain about what to answer in relation to aspects concerning online grocery retailing, which for many respondents still may represent a rather new shopping opportunity. When conducting the surveys, we therefore allowed respondents to answer 'don't know' to questions that they did not feel competent to answer. Several respondents used this opportunity and therefore a large number of 'missing cases' across the items of interest were detected. Because of this applying imputation procedures was deemed inappropriate (see Hair et al., 1998), and we therefore decided to exclude the missing cases from the study. This resulted in the following number of valid cases in each of the three segments: segment 1, n = 207; segment 2, n = 251; and segment 3, n = 91. Checks against item non-response bias (Bosnjak and Tuten, 2001) were performed by conducting χ^2 tests (including gender, age, educational level, and household income) to determine whether the sample corrected for missing scale responses (survey sample) differs systematically from the original (uncorrected) sample. The χ^2 tests for age, educational level, and household income produced all *p*-values > 0.28, which strongly indicates that the corrected sample is not statistically different from the uncorrected sample when evaluated on these demographic characteristics. However, the χ^2 test for gender produced a *p*-value < 0.01 indicating that the corrected sample differs systematically from the original sample when evaluated on this characteristic. Women are relatively underrepresented in the corrected sample (share of women: 51%) as compared with the uncorrected sample (share of women: 60.5%). However, since this systematic sample difference is equally distributed across segments 1, 2 and 3 (refer to 'results section' below) we do not consider this to be a serious problem invalidating the results. Further considerations concerning demographic characteristics of the three segments are presented in the 'results section'.

MEASUREMENTS

Multiple item five-point Likert scales (1 = disagree totally; 5 = agree totally) were developed for all the theoretical constructs used in this study. Perceived social influence was measured by obtaining the respondents' level of agreement to the following two statements: (1) Members of my family think that it is a good idea to buy groceries via the Internet, and (2) most of my friends and acquaintances think that shopping groceries via the Internet is a good idea. These two statements were derived from Thompson et al. (1994). In measuring *perceived Internet grocery risk* we draw on numerous writers, including Belanger et al. (2002), McKnight et al. (2002), and Cho (2004). Four statements measured perceived Internet grocery risk: (1) Return and exchange opportunities are not as good on the Internet as in the supermarket/non-Internet shop, (2) a risk when buying groceries via the Internet is receiving low quality products or incorrect items, (3) security around payment on the Internet is not good enough, and (4) there are too many untrustworthy shops on the Internet. To measure *perceived compatibility* we draw on Frambach et al. (1998): (1) Electronic shopping for groceries is attractive to me in my daily life, and (2) buying groceries via the Internet is well suited to the way in which I normally shop for groceries.

Perceived relative advantage was measured by three statements: (1) Using electronic shopping for groceries saves a lot of time, (2) shopping for groceries via the Internet is favourable as it makes me less dependent on opening hours, and (3) there is a lot of money to save buying groceries on the Internet. Four statements measured *perceived complexity*: (1) Electronic shopping for groceries is complex because I cannot see and feel the products, (2) electronic shopping is in general very complex, (3) it is hard to find the required products when shopping for groceries via the Internet, and (4) with electronic shopping for groceries it is difficult to order products. The statements concerning perceived relative advantage and perceived complexity were all adapted from Verhoef and Langerak (2001).

Validation of Measurement Scales

For the purpose of validating the applied measurements, confirmatory factor analysis modelling was conducted (see Table 6.1). The results of the confirmatory factor model show that all items load significantly (t-value > 1.96) on their corresponding latent construct, which indicates that convergent validity has been obtained. The reliabilities and variance extracted for each variable also indicate that the measurements are reliable and valid. All composite reliabilities were $\geq$ 0.70 except one, namely 'perceived relative advantage' at 0.67. Extracted estimates of variance were all above or very close to 0.40. The reliabilities and variance were computed using indicator standardized loadings and measurement errors (Hair et al., 1998; Shim et al., 2000). Discriminant validity of the applied constructs was tested applying the approach used by Grant (1989). The diagonals in Table 6.2 represent for each construct the variance extracted as reported in Table 6.1.

The other entries represent the squares of correlations among constructs. An examination of the matrix displayed in Table 6.2 shows that the non-diagonal entries do not exceed the diagonals of the specific constructs, except for subjective norm with respect to its squared correlation with perceived compatibility (variance subjective norm = 0.62 < squared correlation subjective norm – perceived compatibility = 0.63) and for perceived compatibility with respect to its squared correlation with perceived relative advantage (variance perceived compatibility = 0.57 < squared correlation perceived compatibility – perceived relative advantage = 0.76), although the squared correlations in both cases are below the suggested threshold of 0.85 (Frambach et al., 2003). Since the investigated concepts are very similar in nature, these results are, however, not surprising. Nevertheless, in the subsequent data analysis the presence of significant bivariate correlations among constructs is taken into account.

The chi square statistic of the confirmatory factor model was 173.93 (df = 55, $p < 0.001$) indicating that the model fails to fit in an absolute sense. However, since the χ^2 test is very powerful when n is large, even a good fitting model (i.e., a model with only small discrepancies between observed and predicted covariances) could be rejected. Several writers (e.g., Hair et al., 1998) therefore recommend that the chi-square measure should be complemented with other goodness-of-fit measures.

Table 6.1 Confirmatory factor model results

Construct/indicator	Standardized factor loading [a]	SE	t-value	Construct reliability [b]	Extracted variance [c]
Subjective norm				0.76	0.62
X1	0.80				
X2	0.77	0.06	13.33		
Perceived complexity				0.73	0.48
X3	0.60				
X4	0.63	0.09	11.01		
X5	0.83	0.11	11.73		
Perceived compatibility				0.73	0.57
X6	0.69				
X7	0.82	0.08	15.53		
Perceived relative advantage				0.67	0.51
X8	0.68				
X9	0.74	0.09	13.13		
Perceived Internet grocery risk				0.71	0.38
X10	0.67				
X11	0.56	0.07	10.27		
X12	0.66	0.09	11.45		
X13	0.59	0.07	10.66		

$\chi^2 = 173.93$ (df. = 55, p–value < 0.001); GFI = 0.953; AGFI = 0.922; CFI = 0.945; RMSEA = 0.063.

Notes:
[a] The first item for each construct was set to 1.
[b] Calculated as $\dfrac{\sum(\text{Std. Loadings})^2}{\sum(\text{Std. Loadings})^2 + \sum \xi i}$
[c] Calculated as $\dfrac{\sum \text{Std. Loadings}^2}{\sum \text{Std. Loadings}^2 + \sum \xi i}$

Table 6.2 Discriminant validity of constructs

Construct	1	2	3	4	5
1. Subjective norm	0.62				
2. Perceived complexity	0.10	0.48			
3. Perceived compatibility	0.63	0.15	0.57		
4. Perceived relative advantage	0.45	0.16	0.76	0.51	
5. Perceived Internet grocery risk	0.13	0.35	0.22	0.07	0.38

Notes: Diagonals represent average amount of extracted variance for each construct. Non-diagonals represent the shared variance between constructs (calculated as the squares of correlations between constructs).

The value of the goodness of fit index (GFI) was 0.953, which is well above the acceptable level of 0.9 (Bollen and Long, 1993) and thus indicates a good overall model fit. The point estimate of RMSEA was 0.063, which indicates an acceptable fit of the model in relation to the degrees of freedom. The incremental fit measures also provide support for the model. The adjusted goodness of fit index (AGFI) showed a value of 0.922, which is above the recommended threshold of 0.9, and the value of the comparative fit index (CFI) was 0.945, which again is well above the 0.90 threshold. To conclude, acceptable support is provided for the applied measurements.

RESULTS

Table 6.3 displays the construct means and standard deviations for each of the three segments and the findings indicate several significant mean differences across them. In each of the three segments, three or more constructs show univariate differences between the considered segment and each of the other two segments.

This suggested that multiple discriminant analysis would be appropriate for the purpose of investigating the research questions and hence this method was used to explore the degree to which respondents' perceptions of Internet characteristics predict segment membership.

To test the assumption of equal variance–covariance Box's M test statistic was applied. The following values were obtained: Box's M = 51.74; approximately $F = 1.64$; df = 30; $p = 0.016$ indicating a violation of the equal variance–covariance assumption. However, this test is sensitive to other factors (e.g., sample size) apart from just covariance differences (Hair et al., 1998). Note also, that the corresponding F-value was only 1.64, suggesting that the departure from the null was not large (Noble and Schewe, 2003). The sample was split into two parts, with the first part covering two-third of the respondents and the second part covering one-third of the respondents. Reflecting that the three segments (s1, s2, s3) are unequally represented in the sample, a proportionally stratified random sampling procedure was applied. The first part (n(s1) = 142, n(s2) = 164, n(s3) = 59) was used to generate the discriminant functions. To assess the internal validity of the results the generated discriminant functions were then used to predict segment membership in the holdout sample (n(s1) = 75, n(s2) = 79, n(s3) = 27).

Table 6.3 Construct means and standard deviations

Segment	Construct	Mean	Std. deviation	n
Segment 1	Subjective norm [c]	2.36	0.84	207
	Perceived complexity [c]	2.79	0.69	207
	Perceived compatibility [b c]	2.62	0.90	207
	Perceived relative advantage [b c]	3.38	0.98	207
	Perceived Internet grocery risk [b c]	3.38	0.70	207
Segment 2	Subjective norm [c]	2.49	0.80	251
	Perceived complexity [c]	2.71	0.76	251
	Perceived compatibility [a c]	2.95	0.98	251
	Perceived relative advantage [a c]	3.64	0.93	251
	Perceived Internet grocery risk [a c]	3.14	0.72	251
Segment 3	Subjective norm [a b]	3.00	0.86	91
	Perceived complexity [a b]	2.38	0.83	91
	Perceived compatibility [a b]	3.59	0.99	91
	Perceived relative advantage [a b]	4.00	0.78	91
	Perceived Internet grocery risk [a b]	2.88	0.74	91

Notes:
[a] Different from segment 1, $p < 0.05$ by LSD.
[b] Different from segment 2, $p < 0.05$ by LSD.
[c] Different from segment 3, $p < 0.05$ by LSD.
Each of the summated scales was divided by the number of scaleitems;
scale values ranged from 1 (disagree totally) to 5 (agree totally).

Only the first discriminant function (Wilks' $\lambda = 0.875$; $\chi^2 = 48.18$; df = 10, p-value < 0.001) was significant and explains 11.2% of the variance in the three segments. Since the second function is not significant, its associated statistics will not be used in the interpretation of the ability of the five constructs to discriminate among segments. The first discriminant function, which accounts for 89.1% of the variance explained by the two functions, correctly classified 50.4% (48.6% of the holdout sample) of the originally grouped respondents (see Table 6.4).

Table 6.4 Classification results

Actual group	Number of cases	Predicted group		
		Segment 1	Segment 2	Segment 3
Analysis sample[a]				
Segment 1	142	*66*	75	1
		(46.5%)	(52.8%)	(0.7%)
Segment 2	164	47	*110*	7
		(28.7%)	(67.1%)	(4.3%)
Segment 3	59	7	44	*8*
		(11.9%)	(74.6%)	(13.6%)
Holdout sample[b]				
Segment 1	75	*37*	34	4
		(49.3%)	(45.3%)	(5.3%)
Segment 2	79	28	*46*	5
		(35.4%)	(58.2%)	(6.3%)
Segment 3	27	8	14	*5*
		(29.6%)	(51.9%)	(18.5%)

Notes:
[a] Percent of analysis sample cases correctly classified: 50.4% ((66 + 110 + 8)/365 = 50.4%)
[b] Percent of holdout sample cases correctly classified: 48.6% ((37 + 46 + 5)/181 = 48.6%)

For the purpose of assessing the overall fit of these classification results, the hit ratios were compared against the proportional chance criterion (Cpro = 38.0%) and the maximum chance criterion (Cmax = 45.0%). The proportional chance criterion determines if the obtained classification is better than chance, while Cmax determines if these results exceed the percent of respondents that would be correctly classified if all observations were assigned to the segment with the greatest probability of occurrence (Noble and Schewe, 2003). Hit ratios for both samples exceed these estimates although they are close to the Cmax criterion. However, since we have unequal group sizes, it is important that the Cmax criterion is complemented with other overall fit measures. The computed Press's Q statistic gave the following results: Qanalysis sample = 47.90; Qholdout sample = 19.03, which in both cases exceeds the critical value of $\chi^2 = 6.63$, df = 1, with a significance level of 0.01. We therefore conclude that the classification of respondents in both samples is significantly better than chance.

Table 6.5 Summary of multiple discriminant results

Construct	Function 1	
	Discriminant loading	Standardized coefficient
Perceived social norm	0.676	0.237
Perceived complexity	−0.502	−0.120
Perceived compatibility	0.841	0.479
Perceived relative advantage	0.638	0.142
Perceived Internet risk	−0.683	−0.419
χ^2	48.18 (df = 10, $p < 0.001$)	
Variance explained	0.112	
Canonical correlation	0.334	
Group centroids		
Segment 1	−0.377	
Segment 2	0.020	
Segment 3	0.636	

The standardized coefficients and discriminant loadings for each construct along with the group centroids are provided in Table 6.5. The standardized coefficients denote the partial contribution of each of the constructs to the discriminant function. The larger the standardized coefficient the greater the contribution of the respective construct to the discrimination between segments. However, several authors (e.g., Hair et al., 1998) warn that the interpretation of the standardized coefficient may lead to misinterpretations. As in regression analysis, a small weight may either indicate that the discriminating power of a construct is low or that it has been partialled out of the relationship because of a high degree of multicollinearity (Hair et al., 1998).

In the present study, several significant bivariate correlations (indicating multicollinearity) were detected among the independent constructs. For example, the bivariate correlations between subjective norm and perceived compatibility ($r = 0.79$), between subjective norm and perceived relative advantage ($r = 0.67$), and between perceived compatibility and perceived relative advantage ($r = 0.87$) were all highly significant (p-values < 0.001). We therefore evaluated the discriminating power of each construct on the basis of discriminant loadings, which are considered relatively more valid than standardized coefficients as a means of interpreting the discriminating power of the independent constructs because of their correlational nature (see Hair et al., 1998). The discriminant loadings denote the correlations between the constructs and the discriminant function.

As can be seen from Table 6.5, perceived compatibility was the main contributing construct (discriminant loading = 0.841) in discriminating between segments. Substantive loadings (> ± 0.30, see Hair et al., 1998) were also obtained for all other constructs: perceived complexity (–0.502), subjective norm (0.676), perceived relative advantage (0.638), and perceived Internet risk (–0.683). F-tests of the equality of group means supported these results. All p-values were < 0.05 indicating that, for each of the five constructs, means are unequal across the three consumer segments. An examination of group centroids clearly suggests that function 1 discriminates between segment 3 and segment 1/segment 2 consumers. When compared to segment 1/segment 2, segment 3 respondents perceive online grocery buying to be more compatible with their existing needs and habits. Segment 3 respondents attach the lowest complexity to online grocery buying and also perceive a higher relative advantage to this way of buying. In addition, segment 3 respondents perceive their social surroundings to have the most positive attitude towards online grocery buying.

Respondent Characteristics across Segments

The profiles of the respondents included in this study are displayed in Table 6.6.

Since the multiple discriminant analysis only suggested discrimination between segment 3 and segment 1/segment 2 (i.e., no discrimination between segment 1 and segment 2 was suggested), respondents belonging to segments 1/2 are grouped together.

For the purpose of evaluating the extent to which the demographic characteristics of the respondents explain segment classification, four demographic variables were measured in the survey: gender, age, educational level, and household income per year. It was also investigated whether segment classification differed with nationality.

The following considerations guided the selection of demographic variables. First, innovators are generally known to have higher educational and income levels and to be younger than other consumers (Gatignon and Robertson, 1985; Martinez et al., 1998). Secondly, several studies (e.g., Raijas, 2002; Hansen, 2003) suggest that women are still responsible for carrying out most of the household's grocery shopping. Since Internet shopping has the possibility of reducing time spent on grocery shopping it was of interest to investigate whether online grocery shopping attracts relatively more women than men. The results of the χ^2 tests show that relatively more Danish than Swedish consumers were found in segments 1 and 2. No demographic variables were significantly different across segments.

Table 6.6 Respondent characteristics

Demographic factor	Segment 1 + 2 ($n = 458$)		Segment 3 ($n = 91$)	
Gender				
Male	232	(50.7%)	37	(40.7%)
Female	226	(49.3%)	54	(59.3%)
Nationality [a]				
Danish	308	(67.2%)	44	(48.4%)
Swedish	150	(32.8%)	47	(51.6%)
Age				
Under 25	49	(10.7%)	8	(8.8%)
25–29	77	(16.8%)	19	(20.9%)
30–34	76	(16.6%)	23	(25.3%)
35–39	61	(13.3%)	17	(18.7%)
40–45	81	(17.7%)	11	(12.1%)
46–50	55	(12.0%)	7	(7.7%)
51–55	28	(6.1%)	5	(5.5%)
56–60	22	(4.8%)	0	(0%)
Over 61	9	(2.0%)	1	(1.1%)
Educational level				
Basic school	23	(5.0%)	3	(3.3%)
High school	75	(16.4%)	10	(11.0%)
Business training	70	(15.3%)	6	(6.6%)
Short advanced study	75	(16.4%)	19	(20.9%)
Medium advanced study	129	(28.2%)	27	(29.7%)
Long advanced study	86	(18.8%)	26	(28.6%)
Household income per year DKK/SEK				
0–99,000	18	(3.9%)	2	(2.2%)
100,000–199,000	32	(7.0%)	3	(3.3%)
200,000–299,000	76	(16.6%)	9	(9.9%)
300,000–399,000	66	(14.4%)	18	(19.8%)
400,000–499,000	81	(17.7%)	12	(13.2%)
500,000–599,000	78	(17.0%)	18	(19.8%)
600,000–699,000	41	(9.0%)	14	(15.4%)
700,000–799,000	31	(6,8%)	6	(6.6%)
800,000–899,000	9	(2.0%)	5	(5.5%)
900,000–	26	(5.7%)	4	(4.4%)

Note: [a] Chi-square test significant at the 0.01 level.

DISCUSSION AND IMPLICATIONS

The overall purpose of this research was to investigate the extent to which consumers who already had purchased groceries via the Internet perceived this innovation differently from other online segments. Three groups of consumer segments were studied. Segment 1 included online consumers who had not yet purchased anything on the Internet, segment 2 consisted of online consumers who had purchased goods or services on the Internet but not groceries, and segment 3 covered online consumers who had purchased goods/services on the Internet, including groceries. A diagrammatic representation of the obtained results is shown in Figure 6.1.

The overall results of an inter-segment comparison showed that segment 3 consumers perceive characteristics of online grocery shopping differently from segment 1/segment 2 consumers. This result clearly indicates that consumers consider online grocery shopping as an innovation that is different from other grocery shopping channels. An inspection of the individual discriminant loadings suggested that perceived compatibility was the primary discriminating construct. Thus online grocery retailing should be compatible with consumers' existing grocery shopping patterns. That is, online grocery retailers should not expect consumers to compromise their existing shopping needs and habits in order to carry out online grocery shopping, and so must adapt themselves to the daily life of consumers. Similar results were obtained in a qualitative study of Danish and Swedish online grocery shoppers (Friese et al., 2002, 2003).

In the survey, perceived social norm was found to discriminate between segment 3 and segment 1/segment 2. At least two possible explanations seem to apply in connection hereto. First, much relevant information concerning online grocery buying may be classified as 'experience information' (see Nelson, 1970). For many grocery products for instance, there may be less opportunity to inspect salient offline search attributes (e.g., odour, physical appearance of fresh fruits and vegetables and meat products) before buying the products on the Internet. From an economics of information perspective, inexperienced online consumers may simply be imperfectly informed and may therefore keep an open mind towards possible guidance from friends and relatives. Secondly, many consumers are members of a household in which major decisions regarding grocery store patronage (off- or online) may not just be a matter for the individual household member but for the entire household. Hence, a consumer may give weight to normative guidance from close social surroundings when considering online grocery shopping.

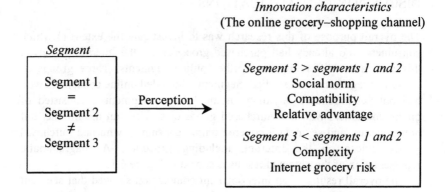

Notes:
Segment 1: Internet users who have not purchased anything over the Internet yet (non-adopters of online shopping).
Segment 2: Internet users who have purchased goods/services over the Internet but not groceries (online shopping adopters).
Segment 3: Internet users who have purchased goods/services over the Internet, including groceries (online shopping adopters and online grocery-shopping adopters).

Figure 6.1 Diagrammatic representation of the obtained results

   Consumers belonging to segment 3 also attach a higher relative advantage (possibilities for saving time and money when shopping for groceries online) to online grocery shopping than do other consumers. Online retail managers may therefore wish to market such benefits of online grocery shopping to the entire household and thereby facilitate more positive family decision-making in relation to online grocery shopping. It also seems important that online retailers design simple and effective information and ordering procedures that are easy to understand and do not require high online navigation skills and effort. This suggestion is derived from the result that perceived complexity (with a negative sign) substantially contributed to the discrimination between segment 3 and segment 1/segment 2. Segment 3 consumers attach a lower perceived risk to online grocery buying than do segment 1 and segment 2 consumers. Hence, the results also suggest that it is still important that online suppliers provide online consumers with 'risk relievers' (Van den Poel and Leunis, 1999) in relation to specific online buying events. Such risk relievers, which may help consumers to reduce their uncertainty when considering online grocery buying, may include 'complaint opportunities', 'security guarantees', 'money-back guarantees', 'privacy guarantees', and the like.

Relatively more Danish than Swedish consumers were found in segments 1 and 2. No demographic variables differed significantly across segments. This result can be contrasted to previous findings (e.g., Donthu and Garcia, 1999; Sin and Tse, 2002), which suggest that Internet buyers tend to be male and to be better educated and have higher income than other consumers. However, while our study concerns a product specific innovation (online grocery shopping) the results obtained by Sin and Tse, among others, concerned the more general innovation of Internet shopping as such. Therefore, the results obtained by for instance Sin and Tse cannot be directly compared to the results obtained in the present study. The present results suggest that online grocery shopping mainly can be described as a domain-specific innovation as none of the investigated innovator variables differed across segments. This suggestion is also supported by the finding that segment 3 consumers perceived all the investigated online grocery shopping characteristics differently from other consumers.

LIMITATIONS AND FUTURE RESEARCH

Research on diffusion processes suggests that cultural, geographic and other differences among countries may lead to different diffusion patterns. For example, in many small countries consumers rarely have to go a long distance to reach the nearest store, which means that the relative advantages of the Internet concerning reduced time spent shopping may be perceived to be of less importance than in some parts of geographically larger countries. This is actually the case in Denmark and Sweden, with particularly Denmark having one of the highest densities of retailers in the world.

This research used a single respondent as a household representative. Since grocery buying concerns the entire household, this procedure assumes that the selected respondent provides answers that are representative of the household's opinion. Future research may wish to verify the proposed framework using multiple household representatives.

Moreover, this study focused on analysing one product category (groceries). This could mean that the results may suffer from a lack of generalizability when other product categories are considered. A cross–section of product categories ought to be studied to improve the generalizability of the results.

As with much other research, this study provides a snapshot of online behaviour rather than a longitudinal study. Hence, when considering the findings obtained in this study one should be aware that the Internet as a grocery-shopping channel is still evolving and that Internet consumer research – as is the case with many other consumer studies – needs to be continuously repeated and modified.

REFERENCES

Anckar, B., Walden, P. and Jelassi, T. (2002), 'Creating constomer value in online grocery shopping', *International Journal of Retail and Distribution Management.* **30**(1), 211–220.

Belanger, F., Hiller, J.S. and Smith, W.J. (2002), 'Trustworthiness in electronic commerce: the role of privacy, security, and site attributes', *Strategic Information Systems.* **11**, 245–270.

Black, N.J., Lockett, A., Winklhofer, H. and Ennew, C. (2001), 'The adoption of Internet financial sevices: a qualitative study', *International Journal of Retail and Distribution Management.* **29**(8/9), 390–398.

Blackwell, R.D., Miniard, P.W. and Engel, J.F. (2001), *Consumer Behavior*, 9th edn, London: Harcourt.

Bollen, K.A. and Long, J.S. (1993), *Testing Structural Equation Models*, London: SAGE Publications.

Bosnjak, M. and Tuten., T.L. (2001). 'Classifying response behaviors in Web–based surveys', *Journal of Computer–Mediated Communication* **6**(3). Available at: http://www.ascusc.org/jcmc/vol6/issue3/boznjak.html

Boyer, K.K., Olson, J.R., Calantone, R.J. and Jackson, E.C. (2002), 'Print versus electronic surveys: a comparison of two data collection methods', *Journal of Operations Management.* **20**, 357–373.

Cheung, C. and Lee, M.K.O. (2000), 'Trust in Internet shopping: a proposed model and measurement instrument', *Proceedings of the 6th Americas Conference on Information Systems*, 681–689.

Cho, J. (2004), 'Likelihood to abort an online transaction: influences from cognitive evaluations, attitudes, and behavioral variables', *Information and Management.* **41**(7), 827–838.

Donthu, N. and Garcia, A. (1999), 'The Internet shopper', *Journal of Advertising Research.* **39**(3), 52–58.

Elliot, S. and Fowell, S. (2000), 'Expectations versus reality: a snapshot of consumer experiences with Internet retailing', *International Journal of Information Management.* **20**, 323–336.

Fishbein, M. and Ajzen, I. (1975), *Belief, Attitude, Intention, and Behavior: An Introduction to Theory and Research*, Reading, MA: Addison Wesley.

Forsythe, S.M. and Shi, B. (2003), 'Consumer patronage and risk perceptions in Internet shopping', *Journal of Business Research.* **56**, 867–875.

Frambach, R.T., Barkema, H.G., Nooteboom, B. and Wedel, M. (1998), 'Adoption of a service innovation in the business market: an empirical test of supply-side Variables', *Journal of Business Research*. **41**, 161–174.

Frambach, R.T., Prabhu, J. and Verhallen, T.M.M. (2003), 'The influence of business strategy on new product activity: the role of market orientation', *International Journal of Research in Marketing*. **20**, 377–97.

Friese, S., Beckmann, S.C., Bjerre, M., Hansen, T., Sestoft, C. and Kornum, N. (2002), 'Motivators and barriers for online shopping of FMCGs', Conference Paper, ANZMAC–EMAC joint symposium: Marketing Networks in a Global Economy, Perth, Australia, 16–17 December.

Friese, S., Bjerre, M., Hansen, T., Kornum, N. and Sestoft, C. (2003), 'Barriers and motivators of online grocery shopping in Denmark', *Research Report, No. 2003–09* January, Department of Marketing, Copenhagen Business School.

Gatignon, H. and Robertson, T.S. (1985), 'A propositional inventory for new diffusion research', *Journal of Consumer Research*. **11**, 849–867.

Gemünden, H.G. (1985), 'Perceived risk and information search. A meta–analysis of the empirical evidence', *International Journal of Research in Marketing*. **2**, 79–100.

Geuens, M., Brengman, M., and S'Jergers, R. (2003), 'Food retailing, now and in the future. A consumer perspective', *Journal of Retailing and Consumer Services*. **10**(4), 241–251.

Giese, J.M. (1996), Place without space, identity without body: the role of cooperative narrative in community and identity formation in a text–based electronic community, Dissertation, Pennsylvania State University, USA.

Goldsmith R.E. and Hofacker C.F. (1991), 'Measuring consumer innovativeness', *Journal of the Academy of Marketing Science*. **19**, 209–21.

Grant, R.A. (1989), 'Building and testing a model of an information technology's impact', in J.I. DeGross, J.C. Henderson and B.R. Konsyniski (eds), *Proceedings of the Tenth International Conference on Information Systems*, Boston, MA, pp. 173–184.

Hair J, Anderson R.E., Tatham R.L. and Black, W.C. (1998), *Multivariate Data Analysis*, 5th edn., New Jersey, Prentice Hall.

Hansen, T. (2003), *The Online Grocery Consumer*, Working Paper No. 1, March, Department of Marketing, Copenhagen Business School.

Jarvenpaa, S.L. and Todd, P.A. (1996), 'Consumer reactions to electronic shopping on the World Wide Web', *International Journal of Electronic Commerce*. **1**(2), 59–88.

Joseph, B. and Vyas, S.J. (1984), 'Concurrent validity of a measure of innovative cognitive style', *Journal of the Academy of Marketing Sciences*. **12**(2), 159–75.

Kaufman–Scarborough, C.K. and Lindquist, J.D. (2002), 'E–shopping in a multiple channel environment', *The Journal of Consumer Marketing.* **19**(4/5), 333–350.

Keh, H.T. and Shieh, E. (2001), 'Online grocery retailing: success factors and potential pitfalls', *Business Horizons.* **44**(4), 73–83.

Korgaonkar, P.K. (1982), 'Non–store retailing and perceived product risk', in B.J. Walker et al. (eds.), *An Assessment of Marketing Thought and Practice*, Chicago, IL: American Marketing Association, 204–207.

LaBay, D.G. and Kinnear, T.C. (1981), 'Exploring the consumer decision process in the adoption of solar energy systems', *Journal of Consumer Research.* **8**(December), 271–278.

Lockett, A. and Litter, D. (1997), 'The adoption of direct banking services', *Journal of Marketing Management.* **13**, 791–811.

Martinez, E., Polo, Y., and Flavián, C. (1998), 'The acceptance and diffusion of new consumer durables: differences between first and last adopters', *Journal of Consumer Marketing.* **15**(4), 323–342.

McCorkle, D.E. (1990), 'The role of perceived risk in mail order catalog shopping', *Journal of Direct Marketing.* **4**, 26–35.

McKnight, D.H., Choudhury, V. and Kacmar, C. (2002), 'The impact of initial consumer trust on intentions to transact with a web site: a trust building model', *Strategic Information Systems.* **11**, 297–323.

Miyazaki, A.D. and Fernandez, A. (2001), 'Consumer perceptions of privacy and security risks for online shopping', *The Journal of Consumer Affairs.* **35**(1), 27–44.

Nelson, P. (1970), 'Advertising as information', *Journal of Political Economy.* **81**, 729–754.

Noble, S.M. and Schewe, C.D. (2003), 'Cohort segmentation: an exploration of its validity'. *Journal of Business Research.* **56**, 979–987.

Odekerken–Schröder, G. and Wetzels, M. (2003), 'Trade-offs in online purchase decisions: two empirical studies in Europe', *European Management Journal.* **21**(6), 731–739.

Raijas, A. (2002), 'The consumer benefits and problems in the electronic grocery store', *Journal of Retailing and Consumer Services.* **9**, 107–113.

Ranganathan, C. and Ganapathy, S. (2002), 'Key dimensions of business–to–consumer web sites', *Information and Management.* **39**, 457–465.

Ring, L.J. and Tigert, D.J. (2001), 'Viewpoint: the decline and fall of Internet grocery retailers', *International Journal of Retail and Distribution Management.* **29**(6), 266–273.

Robertson T. S. (1967), 'The process of innovation and the diffusion of innovation', *Journal of Marketing.* **31**, 14–19.

Rogers, E.M. (1983), *Diffusion of Innovations*, 3rd ed, New York: The Free Press.

Rogers E. M. (1995), *Diffusion of Innovations*, 4th ed, New York: The Free Press.

Roselius, T (1971), 'Consumer rankings of risk reduction methods', *Journal of Marketing*. **35**, 56–61.

Shih, H.P. (2004), 'An empirical study on predicting user acceptance of e–shopping on the Web', *Information and Management*. **41**, 351–368.

Shim, S., Eastlick, M.A., Lotz, S.L. and Warrington, P. (2001), 'An online prepurchase intentions model: the role of intention to search', *Journal of Retailing*. **77**, 397–416.

Sin, L. and Tse, A. (2002), 'Profiling Internet shoppers in Hong Kong: demographic, psychographic, attitudinal and experiential factors', *Journal of International Consumer Marketing*. **15**(1), 7–29.

Thompson, K.E., Haziris, N. and Alekos, P.J. (1994), 'Attitudes and food choice behaviour', *British Food Journal*. **96** (11), 9–17.

Van den Poel D. and Leunis J. (1999), 'Consumer acceptance of the Internet as a channel of distribution', *Journal of Business Research*. **45**(3), 249–56.

Verhoef, P.C. and Langerak, F. (2001), 'Possible determinants of consumers' adoption of electronic grocery shopping in the Netherlands', *Journal of Retailing and Consumer Services*. **8**, 275–85.

Weich, C.W. and Walchli, S.B. (2002), 'Genetically engineered crops and foods: back to the basics of technology diffusion', *Technology in Society*. **24**(3), 265–283.

7. Behind the Values: Understanding Consumer Behaviour and E-Grocery Business from a Dialectic Culture Perspective

Christine Sestoft

INTRODUCTION

E-business is marching on in several markets, but not in one important one: the grocery market. The lesson learned in the last 10 to 15 years, from brick-and-mortar supermarkets going online, is that it is very difficult to profit from digitalizing the daily buying of groceries.

All consumption research shows that the online grocery business still has a lot of functional (e.g. technical and sensory) disadvantages compared with offline grocers. Apparently it is not much easier to plan, choose and buy groceries online than in the traditional retailer/supermarket. Some of the relatively few experienced grocery consumers support the theory that one may save some time and effort getting one's groceries packed and delivered, but to the majority this is obviously just not good enough, especially taking the delivery fee into account.

However, the functional disadvantage explanation cannot stand alone as an answer to why online grocery business is not more of a success and it may even be overrated. New sales channels have always had the 'disadvantage' of not functioning like/as well as the old ones. To me, another interesting issue in the subject seems to be about consumer values and how their practising is not supported in this new sales channel.

New consumer values referring to being a good citizen are expressed in both public and professional discussions on how to be responsible consumers in sustainable societies, that is, political, ethical, healthy, rational and sensible consumers in a multiple-choice world. Such value discussions move the good life in the right direction, such as when pointing out meaningful grocery consumption to follow or learn from. This kind of 'consumer value democracy' can be difficult to exercise in conventional brick-and-mortar supermarkets, but even more so in conventional online grocery shopping, first and foremost because of information and communication overload, especially on the Internet. And that is a strategic business *disadvantage* to online grocery business.

A lot of online consumption research has been concerned with the consumers' problems with the Internet (e.g. Hansen, 2002), not so much with the problem of online businesses strategic relations, such as regarding specific consumer subjects. According to Michael Porter (Porter, 2001) the missing strategy discussion is what explains the lack of online business success. Only very few e-businesses seem to have understood the particular link between themselves, their context and this relation. Therefore, only very few of them have been able to see the specific potential in e-business and consequently they have been unable to penetrate the markets and appeal to consumers and their values.

INTRODUCTION: VALUES IN MARKETING RESEARCH

Consumer behaviour is an expanding field of research. In recent years one of the most interesting new directions is interpretive consumer research (Beckmann and Elliot, 2001). These relatively new directions within consumer research have arisen from the ongoing quest to fully understand consumer relations, for example the relations between having and being, between buying goods and being a consumer, or between societies and consumer subjects.

Today, interpretive research is in general accepted as a progressive trend moving towards the study of how 'goods have meanings for consumers, not only in their individual lives, but also in and for their everyday interactions in their sharing of meaning (i.e. consumption) for their conflicts on taste, that is, in and for all those minor consumption practices that converge into the constitution of society' (Giddens, 1984 quoted in: Beckmann and Elliot, 2001, p. 21). As we see from Giddens, the individual person's, everyday conflicts and taste are deeply involved in, or part of, major cultural and political structures and the link seems to be the converging of norms and values. As a consequence, interpretive research interested in both structures and agency must consider values a conceptual and relatively key driver in broad terms.

Still, not many marketing researchers are concerned with building interpretive theory via the concept of value. As Holbrook explains, scholars in the marketing-related disciplines have habitually neglected this body of knowledge (Holbrook, 1999, p. 3). This may well be linked to the economic paradigm of utility still hidden in a lot of marketing research, and this again may well be linked to the professional tradition in marketing of seeking straight answers to straight questions.

In the traditional marketing field of consumer behaviour, two of the perhaps most prominent descriptive theories include: first, the Theory of Reasoned Action (TRA) that accounts for aggregated behaviours (i.e. consumer actions), representing underlying behavioural dispositions (i.e. personal traits). Second, the Theory of Planned Behaviour (TPB), that deals with how consumer behaviour is influenced in specific contexts, when they have so-called incomplete volitional control (Ajzen, 1991). None of the theories explicitly discusses values, because they all stem from a positivistic tradition, where value is much too vague a concept to measure. The closest we get to values is in the TPB where the concept of perceived behavioural control (PBC) refers to people's *perception* of the ease or difficulty of performing the behaviour of interest (ibid., p. 183).

Recently it has been argued that even the addition of PBC in the TPB model is not as satisfying as it could be. Inspired by interpretive consumer research, the missing link has been argued to be the concept of values (Choi and Geistfeld, 2003; Sestoft and Hansen, 2003). As mentioned, values are increasingly being considered as important drivers of consumer behaviour – some have even called them the ultimate source of choice criteria that drive buying behaviour (Claeys et al., 1995, p. 193). Holbrook further supports this point of view in his saying that 'The Concept of Consumer Value constitutes the *foundation*, defining *basis*, or underlining *rationale* for the Marketing Concept in the sense that each party to a transaction gives up one thing in return for something else of greater *value*' (Holbrook, 1999, p. 2). Next in line is then the problem of how to understand the idea and specific formation of such transactions, for example the relation between consumer values and product characteristics.

Even though Holbrook is one of the most prominent researchers in consumer values, he has been criticized even by himself for previously oversimplifying the concept of value along with many other researchers (Oliver, in: Holbrook, 1999). The argument behind the criticism is that the concept of value is not evident but relative. From such a critical point of view, our efforts in consumer research should be directed by the study of the nature and types of consumer value *within* the underlying determinants of the market space. This means studying how the *dimensions* of the market space represent those characteristics, attributes, or features of brands in the product class that provide *consumer value*, and how this consumer value is located in ideal points indicating different positions of maximum consumer value (Holbrook, 1999, p. 3).

Holbrook argues that values in marketing research, as in interpretive research in general, are conceptual and relatively key drivers. Above all, he is interested in what goes on in the consumer's mind as well as in the consumption process, for example how the characteristics the consumer seeks from the relevant product category represent the market dimensions. As such, his approach to consumer value is now very relativistic. Holbrook defines consumer value as an 'interactive relativistic preference experience' (see Holbrook and Corfman, 1985, p. 23 and Holbrook, 1994a, p. 27). This definition refers to the *nature* of the value concept, Holbrook argues. Besides that, he also makes a typology of consumer value, classifying eight types of value in the consumer experience in a matrix (Holbrook, 1994a, p. 45). Holbrook describes his own treatment of the concept of consumer value as being as radical as a radish (Holbrook, 1999, p. 9), and he seems right in this ironic description, because referring to value as an interactive relativistic preference experience is not new, at least not to culture researchers. Listing and describing eight theoretical types of consumer values as ideal types actually seems more radical.[1]

Even though he recognizes the structural relevance to consumer behaviour studies, that is, the relations between market dimensions and consumer values, as a psychologist Holbrook first and foremost has an inside-out perspective on the subject, relating internal feelings to outside causes or premises. This results in an either or value perspective: you have either extrinsic or intrinsic goals, you are either self-orientated or other-orientated and you are either active or reactive in your actions. What is missing from this interesting but dualistic perspective is the important discussion of how the concepts and their practices determine and influence each other, that is, not only a discussion of the relation between the categories/types of consumer values and the market space, but also a discussion of the power and transformation between consumer values and market space. Instead of just focusing on the market as a determinant and existing conceptual dichotomies (extrinsic/intrinsic, self-orientated/other-orientated, and active/reactive), we should also be interested in how specific values have become generally accepted invisible guidelines in our society and self-conceptions. Although path-breaking, Holbrooks contribution to the study of values in marketing research seems to lack a conceptual discussion of the processes and structures of consumer values in general as well as the different types of value, that is, a discussion of how the relations between market or societal dimensions and consumer values work. This calls for an epistemological shift from dualistic to dialectic consumer behaviour research. Consumer value research should focus on both the genealogy, that is, the 'nature' of the values represented in goods, and how this discursive 'nature' positions itself in different types of subjective consumer values.

Additionally, a research should focus on how the different types of subjective consumer values not only constitute but also potentially transform the discursive 'nature' of the values when practised, because of the cunning of reason.[2] We can find inspiration for such focused research in the culture studies.

In *Keywords. A Vocabulary of Culture and Society* by Raymond Williams (1983, p. 43), the term behaviour is described as follows: 'Behave is a very curious word which still presents difficulties. [...] But the modern word seems to have been introduced in [the 15 [th] century] as a form of qualification of the verb have, and especially in the reflexive sense of "to have (bear) oneself."' Reading this vocabulary piece one understands that consumption and subjectivity meet semantics in the concept of behaviour, through its extensional description of the words having and bearing.[3]

In this chapter, I will try to argue that having and bearing also meet syntax in the logic of contemporary consumption, and further argue that this calls for a culture-specific way of dealing with and understanding the concept of consumer values. More specifically, I will discuss consumer values as virtuous expressions of hegemonic consumption discourses within a specific consumer *Subject*. These virtues are to be understood as the cultural, political and economic defence of state subjects, most often orientated towards defending the nation state as a responsible citizen, but sometimes orientated towards defending international or even global communities taking the position of a responsible 'global-citizen' – in any case always as 'the consumer'.

The main purpose of the present chapter is to reflect upon how one can develop a dialectic theoretical consumer behaviour theory that integrates the concept of values logically within the concepts of society and market.

The chapter presents a draft for a new theory of consumer behaviour that aspires to go beyond structure and hermeneutics. It suggests a framework for analysing consumer behaviour that makes sense on several conceptual levels, a framework that considers consumer behaviour just as much an ideological and political as a practical, daily life phenomenon. This is a dialectic theory that sees consumer subjects, their practices and values, as a part of the processes of ideology and culture fights within a state subject.

The second purpose of the chapter is to reflect upon this theory in relation to the online grocery business. I conclude by answering two questions: Do online grocery businesses have a future – why/why not? And: could they be made (and how) more attractive to contemporary consumers?

TOWARDS A NEW CULTURE THEORY OF CONSUMER BEHAVIOUR

Since *The World of Goods* (Douglas and Isherwood, 2004/1979) invaded the scientific field of consumption studies in 1979 fighting for the anthropological perspective, and successfully challenging the idea of economic man and utility theory, arguing about the ranking of values and discussing how the value assemblage presents a set of meanings more or less coherent, more or less intentional, one cultural theory after another has appeared in consumption studies.[4] In most of these cultural theories, the main argument is 'that the rational being must fail to behave rationally, unless there is some consistency and reliability in the world around him' (ibid., p. viii). Like Aristotle says, 'Man is a necessary part of society. One can only stand outside society if one is an animal or God.' This consistency and reliability is very much embedded in consumption and works behind different values. So, to a cultural researcher, consistency and reliability are 'naturally' behind the values. Douglas and Isherwoods two little words, consistency and reliability, point out why cultural theory has so much to offer consumption studies. They explain why values are essential to all cultural studies, in one way or another. From a cultural study point of view, values constitute the foundation of existence of cultural beings, for example, their meaning and taste.

The way this foundation works in the field of consumption differs in the eye of the beholder. In the following, I point out three different theoretical consumer culture perspectives on the issue, thus leading up to my alternative.

The spectrum within consumer culture theory can be categorized into three main perspectives. One is orientated towards how different *types* of consumer subjects or segments make meaning out of commodities and consumption, because of their different values, rationales and cultural 'needs'. Such theories focus on consumers being consumers, on identity and lifestyle in communities (e.g. Chaney, 1996). It is a kind of fusiontheory where consumer communities are regarded as results of integration of emancipated sub-cultural consumerist identities. Another category of consumer culture theory is that which focuses more on the social and instrumental *structures* that force consumers into their consumerist rationale and in this way determine their values. This second category also focuses on being consumer(s) and making consumer identities through the constitution of values. However, the important difference from the first mentioned theory is that in the second one, consumer cultures and identities result from manipulating political, economic or ideological structures (e.g. Adorno and

Horkheimer, 1979). The third perspective concentrates on the *meta-structures* or paradigms of consumption, often discussed in the form of discourse analysis and the like. Here, values arise from a multitude of sources, such as the spirit, discourses and ideas that unfold in culture and culture differences, that is, constructing modern consumption and modern consumers through consumer 'casting' and 'acting' via self-disciplining technologies (see e.g. Falk, in: Falk and Campbell, 1997). Such perspectives often describe the consumer and his or her values as emancipated believed or felt although actually guided by structural dominance.

In discussing the broad spectrum of consumer culture theory, it is clear that interpretive marketing research has a lot to learn from studying values from a culture theory perspective, whether it is the 'bottom up' (first), 'top down' (second) or 'all around' (third) perspective. The first is suitable for studying concrete consumption and values on an individual level, the second is suitable when focus is on power and politics, while the third is interesting when it comes to hegemonic culture and Identity with a capital i.

Despite the vast variety of theoretical perspectives, the field of consumer culture theory is still left with one problem: what to do if we want to investigate values and consumption from all three perspectives, not one after the other, in a dialectic study?

Having a multiple perspective is actually one of the advantages in qualitative research. It is often possible to interpret the same empirical data from different perspectives within the one study. In a dualistic framework, however, the advantages may turn out to be problematic. The problem is not dealing with both structures and agents within the same consumer theory or –model, but the deductive way in which many of them are built, for example the McCracken-model (McCracken, 1988, p. 71). The McCracken model suffers from the problem of transcendental reciprocity: structure causes agency causes structures and so on.

McCracken wants to analyse consumption research on several levels like the true culture-orientated consumption researcher he is. He does not want to choose between focusing on structures or agents. On the one hand, McCracken discusses how the ritual use of consumer goods filled with cultural meaning represents an agency constituting the meaning of consumption and everyday life and, on the other hand, he describes how the culturally constituted world structures the everyday experiences and practices of consumption (ibid., p. 72). What undermines the reliability of the theory is the fact that it cannot explain what changes the structure (the culturally constituted world) that determines the actions. To me the missing link seem to be concepts describing the *dialectic* between structure and agents, instead of determinant structures vs. determinate agents.

The discussion of how to develop a culture theory that avoids transcendental reciprocity in its understanding of changes vs. permanence has been very important to the Danish ethnology professor Thomas Højrup (Højrup, 1995).[5] In my work on consumer values, I am primarily inspired by the culture theory of specific state forms and life modes by Højrup (ibid.), because of its ability to transgress the dualism between structure and agency when studying culture, life modes and values. This is not a specific consumption theory, but fascinating in relation to consumption studies.

Højrup is interested in the question of why different cultural values when brought together in interaction do not homogenize; what constitutes the structure and relates it is not determination but *interpellation* (Højrup, 1995, p. 207).[6] As such, he is interested in why interaction does not principally lead to integration, such as with questions like why do we stay loyal to different values and why do we not get infected by other people's values all the time? To Højrup, the central idea of the meaning of cultural values seems to equate to relative difference. Højrups so-called fission perspective on values opposes many culture researchers, most importantly Benedict Anderson (1991) and his 'interaction-causes-integration' fusion perspective. The fission perspective brings Højrup to theorize about how *Subjects* in a *Subject* system force each other to defend themselves by promoting similar or complementary new resource-giving life modes (subjects) in the individual societies.[7] Højrup explains his theory in the following way (Højrup, 1995, p. 210): 'Behind this concept [of "the state"] lies the idea that each life-mode concept posits its own economic and political juridical preconditions in the society. The life-modes thus exist in a framework set by the state, while state policy is an arena for the struggle for recognition among various life-modes. Central political direction can be viewed as the state's effort to increase, order and control its internal resource base of significance for its external relations, inasmuch as a state's strength in a state system is based upon how successful it is at increasing and mobilizing its resource base for its own ends.'

With this theory, Højrup makes it possible to talk about cultural practices, values and their transformations without presenting power and attitude as an elite violently manipulating others against their will or a question of 'grass root revolutions' as emancipated or emancipating driving forces of change. Inspired by the writings of Michel Foucault (e.g. 1977), the theory considers power the very basic driver in practice, that is, not harmful but determined, making its way through the interpellation of different values in specific subjects.

The theory makes way for a new definition of culture that works on several conceptual levels. That is, culture as *the processes in which we are categorized as more or less powerful specific subjects with principally different values within superior systems of defence*. This alternative way of talking about culture and values with all its complex details and relations, I think could be a positive contribution to research in consumption studies, and thus consumer values, where we are often confronted with the choice of viewing consumer culture as a result of either ideological manipulation or emancipation, and thus consumer behaviour as a question of consumers being more or less authentic or artificial.

THE SPECIFIC STATE FORM AND LIFE MODE CONSUMPTION THEORY

Robert Bartels has said about 'marketing knowledge' that 'It cannot be stated of what this body of thought consists *as a* whole, for, while its subject matter is marketing, its content is as multiform as the prismatic refractions of a many-sided cut stone' (Bartels, 1976, p. 31). The same goes for consumer behaviour and values as previously discussed in this chapter. We may well talk about *the field* in singular, but in practice we are dealing with a number of issues simultaneously. Because of the realized complexity, culture as a scientific concept is now more useful than ever. As previously argued, culture studies are meant to analyse the complexity of humans and societies (see also Liep and Olwig, 1994).

The introduction of the concept of culture in consumption studies has been a great achievement in understanding the complex relation between societies, consumers and the idea, nature, types or ranking of values. As a positive side-effect, this has enabled consumer researchers to convince others outside the specific profession, such as politicians and fundraisers, that comprehending consumption is important, not only for the structures of economy, but also in relation to our self-conception – personally and from a societal point of view (e.g. convincing researchers like McCracken, 1988; Featherstone, 1991; Miller, 1995 and Bourdieu, 1995). It is clear that a new discourse about consumption has emerged since the 1980s (see note 4), making consumption a matter of *general* interest. Nowadays most – I dare say all – socially interested researchers agree that consumption is pivotal to understanding contemporary society and existence. Some have suggested this to be because we – in western capitalist civilization – live in consumerist societies where people are categorized according to their competences as consumers (e.g. Bauman, 1997, Bourdieu 1995), others that this is because we construct ourselves in order to communicate consumer lifestyles and dreams (e.g. Chaney, 1996, Featherstone, 1991).

Consumer behaviour research investigates consumer norms, beliefs, values, attitudes, intentions, actions, and so on. In practice, it is often easier to grasp such soft and slippery issues if one tries to understand the relation within and between them, focusing on problems and conflicts; who gains and who loses, what is won and lost, what do we not like and what is wrong, and so on, and in doing that it is easy to see that consumer research also examines political culture, cultural fights and consumer strategies. If one does not take an interest in the built-in paradoxes and ambivalences in the system among the consumers, about resources (e.g. time, money, knowledge, rights, morals, etc.), consumption studies miss the opportunity of discussing power. As Karl Marx philosophized, and thinkers within critical theory have discussed (e.g. Horkheimer and Adorno, Habermas, Bauman), the political and cultural dimensions of life are two sides of the same coin. This is exactly what the specific state form and life mode consumption theory intends to help consumer studies to show.

A shift in the consumer discourse from specifically professional to general, of course, deeply affects both how we understand business and how business positions itself in society, at least if one agrees that business and markets are part of culture and society. But even though we acknowledge the importance of understanding the complex relation between societies, business and consumer value through the concept of consumer culture, how are we to comprehend the complexity? How can we understand consumer identity, feelings and preferences in relation not only to market dimensions and strategy, but also to community, norms, beliefs, politics, and so on, without being trapped in a transcendental reciprocity between structures and agents like McCracken. My proposition is that we need a Højrup-like culture theory of consumer behaviour.

In my theory I argue that one of the most important superior defence strategies today is consumption. This is a result of the mentioned change in consumer discourse. The ongoing discussions of progression in freedom and democracy through individualization and globalization of society, and the following logic of 'marketization' of politics and politization of consumption, have elevated the concept of consumption to a strong episteme (historically articulated paradigm) or the essence of our time (see e.g. Daunton and Hilton, 2001). In the modern, progressive free world of today, state *Subjects*, currently in the form of nation states, force each other to defend and improve their political, cultural, moral and economical positions by promoting similar or complementary new resource-giving life modes: specific *consumer-subjects*, in the individual societies. Consumers are 'soldiers' in virtual wars about the formation of future cultures and politics, their weapons are consumer values and their ammunition the abilities to choose and buy.

The theory argues that consumer values are to be seen as specific virtues interpellated to defend the *Subject* within a *Subject* system. This defence takes place not only in the form of more or less extreme consumer boycotts and the like, but especially on a daily basis in the form of consumers consuming the 'right' products for the 'right' reasons and thus ridding themselves of a bad conscience, of feeling guilty. This consumer-specific political/cultural system has unintentionally resulted from the transformation of previous political and cultural systems in western, capitalistic, industrial nations, by the cunning of reason. As such, modern people find it natural to live in consumer societies categorized as consumers according to their competences as consumers, for better or worse. Some call this contemporary condition, post-modern societies (e.g. Firat and Venkatesh, 1995).

In the western part of the world, democracy has gone beyond its institutions to some degree – it has been hyper-democratized in a Baudrillardian sense (refer to Baudrillard, 1997) – due to the politiciation of consumption and hence disciplining of political consumer subjects (Sestoft, 2002). This combined with multiple achievements in science and technology and the internationalization and globalization of politics and economy – and culture for that matter – makes way for a new position for individuals and their consumer values: more or less liberated from rank, class, religion and other hegemonic orders, traditional systems have virtually been eliminated and it is now up to the consumer to make the world a better place through consumption. In this society, it seems to be up to the consumer to try with a little help from her friends[8] to make the world a better place through responsible consumer values and meaningful consumption.

Living up to this new responsibility of course means we have to be skilful consumers. The hyper-democratized system works as illustrated in the model of political consumption discourse in Figure 7.1. Consumer values play a crucial part in this new system, as it is up to the consumer to choose responsibly and wisely thus steering the markets. The model shows why consumer values have become the most important virtues from a *Subject* point of view: Consumer values are weapons on the market battlefield, and this battlefield is the most (maybe the only) rational one in the contemporary era of global capitalism (see Castells, 2003, pp. 119-120).

In Denmark, politicians, institutions and citizens more or less have to rely upon the consumer to choose her way to system improvement – be it a healthier life, a happier family or a better world. But the way we get there is an ongoing paradoxical discussion about whether it should be consumer choices and values that improve the system on the basis of individual cost benefit analysis and free market choice, or whether the system should label the goods, guide the consumer choices and control the market (see Figure 7.1). Some are most focused on the need to institutionalize the consumer society and control the markets, others on the need to enlighten and educate the consumer and further open the markets to free competition.[9]

By now, the ideologies of consumption seem to have overruled the ideologies of production and its powerful instruments of the traditional world. This transition, of course, has consequences for the economy and business, and has created new challenges and problems for businesses to deal with. Mads Øvlisen, the former CEO of Novo Nordisk, one of the largest and most successful Danish businesses, puts is this way: 'The task of businesses today is to legitimize the business' behaviour and get accepted by political consumers' (Fyns Stifttidende, 25/02/04). And the businesses need to get busy, because today the political consumer is a potential virtue within all interpellated (i.e. dependable and acceptable) members of society because of the new *general* consumer discourses.

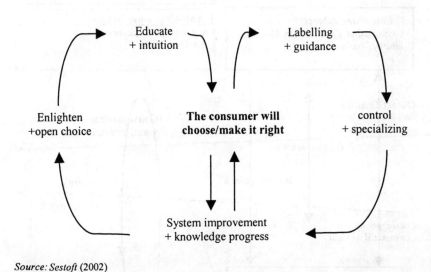

Source: Sestoft (2002)

Figure 7.1 Model of political consumption discourse

Like me, Øvlisen sees general changes in consumer values and behaviours, as well as changes in the specific society and market place within which Novo Nordisk operates. This interesting new system requires new business strategies and a different understanding of marketing as Øvlisen sees it, for example, more focus on sustainability and corporate social values.[10]

One might conclude that from a business director's point of view, we also need a theory that considers the power of consumer practices and values as equal partners in contemporary (consumer) political/cultural systems. In the social and cultural sciences, we have to relate structural changes in society, culture and consumption to specific historical situations, practices or processes. Many consumer culture researchers have done this, and they have all contributed to the explanation of why and how the consumer society was established as it is. Bauman (1997) talks about how consumers are the extreme extension of the disciplining of the working man. McCracken (1988) sees consumerism as a modern and democratic way of redistributing resources. And Bourdieu (1995) explains consumption not as a new but a different way of achieving and maintaining a dominant position within a capitalistic system of classes. I would argue that the *Consumer Subject* is all of this and more. It is the project of enlightenment and re-enchantment of the post-industrial societies (see also Firat and Venkatesh, 1995).

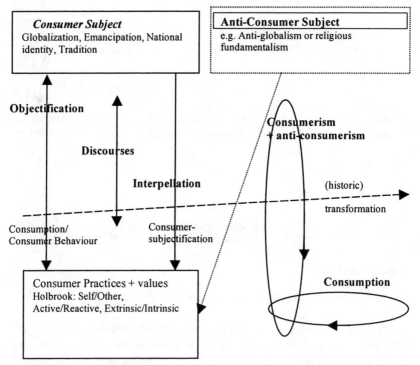

Figure 7.2 The specific state form and life mode consumption theory

Nowadays, we live in a consumer society transformed into 'producing' technical, scientific risks (see also Beck, 1997). As such, consumers of the global community are accessories to social, ecological or safety related problems through 'bad' consumption – and conversely heroes when it comes to 'good' consumption. Consumers are, metaphorically speaking, steering the future development of sustainable and defensible societies. How to consume or not to consume is no longer just an economic and macro-political question, but also a micro-political, social and moral question. As this shows, identifying consumption and consumer values is very much structured and interdependent. The way this structure and interdependence works is shown in Figure 7.2.

The model in Figure 7.2 is the result of my developing a new consumer theory from Højrup's state form and life mode theory. It shows a dialectic cultural theory of consumer behaviour including a dynamic understanding of a transformation of the same. It depicts the conceptualization of the culturally constituted relations of power between the *Consumer Subject* and specific consumer subjects and their practices and values. The model further depicts clean conceptual relations but in messy everyday life they are expressed as differences in behaviour, intentions, preferences, and attitudes, that is, in people's complex consumer practices and values.

The value perspective in the model of the specific state form and life mode consumption theory is open to both Holbrook's definition of consumer values as an interactive relativistic preference experience and his value type dimensions (Holbrook, 1999, pp. 5 and 10 - 12). What Holbrook would call the nature of values in my model becomes the virtuous expressions of the *Consumer Subject*. As such, the nature of values is not an evident thing but a relative one, as against Holbrook's perspective (Holbrook, 1999). A considerable difference from Holbrook is that the model explicates the structure in which this interactive relativistic preference experience takes place, making consumer values more than psychologically interesting – that is, consumer values are interesting from a cultural and societal perspective.

Nowadays consumers are expected to invent and present authentic and autonomic selves from consumption; that is, to create valid preferences and attitudes out of still more complex and scientific information (see also Halkier, 2001; Firat and Venkatesh, 1995; Sestoft 2002). A modern consumer 'instinctively' knows that consumer behaviour identifies who we are, and even though many unique consumers dislike being categorized, segmentation teaches us that we are often authentic and autonomic in the same way as a lot of other people (!) The possibility of feeling unique and fitting into a segment all at the same time suggests that consumer identification is a process of relative differences in specific consumer practices and values in relation to general consumption issues – a *Consumer Subject*.

At the same time as consumers are expected to invent and present authentic and autonomic selves through consumption, it is imperative that they discipline themselves to learn how to value consumption to choose, consume and evaluate goods and services regarding still more complex, political and morally implicated trade-offs in still more complex markets (ibid.). Many of us know the feeling of wearing the right vs. wrong clothes, serving the right vs. wrong food or wanting the right vs. wrong things depending on the situation. Such feelings are expressions of the ongoing discipline of consumption a new kind of soft power or powerful softness. The subject technology of self-discipline fosters virtuous consumers, builds up responsible consumers from the inside. This specific interpellation calls for empathic consumers who are aware that individual consumer behaviour affects present and future developments of markets and societies. The central act of consumer interpellation is the day by day production or fostering of consumer-knowledge and know-how based on information and characteristics about the goods, and the simultaneous incorporation and integration of this knowledge as identity markers: consumer values. To be responsible consumers, that is, subjects of the 'positive' (liberal, capitalistic, democratic) world, people need to know and feel what is good for themselves and others, to be able to steer the local and global communities they are part of in an even more positive direction. As a result of consumerist discourses, responsible consumers are now aware that their behaviour, practices and values are important to themselves, their family, producers, retailers, communities, societies, nations, and so on, and this awareness is reflected in the objectification of groceries that turn out to be very meaningful objects. This contributes to the explanation of why cookbooks, open kitchen environments and TV cookery programmes are trendier and more popular than ever before and why more Danish boys dream of becoming chefs and not firemen or policemen. The interpellated consumer responsibility unfolds within the dimensions of the episteme. Today, this system focuses on the question of how to place nation states and its subjects/citizens in a global market-orientated world. This question drives the ongoing interest in themes such as globalization, emancipation/freedom, traditions or national identity.

Because the theory is based on a notion of power as a relational and relativistic phenomenon, it can be read both ways; from 'consumer practices and values' up or from the '*Consumer Subject*' down. Because it is an episteme, the consumer subject works as a guiding principle behind practices and values – as a superior substance or dominating cultural structure. The '*Consumer Subject*' is the thinkable and speakable consumption related concept, that dominates contemporary society what we as subjects are made of, so to speak.[11] Consumption and consumer virtues represent the most reasonable defence of the state subject in the contemporary state system, because of the difficulty of policy-making in an open international, global-orientated world, which leads to changed political and cultural strategies.

The consumer virtues are interpellated by different institutions of consumerism; for example, the industry of culture, the media, pop-idols, music; and by the aesthetic, ethic or scientific narratives of right, wrong, good or bad, nice or ugly; consumption. This interpellation feels totally natural to individuals as they are subjected as consumers just as natural as values feel! Often this 'natural' feeling is what we describe as our *need* to buy or our *desire* for new things.[12]

Transformation of both principles and practices takes place through the rules of dialectics because of the cunning of reason. Intended or unintended, transformation will always occur even if we try to stabilize the process. The political, cultural and social fights about value categories and definitions are fought out via discourses in a Foucauldian sense (see Foucault, 1977 and 1994). In that way, discourses form and drive consumer attitudes, intentions, preferences, values and feelings, and so on. As such, consumer intentions, preferences, values and feelings are implications of the temporary hegemonic categories and definitions of virtuous consumption, that is, not evident but relative ones.

As a culture consumption researcher, I am especially interested in the relation between subjects and objects, a relation not explicit in Højrups theory, and 'objectification' would seem to be the answer.[13] The concept of objectification comes from Daniel Miller who gets it from Hegel (Miller, 1987). Miller defines objectification as 'a series of processes consisting of externalization (self-alienation) and sublation (reabsorption) through which the subject of such a process is created and developed' (Miller, 1987, p. 12). This definition lies within Højrup's definition of culture as the processes in which we are categorized as more or less powerful specific subjects in superior systems of defence, but the concept of objectification focuses more on the specific subject object relation. So, in the model, consumer subjectification relates to how consumers are subject to ideologies within consumerism, and objectification relates to the part material objects and consumer behaviour play in this interpellation.

Of course it is possible to be subjected to another *Subject*, such as anti-globalism or religious fundamentalism (see Figure 7.1). This could explain existential crises, cultural confusion and clashes of values, because such subjects would be interpellated with other values possibly opposing or disturbing to the responsible *consumer* values. From a dialectic perspective, in theory as well as in practice, value crises, confusion and clashes must take part in the constellation of consumer preferences. What or who to believe as a responsible consumer, how to act and where to prioritize is, in the end, all up to the individual consumer to figure out for herself, which calls for some thinking and reflecting. From time to time, the consumer will need help though, and buying well-known, recommended, publicly tested, branded or otherwise marked or guaranteed goods is a solution to many consumers (e.g. 'Max Harvelar', the Nordic 'Swan', EU's 'Flower' or different 'organic' brands). Another very popular type of guidance/help, is found in the massive amount of consumption-oriented programmes in the mass media, where consumers learn about 'the right' consumption from various aesthetic, ethical and political perspectives (e.g. infotainment programmes, magazines and articles on 'find a new style', 'make your house attractive', learn about products' etc.).

A NOTE ON METHODS

In my pursuit of a general understanding of the processes behind the consumer values, how consumers choose, consume, evaluate, understand themselves and reflect each other within a *Consumer Subject*, I have argued for a general consumption theory. One way of validating my specific point of view (/theory) is to test it using empirical material to see if it makes sense of a complex reality.

The purpose of empirical data in relation to the specific state form and life mode consumer theory is to describe different expressions of the structures and ideologies of consumerism, that is, the *Consumer Subject*. As previously discussed, this is expressed in consumer subjects' relation to the objects (/goods and services), in consumer self-conceptions, and in consumer perceptions of the relations between different categories of consumer subjects.

The theoretical approach in this chapter has the methodological implication that consumer values can be analysed from ideological, societal and subject perspectives. This is due to the fact that in my theory, ideology does not just equal spirit, society not only practice and subjects not exactly individuals. From this Althusserian point of view, ideology is always located in practice and practice is always ideologically constituted (Althusser, 1999). Despite the theoretical complexity, the methodological advantage is that empirical data becomes multi-analytical. This also means that interpretation – the reading of the text in a broad sense is crucial to this kind of research, which inscribes it in the hermeneutic tradition and results in a type of analysis of the material, that is, more a discussion or reflection than a presentation of 'the facts'.

All discussions in the chapter are guided by the method of discourse analysis. This method is actually more than a method. Discourse analysis is a specific way of reading a text, that is, of viewing the empirical reality as specific social and cultural constructions. As Foucault shows (e.g. Foucault, 1977 and 1994), these specific social and cultural constructions are transformed by social and cultural powers that are specific epistemic perceptions of reason, knowledge and science.

The specific empirical material in this chapter is aimed at understanding what lies behind the practices and values of online consumer intentions and actual online behaviour. The data here analysed consists of interviews, photographs, observations and diaries, collected with the intention of enabling 'texts' (/informants) to talk about daily life consumption, ITC and online grocery consumption. The informants were found via the databases of an online supermarket and an online grocery service business. In general, the informants were not particularly experienced with online grocery business, especially not the consumers from the database of the online supermarket. But they all had some experience of online grocery shopping, which was enough to secure the reliability of their answers.

The data collection was based on four practice-oriented research questions:

1. What are the advantages and disadvantages experienced by consumers with off- and online buying of fast moving consumer goods (FMCG)?
2. What kind of items are preferably purchased off- or online and for what reasons?
3. What aspects are important for consumers in relation to the delivery of goods purchased online?
4. What happens after delivery? How are goods and packaging handled, stored and disposed of?

Table 7.1 Respondents characteristics

Online grocery service customers: 2 women, ages 40, 48. 1 man, age 50 Children: School children or grown up
Mixed experience (online grocery service + online supermarkets): 3 women, ages 27, 41, 42 1 man, age 50 Children: No children, toddler, not living at home
Online supermarkets: 3 women, ages 29, 30, 51 1 man, age 47 Children: Baby, kindergarten, school children, grown up

Ten in-depth semi-structured interviews were conducted with customers from the online grocery service and online supermarket, after they had written a consumer diary for a week.[14] The questions asked varied from very general ones about their consumer lives to more specific ones about online and grocery buying.[15] Photographs of where the respondents store their groceries and return packaging were taken as well.

The respondents were characterized by the following [16] (The total number of respondents was 11, because one interview was conducted with both husband and wife).

The concrete consumer practices and values are empirical expressions of the *Consumer Subject* and they refer to all the different categories of consumer subjects and different consumer lives across different means and resources. This means that nobody can fit the theory perfectly because nobody is a perfect consumer. The theory is a tool to gain understanding and obviously a specific scientific perspective. From this point of view, the purpose of the analysis is to understand the grand narratives consumer subjects are interpellated and socialized within, as well as the individual narratives realized from the ongoing categorizations of more or less acceptable things and meanings – that is, lifestyles, values, feelings, 'good people' and 'good life'

CASE DISCUSSION

The Problem of Technology

Since the 1990s, the problem of how to include information and communication technology (ICT) in our still more modern, effective and rational society has been an ongoing discussion in every part of our culture in relation to grocery consumption too. Ten to fifteen years ago, technology experts predicted e-business would take over most consumption, because of the convenience and effectiveness of the technology. Such predictions suffered from an early kind of techno-seduction, which disregarded all kinds of consumer behaviour perspectives and considerations about groceries as cultural objects and social expressions.[17] The seductive perspective was quickly seriously challenged by social and cultural research pointing out the less attractive sides of ICT stress, isolation, loneliness, fraud, safety, and so on, making the technology discourse complex and hard to follow for some.

Despite 15 years of public discussion about ICT and the fact that today almost everyone in Denmark owns a PC and almost everyone has access to the Internet, it still seems to be difficult to match technology and grocery consumption mentally as well as practically. Technology does not seem to belong to the consumer subject category it is considered special and smart, whereas grocery consumption is considered general, relevant and easy. The attitude that follows is that technology we may do without (many of us did a short time ago), but grocery consumption is important. Of course this may change in the future, but as for now grocery consumption technology is not something we need, and even more interesting, it is not something we want. As such, only about 3 per thousand of the total grocery consumption in Denmark comes from online business.[18]

Everybody agrees that the grocery business in Denmark almost like everywhere else today, is not a success. If you look at busy consumers' fragmented daily lives, consumers' constant aspirations to experience and enjoy themselves and their general effort to engage in the transforming market as consumer subjects, you could say that in theory online grocery business should be successful: buying groceries on the Internet, you can buy what you need, when you have the time and you get your 'smart' groceries packed and delivered. So, why is it not a huge success?

One problem is the medium itself. Technology and not least the Internet have affected our conditions of life and by that possibly our practices, values and self-conceptions (e.g. Castells, 2003), but apparently not when it comes to grocery consumption. Mark Poster points out (Venkatesh, 2002) that Internet technology threw the consumer into virtual space where objects are 'underdeterminated' meaning relatively unspecified regarding physical goods and real-life situations. In my theory, this underdetermination could be explained as a lack of objectification, hence the alienated consumer behaviour, that is, consumers do not feel like *consumers* on the Internet. Moving on from technology itself, another problem is information what the medium mediates. The need for more information and specifications is an argument that gets support from many online business researchers, such as Degeratu (Degeratu et al., 2000). They find that consumer behaviour on the Internet in particular is sensitive to information, that is, price, brand and especially factual information, than conventional stores. As a result, e-businesses have to take extra care in supporting the information and specification needs in the sales channel. However, it also means that e-consumers have to enhance their search for information and trust their 'sense-less' evaluations of the goods.

My data material and observations tell me the conventional e-grocery business[19] does not support the extra need for information and specification in the sales channel. But then again, maybe more information and specification here is not in itself the right solution. At least not if you ask my informants, who all agree that they do not want to spend much time searching for information about their daily groceries. Buying groceries online you first and foremost want to save time. When the consumers are asked directly, there are a lot of rational explanations for why they do not buy groceries online. From the interviews, we can see that money is an issue:

> (Translated from Danish) Yes, I have to say that the disadvantages [of online grocery shopping] is both that it can go wrong during the delivery process, and, in general, I don't think that the prices are cheap. And of course one looks at the prices! (Woman, age 40)

Another anxiety relates to being electronically mugged when buying on the Internet:

> (Translated from Danish) Well, you see, it's just this (ha, ha) fear of having to give your Visa-card number and all that, you know. I'm still uncomfortable with that, you know. And I even have a friend who does it all the time, who has never had any problems, so... (Woman, age 51)

But these issues should not count as factishes (Latour, 2000), not as a fetish-like fact, because as we know from Holbrook, consumer values, both perceived prices and safety, are relative experiences. History also supports this perspective, since in the last decade Danes have generally become richer and much better acquainted with being online, for example, seeking information, chatting and surfing on the Internet, and so on, all the while almost no one has become interested in integrating online grocery business in their daily lives. It is evident that consumers have a fundamental problem with letting go of the daily grocery shopping experience, even though they are somewhat bored with it or even dislike it. This is clear in the following dialogue between this married couple from one of the interviews:

> (Translated from Danish)
> Husband: ... we love to shop ... we surely don't have anything against it.
> Wife: *You* love to shop!
> Husband: (ha, ha) so do you!
> Wife: No, actually I don't! It's *you* who loves to go shopping. You love to 'fiddle around' in the stores – I don't! I really don't!... [Addressed to the interviewer:] You know, when we go shopping [husband] loves to 'potter about' in the stores. That's not me! I have my shopping list, and off I go...

Technological incorporation, specification or even technological alienation, cannot in itself explain the general structural conditions consumer (online) values are part of, even though there *are* considerable problems with ITC in relation to the e-grocery business. For this reason, it is important to understand the practice of technology, lifestyles and society in dialectic relation to their structural conditions. To not include this would be like describing anti-Semitism and the holocaust without understanding the structural conditions of modernity (refer to Bauman, 1989).

The Problem of Daily Life

Explanations such as lack of trust, low hedonic shopping value, bad service management, technological difficulties or inability to use the senses when buying groceries on the Internet, all seem reasonable reasons not to buy, and so does low supply. To the respondents, grocery businesses do not appear to be much interested in selling on the Internet. As one of them explains:

> (Translated from Danish) ...you know when I go on the Internet to look around or something, Well, there is almost nothing! (Woman, age 51)

or another, referring to the difficulties of web-page surfing:

> (Translated from Danish) Hum, yes, well, I have to say ... for instance when I bought groceries on the Internet... well it takes a lot of time, you know - ticking off and so on... Also because I had to see the special offers (ha, ha). Sure it would have gone faster if only I knew what precisely I wanted of this or that. But it takes time to order groceries on the Internet, it surely does. It could take half an hour... three quarters of an hour... (Woman, age 51)

By buying groceries on the Internet, consumers are introduced to a number of advantages and disadvantages compared to offline shopping. As discussed, the majority seem to focus mainly on the disadvantages, this may be because online shopping makes consumers unable to use their senses, that it is too difficult or expensive to use or that overall they do not see any advantages to online business (Raijas, 2002; Hansen, 2003). Both Raijas and Hansen argue (ibid.) that the reason why many consumers are relatively more interested in seeking information and evaluating goods on the Internet than actual e-shopping, is because they have not incorporated e-business into their daily life.

From a social and cultural point of view, changes in social and cultural structures and practices must never be reduced to causal explanations of technological changes not even the invention of the Internet. As Raijes and Hansen point out, ICT is still a foreign body in consumers' lives, but groceries are not. Groceries are just as natural a part of consumer daily life as making a living has been for working people for centuries. As such, buying groceries is a cultural routine, one of those things people do not think they think much about. This explains why consumers categorize groceries as what Bucklin (1963) calls 'convenience goods', and value them on a short-term basis (prefer them), and when short on individual resources (time, money or information) often in relation to use-value of the goods.

From a functional and rational perspective, buying groceries is very much one of those things you do not give much thought to in daily life. Accordingly, the respondents did not categorize grocery products in general as especially 'bad' or 'good' but as 'normal'. Because grocery shopping is so normal, several of the respondents thought their daily shopping routines were 'not interesting' or 'too banal' to talk about. Some even felt a little embarrassed, joking about their so normal lives, during the interview:

(Translated from Danish) Well, I run around buying groceries. Oddly enough I find it funny, uh? (Man, age 50)

(Translated from Danish) But ...eh... I just think it's nice to go shopping in (supermarkets) to see their new products ... it's not a big deal to me. (Woman, age 27)

'There is nothing to it' seemed to be the general opinion. Naturally grocery shopping feels a little better when you are not pressed for time, shop for special occasions or discover new products, and a little worse when you are busy, disappointed in the store choice or in the quality of goods, the respondents argued, but overall buying groceries is just an everyday personal experience.

On the other hand, when digging deeper into the interview, asking the respondents to reflect more on grocery shopping, other more long-term and explicit culture-specific value perspectives appeared, referring to specific discourses about health/risk, identity or social/moral responsibility. For instance, when talking about changing habits and behaviour around grocery shopping, those routines seem to have a snowball-like effect on the rest of the daily life in thought as well as in practice changing habits would also mean changing positions on important political and cultural discourses invisibly related to the practices of daily life and grocery shopping. So behind the normality and neutrality of groceries, deeply constituted values appeared. Values referring to discourses of responsibility, risk vs. health and identity/individualization. To illustrate this, several of the subscribers to the online grocery delivery system would talk about how they were (self)disciplined to eat healthier food because of the subscription. To these respondents, changing their view (/discursive position) of health because of a feeling of individual responsibility to live healthy lives seemed to have been an argument for subscribing in the first place a good example of how subjectification and objectification work hand in hand, mediated through consumer practices and values interpellated by a *Consumer Subject* (refer to Figure 7.1).

The Problem of Virtuous Consumers

Reflecting on why and how they have or could have imagined changing their grocery shopping routines, most respondents refer to comments within the episteme of the *Consumer Subject* about welfare (/health/safety/lifestyle), experience (/personal/family/friends) or consumer responsibility (/local/global), and all of a sudden the same goods 'transform' from convenience goods to special goods. This is especially the case when it comes to vegetables. From a societal perspective, this discursive change in groceries and food categories from convenience to special is a sign of successfully interpellated virtues – that is, responsible consumer values. Such values are an empirical expression of the fostering of a trustworthy consumer subject who in a naturally felt way is concerned with being capable of classifying and integrating new responsible products in to daily routines and at the same time having fun, getting to know things – progressing and refining as a consumer subject. The respondents, of course, have different opinions about these discursive comments, because of their different life modes, resources and discursive positions, be it eating more vegetables, losing weight, saving time, saving money, surprising others, just enjoying, buying organic food or boycotting Israel (all examples from the interviews). However, despite the differences, they all agree that consumption is very meaningful and very important now and in the future: society could not do without it and neither could the consumers.

As the interpellation of a responsible consumer subject and objectification of groceries are important to the defence of our culture, it means that even though the respondents first comment on groceries as something conventional and convenient and on grocery shopping as something boring and normal, after some reflection they talk about how they expect the grocery shopping experience to surprise and delight them – to mean something and awake feelings:

(Translated from Danish) So…it became like new inspiration to…to cooking and doing new stuff [...] and I think it has enhanced the quality of our daily-life – a lot, actually. I think so. (Woman, age 48)

(Translated from Danish) But, you know ...buying ten litres of milk is not something you learn a lot from [...] But, there is always something new and that's a bit exciting. (Woman, age 41)

(Translated from Danish) You know, sometimes I find it nice to go around in (supermarkets), and like "Oh, they have rabbit-roast today – we've got to try that." So we buy a rabbit-roast. (Woman, age 51)

As groceries have become objectified as objects of health, safety, lifestyle and morals, because of similar discourses including scientific information and expert recommendations about the best/worst consumption, groceries (/food) have become a natural yet value-based categorizing part of life. Responsible consumers know that not much in this world changes if the consumer does not care and does not act responsibly. You can try to resign from this responsibility, but it is impossible and in any case unavoidable because of the constant reminder from everywhere – school, TV/media, public campaigns, and so on.

When it comes to the Internet, there is a problem though: because the Internet, as mentioned, is low on information, specifications are underdetermined, and because the consumers lack experience (/have not integrated e-business in to their daily lives) it is neither easy for them to think for themselves nor to be guided on the Internet. These arguments are supported by statements from the interviews that when the respondents buy on the Internet they either buy special offers and cheap standard goods or highly branded specialty goods. These practices reflect different strategies for reducing risk, but build on the same consumer values, namely seeking experience albeit in a virtuous manner, while classifying and potentially integrating new responsible preferences.[20]

(Translated from Danish)
I: Please tell me why online-shopping sometimes works for you?
R: That's because it's standard goods. You know, you only have to ship it back if it doesn't work.
I: But why prefer it to a 'normal' [offline] store?
R: Because it's cheap!
I: Okay. Any other reasons?
R: Yes well, 'Wall Paper'. ...I don't think you can subscribe [offline]...well...there are some things you can't get anywhere else.

The dilemma between choosing for themselves and being guided (/recommended) is a consumer paradox, especially in the case of groceries (/food), a bodily embedded dilemma that deeply affects consumer behaviour. This is a paradox that in our daily lives makes consumption a complex and sometimes contradictory experience; so demanding, frustrating and at the same time emancipating and exciting.

Because consumers are expected to invent and present themselves from consumption (subject to consumption), and hence create valid preferences out of still more complex and scientific information, and because it is so impelling that we learn and re-learn all the time how to behave choose, live and consume regarding still more complex, politically and morally implicated trade-offs to still more complex markets, some consumers feel shopping can be stressful:

> (Translated from Danish)
> I: [What do you in general think about going shopping?]
> R: It depends on how much time you've got and such. And if you're busy it's not at all great...I know about that! ...hum, it depends on how much time you've got...

In our daily lives, we have to balance our demands for personal experience from consumption with the interpellated virtue of consumption, and we have to integrate the ongoing objectification meaningfully as identity while classifying consumption and classifying ourselves and others as consumers, according to what is scientifically and morally 'right' or 'wrong' at a given time in given products and services.

Not all people are equally comfortable about their consumer practice, far from it, and some have more or less given up on the virtuous consumer values; this may be because of the different means and resources, such as time, money, know-how or knowledge, or because of a moral or political opposition to the *Consumer Subject* itself.

> (Translated from Danish) Actually, I think I get quite irritated quite fast, because of the web-pages and think: 'This I don't understand!' And then you know, you move on and away from it. So, it's only if I can see an advantage I try to understand what's going on. (Woman, age 27)

Some of the consumers have even grown to like not to choose (/shop) because of all the arguments we often have to consider in the decision-making process. These respondents explain that it feels like Christmas, like getting gifts, when the online grocery system delivers the goods:

> (Translated from Danish) So I have to say, it has become like a fixed point (ha, ha), this box of vegetables, from... I can't remember...She [his wife] gets it every Friday. They [the vegetables] are lined up in long rows, ok, and then we look at them (ha, ha). We almost take pictures of it! (ha, ha). It's funny [...] It's real exciting, you know. You think you get something and then maybe you get something else you have to find out how to use. (Man, age 50)

This attitude to consumption opens a niche where online business could gain an advantage, integrating some of the problems from the practices of the consumers such as corporate social responsibility (CSR) and strategic marketing (see figure 7.3).

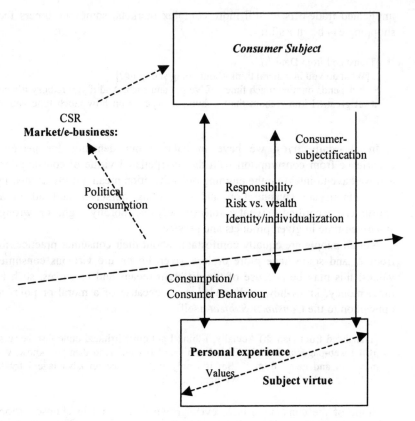

Figure 7.3 Model of new business from a behind the values perspective

A NEW KIND OF BUSINESS

We can easily agree that the supply of groceries on the Internet is very poor in Denmark today.[21] But my main point would be that consumers still did not buy groceries on the Internet even when the special offers and supply were much more plentiful, such as when the Danish supermarket ISO launched its Internet grocery shop at the beginning of the 1990s. Despite sales campaigns and TV commercials, Internet ISO turned out to be an economic fiasco and eventually closed.

Because Holbrook focuses on the relation between the dimensions of market space and relative consumer values, his specific value types become useful to my theory of consumer values. In relation to the Holbrook typology of values, conventional e-grocery businesses apparently think they ought to support the extrinsic (functional, utilitarian, or instrumental), self-oriented and active dimensions of consumer value, that is, types of value like efficiency, play, excellence and aesthetics, in their efforts to look like brick-and-mortar supermarkets. But those values are not as transposable to the practice of online service as believed, hence the consumers' feelings of disadvantage with online-grocery shopping. This means that both consumers with the above mentioned values and consumers with other-oriented, intrinsic and reactive consumer values are discouraged to use the Internet as a shopping channel.

The objectification of meaningful groceries and the subjectification of virtuous grocery consumers make grocery shopping part of complex and politically implicated discourses about responsibility across different life-modes, without people realizing it on a daily basis. I think e-businesses have overlooked this new culture system, and instead, they have been focusing on the general positive attitude to technology and the stressful consumer life of modern society. The fact that most people agree that the Internet it is a smart technology, combined with the consumers' call for convenience may have confused the businesses into making online supermarkets look-alikes.

As is often the case in marketing and product development, online-consumers do not know what they want at least not until they get it. Many consumers refer to online grocery shopping as a good idea, because they perceive ITC to be a smart and rational thing, but most consumers do not choose online grocery shopping because they are unable to apply their values within the virtual business concept and groceries are too culturally important for them not to be able to do that, not least because of the discursive politiciation of consumption, and consequently the interpellation of the political consumer.

When it comes to buying groceries, it is obvious that the online businesses have to reflect much more on how consumers struggle (e.g. consumers' ability to value groceries) to live coherent lives as consumer subjects 'outside the Internet' according to the positions they posit as responsible subjects of the *Consumer Subject*, disciplined to seek personal experience in a virtuous manner, while classifying and potentially integrating new responsible preferences. To follow this recommendation, businesses should not focus on technology because, in practice, information technology is not in itself of particular interest to the consumers. One respondent put it as follows:

(Translated from Danish) Yes, well, it's [the Internet] just a practical way of finding things. It's not such an experience in itself. You just sit and look at something. I think it is already sort of an everyday occurrence. It's just there. (Woman, age 51)

I lean towards the conclusion that on a strategic level the Internet cannot compete with offline supermarkets and the like, in servicing interpellated responsible consumer practices and values. Shopping for groceries on the Internet does not seem to give people a feeling of personal experience. That is one thing, while another and more important issue is that it is too difficult to act as a virtuous consumer subject online – the information on the goods is too comprehensive, incontrollable and diverse for consumers to trust themselves (to be fully and adequately informed) and their choices.

Based on the interviews, the lesson to be learnt must be that 'conventional' online grocery business is more or less a dead-end. To use the words of one of the respondents, *It's just there* and *not an experience in itself.* The main point in this chapter is that the future for online grocery-business should not be an extension of a brick-and-mortar store; at least not in Denmark where the discount brick-and-mortar stores especially are growing (Stockmann gruppen, 2004). According to this study, conventional Internet-based online grocery businesses have the disadvantage of not meeting the consumer values or solving the problems of the virtuous consumer subject any better than a traditional retailer/supermarket: it is not easier to choose and classify, it does not improve your planning and integration of new products, and you still cannot be sure of quality and other positive experiences in broad terms. Everybody knows you may save some time getting your groceries delivered, but to the majority this is obviously just not enough when you include the delivery fee. From a conventional supermarket point of view, it seems almost impossible to digitalize the daily buying of groceries, this simply does not correspond with the dominant discourse that holds consumers responsible for good or bad consumption, regarding issues such as health, happiness or viability in their personal life, within the family or the nation, even the globe. The positive perception of being in control of grocery shopping may be difficult in conventional brick-and-mortar supermarkets, but it is almost impossible with online-grocery shopping. In practice, online grocery shopping means consumers have to trust their practice of consumer values to digital technology and total strangers, and from this realization the potential for a new kind of e-grocery business arises. Many researchers have been concerned with the consumers' problems with the Internet (e.g. Hansen, 2002), not so many with the problem of online business itself. In Denmark, apparently only one of the online grocery businesses (aarstiderne.com) has understood and linked itself to the complex relations between the powerful discourses that shape consumer behaviour, practices and values of the *Consumer Subject*. Also, according to Michael Porter (Porter, 2001), only very few e-businesses seem to have understood the principal difference and special circumstance of the virtual business reality. Therefore, only very few of them have been able to see the specific potential in e-business and consequently they have been unable to penetrate the markets and appeal to consumers. Instead of the sales channel and form, e-businesses should focus on content and communication, for example, their corporate values, the quality/specificity of the goods and services and business strategies. Online grocery businesses need to focus much more on the practices and values of consumers, especially on the consumer problems of being virtuous, that is, buying, cooking and eating the right, responsible, not too risky, not too expensive, but interesting/educating products. They have to rethink themselves strategically as a new type of business concerned with the total welfare of consumers, attentive to consumer values and discursive disciplining of (grocery) consumer behaviour. If online businesses want a strategic advantage, they need to focus more on what they can do better than traditional supermarkets, and at the same time focus on solving some of the issues from the daily lives of consumers. Two very different business strategies for the future online grocery businesses are suggested in the following, inspired by Porter (2001). One focuses on total self-service, supporting the extrinsic, self-oriented and active dimensions of consumer values, and the other focuses on total service, supporting the intrinsic, other-oriented and reactive dimensions of consumer value. The first type of strategy, the total self-service grocery business, is actually a brick-and-mortar store, albeit totally integrated within information technology. This business supports the free choice and values-at-work perspective. We already know this strategy from 'The Future Store'[22]. In the Future Store, the shopping cart gives the consumers all the information needed about the goods to match what the business knows/believes to represent consumer values as they shop. Of course it also registers the prices and weights of the goods. The business strategy is to make grocery shopping as cheap and convenient as possible, concentrating the time consumers spend on buying groceries on value-based *shopping* – not queuing, seeking staff, and so on – and at the same time maximizing the consumer choices. Some might say this is not e-business, and maybe they are right, as it is in fact a brick-and-mortar shop. But even though the shopping site is physical, the shopping experience must be hyper-real (more real than real) because of the massive amount of available information about the goods, that is, about their production, manufacturer, declarations, advisories, use, and so on. What this kind of business does not address is the communication with the consumer, which may be a problem.

The second business strategy is much more interesting, revolutionary and focused on the principal difference and special circumstance of the virtual reality of business. It is the 'subscription-delivery' business strategy, as we know it in Denmark from Aarstiderne.com,[23] just much wider-ranging. The idea is that the online grocery business takes over the consumer's grocery shopping dilemmas, because it more or less takes over grocery shopping. The business strategy is ICT-radical, as almost all communication is digitalized, but the technology involvement is reduced to a minimum for the consumer. In this kind of business, the business plans, chooses and delivers all groceries needed in a household. The consumers are able to choose between different 'lifestyles menus', but ultimately it is the business that chooses groceries for the consumers and guarantees that the diet is both exciting, healthy and socially responsible. This strategy resembles that of being a member of a grocery club or a grocery party, where consumers leave their grocery values up to others. It is evident that CSR becomes a crucial point in such a business (see Figure 7.3). A business that takes over the practice of consumer values must not only be in constant contact and dialogue with consumer values, but must also be aware of the part the business plays in the interpellation of such values. Naturally, it is very important that a total-service business is sincere about its strategy and its values, because trust means everything to the customers of such a business. Such an e-business would be able to create the crucial relation of 'love' with the customer (refer to Frostling-Henningsson, 2003) no other (e-)grocery business can do.

FINAL REMARKS AND FURTHER RESEARCH

Building a consumption theory that aspires to go beyond structure and hermeneutics is crazy talk to many. However, this is what is needed if one agrees that 'The Consumer', consumer behaviour and consumer values are incomprehensible in themselves and one further agrees that researchers in social sciences and humanities also have to be explicit about their worldview and interpretive framework to be reliable and open to discussion.

Many contemporary but otherwise strange situations and identities make sense in the perspective of consumer practices and values as defences of the *Consumer Subject*. For instance, the perspective made sense to the US President George Bush when the day after the September 11 terrorist attacks, he first of all urged people: Go buy! If we don't buy, other *Subjects* have won was the message, and even though the message sounded somewhat hollow and misplaced at the time, deep down we knew he was right: consumption and consumer values are a central and constituting part of our life and society.

The state forms and life modes have transformed consumer practices and values into powerful expressions of hyper-modern cultural and political defences. Such a perspective and consumer behaviour theory is not only beyond structure and hermeneutics, it is also beyond marketing, thus placing marketing in a very important role and business in a very responsible position in contemporary society, for better or worse. I think the e-grocery business has an opportunity to make it better rather than worse because of its potential ability to communicate with the consumers, for example about values.

Taking the cultural perspective I do on consumer behaviour and online grocery business: integrating consumer discourses, interpellation and behaviour within a state and life mode perspective, I hope to contribute to the discussions of the processes of making and being consumers in contemporary society, and to the discussions of the different role online grocery businesses could play in future consumerism and in the improvement of the life of consumers. Obviously, my points are developed from a mandatory bird-perspective. Thus further research into which discourses are relevant to the strategic practices of consumers and how interpellation unfolds in the empirical realities will continue to be of utmost importance.

NOTES

1. The eight types of value: efficiency, play, excellence, aesthetics, status, ethics, esteem, spirituality, are described from combining three dichotomies; extrinsic vs. intrinsic value, self-oriented vs. other-oriented value and active vs. reactive value into a 2x2x2 cross-classification (see Holbrook, 1999).
2. The fact that reason transcends itself dialectically.
3. Bearing: Having manners or being good in a general moral sense (Williams, 1983, p. 43). In my terms having a virtuous attitude.
4. Studies in values and material culture have always existed in the humanities and social studies (e.g. Karl Marx and Max Weber) and especially within the disciplines of anthropology, ethnology and archaeology. Material culture within these disciplines is often related to consumption as well as production/reproduction issues. However, the professional discourse before 1979 seems to be more about structures and agency of daily life, household or community, etc., and not 'consumption'.
5. Højrup has specified a dialectic theory of how specific state forms and life modes constitute each other's subjects, building on Marx' concepts of life (production reproduction cycle) and production mode, Hegel's concepts of subject and state (*Subject*), Althusser's concepts of ideology and interpellation and Clausewitch's theory of war (and peace = virtual war).
6. Louis Althusser (1999) describes the concept of interpellation as the call for subjectivity. He explains the process of interpellation as the disciplining whereby individuals become attentive to whom and what they are, in relation to

others. The process is a fostering of personality, and it takes place as ideology interpellates concrete individuals as specific subjects.

7. The *Subject* can be defined as the cultural precondition for the internal organization of society or the essence of substantial subjectivity. This concept is somewhat parallel to the sociologist Emile Durkheim's concept of social reality or rules. However, to Højrup the *Subject* is not a social fact, not a cause or function and not determinant ideology existing outside or independent of individuals, because reality in the Hegelian sense is not a question of existence, but of essence.

8. Margot C. Finn (in Daunton and Hilton, 2001, p. 90): 'Closely intertwined with this representation [of customers increasingly acquiring objects in impersonal interactions in impersonal institutions] of the mass market is a prevailing historiographical tendency to depict the middle class female consumer and the department store as the archetypical agents of commercial modernity', hence my choice of a female subject.

9. Enlighten and educate is the closest – but not precise translation of the German phrase 'Bildung'. In Danish we have the word 'dannelse', which captures the meaning better.

10. See: http://www.novonordisk.com/sustainability/default.asp

11. Other consumer researchers have tried to describe this conceptual level as 'class system' (Bourdieu, 1995), 'spirit'(Campbell in: Falk and Campbell, 1997), 'paradigm' or 'discourse' (Falk and Campbell, 1997; Hirshmann and Holbrook 1992). A problematic tendency, however, has been that this conceptual macro level has been described as manipulating structures oppressing all or some of the subjects (e.g. the habitus of the middle class oppressing the lower classes (Bourdieu, 1995)), no matter whether the subjects feel good and even emancipated in their own terms. It is important that the *Subject* level is dialectically related to the subject (practice and value) level, so that the (conceptual) communication between structure and process works both ways because of the cunning of reason – how else can one explain transformation?

12. Often, other *Subjects* besides nation states, e.g. EU or UN, act like the *Consumer Subject,* communicating consumer politics and consumer practices and values as a matter of general political, economic or ethical interest.

13. This expansion does not disturb the logic of the model. It is just another side of Hegel's subject definition.

14. The interviews lasted between 2½ to 4 hours, were tape-recorded and transcribed verbatim.

15. The interview transcripts were coded with the software ATLAS.ti. For more information see http://www.atlasti.de/

16. Fore a more detailed description of the respondents see *E-bizz Øresund Report: Barriers and Motivators of Online Grocery Shopping in Denmark*, Jan. 2003.

17. Groceries may even be more culturally representative than other goods. First, because they represent a basic and obvious transformation of nature to culture, second, because groceries are consumed on more or less a daily basis and thus present in our minds all the time, and third, because different discourses of e.g. health, risk and sustainability have made us aware us that foods directly affect our bodies and well-being, and thus controlling our food is the same as body control.

18. 300 million Danish kroner out of of 91 billion Danish kroner

19. Conventional e-grocery business: e-businesses where the web-pages are constructed to remind us of the traditional brick-and-mortar supermarkets.

20. Compare Holbrook's definition of consumer value: an interactive relativistic preference experience (Holbrook, 1999, p. 5)

21. In Denmark, we have had four Internet supermarkets: ISO.dk, Coop's NETbutik, SuperBest.dk. and Intervare.dk. They offered their services mainly to people of Copenhagen and Copenhagen suburbs. Today only Intervare.dk and Coop NETbutik exist and cover Denmark as an area, however you have to pick up your order in one of Coop's brick-and mortar stores. Additionally, there are several other specialized Internet shops that sell all kinds of things from Cuban Cigars (http://cubacigar.subnet.dk) to lamb meat (http://www.dk-lam.dk). See: http://www.oxygen.ro/Top/World/Dansk/Netbutikker/Dagligvarer. The biggest and most successful of the specialized Internet shops is no doubt Aarstiderne.com.

22. Future Store is the METRO Group Future Store Initiative. It is a cooperation project between METRO Group, SAP, Intel and IBM as well as other partner companies from the information technology and consumer goods industries. The METRO Group Future Store Initiative develops innovative technologies, which will decisively shape the retail trade of the future. These technologies are aimed at making shopping more convenient for consumers through better service and at improving processes in retailing. In a test store, the use and combination of different technical applications are tested, in which a completely integrated system is implemented for inventory management, information and check out. See http://www.future-store.org

23. Aarstiderne.com is the biggest (and one of the few) successful online grocery services in Denmark. For more information see http://www.aarstiderne.com

REFERENCES

Adorno, T.W. and Horkheimer, M. (1979), *Dialectic of Enlightenment*, London: Verso.

Ajzen, Icek (1991), 'The Theory of Planned Behaviour', *Organizational Behaviour and Human Decision Processes*, 50, 179 - 211.

Althusser, Louis (1999), 'Ideology and Ideological State Apparatuses - Notes towards an Investigation', in Jessica Evans and Stuart Hall (eds), *Visual Culture – The Reader*, London: Sage Publications Ltd., pp. 317 - 323.

Anderson, Benedict (1991), *Imagined Communities*, New York: Verso.

Bartels, Robert (1976), *A History of Marketing Thought*, Ohio: Columbus.

Baudrillard, Jean (1997), *Forførelse. Essay om begær og spil, skin og simulation* (in French: De la seduction), Frederiksberg, DK: DET lille FORLAG.

Bauman, Zygmunt (1989), *Modernity and the Holocaust*, Cambridge: Polity Press.

Bauman, Zygmunt (1997), *Work, Consumerism and the New Poor*, London: Open University Press.

Beck, Ulrich (1997), *Risikosamfundet – på vej mod en ny modernitet* (in English: Risk Society), Copenhagen: Hans Reitzels Forlag.

Beckmann, Suzanne and Elliot, Richard E. (eds.) (2001), *Interpretive Consumer Research. Paradigms, Methodologies & Applications*, Copenhagen: Copenhagen Business School Press.

Bourdieu, Pierre (1995), *Distinksjonen - en sosiologisk kritikk av dømmekraften* (in English: Distinction - a Social Critique of the Judgement of Taste), Oslo: Pax Forlag.

Bucklin, L.P. (1963), 'Retail Strategy and the Classification of Consumer Goods', *Journal of Marketing Research*, January.

Castells, Manuel (2003), *Netværkssamfundet og dets opståen. Informationsalderen: Økonomi, samfund og kultur. Bind 1* (in English: The Rise of the Network Society. 2nd ed.), Copenhagen: Reitzel.

Chaney, David (1996), *Lifestyles*, London and New York: Routledge.

Choi, Jayoung and Geistfeld, Loren V. (2003), 'Cross-cultural Investigation of Consumer E-shopping Adoption', *Journal of Economic Psychology*, 25 (6), 821-838.

Claeys, C., Swinnen, P. and Abeele, P. Vanden (1995), 'Consumers' Means-end Chains for "Think" and "Feel" Products', *International Journal of Research in Marketing*, 12 (3), 193 - 208.

Daunton, Martin and Hilton, Matthew (eds) (2001), *The Politics of Consumption. Material Culture and Citizenship in Europe and America*, Oxford: Berg.

Degeratu, Alexandru M., Rangaswamy and Wu Jinan Arvind, (2000), 'Consumer Choice Behaviour in Online and Traditional Supermarkets: the effects of brand, price and other search attributes', *International Journal of Research in Marketing*, 17 (1), 55-78.

Douglas, Mary and Isherwood, Baron (2004), *The World of Goods: towards an anthropology of consumption*, London and New York: Routledge.

Falk, Pasi and Campbell, Colin (eds) (1997), *The Shopping Experience*, London: SAGE Publications.

Featherstone, Mike (1991), *Consumer Culture and Postmodernism*, London: SAGE Publications.

Firat, Fuat and Venkatesh, Alladi (1995), 'Liberatory Postmodernism and the Reenchantment of Consumption', *Journal of Consumer Research*, 22 (3), 239-267

Fishbein, Martin and Ajzen, Icek (1975), *Belief, Attitude, Intention and Behavior – An Introduction to Theory and Research*, Reading, MA: Addison-Wesley Publishing Company.

Foucault, Michel (1977), *Overvågning og straf - fængslets fødsel* (in English: Surveillance and Punishment – The Birth of the Prison), Copenhagen: Rhodos Radius.

Foucault, Michel (1994), *Viljen til viden – seksualitetens historie 1*, (in English: The history of Sexuality. Vol. 1. The Will to Knowledge), Frederiksberg, DK: DET lille FORLAG.

Friedman, Monroe (1999), *Consumer Boycotts. Effecting Change through the Marketplace and the Media*, New York and London: Routledge.

Friese, Susanne et al. (2003), *E-bizz Øresund Report: Barriers and Motivators of Online Grocery Shopping in Denmark*, Research Report, Copenhagen Business School, Department of Marketing.

Frostling-Henningsson, Maria (2000), *D@gligvaruhandel over nätet...vad innebär det? - en kvalitativ studie av 22 svenska hushåll 1998-1999*, Research Report, Stockholm University, School of Business.

Frostling-Henningsson, Maria (2003), *Internet Grocery Shopping. A Necessity, A Pleasurable Adventure Or An Act of Love*, Research Report No. 2003: 8, Stockholm University, School of Business.

Halkier, Bente (2001), 'Consuming Ambivalences – Consumer Handling of Environmentally Related Risks in Food', *Journal of Consumer Culture*, 1 (2), 205-224.

Hansen, Torben (2002), 'Forbrugeren og Internettet - en litteraturgennemgang og forslag til yderligere forskning' (in English: The Consumer and the Internet), Working Paper, Copenhagen Business School, Department of Marketing.

Hansen, Torben (2003), *Kvantitativ Rapport, Project Ebizz Öresund*, Research Report, Copenhagen Business School, Department of Marketing.

Hansen, Torben; Jensen, Jan Møller and Solgaard, Hans Stubbe (2004), 'Predicting Online Grocery Buying Intention: a comparison of the theory of reasoned action and the theory of planned behaviour', *International Journal of Information Management*, 24 (6), 539-550.

Hirshmann, Elizabeth and Holbrook, Morrris B. (1992), *Postmodern Consumer Research - the Study of Consumption as Text*, Newbury Park, CA: Sage.

Hjelmslev, Louis (1966), *Omkring Sprogteoriens Grundlæggelse* (in English: The Foundations of Language Analysis), Copenhagen: Akademisk Forlag.

Holbrook, Morris B. and Corfman, Kim P. (1985), 'Quality and Value in the Consumer Experience: Phaedrus Rides Again', in . J. Jacoby and J. Olson (eds), *Percieved Quality*, Lexington, MA: Lexington Books.

Holbrook, Morris B. (1994a), 'Defining Service Quality', in R.T. Rust and R.L. Oliver (eds), *Service Quality- New directions in Theory and Practise*, Thousand Oaks, CA: Sage Publications.

Holbrook, Morris B. (1994b), 'The Nature of Consumer Value: an axiology of services in the consumption experiences', in: R.T. Rust and R.L. Oliver (eds), *Aesthetics of Textiles and Clothing: Advancing Multi-Disciplinary Perspectives*, Monument, CO: International Textile and Apparel Association.

Holbrook, Morris B. (eds) (1999), *Consumer Value. A Framework for Analysis and Research*, New York: Routledge.

Højrup, Thomas (1995), *Omkring Livsformsanalysens Udvikling*, Copenhagen: Museum Tusculanums Forlag.

Højrup, Thomas (2002), *Dannelsens dialektik - etnologiske udfordringer til det glemte folk*, Copenhagen: Museum Tusculanum.

Højrup, Thomas (2003), *State, Culture and Life-modes - the Foundations of Life-mode Analysis*, Burlington, VT: Ashgate.

Lash, Scott and Friedman, Jonathan (1992), *Modernity and Identity*, Oxford: Blackwell.

Latour, Bruno (2000), 'When Things Strike Back: a possible contribution of "science studies" to the social sciences', *British Journal of Sociology*, 51 (1), 107-123.

Liep, John and Olwig, Karen (eds) (1994), *Komplekse liv. Kulturel mangfoldighed i Danmark*, Copenhagen: Akademisk Forlag A/S.

McCracken, Grant (1988), *Culture and Consumption*, Bloomington and Indianapolis: Indiana University Press.

Mauss, Marcel (2000/1925), *Gaven – Gaveudvekslingens form og logik i arkaiske samfund/The Gift*, Copenhagen: Spektrum.

Miller, Daniel (1987), *Material Culture and Mass Consumption,* Oxford: Basil Blackwell Ltd.

Miller, Daniel (eds.) (1995), *Acknowledging Consumption. A Review of New Studies*, London and New York: Routledge.

Porter, Michael (2001), 'Strategy and the Internet', *Harvard Business Review*, 79 (3), 62-79.

Raijas, Anu (2002), 'The consumer Benefits and Problems in the Electronic Grocery Store', *Journal of Retailing and Consumer Services*, 9 (2), 107-113.

Sestoft, Christine (2002), *Med hensyn til den politiske forbruger* (in English: Regarding the Political Consumer), Copenhagen: Akademisk Forlag.

Sestoft, Christine and Hansen, Torben (2003), 'Value-driven Planned Behaviour: a model for predicting consumer online grocery buying intention', in: C. Veloutsou ed.), *Communicating With Customers: Trends and Developments*, ATINER, Athens.

Shim, S., Eastlick, M.A., Lotz, S.L. and Warrington, P (2001), 'An online Prepurchase Intentions Model: the role of intention to search', *Journal of Retailing*, 77 (3), 397-416.

Storey, John (1999), *Cultural Consumption and Everyday life*, New York: Oxford University Press.

Stockmann gruppen (2004), *Supermarkedshåndbogen*.

Venkatesh, Alladi (2000), 'The mode of Information and the Cultures of the Internet – A Conversation with Mark Poster', *Consumption, Markets and Culture*, 3 (3), 195-213.

Weber, Max (1995/1930), *The Protestant Ethic and the Spirit of Capitalism*, London: Routledge.

Williams, Raymond (1983), *Keywords. A Vocabulary of Culture and Society*, London: Fontana Press.

Other:

Fyns Stifttidende (25/2/04) 'Klar. Parat – omstil'.

8. Effective E-Grocery Logistics

Hannu Yrjölä and Kari Tanskanen

WHY LOGISTICAL EFFECTIVENESS IS CRUCIAL IN E-GROCERY

From E-Business Hype to Collapse and Revival

The history of electronic grocery shopping (EGS) is quite short but dramatic. At the end of last decade several online players challenged the old brick-and-mortar groceries, especially in the USA. For example Webvan, Streamline and Peapod invested billions of dollars in the new business models, believing in a fast victory over the established supermarkets. Also numerous old players in the grocery retailing business all over the world introduced electronic shopping channels. However, most of the old players were very cautious in their e-channel development, fearing the new channel would cannibalize their established business. The different competence requirements of e-grocery compared to supermarkets and ambivalence about customer reactions also slowed down development. Only a few old players really forcefully invested in and developed e-shopping models for consumers.

Most of the purely online players quite soon ran into serious troubles and were forced to cease their operations. The old brick-and-mortar retailers took over the best parts of their former challengers businesses and continued the development of the e-grocery business from a new basis. Examples in the USA are Ahold with Peapod and Safeway and Tesco with GroceryWorks. Also most of the old players struggled to make the electronic channel profitable, and many have closed their e-stores. The most successful old player has been Tesco, which is currently (2004) the biggest e-grocer in the world, and which claims to be profitable. After the e-boom years of the late 1990s, the beginning of this century has been a period of gradual development. The growth of electronic retailing has continued with less bluster, and recently there have been signs of a wider rebirth of e-grocery. Many online retailers turned profitable in 2003, and continued a rapid growth (Tedes,hic 2004). New players have also again entered the markets. In 2002 Ocado, a pure electronic grocer was founded in the UK and is partnering with an established supermarket Waitrose. It has grown fast but has not yet reached profitability (www.Hoovers.com). Also one of the oldest and biggest e-retailers, Amazon, has started to sell also groceries online.

Logistics - the Profit Killer of E-Grocery

Overall, electronic grocery retailing has turned out to be extremely difficult to operate profitably. Numerous reasons can be identified for the difficulties and failures ranging from difficulties in changing customers' buying habits to poor purchasing power of the new entrants. It is, however, clear that logistics is an important reason for poor profitability for all players. There have been serious problems in managing both information and material flows, leading to skyhigh logistics costs and low value to customers. Difficulties have appeared in many ways in all parts of logistics. This is discussed in the following sections.

Order Assembly

The e-channel solutions of the old brick-and-mortar supermarkets have mostly been based on picking from store, while many pure players started with dedicated order assembly and distribution centres. At the beginning of the e-grocery business, store picking seemed to be more efficient, even though only Tesco has reported it to be profitable. The biggest failure was Webvan, which invested hundreds of millions of dollars in highly automated distribution centres that were never even close to breaking even before the company ran out of money and closed its operations. Ahold/Peapod, which recently has been the most successful e-grocer in the USA, has combined different order assembly and distribution concepts. In addition to dedicated warehouses that serve customers in high selling markets they use *warerooms*, which are dedicated areas attached to Ahold stores. Warerooms are used as business is developing in new markets and they leverage the stores' infrastructures.

All options for organizing order assembly have involved difficult problems:

- Order picking in stores has been ineffective, because supermarkets are not designed for fast picking. On the contrary, stores are often designed so that customers must walk a long way, during which they do impulse purchases.
- The distribution centres that deliver to supermarkets cannot be used for order assembly of individual shopping baskets, because their

logistics systems are designed for handling big batches.

- Building a dedicated distribution centre for home deliveries of groceries is a huge investment. It is difficult to automate the order assembly of a shopping basket, and the high requirements for temperature control increase the costs. Therefore high volumes are required to break even. Also the peaks in demand on certain days of the week and at certain times of the day make it difficult to utilize capacity effectively.

The stock-outs that are common in supermarkets also create problems and additional costs in the order assembly. According to a recent study (Corsten and Gruen, 2004), stock-out rates in supermarkets are around 8%, worldwide. In electronic grocery shopping, stock-outs are much more visible to customers compared to supermarketshopping. In a supermarket the seller do not usually know if a customer missed some item because it was out of stock. In EGS the customer has identified each item she wants to buy, and a missing item always needs some kind of exceptional handling. This problem could potentially be turned into an advantage, because the e-grocer receives systematic information about customers' real needs.

Home Delivery and Goods Reception

The most common home delivery modes in EGS have been next day delivery, a two hour delivery window and manned goods reception. Yet, there are different operating modes as well as different home delivery fees; Table 8.1 summarizes some examples of existing e-grocers. In many companies the practices and service fees have been changed several times over time. Let us use Webvan as an illustrative example about the importance of home delivery mode.

Webvan launched its e-grocery business in June 1999. To reach market dominance, Webvan offered home delivery with attended reception and delivery time windows of 30 minutes, free of charge, for orders above $50. However, Webvan was unable to create sufficient demand to reach economically viable home delivery operations. Low customer density, attended reception, and short delivery time windows together resulted in extremely high delivery costs. In November 2000 Webvan started to charge $4.95 for deliveries less than $75. In December 2000 Webvan tried to decrease the home delivery costs by cutting down its service level to 60-minute delivery time windows. Then again in May 2001 Webvan raised the delivery fees for orders under $75 from $4.95 to $9.95 and imposed a new fee of $4.95 for orders between $75 and $100, leaving free delivery only for orders over $100. Later, in June 2001, it offered a home delivery scheduling system whereby the customer earned bonus points by selecting the same delivery timetable as had already been selected for the neighbourhood. Even rationalizsing and pricing its home delivery service was not enough to prevent Webvan from running out of money as a result of an unexpected drop-off in incoming orders when delivery fees were introduced. Finally, in July 2001 Webvan ceased operations.

Table 8.1 Delivery concepts of some existing e-grocers

	Tesco UK	Peapod/Ahold USA	Ocado UK	Ruokavarasto Finland
Minimum delivery time	Varies depending on available delivery slots 6 days a week	Next day 7 days a week	Next day 6 days a week	Same day if order placed before 2 p.m. 6 days a week
Delivery window	2 hour	2 hour	1 hour	2 - 4 hours
Reception	Attended	Attended	Attended	Attended and reception box
Delivery fee	Between £3.99 and £5.99 in UK €7.62 in Ireland	As low as $4.95; fees vary according to basket size and location	£5 for orders less than £75 others free of charge	7 or 9 Euros in attended delivery Reception box customers pay 36 Euros rent per month, no separate delivery fee
Order assembly	In Tesco stores	2 dedicated warehouses 8 warerooms	1 dedicated distribution centre	In stores

The basic problem with home delivery transportation has been that short delivery times and short delivery windows (= time between earliest and latest possible delivery) have in many cases inhibited effective combining of home deliveries. Delivering a single shopping basket by a delivery van is very expensive. In many urban areas traffic jams create additional problems for home deliveries as they increase transportation times and create uncertainty that makes transportation planning difficult. Also daily changes in the amount of orders make it difficult to effectively utilize transportation facilities. The delivery vans need to be temperature controlled, which adds additional costs.

Reception of goods is in many ways an important phase of the logistics process of home deliveries. The way it is organized affects both the efficiency of the entire logistics system and the value to customers. The basic alternatives are manned and unmanned goods reception. In manned reception the customer has to receive the delivery at home at the agreed time, while in unmanned reception the shopping basket can be left in the proximity of the customer's home or in another agreed place without the customer being present. These both involve several problems and challenges:

- In manned reception it is quite common that the customer is not at home when the shopping basket is delivered. In these cases the goods must be taken back and re-delivered later. There might also be things that take time away from the person delivering the orders and increase delivery costs in the manned reception. Refunding money, checking the goods or in some cultures simply the habit of making small talk with the customer may multiply the dropping time of home deliveries.

- Unmanned reception solves some of the before mentioned problems, but has its own challenges. When unmanned reception is achieved by using reception boxes, the investment is quite high because there need to be departments for different temperatures. Many customers are not willing to pay this investment. When unmanned reception is achieved by using delivery boxes that can be left and possibly locked to a customer's home, there are often problems with temperature control. The collection of the boxes might also cause additional costs.

Information Flows and Ordering Process

The fundamental problem in the e-grocery ordering process is that it commonly takes a long time to make the first orders. The ordering time shortens remarkably when the customer learns how to use the ordering system and can take the advantage of standard shopping lists that can be created in most ordering systems. Ordering time is a critical issue because time saving is one of the biggest motivators to use e-grocery. Many customers are not patient enough to learn the effective use of the ordering system. Also, many of the first ordering systems did not support fast ordering to a satisfactory degree.

Also Internet connections have often turned out to be too slow and vulnerable to faults for making orders. Customers soon became frustrated if they had to restart the ordering process. In practice most of the e-grocery ordering systems require broadband Internet connections to work properly.

The third major problem has been that the ordering systems often provide insufficient product information to the customer. One of the most important obstacles to adopting the e-channel is that many customers want to see and touch the products that they buy. Touching the products is impossible in an e-grocery, but rich and updated product information is crucial. It is also a potential advantage to the e-channel if the ordering system is well designed.

A common problem in EGS is that the customer cannot see which products are out of stock. This leads to either incomplete deliveries or the use of substitutes. It is often problematic to make decisions about substituting a product with another. Some e-grocers call the customer in these situations, which is an additional cost.

Many existing e-grocers have developed their ordering systems to overcome these problems. Also broadband Internet connection penetration has increased significantly during recent years. Some e-grocers have also developed solutions to overcome the out-of-stock and substitution problems. For example Ocado provides the customer information about product availability. This way customers can avoid ordering items that are out of stock and select the substitute selves.

The E-Grocery Logistics Challenge

To summarize, the early years of electronic grocery shopping involved numerous problems in all fields of logistics. These problems have in many cases been among the most important reasons for disastrous failures of some of the early pure player e-grocers. Logistics problems have also slowed down the growth of the e-channel of the traditional supermarkets. In the brick-and-mortar supermarkets these logistics problems have been avoided by self-service: the customer acts as voluntary and unpaid workforce in order picking and last mile transportation of groceries. According to studies conducted in Finland (LTT, 1995 and 1997), households visit shops on average 4.6 times a week, spending on average 48 minutes on weekdays and 58 minutes at weekends, with 57% of the time being spent in cars and the rest in shops selecting and paying for the goods. This is approximately 200 hours per year, which means that households spend on average 5 full 40-hour working weeks annually doing their grocery shopping! In the case of combined trips the time spent on other shopping was eliminated, so the result is the actual extra time required for shopping for groceries.

However, people do not usually see the time they use and kilometres they drive their own cars for buying their groceries as additional cost. Therefore self-service has been an excellent solution from the viewpoint of the supermarket. For the customer any fees paid in e-grocery are additional costs, no matter how much more effective the logistics system really is. Therefore efficient logistics is a basic requirement for e-grocery business, and to succeed an e-grocer must have logistics solutions that provide customers value that brick-and-mortar supermarkets cannot provide.

Searching for Solutions: the ECOMLOG-Project

The logistics challenges of e-grocery business were addressed in a three-year, €1.5 million Supply Chain Management for Electronic Commerce ECOMLOG[1] research programme at Helsinki University of Technology. The first phase of the project was current state analysis, which aimed at identifying the essential supply chain issues involved in the emerging e-grocery business. In the second phase the main question was: 'What is the effective supply chain for electronic grocery shopping?' During this phase, alternative solutions were constructed, analysed and tested for order assembly, home delivery and goods reception. This was done in close cooperation with major Finish grocery retailers and suppliers. The third phase of the research focused on specific logistics issues and on strategic implications. First, the cost structure of EGS was analysed in more detail. Then the research focused on the question: 'What is the required growth and customer acquisition strategy for EGS from operational efficiency viewpoint?' Also several questions related to unattended reception with reception boxes were studied.

The research programme involved a set of research methodologies: case studies, modelling and simulation (mostly with real company data), and surveys. Also a pilot e-grocery operation was set up in a suburban area of Helsinki. In this pilot, a Finish supermarket offered e-grocery service to 40 households, who were provided with a customer-specific reception box. The pilot worked also as our research platform.

In this article we summarize the main findings of the ECOMLOG-project, describe the elements of an effective logistics solution for electronic grocery shopping, and propose how logistics should be leveraged to make a profitable e-grocery business.

A FRAMEWORK FOR E-GROCERY LOGISTICS

Kämäräinen et al. (2001) identify two basic models for logistical operations in e-grocery. The first is based on home deliveries from existing supermarkets. This so called intermediary model requires low investment but has very high operating costs. The products are first put on shelves in the supermarket and then picked for home delivery, which causes a lot of materials handling work. Supermarkets are not designed for efficient picking of goods; instead the purpose is to get the customers to walk through the entire shop to maximize their impulse buying. Examples of the intermediary model are Tesco (UK), Ruokanet (Finland). Peapod (USA) is also partly operating by this model.

The second model is based on deliveries from a dedicated distribution centre (DC). This model in turn has high investment costs but low operating costs if there enough sales that the utilization rate is high enough. The major reasons for low operating costs are that the DC can be designed for effective picking, and less space is required because the shelves do not have to look as attractive as in supermarkets. The DC may also in be located in a cheaper location than a supermarket. Examples of this so-called channel model are Peapod (USA) and Ocado (UK).

Yrjölä and Tanskanen (1999) have presented a model that combines the advantages of the channel model and those of intermediary model. This so-called 'hybrid model' is specially designed for the traditional brick-and-mortar supermarkets that are making their move to e-grocery. The basic principle of the 'hybrid model' is that the grocery products are divided into A, B and C categories applying the Pareto principle. A products are delivered to the distribution centre according to end-customer order and are only cross-docked at the DC. B products have inventory in the DC, and the emphasis is on efficient picking. For C category products the supermarket is used as an inventory. In this model the DC and the supermarket are close to each other to enable combining A, B, and C products to the home delivery effectively. However, there are yet no examples of e-grocers operating by the hybrid model.

From these studies we may derive three alternatives for the distribution channel solution:

1. Deliveries from the dedicated distribution centre.
2. Deliveries from the shop.
3. Deliveries from combined DC/shop (the hybrid model).

Another factor that has remarkable impact on the effectiveness of home delivery distribution is the mode of goods reception. The basic alternatives are:

1. Attended (somebody needs to be at home to receive the goods, agreed time window for goods reception).
2. Unattended (deliveries are to a locked reception box with temperatures needed for groceries).

The reception boxes may either be located at consumers' homes or be shared between several customers and located at some point that is close to them. Reception boxes have mechanically maintained temperatures for groceries. Delivery boxes are returnable boxes that have no mechanical temperature control, but they can keep the required temperature for a short time.

When the two main factors of e-grocery logistics system are put together, we end up with four basic scenarios that are described briefly.

Delivery from shop/attended goods reception

This model has the lowest investment costs, but the highest operating costs because materials handling operations in the shop (picking and shelving) are ineffective and delivery costs are high because attended reception of goods restricts optimization of transportation. The potential for developing value-added services is restricted to those that can be offered at the web-site (for example recipes). This may be a 'fast entry' strategy for an e-grocer, but it is very difficult to make this profitable even by developing the picking methods.

Delivery from shop/unattended goods reception

This model requires investment in reception boxes either by the vendor or by the customer. The investment depends on the number of customers, but is moderate in the early stages. Use of returnable boxes would decrease the investment costs, but also restrict the possibility to develop new services and decrease customer loyalty. Picking costs are still high, but transportation costs can be optimized through better planning possibilities. Transportation effectiveness can be reached at quite a small customer base and it is also possible to combine this model with the shop/attended model so that some parts of the deliveries are to reception boxes and some parts require customers to be at home to receive the goods. However, the transportation cost advantage is soon lost if unattended reception is mixed with attended reception. According to simulation studies, 10% of attended deliveries during the route will double the number of vehicles needed compared with the totally unattended home delivery concept (Punakivi and Saranen, 2001).

This model also enables the introduction of new kinds of value-added services like Streamline's 'don't run out'. This means that the e-grocer automatically replenishes the customer's inventory of continuously consumed goods without a separate order.

Delivery from Dedicated Distribution Centre/Attended Goods Reception

This model has high investment costs, but the picking is much more effective than in the previous models. Both the size of the investment and the picking efficiency depend on the level of automation in the distribution centre. The automation level should be optimized taking into account the capacity utilization point of view (Kämäräinen et al., 2001). To break even this model requires a large customer base. The exact number of customers required depends on the size and automation level of the DC. Streamline estimated that the break-even point for a distribution centre is 1600 households, and the maximum number of households that can be served by one DC is 4000 (Dagher, 1998). In this model transportation costs remain high and the possibility to offer value-added services is limited. A major problem in this model is also that there are very poor possibilities to even the capacity load. There are high peaks in demand on certain weekdays and times of the day, and the capacity has to be built to meet these peaks.

Delivery from Dedicated Distribution Centre/Unattended Goods Reception

This model has the highest investment cost, but the lowest operating costs as both picking and transportation can be optimized. This model also provides numerous possibilities to develop value-added services. The traditional supermarket mode of operation can be totally rejected. New operation and service modes can be developed that maximize the value to the consumer and optimize the operating costs. This model provides also the best platform for adding new products and services to offer to customers in addition to groceries. The e-grocer is in a very strong position in its customer relationship, which enables it to become a 'purveyor' that supplies customers with an increasing share of their purchases. This model is the most difficult to learn to operate, because it differs the most from traditional ways of operating. However, the high investments require a relatively big sales volume to break even. These two things together make starting with this model problematic.

Table 8.2 Summary of the major characteristics of the alternative models

	Shop/ attended	DC/ attended	Shop/ unattended	DC/ unattended
Required investment	Low	High	Moderate	High
Picking costs	High	Low	High	Low
Transportation costs	High	High	Low	Low
Convenience to customer	Poor	Poor	Good	Good
Possibility to grow fast	Poor	Good	Moderate	Problematic
Possibility for value-added services	Limited	Limited	Moderate	Excellent
Customer loyalty	Low	Low	High	High
Possibility to add new products	Poor	Limited	Limited	Excellent
Examples of e-grocers	Tesco	Ocado	Ruokavarasto	Streamline

LOGISTICS COSTS ANALYSIS

This section summarizes the findings of various research activities around the cost structure of the Electronic Grocery Shopping supply chain. It is divided into four parts: shopping basket assembly, home delivery, implications for suppliers and primary distribution, and comparison, with the conventional grocery supply chain. The details of the research have been published in three doctoral dissertations, numerous articles and conference papers during five years. All references cannot be listed here but most of the publications are available online at www.tuta.hut.fi/logistics. A very extensive list of references can be found in Yrjölä (2003).

Shopping Basket Assembly

The previous chapter illustrated that there are a number of different strategies to launch new EGS services. In practice, most of the established brick-and-mortar grocery chains have chosen to use the store for picking. Most successful in this strategy is Tesco in the UK. Tesco has been able to develop the new service without massive investment and to make a nationwide rollout reasonably quickly, covering now over 90 per cent of potential customer households in the UK today. Based on the research the costs for store-based picking are 19 per cent of the value of the goods. This figure is not very much dependent on the business volume and it seems to be the best business model when the business volume is reasonably low. Store-based picking cost structure will be a fruitful area of further research when the business volume grows, and specially when the EGS volume is a substantial part of the store's total business. It is anticipated that there is even the possibility that the picking cost could be higher with large volumes, because the large number of pickers and customers shopping in the store will make the process slower. However, there is no hard evidence as yet of on how this will affect the cost.

The other approach mainly used by the new pure play e-grocers was to build a dedicated outlet for the picking. The cost structure of a local distribution centre (LDC) was researched by benchmarking all available data from the operating companies and on the other hand building a virtual LDC in an operating supermarket. The cost structure of an LDC is presented as per centage of turnover in Figure 8.1.

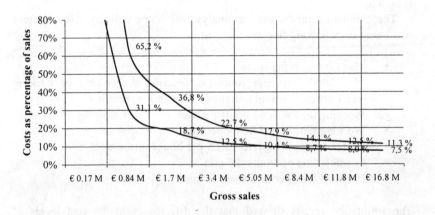

Figure 8.1 The costs of the Local Distribution Centre

With turnover of less than €2 million the costs of a dedicated outlet are very high. This is due to all fixed costs being allocated to a small sales volume. When the sales volume is between €2 and €5 million the costs are in the same area as picking from a store. When sales volume goes over €5 million the research results suggest that using a dedicated outlet is clearly more cost efficient than store-based picking. Most of the early practitioners ran out of money by investing heavily in automation and then having very low utilization rates for their dedicated outlets.

Home Delivery

The early practitioners in EGS did not usually understand the crucial importance of service models in home delivery. Public transportation gives a good and simple example of how different service models have to be priced to enable profitable operation. A bus or a train has a pre-set timetable and route and people wishing to use the service adjust their own timetable according to that. If they want to decide the timing and routing they can order a taxi. Everybody understands that the cost of providing taxi service is much higher and the price must be higher, too. Webvan tried to deliver in half-hour time windows at the beginning of its operation, which is comparable to taxi service.

The research of Punakivi and Saranen (2001) showed that the production cost of even one hour time window delivery is close to three times the production cost of once a week unattended delivery, which was the operational model of Streamline. The research analysed the most common service models added used in the early age of EGS. These are described in table 8.3.

The simulation model used to analyse the home delivery cost structure was based on following fleet characteristics:

- Max 60 orders per route
- Max 3000 litres per route (to describe the volume of packing materials etc; the real volume of the van is normally 6 - 12 m^3)
- Working time max 11 hours per van
- Working time max 5 hours per route
- Costs of van plus driver: €22.5 per hour (outsourced)
- Loading time per route: 20 min
- Drop-off time per customer: 2 min.

The simulation results showed that the differences in the cost levels of different service models are huge. The smaller the time windows for attended delivery, the more the delivery vehicles need to drive back and forth in the distribution area to meet the promised delivery time windows. Just to demonstrate that do-it-yourself shopping also includes cost, the average cost of consumers doing their shopping by private car has been calculated and indexed at 100. Using that index, the transportation cost of case 2 (next day 1 hour slots) is 150, the cost of case 1 (3 times 2 hour slots same day) is 100, case 3 (next day to reception box) is 73 and in case 4 (1 order/customer/week to reception box) only 57.

Table 8.3 Different service models analysed (Punakivi and& Saranen, 2001)

Case	Order	Delivery	Reception	Delivery time	Example
1	by 10.00	same day	manned	3 delivery time windows: 17-19, 18-20, 19-21	Matomera, Sweden Ruok@net
2	by 24.00	next day	manned	1 hour delivery time between 12 and 21	Ykköshalli Eurospar, Finland WebVan (½h), USA Tesco (2h)
3	by 24.00	next day	unmanned reception	delivery between 8 and 18	Streamline, USA S-kanava
4 *	by 24.00	next day (fixed day)	unmanned reception	delivery between 8 and 18, once a week chosen by customer	Optimal case in concept
5 **				all orders delivered with car, simulating the situation where households are doing the shopping themselves	Traditional shopping
6	by 24.00	next day	manned / unmanned reception	unmanned: delivery between 8 and 18 manned: 1 hour chosen delivery time between 8 and 18. The amount of manned reception: 0 – 100 %	

* Case 4 simulates the best possible case from the e-grocers point of view, meaning that orders are sorted by postal code and divided evenly on all delivery days. This kind of situation can be reached by, for example, pricing
** Case 5 enables the comparison of the different e-grocery cases to the current situation where customers visit supermarkets

The first objective of the research was to analyse the different service models and their cost differences. The other important objective was to understand how the cost of home delivery reacts to drop density. To test the sensitivity of drop density, different 'market share' projections were generated by multiplying the basic data set for the same test area. Based on simulations for different sales projections the cost of home delivery is presented as per centage of the value of the groceries in Figure 8.2

Home delivery cost

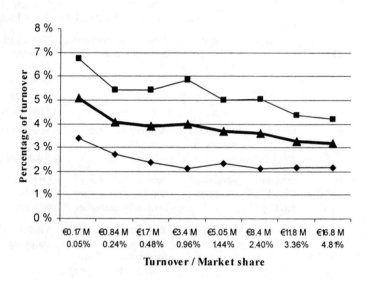

Figure 8.2 Home delivery cost structure. The cost structure of home delivery is shown as a per centage of the value of the groceries (Yrjölä, 2001)

The upper curve represents attended delivery in one-hour time windows and the lower case is the most effective service model, once-a-week unattended delivery using reception boxes. The research indicates that the low density home delivery with attended reception costs around 7 per cent of the value of the groceries. This happens to be exactly the same figure given by Tesco for their home delivery cost (Business Week, 2001). The lower curve shows that when the drop density grows, the home delivery cost starts to approach 2 per cent of the value of the groceries. The critical threshold in the business volume was €170,000 of annual sales per square kilometre, evenly spread over all 12 months of the year. Further increases in drop density do not have a substantial impact on the costs. The costs of loading and unloading are not affected by the drop density and after this point their costs become the decisive factors in the total cost.

Implications for Primary Distributions and Suppliers

EGS, especially with dedicated shopping basket assembly outlets, will change the downstream of the grocery supply chain extensively. To be able to investigate for the whole supply chain cost structure, the implications of EGS supplier operations and primary distribution have to be analysed. Since there are no substantial EGS operations anywhere, quantitative analyses cannot be carried out. The intention of the research was only to find evidence of the direction of the potential changes, not to quantify them. This is why the use of weaker methodology was seen as appropriate and sufficiently reliable.

The data for this exercise were collected by interviews with three different types of supplier executives and managers: a brewery, a dairy products manufacturer and a meat packaging company. Persons interviewed were involved in general management, logistics, manufacturing and marketing. The data were analysed as cases using case methodology (Eisenhardt, 1989). The difference in this research was that the purpose was not theory building, just finding the answer to the direction of potential changes. The implications for these industries summarized in Table 8.4. The impact on costs in various functions is indicated with the following scale:

(---) = extremely negative impact
(--) = substantially negative impact
(-) = slightly negative impact
(+) = no impact
(+) = slightly positive impact
(++) = substantially positive impact
(+++) = extremely positive impact.

Even if the evidence is not very strong and the number of the cases is limited, the general conclusion is that the overall implication for the suppliers is not negative. There are implications that are expected to increase costs in some functions, but there are others that will at least offset the increase.

Table 8.4 The implications of customer order-based operation for the middle and upstream operations of the supply chain

	Sourcing and production planning	Manufacturing	Packaging and dispatching	Distribution
Breweries	+-	+-	--	+++
Dairy industry	++	+-	++	+
Meat packaging	++	+-	+-	+
Average	+	+-	+-	++

Comparison to Conventional Supply Chain

Based on the earlier section findings, the EGS-based supply chain total cost estimate can be derived by adding up the order assembly costs and home delivery costs. The overall impact of the downstream changes is more likely to be positive than negative for the upstream operations. This is why in a conservative estimate the upstream implications are not estimated or taken into account. Figure 8.3 illustrates the total costs of EGS downstream operations as a per centage of the sales volume. The bold line in the middle is the sum of averages of optimistic and pessimistic curves in Figures 8.1 and 8.2. In the dotted lines in the chart the deviations of optimistic and pessimistic scenarios are halved and summed to give the most likely range of the overall cost.

The comparable cost in the conventional supermarket supply chain is the running cost of a supermarket. It could be argued that the consumer's cost of driving the supermarket and even the cost of shopping time should be taken into account to make the comparison correct. However, in the research it was noted that consumers do not see driving to a supermarket as a cost, even if the out-of-the-pocket costs are at the same level as once weekly unattended delivery cost at high volumes.

Distribution centre costs with home delivery

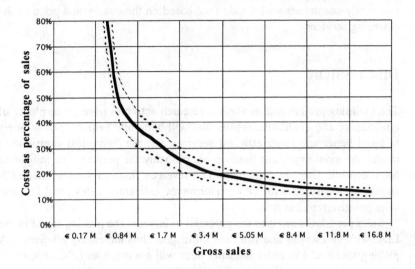

Figure 8.3 The EGS downstream cost structure (Yrjölä, 2001)

In the simulation model the target households were situated within a geographical area of 60 square kilometres. The cost of EGS operation in this area reaches 17 per cent overall cost at a sales volume of €6.7 million annually. This is the same cost as a typical supermarket in the United States (Macht, 1996). However, there is some 2 per cent supermarket level marketing cost in that 17 per cent figure, which makes the comparable pure operating cost 15 per cent. This coincides with the cost figures derived from the UK market as well as a confidential analysis made in Finland.

This cost level is achieved with a sales volume of €8.4 million with the average curve and €12.6 million with the pessimistic scenario. The pessimistic scenario can probably be achieved without unattended delivery, which usually involves some debatable cost items. Therefore it is safer to take the pessimistic scenario as the basis for comparison. Based on all this the overall cost structure of the Electronic Grocery Shopping supply chain becomes more efficient at asales volume of some €200,000 per square kilometre annually.

The success of Tesco in the UK shows that a supermarket-based operation with operational costs of some 26 per cent (12 per cent store-based costs, 7 per cent picking and 7 per cent home delivery) can be a viable business. The research suggests that a dedicated supply chain should be much more efficient and with volume become even more efficient than the traditional supply chain. Future development is hard to predict and eventually consumers will decide this, based on the quality and price of the emerging services.

DISCUSSION

The Ecomlog project and its various research activities have given plenty of quantitative and qualitative results that will hopefully help the practitioners to build better and more efficient services. On the theoretical contribution maybe the most important findings are probably the performance indicators for Electronic Grocery Shopping. The research findings suggest that EGS should be measured with new performance indicators: sales per LDC and sales per geographical area.

Sales per LDC describes the potential to increase the picking speed in the LDC with investment and full-time utilization, thus increasing efficiency. A picking speed of 450 order lines per hour will not make an LDC efficient if it is used for only two hours a day (Kämäräinen et al., 2001). The sales per square metre in an LDC can naturally still be used as a performance indicator, but it will not be very important. The LDC can be placed in areas where space can be hired with low cost and the size of the outlet can be more flexible, because there are no visiting consumers who have to be taken into account.

Sales per geographical area (square kilometre or square mile) gives an overall indication of the efficiency potential for an EGS business in a certain area. Even if sales per LDC are sufficient, the geographical distribution area has to be small enough to enable efficient home delivery. These two performance indicators are likely to be useful for any electronic consumer trade with home delivery.

EGS efficiency is based on direct demand information from consumers that can be made immediately available to all parties in the supply chain. The demand information is not distorted by intermediaries who will modify it on the basis of their own estimates of real demand as is the case in the conventional grocery supply chain. Furthermore, demand forecasting accuracy improves with a shorter supply chain. EGS does not only shorten the supply chain, with higher volumes it is expected to stabilize the demand or at least make it more predictable.

On the practical contribution side the lessons learned during the three years of this research project can be summarized in six pieces of advice that can be used as guidelines on the way to run a profitable EGS (these lessons are discussed more fully in Tanskanen et al. (2002):

1. Focus on customer density and build operative systems locally – copy and paste the working system to make it big.

The effectiveness of the e-grocery operations depends critically on local customer density. From a logistical viewpoint home delivery of groceries is quite similar to a garbage collection business; the markets should be taken over street by street. After an effective system for operating locally is developed, the way to make the business big is just copying the concept to new local areas.

2. E-grocery is loyalty business – build and maintain trust.

The cost of acquiring a new e-grocery customer is high, especially in relation to the low margins of grocery business. Achieving customer loyalty requires systematic building and maintaining of trust. Customer loyalty is also the cornerstone of effective logistics. The logistical cost of serving occasional customers' momentary needs is very high in relation to serving the continuous needs of permanent customers.

3. The buying power should be at least as strong as the supermarkets have.

Starting a business from scratch is difficult and in grocery retailing even more difficult because the merchandise comes from so many different suppliers all having long-lasting relations with the established businesses. The customers of an e-grocery are not willing to pay more for their groceries than in the average supermarket. They might be willing to pay something for the home delivery but definitely not more than is needed to cover the cost. To be able to offer competitive prices the purchase prices should be at the same level as the competition.

4. Take care of operational efficiency and provide a high service level – utilize reception boxes and start with a store-based service – switch to a hybrid model and build dedicated fulfilment centres when the local business volume justifies it.

The home delivery cost does not depend only on the density of drops, the service model and the way the delivery is received also have a substantial effect on the cost structure. The key to efficient home delivery is unattended reception of goods. This can be achieved with a refrigerated reception box at the customer location or a delivery box. Picking from an existing store is the least expensive alternative to start the service. Once the volume grows, picking from a dedicated outlet or using a hybrid model – combination of a store and fulfilment centre becomes less expensive.

5. A good ordering interface and the availability of product information are basic requirements – eDemand and eCategory management are powerful new opportunities.

A good ordering interface does not only display the products well, it also makes buying easy. A standard shopping basket is a popular solution. New opportunities arise with information technology – every customer can have a tailored grocery offering based on personal budget constraints, dietary preferences, medical treatments and even possible food allergies. Further opportunity is gained by integrating the service with activity planning. The e-grocer can, for example, propose a menu for a party and create the shopping list for the number of people attending.

6. Enlarge the product range you offer to include high margin non-grocery items when an effective logistics system for households has been built and there is a base of loyal customers.

The e-grocery home delivery can help in building a new delivery network from suppliers of tangible products to the households. In this network adding a new product group into the selection is like adding a new TV channel for a cable TV subscriber. The home delivery network could become part of the community infrastructure (like water mains, electricity supply and garbage collection). When it has reached the critical volume of business and density of drops it will also be economical to include mail delivery and smaller local distribution tasks from other freight carriers.

These six lessons are focused on the logistical feasibility of EGS and there is no new evidence as per October 2004 to make the authors change their list. Once the current practitioners manage to grow their businesses and more data become available, further research will show the validity of these general guidelines. Following these pieces of advice is no guarantee for automatic success but it will prevent the making of the same costly mistakes that most of the early practitioners have made.

NOTE

1. The detailed results from the ECOMLOG programme have been reported in several journal rticles: *International Journal of Retail & Distribution Management, International Journal of Physical Distribution and Logistics Management, International Journal of Logistics Management, Supply Chain Management: an International Journal.* Detailed information about the ECOMLOG programme can be found at www.tuta.hut.fi/logistics.

REFERENCES

Business Week (2001), 'Tesco's advantage by the numbers' 1 October 2001, available at: http://www.businessweek.com/magazine/content/01_40/ b3751625. htm

Corsten, D. and Gruen, T. (2004), 'Stock-outs cause walkouts', *Harvard Business Review*, May 2004, 26 - 27.

Dagher, N. (1998), 'Online grocery shopping', Working Paper, 1998 INSEAD, Fontainebleau, France.

Eisenhardt, K. (1989), 'Building theories from case study research', *Academy of Management Review*, 14 (4), 535 – 556.

Kämäräinen, V., Småros, J., Jaakola, T.and Holmström, J.(2001), 'ost-effectiveness in the e-grocery business', *International Journal of Retail & Distribution Management*, 29 (1), 41 – 48.

LTT (1995), 'Kotitalouksien päivittäistavaroiden ostotavat 1994 sekä ostostenteon ongelmat', LTT publication series B119, Helsinki (The Helsinki Research Institute for Business Administration LTT, 'Households' buying habits for daily consumer goods 1994 and problems experienced by customers in shopping', in Finnish).

LTT (1997), 'Päivittäistavaroiden kauppapalveluiden koettu saavutettavuus, LTT publication series B139, Helsinki (The Helsinki Research Institute for Business Administration LTT, 'The perceived availability of daily consumer goods shopping services', in Finnish).

Macht, J. (1996), 'Errand boy', *Inc.Magazine*, November 1996, p. 60, available at: http://www.inc.com/incmagazine/

Punakivi, M. and Saranen, J. (2001), 'Identifying the success factors in e-grocery home delivery', *International Journal of Retail & Distribution Management*, 29 (4), 156 - 163.

Tanskanen, K., Yrjölä, H. and Holmström, J. (2002), 'The way to profitable internet grocery retailing – 6 lessons learned', *International Journal of Retail & Distribution Management*, 30 (4), 169 - 178.

Tedeschi, B. (2004), 'After many have fallen by the wayside, retailers have begun to find a profit in online sales', *The New York Times*, 31 May 2004.

www.ocado.com (26.8.2004)

www.hoovers.com (26.8.2004)

www.peapod.com (26.8.2004)

www.tesco.com (26.8.2004)

www.ruokavarasto.fi (26.8.2004)

Yrjölä, H. and Tanskanen, K. (1999), 'An evolutionary approach for developing physical distribution in Electronic Grocery Shopping', *Proceedings of the Logistics Research Network Conference 1999 at Newcastle: Newcastle Business School*, The Institute of Logistics and Transport.

Yrjölä, H. (2001) 'Physical distribution considerations for electronic grocery shopping', *International Journal of Physical Distribution and Logistics Management*, 31 (10), 746 - 761.

Yrjölä, H. (2003), *Supply Chain Considerations for Electronic Grocery Shopping*, HUT Industrial Management and Organisational Psychology Dissertation series No 3, Espoo 2003.

9. Cost Drivers and Profitability of DC Based Grocery Home Delivery Systems

Niels Kornum and Mads Vangkilde

INTRODUCTION

The pioneering e-grocers have learned some initial and harsh lessons trying to become profitable. Webvan, as one of the more extreme examples, failed for rather obvious reasons. They invested more than €625 million[1] in infrastructure, albeit having relatively few customers. Many other e-grocers with far more modest investment rates also ceased operations, for example, Streamline (USA), Rema Hem til Dig (Norway), Matomera (Sweden), ISO Telekøb and Super Best (Denmark). From the early days of e-grocery shopping, it has been hard to obtain the right mix of customer interest and operational profitability to support sustained businesses.

However, with Tesco.com's apparent success,[2] it would *not* be fair to say that e-grocery businesses will never be profitable at all. In Denmark, the organic e-grocer Aarstiderne.com managed not only to stay afloat, but also gradually to broaden its services; and in its 5th year, there are no signs of cutting back as it services 35,000 regular customers and ships 25,000 boxes of food per week (Skouboe 2004). In light of these cases – although few and far between, the question should not be whether e-grocers will survive, rather under what conditions will they be profitable?

Although consumers may slowly become aware of the advantages of e-grocery shopping (Hansen 2003), this does not make it profitable over night – even when adopting more reasonable operational settings than Webvan. Where is the balance that Tesco.com seems to have found? Internet-based grocery shopping on the same scale as Tesco in the UK is unimaginable in Denmark at the moment. Still the question remains – what would it take?

Reported information on potential profit in grocery e-commerce based on Tesco figures indicates that despite a four times higher net margin for Internet sales as compared to store sales, a delivery fee is necessary to cover fulfilment costs (Ramaswamy and Dikalov 2000). The calculations are based on annual sales of €780 million, so despite large volumes, grocery e-commerce will only be profitable if a delivery fee is included. From the presented evidence, it is not possible to identify how the different cost drivers are interrelated and how this will influence profit. For example, some costs are primarily related to order size, such as picking and packing costs, others primarily to volume, such as transportation costs, and others again are relatively fixed despite short-term variances in volume, for example, warehouse size. There is an obvious need to identify the proportions and interrelatedness of these cost drivers and to what extent they contribute to making e-grocers profitable. Identifying these cost drivers and determining the most favourable composition of volume and order size is the purpose of this chapter.

Although this task is fairly simple to formulate, the actual dissemination hereof is very cumbersome. First, a realistic picture must be drawn of the processes involved in the business of e-grocery. This involves knowledge of how such businesses are structured or could be structured. Secondly, reliable data must be gathered for all steps in the processes. In order to be able to proceed with calculations, ratios for scaling data to higher or lower stages must be determined. Scaling proved to be a critical issue and one that was difficult to overcome.

Furthermore, conscious choices had to be made concerning set-up. One such choice involved the format of the delivery system. There are at least two different types of formats (Kornum 2002) of delivery systems for a grocery e-commerce service. With the first solution, picking and packing operations are situated in the existing store, and with the second solution, these operations are located at a distribution centre. There are obvious advantages with regard to layout (and the ensuing efficiency of picking orders) with the distribution centre-based approach. The store-based approach, on the other hand, will have advantages related to the use of existing capacities in the shops, such as staff capacity and assortment.

This chapter focuses on a model of distribution centre-based picking and packing while results from store-based picking and packing will be reported elsewhere although a comparison would interesting as Tesco still seems to prefer store picking (Child 2002). On this basis, the chapter intends to answer the following questions:

- What are the primary cost drivers of a DC-based grocery home delivery system, what are their proportions and how are they interrelated?

- And under which conditions will such a system break even or be profitable?

THEORETICAL FOUNDATION

As already mentioned, many of the pioneering players, like Streamline, using a DC-based solution had problems making a profit from their business, which may be due to insufficient volumes. With this in mind, it becomes relevant to ask what is the size of volume needed to reach break-even? The crucial point for grocery e-commerce is whether the variable and fixed cost curves will follow the increase in volume and then never break even. Or will the variable (and fixed) cost curve at some (high) level of volume tend to be more flat and consequently reach the point of break-even and profit?

It is a well-known fact that break-even is obtained when the total costs are equal to the generated sales revenue. Variable costs normally change as the volume of activities changes. By the same token, fixed costs will stay constant even when volume of activities changes, however, this only holds true for changes within a given volume range (Harrison and van Hoek, 2002). What is of special interest and needs to be uncovered is the composition of variable costs. Dissecting this parameter unveils the answer to the question of whether DC-based home deliveries are economically viable. Variable costs as a cost pool include the critical elements of picking, packing and delivering the goods. Correctly estimating and gauging the variable costs yields an understanding of the required sales revenues and the realistic size of the fixed costs. In order to perform this analysis, we applied the concept of activity-based costing (ABC).

Robin Cooper and Robert S. Kaplan first introduced the notion of an activity-based cost accounting system in the 1980s. Activity-based cost accounting was developed because of the lack of proportional connection between the number of activities performed and the bulk of goods produced in the traditional accounting systems. The need for this information arose out of increased competition. It involves resource consumption (time, machinery cost, etc.) to move units from receiving to manufacturing (e.g. writing invoices, manufacture a product, etc). If the number of activities performed per finished output is always the same, then traditional volume-based accounting systems suffice very well – the problem is that this is rarely the case. ABC represents an accounting system designed to avoid arbitrary allocation of costs to functions. Moreover, it seeks to determine costs associated with activities or specific processes (Kaplan and Cooper 1998).

ABC was quickly embraced by the manufacturing discipline, but not within the field of logistics (Pohlen and La Londe, 1994). Perttilä and

Hautaniemi (1995) argue for the benefits of ABC in logistics emphasizing the accuracy of cost information. An accuracy that, if applied correctly, ABC can provide. This cost information is more accurate than that provided by traditional systems and therefore it supports managers in decision making within several areas: logistics strategy and policy decisions, control of logistics activities, marketing strategies and policies and finally pricing decisions. All areas are affected by the logistical set-up and hence make for potential areas of improvement via ABC. The ABC system can shortly be described as follows:

ABC/M[3] systems are designed and implemented on the premise that products consume activities, activities consume resources and resources consume costs. ABC/M systems assign costs to activities based on their consumption of resources and then activity costs are assigned to products or services in proportion to a selected measure to their individual workloads. ABC/M systems examine all processes (or activities) that are actually relevant to the production of a product and attempt to determine exactly what proportion of each resource is consumed i.e. which activity a particular product uses. (Gupta and Galloway 2003, p. 132).

Costs are allocated from resources to activities and thereafter from activities to products. The distribution of company resources onto activities can, in principle, be performed to a fully disaggregated level, for example, specific activities such as 'writing of invoices' would be assigned as a spending of resources (Pohlen and La Londe, 1994). Although a fully disaggregated account is possible, it is hardly desired, as it would require extensive work to define and programme all the activities involved. In practice, the identification of groups of activities is sought. These groups are characterized by a common spending of resources and this spending being attributed to a single cost-driver – and a single cost-pool. Such an approach – although still resource consuming – is much less demanding for company accountants and company information systems. Decreasing the complexity of the task and the resources required to perform it, increases the likelihood of it succeeding (Innes and Mitchell 1998).

The theoretical basis for this study is therefore the principles of activity-based costing conceptualizations (Innes and Mitchell 1998; Kaplan and Cooper 1998; Gupta and Galloway 2003). Also, we partly rely on different perspectives on cost accounting in logistics (Harrison and van Hoek 2002; Vangkilde 2004) in order to achieve optimal adaptation to the logistical issues.

METHODOLOGY

The chosen method is a scenario-based study. Different levels of sales (volume) and order sizes are examined in order to clarify if the system will break even at all and at which level this will potentially happen. Adopting a model that allows us to scale each of these variables enables us to investigate the possibility of ever reaching break-even, and understanding the mechanisms for this to occur. To handle the scenarios, an Excel spreadsheet was used. Data were collected from both primary and secondary sources. Trend analyses were performed to accurately determine the scale ratios.

Several independent and yet interconnected issues needed to be addressed in attempting to answer the proposed research questions. As found via the concept of ABC, we needed to break down the process of DC-based grocery deliveries. That is, we needed to determine the appropriate levels for analysing activities performed in the process. Gauging them too broadly would not yield satisfactory information. Gauging too narrowly would make the process unnecessarily cumbersome and potentially incomputable. This implied an in-depth understanding of the processes involved in the facilitation of home deliveries from a distribution centre. Secondly, we needed accurate and reliable data concerning the different activities. These data involved all aspects from warehouse rent over average packing speed to transportation costs. Thirdly, as the breakdown of activities addresses the variable costs via the ABC principles, determining fixed costs also became an issue. Although easier to identify, the aspect of scale proved a significant factor. We structured our model to encompass several key functions: turnover, order size, profits, costs, number of orders, and orders handled per day.

Turnover and order size were our prime variables. In a pre-test, we ran 36 samples, with six different order sizes (ranging from €26.5 to €159) and six different turnovers (from €2.65 million to €68.8 million).[4] Although we assumed that an average order size of €159 would be unrealistic, we included these ranges to allow a broader analysis. However, in the final model, only the €106 order size was chosen based on the considerations discussed below. The pre-test also indicated that the break-even point was not obtained at a sales revenue of around €13.2 million, but rather at a figure approximately 5 times higher.

Two of the cost categories in Figure 9.1 fluctuate with changes in costs per order: costs of transportation and picking/packing. When addressing the element of picking and packing, the insights from the ABC principles turned out to be valuable. While a thorough breakdown appears attractive, the question of relevance and manageability is important. We relied on two different sources of input for these factors. With this data, we ran trend analyses to project a realistic cost assessment of the component of picking and packing. The analyses provided us with insight on the correlation between price and time to pick/pack the order and, correspondingly, the price measured against the number of SKU in an order, (see the specification below). In our model, these costs vary according to the total turnover and are subject to scale advantages – the more that needs to be processed, the higher the probability of lower costs per unit will be. The inputs for these factors are primarily derived from secondary sources. These cost categories comprise: interest in connection with stock-keeping, warehouse facility costs, warehouse investment depreciation, IT&C and administration costs, and finally, other warehouse handling costs. Understanding the relationship between all these factors is pivotal. For a detailed schematic of the correlation between the different cost drivers, please refer to Appendix A. Figure 9.1 shows a model of the analysis performed.

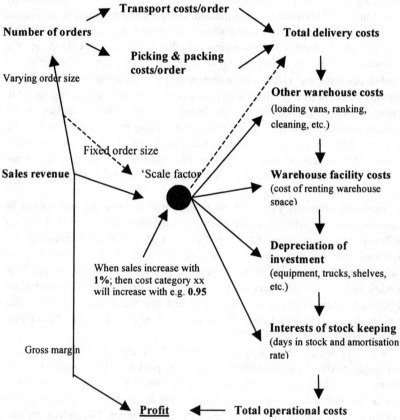

Figure 9.1 Model of analysis

As illustrated in Figure 9.1, scaling is important in our investigation. It has therefore been crucial not only to have precise input, but also to have realistic estimates on how to scale these basic numbers up and down, respectively. The issue of scaling touched all aspects of our study – fixed costs are only fixed to a certain point. Where is that point and at what ratio do we scale it accordingly?

MODEL SPECIFICATION

In the following sections, the more detailed preconditions for the model are presented. First, some general issues concerning choice of order size and gross margin are addressed, then the individual cost categories and available background are considered and the composition of costs corresponding to a sales revenue of €2.6, €16, €29, €43, €56 and €69 million is analysed.

General Issues

The results from the Swedish and Danish surveys in the Ebizz Øresund project indicate that customers are not especially interested in buying groceries in large quantities (order sizes). Most respondents find that outlay sizes of €26.5 to €79 would be sufficient to gain deliveries free of charge (Hansen 2003). But how can the e-grocers possibly meet this demand. As can be seen from Figure 9.2, small order sizes are costly regardless of sales revenue size.

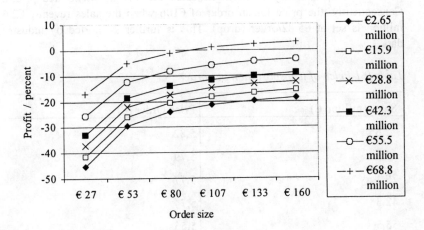

Figure 9.2 Impact of order size on profitability

The effect of operating bigger order sizes is considerable when the order size increases from €26.5 to €106, but the curve becomes flatter when order sizes are over €106. Thus, proposing bigger order sizes will only increase profitability to a minor degree.

In addition, international experience from the e-grocery sector supports the proposition that the *average order size is high* (higher than in a supermarket). Webvan's average order size was reported to be 'above €78'[5] (Bakshi and Deighton 2000) and by April 2001 €89 (Langberg 2001). Similarly, Tesco's average order size amounted to €98, Albertson's (US) about €78 (Said 2001) and Home Grocer and Streamline (US) €86 (Bakshi and Deighton 2000). From this background, the order size in the model is set at €106. Based on industry sources, the gross margin is set at an average of 20% for groceries (VAT excluded). These figures are basic elements in the calculation of profitability in the model.

Transport Cost

Definition: Transport costs are the costs the e-grocer pays per drop/order either into its own transport system or to an external carrier.

Data background: According to Kornum et al. (1999, pp. 140, 146), in interviews two carriers suggested the transport cost per order/drop to be €4.63 and €3.97, respectively. Yrjölä (2003) mentions a cost per drop for unattended delivery of €4.20 (Pilot with S-Group). This information does not include order size. An estimate shows that order sizes of €106 generate a need for four transport boxes (79–3, 53–2, 26.5–1). This indicates that the price per drop is likely to be higher than the already mentioned prices. Consequently, the price for an order of €106 when the sales revenue €2.6 million is set at €5.82/order (drop). This is further supported by industry data.

Table 9.1 Price of transportation per order

Sales (million €)	Price/Order (€)
2.65	5.82
15.9	5.79
29.1	5.77
42.3	5.74
55.5	5.55
68.8	5.29

Increasing sales revenue (€2.6, €16, €29, €43, €56 and €69 million) only slightly improves the efficiency of transport (cost per drop). Every customer must be visited and this generates a specific time usage per customer (stop time), independent of driving time. Thus gaining economies of scale is difficult. Still, higher sales revenue will increase the spatial density of customers, which especially in lower density areas will lead to considerable reductions in driving time Furthermore, larger size transport firms can reduce communication costs, for example, EDI and routing software can contribute to the reduction of driving time. On this basis, the price per order of €5.82/order (at sales revenue €2.6 million) is only set to decrease at low rates, but when the sales revenue is around €56 to €69 million, the price per order is set to decrease at higher rates, because significant scale advantages are found to be realistic. Table 9.1 shows the estimated figures.

Picking and Packing Costs

Definitions: These costs include the time used for the following activity cycle: worker picks up the order, picks the goods on the shelves, packs the goods in the transport boxes, places the boxes at a proper location (ranking) and returns to pick up the next order. The costs are calculated per order.

Data background: Yrjölä (2003) mentions an increase in order lines per employee per hour from 200 (manual DC-based picking – Matomera) to 450 (highly automated DC-based picking – Webvan). Industry data indicate that one order of €106 corresponds to around 28 order lines. If these data hold true, the Matomera DC can handle 7.14 orders/hour (8.4 minutes/order), whereas Webvan was capable of handling 16 orders/hour (3.75 minutes/order). The ordinary average warehouse worker's gross wage is set at €16/hour (€0.26/minutes).

Table 9.2 Price of picking and packing per order

Sales (million €)	Price/Order (€)
2.65	2.65
15.9	2.38
29.1	2.12
42.3	1.85
55.5	1.45
68.8	1.05

Therefore the cost per order is estimated to be between €1 and €2.2. From the background of possible efficiency improvements in picking and packing per order, the cost is suggested to vary between €2.6 and €1.05 per order as shown in Table 9.2.

Other Warehouse Handling Costs

Definitions: These costs comprise the following: receipt of items/goods, stacking, loading and cleaning. These costs are related to the size of sales revenue.

Data background: The data set at the lower end of the sales revenue scale is supported by industry evidence, however when scaled up to sales revenue of €69 million, this is based on an estimate. This scale factor is, of course, difficult to estimate; still it is reasonable to suggest that this business would be able to gain higher efficiency as sales revenue rises, for example, based on higher capacity utilization of resources (working force and equipment) and increased utilization of IT&C, such as scanners, radio guided trucks, and so on.

The estimate is based on the rule of thumb that 'Other Warehouse Handling Costs' should not represent a higher share of sales revenue than 'Picking & Packing Costs'. Thus it is not very likely that when the business is more mature the support function ('Other Warehouse Handling Costs') would make up a higher share than the main function ('Picking & Packing Costs'). This estimation is presented in Table 9.3.

Table 9.3 Percentage of total sales of other warehouse handling costs

Sales (million €)	Percentage of sales revenue
2.65	2.7
15.9	2.4
29.1	2.1
42.3	1.8
55.5	1.4
68.8	1.0

Warehouse Facility Cost

Definitions: Warehouse facility costs consist of the costs of providing the e-grocer with a(n) (empty) warehouse facility suitable for picking and packing, other warehouse handling tasks and administrative tasks.

Data background: One important factor when considering the 'Warehouse Facility Cost' dimension is how the need for warehouse space is related to the size of sales revenue. From this the needed square meters multiplied by an average price for renting a warehouse leads to the estimate of the 'Warehouse Facility Costs'. Table 9.4 lists data on the relation between sales revenue and need for warehouse space.

Table 9.4 Correlation between sales revenue and square meters

E-grocer	Sq. meters	Sales revenue $\mathcal{E}$[6]
ISO	1.800[7]	3.968.253[8]
Webvan[9]	32.500[10]	12.500.000
Streamline	5.200[11]	21.164.021[12]
Homegrocer	11.820[13]	39.682.539[14]

There are no data on capacity utilization, but if an estimate is set at say 70%, this will lead to a need for between 22 (the largest warehouse/sales revenues) and 42 square meters (smallest warehouse/sales revenues) warehouse space per million $\mathcal{E}$ sales revenue. From this background, it is possible to estimate what percentage of sales revenue the 'Warehouse Facility Costs' represent, because the average warehouse rent per square meter is common and available business knowledge, for example, $\mathcal{E}$5.88 per sq. m/month Yrjölä (2003). The result of these considerations is presented in Table 9.5.

Table 9.5 Percentage of total sales of warehouse facility costs

Sales (million €)	Percentage of sales revenue
2.65	2.34
15.9	2.07
29.1	1.81
42.3	1.57
55.5	1.34
68.8	1.12

Warehouse Investment Depreciations

Definitions: Warehouse investment depreciations consist of depreciations of investments in handling equipment (trucks, etc.), shelves, temperature-regulated areas, IT&C warehouse equipment and the like.

Data background: In Ramaswamy and Dikalov (2000, p. 13), depreciations are between 0.14 and 1.01% of sales revenue depending on the retail format and based on assumed sales of €780 million. As the present data set consists of smaller sales figures, the share of sales revenue is estimated to be higher, as illustrated in Table 9.6.

Table 9.6 Percentage of total sales of warehouse investment depreciation

Sales (million €)	Percentage of sales revenue
2.65	4.0
15.9	3.5
29.1	3.0
42.3	2.5
55.5	2.0
68.8	1.5

Administrative Costs

Definitions: Administration, overall management, marketing, web store (homepage), customer service, order processing, purchasing and miscellaneous administration

Data background: Ramaswamy and Dikalov (2000, p. 13) present projected costs as a percentage of sales revenue in alternative grocery models and assumes sales of €780 million. Projected figures relating to cost categories similar to the above definition of administrative costs are shown here. These represent the costs of a 'pure player' Kornum (2002). The pure player is here assumed to have an advertising expenditure of 10% of sales. However, this does not correspond with Swedish/Danish experience, namely Matomera and Aarstiderne.com, indicating that low budget marketing (Events, PR, etc.) can generate sales and that ordinary marketing efforts like advertising have very little effect (Carlheim-Gyllenskjold and Rangefeld 2002). Therefore, the advertising category from "Bricks & Clicks warehouse picking, In-house delivery" has been chosen.

Table 9.7 Percentage of total sales of administrative costs

Category	Percentage of sales revenue
Labour costs	3.3
Administrative costs	1.5
Advertising	2.5
Other expenses	1.0
Total	8.3

As shown in Table 9.7, the total labour costs, administrative costs, advertising and other expenses represent 8.3 % of the sales revenue. This total represents the cost categories that are not 'delivery costs'. In the present model, based on sales revenue of €69 million, the administrative cost category amounts to a total of 8% of sales revenue and therefore seems to be comparable in size (ibid.), although the individual cost category is not directly comparable as shown in Table 9.8 below.

On this basis, administrative costs representing 5% of sales revenue are probably suitable for e-grocers with sales revenues that are higher than €69 million, and industry sources indicate that at lower levels of sales revenue, administrative costs might be as high as 20%. Table 9.9 contains these figures, where the relative share of administrative costs only decreases at low rates when the sales revenue is between €2.6 and €42 million, but economies of scale are expected to gain full momentum at higher sales revenues.

Table 9.8 Percentage of total sales of other administrative costs

Category	Percentage of sales revenue
Warehouse facility cost	1.1
Depreciation of investments WH	1.5
Interest stock	0.5
Administrative cost	5.0
Total	8.0

Table 9.9 Percentage of total administrative costs of sales revenue

Sales (million €)	Percentage of sales revenue
2.65	20
15.9	18
29.1	16
42.3	14
55.5	10
68.8	5

Interest on Stock

Experiences from Matomera (see Carlheim-Gyllenskjold and Rangefeld 2002) show that it is difficult to predict the pattern of product types ordered by customers and therefore they began to operate with stock instead of practically no stock. Stock-outs can be very demanding on other cost categories, such as transportation, and therefore stock-keepings days are set at 30. Furthermore, interest generated from stock represents such an insignificant share of sales revenue that 30 days of stock has very little impact on when the e-grocery business breaks even, at least when the interest rate is as low as it is today. The interest rate is set at 7% per year.

RESULTS

Based on the above-mentioned preconditions, calculations were run in the Excel model. The results from these calculations are presented in Figure 9.3. The good news is that it *is* possible for an e-grocery pure player to break even without including a delivery fee.

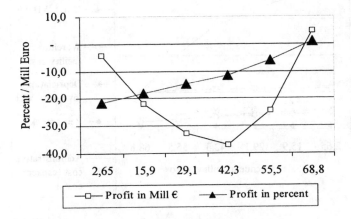

Figure 9.3 Break-even of e-grocers

The bad news is that until a turnover of around €67 million is reached, the e-grocer will accumulate a debt around €15.8 million, amortization not included. With amortization included, this sum will, of course, be considerable higher. Unless the e-grocer grows very fast or has a persistent and affluent financial source, this debt seems impossible to handle. Still, the grocery market is huge (€7.9 to €9.3 billion in Denmark), so there is potential for fast expansion even when only a small proportion of the total market is accessed. However, there is a risk for a first mover in this market. To what extent are second movers able to enter the market and to what extent can they benefit from the fact that they do not have to pay the interests and depreciation of the debt generated by the first mover in the process of creating this market. (See Vangkilde, Chapter 12 in this book).

The process of break-even is filled with harsh demands that the operations must be more efficient as the e-grocer grows. As shown in Figure 9.4, the e-grocer should be able to reduce administrative costs from 20% to 5% of sales revenue. Although not representing as a large a share as administrative costs, the e-grocer should also be able to reduce the cost level

significantly in other categories. Only interest paid on stock holding appears
to have no important influence on the possibility of gaining a profit.

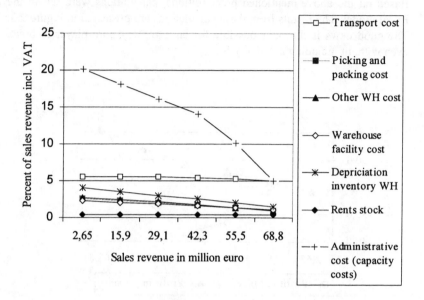

Figure 9.4 E-grocers' cost categories

Another possible way to reach break-even faster is to start the business with
a delivery fee and promise the customers to reduce the fee when this is
possible. The pioneers will then pay the direct cost of the service, but when
the e-grocer's sales revenue gets closer to the break-even point, the delivery
fee can be reduced and thereby the e-grocer will appeal to a broader segment
of customers (Hansen 2003). Figure 9.5 shows how large the delivery fee per
order should be to break even.

According to Ramaswamy and Dikalov (2000), Tesco charges €7.2 for
delivery, ISO in Denmark first charged €7.9 and then €10.6 and Matomera
charges €8.8. This level is reached based on €46.3 and €52.9 million in sales
revenue. It is unlikely that the consumers will accept a delivery fee of €23
(Hansen 2003), but there is also the alternative concept that the e-grocer
generates some debt, such as the difference between €9.52 and €9.26 in
delivery fee per order. Still, this strategy impedes the possibility of rapid
growth, because many consumers expect the delivery fee to be waived on
any substantial order size and this growth is necessary to get the volume to
break-even point.

As mentioned in Kornum (2002), the pure player as a format has some disadvantages as compared to existing supermarkets (store-based e-grocer) providing a supplementary home shopping service (Bricks & Clicks), but also compared to the specialty e-grocer with a narrower and niche-like assortment. Obviously these two formats have survived part of the phase one e-grocery battle with Tesco.com representing the former and specialty e-grocers like Harry and David, Fresh Direct in USA and Aarstiderne.com in Denmark representing the latter. Store-based E-grocers like Tesco have fewer costs, especially in the initial phases, because infrastructure and staff resources can be shared with the existing shops. Outside the UK the delivery fee has probably been an impeding factor for the expansion of this concept (Hansen 2003) and many initiatives have failed (Kornum 2002).

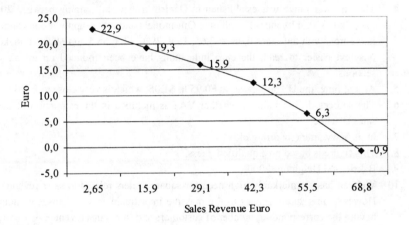

Figure 9.5 Delivery fee size to break-even

The specialty e-grocer focuses on a narrower assortment than an ordinary supermarket and on premium assortments normally difficult to access, such as organic, ethnic and similar products, which should lead to higher margins and to a quicker profit. In addition, these types of businesses do not ask their customers to pay a delivery fee if customers exceed a certain order size. These e-grocery formats have the possibility of expanding into larger parts of the grocery assortment and thereby becoming a competitor to this segment too. However, this strategy can cause some trouble by potentially corroding the existing (corporate) brand of the specialty e-grocer, so the specialty e-grocer may need to make a strategic choice between expanding to new markets (geographical expansion) with the same assortment, motivating the existing customers to buy more of the existing assortment or expanding the assortment to cover a wider range of the ordinary grocery assortment.

NOTES

1. *Chicago Tribune* 18 July 2001, What Killed Webvan was Bricks, not Clicks. By Jorge Rufat-Latre.
2. Tesco launched online sales in February 2000 in 100 of its stores (Economist 2000).
3. Some authors use the terms Activity-Based Costing and Activity-Based Management interchangeably.
4. The turnover range was established in Danish kroner and ranging between 20, 120, 220, 320, 420 and 520 millions. Our models and tables apply a translation into euros, with the exact figures: 2.65, 15.9, 29.1, 42.3, 55.5 and 68.8. To make this text easier to read, the euro indications have been rounded up in many sections.
5. At that time, the US dollar was at €0.95 to $1.05, which is very close to €106.
6. The sources do not indicate whether VAT is included in the estimation of the sales revenue.
7. http://www.markedsforing.dk/
8. This figure is based on a qualified guess.
9. Bakshi and Deighton (2000).
10. Webvan has a remarkably high need for square meters related to sales revenue. However, this surely relates to the massive investment in warehouses without having the corresponding number of customers and thus sales revenue.
11. Yrjölä (2003).
12. Bakshi and Deighton (2000).
13. Ibid.
14. Ibid.

APPENDIX A

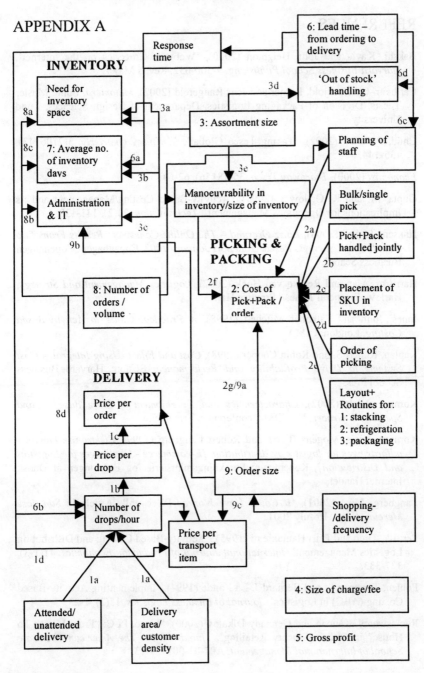

Source: Own Illustration

REFERENCES

Bakshi, Kayla and John Deighton (2000), 'Webvan: Groceries on the Internet'. *Harvard Business School Publishing.* 9-500-052. Rev. 5 May.

Carlheim-Gyllenskjold, Rutger and Jens Rangefeld (2002), *Matomera*, Lund: Master Thesis, Division of Packaging Logistics, Department of Design Sciences, Lund University.

Child, Peter N. (2002), 'Taking Tesco Global'. *McKinsey Quarterly.* 3(7106143), 135-144.

Economist (2000), *Tearaway Tesco.* 354(8156), 62-64.

Gupta, M. and K. Galloway (2003), 'Activity-Based Costing/Management and its Implications for Operations Management'. *Technovation.* 23(2), 131-138.

Hansen, Torben (2003), *Ebizz Øresund – The Online Consumer: Results From Two Scandinavian Surveys; Research Report January 2003*, Copenhagen: Copenhagen Business School.

Harrison, Alan and Remko van Hoek (2002), *Logistics Management and Strategy*, Harlow: Financial Times / Prentice Hall.

Innes, John and Falkoner Mitchell (1998), *A Practical Guide to Activity-Based Costing*, London: CIMA.

Kaplan, Robert S. and Robin Cooper (1998), *Cost and Effect: Using Integrated Cost Systems to Drive Profitability and Performance*, Boston: Harvard Business School Press.

Kornum, Niels (2002), *Characteristics and Development of Store Based – and Specialty E-Grocer.* NOFOMA conference, Trondheim.

Kornum, Niels, Mogens Bjerre and Robert Langberg (1999), *Elektronisk handel - udfordringer for logistik og distribution. [E-commerce - Challenges for Logistics and Distribution]*, København: Forskningsministeriet og Foreningen af Dansk Internet Handel.

Langberg, Mike (2001), '*It Could Have Worked* [Webvan]', Article in *San Jose Mercury News*, 16 July 2001.

Perttilä, Timo and Petri Hautaniemi (1995), 'Activity-Based Costing and Distribution Logistics Management'. *International Journal of Production Economics.* 41(1-3), 327-333.

Pohlen, Terrance L. and Bernard J. La Londe (1994). 'Implementing Activity-Based Costing (ABC) in Logistics'. *Journal of Business Logistics.* 15(2), 1-23.

Ramaswamy, Kannan and Gennady Dikalov (2000), 'Tesco, PLC: "From Mouse To House" in Online Grocery Retailing', *Thunderbird – The American Graduate School of International Management.* A07-01-0011, 1-13.

Rufat-Latre, J. (2001), 'What Killed Webvan was Bricks, not Clicks', *Chicago Tribune*. 18/07/2001.

Said, Carolyn (2001), *'Life after WEBVAN Safeway, Albertson's Hope to Capitalize on Online Grocery Market'*. Chronicle Staff Writer, Monday 16 July 2001 [www.sfchronicle.com].

Skouboe, J. (2004), 'Butikken der overlevede dotcom' (The stores that survived the dotcom). *Berlingske Tidende*. 12/07/2004.

Vangkilde, M. (2004), *Cost Accounting in Logistics and Supply Chain Management*. Copenhagen: CBS Working Paper.

Yrjölä, Hannu (2003), *Supply Chain Considerations for Electronic Grocery Shopping*. Helsinki: PhD Dissertation.

http://www.markedsforing.dk/

10. A Reality Check on E-Grocery Delivery Options – The Swedish Case

Elisabeth Karlsson

INTRODUCTION

There is no widely accepted definition of the term electronic commerce. The definition chosen as the starting point in this chapter is the OECD narrow definition of e-commerce transactions (OECD 2002):

> An electronic transaction is the sale or purchase of goods or services, whether between businesses, households, individuals, governments, and other public or private organizations, conducted over the Internet. The goods and services are ordered over those networks, but the payment and the ultimate delivery of the good or service may be conducted on or off-line.

E-grocery is a combination of the words e-commerce and grocery. In line with the OECD definition of e-commerce, e-grocery here means groceries ordered over the Internet. Usually e-commerce transactions are divided between transactions that take place among businesses, called business-to-business (B2B) and between businesses and consumers, called business-to-consumer (B2C). This chapter deals with B2C transactions. Moreover, only e-grocery stores that substitute rather than complete traditional grocery shopping are focused here, meaning that the customer can do the greater part of their grocery shopping in the e-grocery store. Therefore only full assortment e-grocery stores are included in this study, that is e-grocery stores that carry groceries, of course, but also perishables, chemico-technical products (e.g. cosmetics and detergents) and other products that by tradition are found in grocery stores. Thus it should be pointed out that stores that do not have a full assortment, such as niche stores that only carry delicatessen or some other narrow range of assortments are not included in this study. Niche stores can (and often do) specialize in products with high margin and/or products that are logistically easy to handle. These stores have better prospects of covering costs associated with home delivery than do full assortment e-grocery stores. The latter have to manage products within at least three different temperature zones; products that are often voluminous and have a low margin; and products that are irregular in form and also sensitive to pressure and thrusts which in turn obstruct automation of handling. These conditions make full assortment e-grocery store orders more complex and challenging to handle and deliver – and also to study.

Background to 'The Swedish Case'

In Sweden, e-grocery was introduced in 1996, when a couple of independent e-grocery stores opened (e.g. NK-hallen in Stockholm). The major grocery actors followed with centralized e-grocery stores in the following years (www.expressfood.kf.se and www.netxtra.se in 1997, www.matomera.se in 1998, www.spar.nu in 1999 (later on www.hemkop.se), www.willys.nu and www.billhalls.se in 2000 and finally www.ica.se in 2001). In addition to these centralized initiatives, independent e-grocery stores sprang up like mushrooms. In the early years the optimism was practically boundless. In 1998 one of the pioneering Swedish e-grocers (www.expressfood.kf.se) expected e-grocery to account for at least 20% of total grocery sales within five years, and additional e-grocery stores were planned in several Swedish cities (Forsebäck 2001). Two years later, in 2000, other predictions of e-grocery's market share of total grocery sales ranged between 5% and 25% (Delden, Hansson et al. 2001). It was not only the industry that was optimistic about the future of e-grocery. According to a survey conducted by Sifo in 2000 as many as 28% of questioned consumers expected to use e-grocery services within five years (Jansson 2000). Above all, e-grocery was predicted to be an attractive solution for double-income households with lack of time. With a majority of the population being active Internet users, a prediction of being Europe's most dense area regarding broadband connection, and the highest proportion of double-income households in Europe, Sweden was perceived to have the main prerequisites needed to adapt to e-grocery (Frostling-Henningsson 2002).

However, e-grocery has not proven to be a success in Sweden so far. It accounts for only a fraction of e-commerce in total, which at the last measurement in 2002 accounted for 1.7% of the total retail sales in Sweden[1] (Internetindikatorn 1999-2002). As shown in Figure 10.1 below, all but one of the centralized e-grocery stores have closed (www.matomera.se, www.expressfood.kf.se, www.hemkop.se, www.willys.nu and www.bill-halls.se in 2001 and www.ica.se in 2003). Many of the independent e-grocery stores have also closed. A similar development can be found in the USA where e-grocers such as Webvan, Streamline, HomeRuns, Homegrocer and ShopLink have closed.

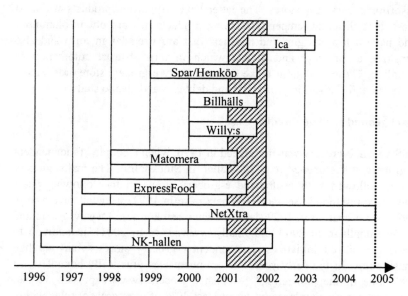

Figure 10.1 The development of e-grocery in Sweden

While several of the mentioned stores in the USA were different regarding deployed distribution strategy as well as offered delivery options, the Swedish e-grocers were very similar in both senses. In Sweden, the only offered delivery options were almost exclusively based upon attended home delivery, which implies that someone in the household is at home in order to receive the groceries. Usually, home delivery was offered Monday to Friday in two or three delivery time windows per day. The delivery time windows were generally between two and three hours. To offer delivery options where the customer has a freedom of choice to this extent can result in low resource utilization as well as low profitability unless the volumes are large enough. The Swedish e-grocers that have been forced to close, gave profitability problems as a reason, partly caused by inability to cover costs in their distribution activities. However, it should be pointed out that there are successful examples among those e-grocers that offer delivery options with a high degree of freedom of choice regarding day of delivery as well as delivery time window. In Sweden the only remaining centralized e-grocery initiative, www.netxtra.se, finally showed a profit in 2004 (Englund 2004). This is also true for www.peapod.com that went on the Internet in 1996 and achieved profitability in four out of five markets in 2003 (http://www.peapod.com/corpinfo/GW_index.jhtml 2004-10-31). Worth mentioning among successful examples of e-grocers is also www.tesco.co.uk in the UK who also show profit in their online business (Moore et al. 2004).

Purpose and Research Questions

In the light of the profitability problems that Swedish e-grocers have encountered, the purpose of this chapter is to identify realistic e-grocery delivery options given the conditions on the Swedish market in 2001 and 2002.[2] The term 'realistic' refers to the delivery options' potential for becoming profitable as well as their ability to meet the customers' demands and preferences regarding the service characteristics of e-grocery delivery options. An initial explorative study revealed that no profound studies had been carried out yet in Sweden regarding customers' preferences and demands concerning different e-grocery delivery options, and this knowledge is vital (Karlsson and Rosén 2002). In order to fulfil the purpose of this chapter, the following three research questions were specified:

- What different e-grocery delivery options can be found in the literature?
- What profitability potential have e-grocery delivery options put into practice in Sweden up to now?
- What needs and demands do consumers have concerning the design of e-grocery delivery options with respect to different service characteristics?

RESEARCH METHOD

The research questions have been dealt with in three different studies, a literature review followed by two empirical studies. The initial literature review addressed the first research question by identifying possible e-grocery delivery options presented in scientific journals and research reports. The second research question is discussed in the light of an evaluation study using a routing and scheduling tool, where a few typical cases of e-grocery delivery options have been evaluated regarding profitability potential. Finally, the third research question was analysed by means of a consumer study consisting of a focus group study and a web survey. The evaluation study was performed by means of a routing and scheduling system called Plan-LogiX.[3] Plan LogiX consists of a number of modules, of which the optimization module has been used in this study. The overall purpose of the system is to calculate the most cost-efficient transport solution, based on input data on customers, orders and resources. Plan LogiX uses a map database (here of the Swedish city Göteborg) to generate detailed travel plans for the routes. The consumer study was made using a combination of a qualitative method (focus groups) and a quantitative method (web survey). By combining these two methods, one can benefit from their respective advantages. The focus group study was of an explorative nature with two aims: the first aim was to capture the consumers' attitudes towards e-commerce in general and different service characteristics in e-grocery delivery options in particular; the second aim was to contribute to the creation of survey items by (a) capturing all the domains that need to be measured in the survey, (b) determining the dimensions that make up each of these domains, and (c) providing item wordings that effectively convey the researcher's intent to the survey respondent, improve validity and reduces unreliability in the subsequent web survey (Morgan 1997). Since the number of focus groups was determined by the phase where theoretic saturation was achieved, a solid foundation creating survey items was obtained. The aim of the web survey was partly to validate the results from the focus group study; partly to do a more detailed investigation of the consumers' perceived value of e-grocery delivery options regarding different service characteristics. Moreover, a quantitative web survey provides a better basis for generalization of the results. The survey population of both consumer studies was intentionally restricted to individuals with experience of e-grocery shopping. The reason why is the belief that the respondents' perceived benefits of different e-grocery delivery options (both real and hypothetical) become more valid if they have personal experience of e-grocery shopping. (See e.g. Hansen and Beckmann in Chapter 6 for findings indicating that consumers with experience of e-grocery shopping perceive characteristics of e-grocery shopping differently from consumers without such experience. Also Wilson-Jeanselme and Reynolds in Chapter 2 show a difference in preference structures between offline shoppers and online shoppers.) In the focus group study, four focus group sessions were held, two male and two female, with 23 experienced web customers participating in total. An invitation to participate in a focus group session was sent to all customers ordering home delivery from two e-grocers in Göteborg during a period of three days. The invitation was followed by a telephone call and those customers that were interested in participating were booked for a focus group session. The survey population in the web survey consisted of all customers of three e-grocers (two situated in Göteborg and one in Stockholm) that placed an order during the period of time (three weeks) that the web survey was accessible on the Internet. In order to only catch the customers of these three e-grocers and make sure that nobody else could answer the questionnaire, the web survey was constructed as a hidden web page questionnaire, which means that the customer confirming his/her order triggered a pop-up window with a request to participate in a survey. In total, the questionnaire was answered by 1587 customers. During the time of the web survey a total number of 2155 orders were placed in the three e-grocery stores. Thus the total response rate was 74% (for the individual e-grocery stores the response rates were 75.5%, 74.4% and 67% respectively). The analysis of focus group data can (a) take a conversation analytic approach, (b) concentrate on group dynamics, or (c) concentrate on providing an understanding of substantive issues in the data (Bloor, Frankland et al. 2001). The latter approach (c) was chosen for analysing the focus group data. Regarding the web survey, it should be pointed out that only results from the descriptive analysis are presented in this chapter. Further statistical analysis will be presented in a forthcoming article.

CLASSIFICATION OF DIFFERENT DELIVERY OPTIONS

When classifying e-grocery delivery options, the physical interface between household and retailer can be taken as a starting-point. The interface between retailer and household differs first depending on where the goods are delivered (if any delivery at all), and secondly whether any physical interaction between the driver and the goods receiver is required. Consequently, the different e-grocery delivery options can be classified according to Figure 10.2 below. Collection points do not include any delivery at all, instead the customer collects the goods from the picking facility. Since no delivery is included, a better name for collection points might be service offer. However, for uniformity reasons and since most e-grocers in Sweden offer their customers this option, it is included here as a delivery option.

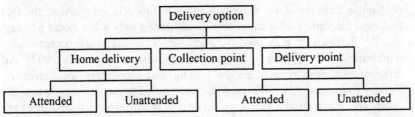

Figure 10.2 E-grocery delivery options

When delivery is included, it can be attended or unattended. Attended delivery can be made either to delivery points (e.g. places of work, service stations and after-hours supermarkets) or to order-specific street addresses (i.e. home delivery). Attended home delivery implies that someone in the household must be at home to receive the groceries. Unattended delivery can be based on either common or personal reception facilities. Common reception facilities can be placed close to places of work, bus stations, subway stations, service stations, shopping centres or other places where it might be convenient for the customers to collect their groceries. Therefore, common reception facilities can be classified as unattended delivery points. Personal reception facilities on the other hand are attached to the customer's house or block of flats, thereby making unattended home delivery possible. Furthermore, personal reception facilities can be subdivided into reception boxes and delivery boxes. Both types of boxes are lockable and refrigerated, thus making deliveries day and night possible. The difference between the two boxes is that the reception box is attached to the house, whereas the delivery box is a container in which the goods are delivered and then connected with a docking station near the house.

Factors Influencing Efficiency

The design of the delivery options influences their efficiency to a great extent. First of all, whether delivery is attended or unattended is decisive. As mentioned above, delivery options based on attended home delivery imply that someone in the household must be at home to receive the goods. Therefore, deliveries have to be scheduled within a predetermined and relatively short delivery time window on the specified day of delivery. Obviously, the customers want the delivery time window to be as short as possible. However, shorter delivery time windows result in more extensive restrictions for the distribution company in generating efficient distribution routes. Moreover, attended home delivery involves physical interaction (e.g. payment procedures and answering of questions), which causes time-consuming delivery stops, thereby leading to low efficiency. Also, the fact that most customers want to receive goods during only a few hours per day, usually between 5 p.m. and 9 p.m., leads to high and concentrated requirements for vehicles and manpower (Karlsson and Rosén 2002). All these factors pose restrictions on routing and scheduling the deliveries, thereby influencing the efficiency for unattended home delivery, when the goods are delivered to a reception facility, it is sufficient that deliveries are scheduled on a predetermined day, or at least within a considerably longer delivery time window than for attended home delivery. Delivery options based on unattended home delivery create better conditions for efficient scheduling of vehicles and manpower, thus reducing the requirements for resources. Moreover, the numbers of unsuccessful deliveries, when nobody is at home to receive the goods, are eliminated. Several studies have shown that delivery options based on unattended home delivery lead to a significantly lower delivery cost than options based on attended home delivery (Kämäräinen 2001b; Punakivi and Saranen 2001; Punakivi et al. 2001; Yrjölä 2001).

Another important advantage of unattended home delivery is that it offers a higher degree of customer service, meaning that the customer gets the same service as with attended home delivery but with less effort, since there is no need to be at home in order to receive the goods. One significant disadvantage of unattended home delivery, however, is the need for investment in reception facilities. High investment costs and time consuming installation of reception facilities lead to lower growth rate for delivery options based on unattended home delivery than for attended home delivery. Therefore, if a high growth rate is considered important, attended home delivery is the preferred delivery option. However, the financing of the investment in reception facilities must be solved. As mentioned, unattended home delivery can be based on either reception boxes or delivery boxes. The two options influence efficiency in different ways. The investment cost is higher for the reception box. According to Punakivi et al. (2001) the costs for a reception box and a delivery box are €400-900 and approximately €170 respectively (Punakivi et al. 2001). The higher cost of the reception boxes results in longer payback times, unless the customer carries the investment fully or partially. Thus delivery boxes are associated with lower investment costs, which lead to a faster growth rate and more flexibility (Punakivi et al. 2001; Punakivi and Tanskanen 2002). A major drawback of the delivery box system, however, is that it generates a reverse flow of empty delivery boxes. From this perspective, the prerequisites of efficiency in unattended home delivery seem better in the case of reception boxes. Secondly, one significant factor that influences the efficiency is whether deliveries are home deliveries or deliveries to delivery points. From a distribution perspective, there is a big difference between delivering to delivery points and to specific street addresses. Delivery points make coordination of deliveries possible, in the sense that several orders can be delivered at one delivery stop, in contrast to home delivery, where only one order per delivery stop is possible. Thus delivery points ought to lead to higher efficiency because of better conditions for scheduling and planning of resources (vehicles and manpower). One problem associated with attended delivery points, however, is that many existing establishments that could be used as delivery points, such as service stations and after-hours supermarkets normally do not have enough cold storage floor space for the goods (Kämäräinen 2000). Investment in dedicated attended delivery points or unattended delivery points, that is, common reception facilities, might therefore be required. From a consumer's point of view, both attended and unattended home delivery ought to be considered more convenient than attended or unattended delivery points, since delivery points imply that the customers themselves have to take care of the final distance to their homes – often by means of their private car. As we have seen, the efficiency of different delivery options has been analysed in several studies (Kämäräinen 2001b; Kämäräinen et al. 2001; Punakivi and Saranen 2001; Punakivi et al. 2001; Yrjölä 2001; Karlsson and Rosén 2002; Punakivi and Tanskanen 2002). First of all these studies indicate that an important determinant for efficiency is whether the customer interface is attended or unattended. Moreover, efficiency is determined by the number and length of delivery time windows offered to the customers. Finally, a factor that has great influence on efficiency is the amount of freedom of choice that is given to the customers with respect to specifying day and time of delivery. The more freedom of choice to the customers, the more restrictions are placed on possibilities to achieve efficient routing and scheduling.

EVALUATION OF TYPICAL CASES OF E-GROCERY DELIVERY OPTIONS

As mentioned earlier, e-grocery in Sweden has experienced profitability problems among other things in consequence of its inability to cover costs of the distribution activities. With the aim of finding out the profitability potential for delivery options offered in Sweden up to now, two typical cases of delivery options have been evaluated. As shown in Table 10.1 below, both options entail attended home delivery. The only difference between them is the number and the length of the time windows.

Table 10.1 Evaluated delivery options

	Interface	Days of delivery	Delivery time windows
Delivery option 1	Attended	Monday – Friday	13–16, 17–19, 19–21
Delivery option 2	Attended	Monday – Friday	13–16, 18–21

In this evaluation study profitability potential has been delimited to mean coverage of costs in distribution activities. Thus, if the average cost of delivery for one of the above delivery options falls below the amount charged for delivery, this delivery option will be considered to have potential for becoming profitable. At the time data were collected for this evaluation the amount charged for attended home delivery was between €9 and €11.[4]

Evaluation Process

The central performance measure in the evaluation study is delivery cost per order. However, a number of physical performance measures will also be briefly analysed: vehicle load factor, number of deliveries per hour, number of kilometres per delivery, and finally number of vehicles required to satisfy demand. Parameter values were acquired from one of the leading Swedish distribution companies with vast experience of e-grocery home deliveries. Table 10.2 below shows the parameter values in the evaluation process.

Table 10.2 Parameter values

Parameter	Value
Loading time at depot	30 min
Unloading time at depot	15 min
Unloading time at customers' doorsteps	7 min
Vehicle capacity	12 m^3
Vehicle cost per hour	€10
Number of vehicles	Unlimited
Manpower cost per hour (driver)	€23
Minimum driving time between delivery stops	2 min

Manpower cost includes bonuses for inconvenient working hours, since some of the delivery time windows take place in the evening. Minimum driving time between delivery stops was set to two minutes, since Plan-LogiX would otherwise (as a consequence of a restriction of details in the map database) aggregate adjacent delivery stops and thereby risks giving deceptive results. The parameter value for vehicle capacity applies to a refrigerated van with a capacity of 12 m^3, which equals approximately 15 average e-grocery orders in the stores included in this study.

The two typical cases of delivery options included in the evaluation process were analysed through the results from iterations in the optimization module of Plan-LogiX during three incremental scenarios with reference to daily demand (see Table 10.3 below). Scenario A, 104 deliveries per day, reflects the situation for one of the major Swedish e-grocers in the autumn of 2001. In scenario B, daily demand is doubled and in scenario C it is multiplied by four, resulting in 208 and 416 deliveries per day respectively.

Table 10.3 Scenarios for evaluated delivery options

Scenario	Number of deliveries per day
A	104
B	208
C	416

Order data for each scenario were generated through a random sample from a customer database with 1656 real order data from a major e-grocer. Thus 20 iterations of order data, based on a random sample with different random seeds, were run in the optimization module for each delivery option, during the three scenarios above. Mean and standard deviation (std.) for every performance measure were calculated for each scenario. The results are presented in Table 10.4.

Evaluation Results

Vehicle load factor is here measured as utilization of the vehicle loading capacity at the beginning of the route. As expected, the load factor increases with a rise in daily demand (see Table 10.4). One would possibly have expected a considerably higher load factor for delivery option 2, since deliveries are carried out within only two delivery time windows, compared with three time windows for delivery option 1. The absence of a significant difference in load factor during scenarios A and B is however a result of insufficient daily demand for creating efficient routes within all three time windows. As a consequence of this, the planned routes for delivery option 1 will extend over two time windows, without the vehicle returning to the depot in between.

Number of deliveries per hour is determined partly by driving time between delivery stops, and partly by time for unloading at customers' doorsteps. The evaluation shows that a rise in daily demand as well as fewer delivery time windows results in increased delivery stop density and, as a consequence of improved conditions for creating efficient routes, driving time between delivery stops is reduced. The improved conditions for efficient routing and scheduling as a consequence of increased delivery stop density are also reflected through number of kilometres per delivery. In scenario A the average *number of kilometres per delivery* was 8.2 for delivery option 1 and 7.7 for delivery option 2. During scenario C the average number of kilometres per delivery decreased to 6.1 and 5.4 respectively.

Table 10.4 Synopsis of evaluation results

Performance measure	Scenario					
	A		B		C	
	Mean	Std	Mean	Std	Mean	Std
Vehicle load factor (%)						
Delivery option 1	70.80	7.40	75.50	8.10	81.20	6.10
Delivery option 2	72.10	10.00	75.40	8.50	86.50	5.90
No. of deliveries/hour						
Delivery option 1	3.10	0.24	3.40	0.18	3.60	0.12
Delivery option 2	3.20	0.26	3.50	0.16	3.80	0.19
No. of km/delivery						
Delivery option 1	8.20	0.94	7.00	0.68	6.10	0.39
Delivery option 2	7.70	0.87	6.40	0.45	5.40	0.24
No. of vehicles required						
Delivery option 1	8.80	0.70	15.90	1.10	30.70	1.30
Delivery option 2	9.10	0.80	16.10	1.00	30.00	3.00
Delivery cost/order (€)						
Delivery option 1	10.60	0.68	9.70	0.51	9.00	0.28
Delivery option 2	10.30	0.75	9.30	0.40	8.70	0.37

Time for unloading at customers' doorsteps includes carrying the goods from the vehicle to the doorstep, unloading the groceries from the packing, receiving payment, and dealing with possible opinions and questions. The period of time required for these activities is not affected by daily demand. The parameter value for unloading time at the customer is set to seven minutes (see Table 10.2). This implies that even if experimenting with very high daily demand, which leads to negligible driving time between delivery stops, the theoretical maximum for this performance measure would be 8.5 deliveries per hour. Since the driving time between two delivery stops was set to a minimum of two minutes in the evaluation, the maximum of the performance measure is restricted to 6.5 deliveries per hour. The only way to increase the number of deliveries per hour is to reduce the unloading time at customers' doorsteps, which can be achieved through implementing distribution solutions based on delivery points or unattended home delivery.

In order to measure *number of vehicles required* for satisfying daily demand during the three scenarios, the parameter value for 'number of vehicles' was set to unlimited. Naturally, the vehicles were allowed to perform several routes per day as well as within each delivery time window, as long as all orders were delivered within the agreed time window. Total numbers of vehicles required to satisfy daily demand during the different scenarios are more or less the same for both delivery options. To meet a daily demand of 416 orders (scenario C) within the agreed delivery time windows, approximately 30 vehicles are required. Delivery options that facilitate evening out of demand over the day would lead to a better degree of utilization of vehicles (more hours per day) and thus reduce the total requirements of resources.

Delivery cost per order has been calculated as total variable cost (vehicle and driver) per route, divided by number of orders in the route. As shown in Figure 10.3 the delivery cost decreases with a rise in daily demand. The development of cost is almost identical for both delivery options, with the difference that the delivery cost is a bit lower for delivery option 2. Thus the evaluation reveals that a delivery option with only two delivery time windows results in a higher cost-efficiency than a delivery option with three delivery time windows.

From the results on delivery cost, it is estimated that delivery options based on attended home delivery can reach profitability provided that daily demand is high enough and that the charge for providing this service remains more or less the same. In other words, with a daily demand of approximately 400 orders (scenario C), it should be possible to cover the variable costs associated with attended home delivery for e-grocery. As shown in Figure 10.3 the delivery cost for scenario C is €9.0 and €8.7 for delivery options 1 and 2 respectively, and these costs equal or fall below the delivery fees (€9–11) charged at the time of the data collection (autumn 2001).

At the time of the data collection, the major Swedish e-grocery actors had a daily demand of 400 to 900 orders *per week*, which is far from the critical volume of approximately 400 orders *per day*. In order to be able to offer customers such freedom of choice regarding day of delivery and delivery time window as in delivery options 1 and 2, a considerable increase in daily demand is required in order to cover delivery costs. As we have already seen, the majority of the early e-grocery initiatives in Sweden have terminated with profitability problems as the main reason, in part as a result of inability to cover variable costs related to delivering the goods.

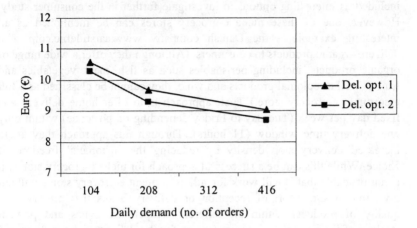

Figure 10.3 Delivery cost per order (€)

The evaluation study illustrates that an increase in daily demand leads to improved conditions for efficient routing and scheduling, thereby lowering the delivery cost per order. However, the scope for cost savings diminishes as daily demand increases. A breakpoint will appear at a certain level of daily demand, above which the conditions for efficient routing and scheduling hardly improve at all. For this reason, it is of great importance that a satisfactory level of delivery cost is achieved at that point. At the moment it seems uncertain if or at least when the market for e-grocery will become large enough for delivery options like those evaluated in this study to break even. Therefore alternative ways of creating *forced* delivery stop density must be looked for. Forced density can be explained as a way of achieving increased delivery stop density by means of offering restricted delivery options with respect to freedom of choice. One approach to create forced density is to divide the market area into different geographical zones, within which the customers are restricted to choosing delivery on only a few days per week, depending on zone. This approach guarantees that deliveries to the different zones are aggregated on the same days, thus creating a forced delivery stop density. Examples of delivery options other than those evaluated in this study that can be assumed to have potential to become profitable at lower levels of daily demand are: delivery options with longer delivery time windows; delivery options based on delivery points; and finally unattended home delivery. Since this chapter only deals with full assortment e-grocery stores (see first page for definition), other delivery options that might be successful for different niche e-grocery stores are not included as interesting options to investigate further in the consumer study. However, one of these niche e-grocery stores can be mentioned as an interesting example – the Danish company www.aarstiderne.com who delivers organic products to consumers. (Although they offer a wide range of organic products, including perishables such as fish, meat, vegetables and fruit as well as colonial products and wine, they cannot be classified as a full assortment e-grocery store.) Their approach is to offer home delivery one fixed day per week (Tuesday to Friday depending on postcode) within only one delivery time window (11 hours). Through this approach they attain increased delivery stop density by reducing the customers' freedom of choice. While this can be a successful approach for niche e-grocery stores, it is not probable that it will work for full assortment e-grocery stores without investing in some sort of reception or delivery boxes that preserve the quality of products within all different temperature zones and prevent stealing of the goods. A common feature for the delivery options discussed above, which all aim at creating forced density, is an adaptation to conditions from the distribution point of view, with the primary objective to create opportunities for more efficient routing and scheduling. Some of the options entail limitations of the customers' freedom of choice. Besides, for options based on unattended home delivery it is unclear who should bear the financial risk associated with investment in reception facilities. Is it possible to expect customers to participate in developing delivery options based on unattended home delivery by partially bearing the investment cost? The answer to this and other questions related to the consumers' attitudes to the above mentioned delivery options, which according to the evaluation study have potential to become profitable, will be presented in the next section.

CONSUMER STUDY – RESULTS

In Table 10.5, background data of the participants in the focus group study and the respondents of the web survey are shown. As expected, the majority of consumers are relatively young, with about 80% being below 40 years of age. Also the majority of the web respondents (70%) are women. Regarding household composition, normally two adults live together with one or more children.

An unexpectedly high share of the focus group participants have no access to cars and live in blocks of flats. The common opinion, which has been confirmed in interviews with e-grocers, is that the majority of e-grocery customers live in single-family houses in the suburbs, and that they normally have access to a car (Karlsson and Rosén 2002). One possible explanation for the deviation in the focus group study is that the sessions were held at the School of Economics and Commercial Law in central Göteborg, and that persons living nearby were more willing to participate since it was more convenient for them than persons living in more distant housing areas.

Table 10.5 Descriptive statistics of the participant and respondent profile (%)

Measure	Item	Focus group	Web survey
Gender	Female	52*	70
	Male	48*	30
Age	< 40	83	80
	> 40	17	20
Household with children	Yes	70	81
	No	30	19
Number of adults in household	One	0	12
	Two	96	85
	Three	4	3
Number of children in household	Zero	31	19
	One	17	21
	Two	31	43
	Three	17	13
	Four or more	4	4
Type of housing	Single-family house	13	49
	Block of flats	87	51
Access to car	Yes	48	77
	No	52	23

Notes:
* Governed by the criteria of selection (two female groups and two male groups).

An explanation for the palpable difference between focus group participants and web survey respondents regarding access to a car could be derived from the difference in type of housing, since a higher share of web survey respondents live in single-family houses (often in the suburbs), where access to a car is more probable than in housing areas with block of flats (often in the inner cities).

Focus Group Study

In all four focus group sessions much time and attention was given to discussing the significance as well as the meaning of the term 'convenience', above all in relation to e-grocery. The primary reason for the participants to use e-grocery services is convenience. The participants' definition of the term convenience (related to e-grocery shopping) can be divided into two categories: on the one hand convenience is seen as *not* having to visit a traditional grocery store with all its related stressful moments, on the other hand the foremost meaning of convenience is *not* having to carry heavy grocery bags from the store (or the car) to the doorstep. The focus group study states very clearly that possibility of having home delivery is a question of vital importance for using e-grocery services.

A majority of the participants did not consider delivery points a feasible option at all. However, those participants that found delivery points a feasible option had one condition: that the delivery point is located within easy reach either along the way to work or near the house. Moreover, the delivery points' opening hours would have to be generous, above all in the evening. Finally, the price charged for delivering the goods is an important factor when considering different delivery options. Since the participants consider delivery point an inferior option with respect to service content, this must be reflected in a lower price.

A majority of the participants did not consider unattended home delivery based upon reception boxes as a conceivable delivery option. The immediate reactions were centred on potential problems related to such a system. First, reception boxes were not seen as a realistic solution for people living in blocks of flats, and second, the participants were concerned about their boxes being damaged. About a third of the participants expressed a positive attitude to the extra service content that the reception boxes imply, namely not having to stay at home during the entire delivery time window in order to receive the goods. The fact that as many as two thirds of the participants expressed a negative attitude towards reception boxes, could be explained by the circumstance that the great majority live in blocks of flats. Furthermore, the fact that only a few of the participants had ever heard of reception boxes prior to the focus group session probably contributes to their opinion of the solution as being unrealistic. Even though the focus group participants thought of a delivery option based on attended home delivery with a two to three hour delivery time window as acceptable, the majority would appreciate an introduction of different service levels with the possibility of choosing a shorter delivery time window in exchange for a higher delivery fee and vice versa. Primarily the participants living in households without children would appreciate a higher service level with shorter delivery time windows.

Thus the focus group study indicates that e-grocery is very strongly associated with home delivery. Many of the participants clearly expressed that attended home delivery is a prerequisite for them to use e-grocery services. Other delivery options (i.e. mainly unattended home delivery and delivery points) discussed in the focus group sessions were in general considered to be inferior e-grocery delivery options, and should consequently be priced lower. The results from the focus group study thus indicate that attended home delivery and possibly unattended home delivery (provided that the potential problems the participants were concerned about can be avoided) can be considered to be realistic e-grocery delivery options.

Web survey

The web survey confirms that the preferred delivery option is attended home delivery, with unrestricted freedom of choice regarding both delivery day and delivery time window. As shown in Table 10.6 as many as 84% of the respondents consider attended home delivery to be a good or a very good delivery option. Many of the respondents seized the opportunity to make a comment that the very point of using e-grocery is the home delivery service. If the possibility to get home delivery disappeared, they would stop using e-grocery services and go back to do their shopping in the traditional way.

Besides attended home delivery, collection points are the delivery option valued highest by the web survey respondents. About 38% of them regard collection points as a good or very good delivery option. It should be noted that attended home delivery and collection points were the only eligible options for most respondents. More than 77% of them have experience of attended home delivery, and 36% have experience of collection points. Only a fraction of the respondents (about 6%) have experience of either delivery points or unattended home delivery.

The reason for including attended home delivery with a fixed timetable is to study the respondents' adjustment between freedom of choice regarding day of delivery and the length of the delivery time window. This delivery option was restricted in the sense that the customer was permitted to book delivery either in the daytime or in the evening on only two predetermined days per week. It is the distributor who decides within which delivery time window the goods will be delivered, and in exchange for this reduction in freedom of choice, the delivery time window is reduced to 30 minutes.

About 40% of the respondents found this delivery option to be good or very good.

Table 10.6 Customers' valuation of different delivery options (%)

Delivery option	Bad/ Very bad	Indifferent	Good/ Very good
Attended home delivery [a]	4	8	84
Attended home delivery - fixed timetable [b]	35	22	40
Delivery points in general	42	27	22
Place of work	43	19	30
Preschool or similar [c]	35	26	36
Collection points	34	21	38
Unattended home delivery (reception box)	28	27	37

Notes:
a Freedom of choice regarding both day of delivery and delivery time window
b Delivery can be booked both in the daytime and in the evening on two predetermined days per week. The distributor decides within what delivery time window the goods shall be delivered. In exchange for the reduction in freedom of choice, the delivery time window is reduced to 30 minutes.
c Since e-grocery customers often live in households with children the idea behind this option is that it might be appealing for these customers to be able to collect their groceries at the preschool, kindergarten, etc. at the same time as they pick up their children.

In addition to the options in Table 10.6 the respondents were asked to value two more delivery options in order to study how different service levels are valued by the customers in monetary terms. The first of these options meant that the customer could get a reduction in delivery fee if the distributor (according to operational conditions) decided which day the customer would get his/her delivery. About 63% of the respondents would accept this delivery option provided that the delivery fee was reduced by approximately €5 on average. Thus it is obvious that the customers require a significant incentive (here in the shape of a price reduction) in order to be forced to accept delivery on a day determined by the distributor.

The second of these additional options examines how the respondents value the length of the delivery time window in monetary terms. The great majority, more than 80%, showed no interest in having a shorter delivery time window in return for an increased delivery fee. A hypothetical option where the delivery time window was reduced from three hours to two and one hours respectively was found appealing to no more than 10% and 16% respectively. On average, these respondents were willing to accept a €2.6

increase in price in return for a two hour delivery time window, and a €4.6 increase in price in return for a one hour delivery time window. Correspondingly, 77% of the respondents showed no interest in having a reduced delivery fee in return for a prolonged delivery time window. A hypothetical option where the delivery time window was prolonged from three hours to four and five hours respectively, was found appealing to 17% and 16% respectively. On average, these respondents wanted the delivery fee to decrease by €4.4 in order to accept a four hour delivery time window and by €5.8 in order to accept a five hour delivery time window.

As shown in Table 10.6, 22% of the respondents regard delivery points in general as a good or a very good delivery option. It should be noted though, that the special cases of delivery points, at place of work and pre-school or similar, are regarded as a good or a very good delivery option by a significantly higher share of the respondents compared with delivery points in general. Only 11% of the respondents would unconditionally consider choosing delivery points as an alternative to attended home delivery. On the other hand, 55% would consider choosing delivery points if at least one of the following conditions applied:

- Delivery points render a lower delivery fee than attended home delivery
- The delivery point is located near the house
- The delivery point has very generous opening hours.

The most important condition for accepting delivery points as a delivery option is that they are located near the respondents' houses. For about 40% this is a paramount condition. For 24% of the respondents, a lower delivery fee for delivery points compared with attended home delivery was a prerequisite for considering choosing them. On average, the respondents required the delivery fee to be about €5 lower than for attended home delivery. Thus, for these respondents, a significant reduction in delivery fee was necessary for delivery points to be considered equal to attended home delivery. At the time of the web survey (December 2001), the leading Swedish e-grocers charged €9–11 for attended home delivery. More than 30% of the respondents would not, even though all three conditions existed, consider choosing delivery points as an alternative to attended home delivery. The most frequent reason for this was that the respondents did not want to carry heavy grocery bags from the delivery point (or the car, if the delivery point is not located near the house) to the house.

As shown in Table 10.6, 37% of the respondents found unattended home delivery based on a reception box to be an interesting option. Earlier studies have pointed out the potential for savings that lie in delivery options based on reception boxes (Punakivi and Tanskanen 2002). The potential for savings is created by improved conditions for efficient routing and scheduling for the distributor as a consequence of not having restrictions for every order to be delivered within a specified delivery time window. The drawback of a delivery option based on reception boxes is, as we have seen earlier, high investment costs, and moreover, savings (as a result of more efficient routing and scheduling) are not big enough to cover the investment costs (see e.g. Kämäräinen 2001b). According to calculations on payback time for an investment in reception boxes, the customers have to contribute to the financing of the investment (Punakivi et al. 2001). With the purpose of revealing the web customers' attitudes towards contributing to financing an investment in reception boxes, they were asked to value the following four offers on a five point scale from very bad to very good:

1. The respondent buys a personal reception box for €500 and gets 50% off on all deliveries.

2. The respondent hires a personal reception box for €60 per month and gets four free deliveries per month.

3. The respondent buys a reception box jointly with other households (neighbours)[5] for €500 and they get 50% off on all their deliveries.

4. The respondent hires a reception box jointly with other households (neighbours)[5] for €60 per month and together they get four free deliveries per month.

The results from the customers' valuation of these offers are summarized in Table 10.7, indicating a clear negative attitude towards contributing to the financing of the reception boxes.

Table 10.7 Customers' attitudes towards different ways of financing reception boxes (%)

Offer	Bad/ Very bad	Indifferent	Good/ Very good
1	90	7	3
2	72	15	13
3	79	14	7
4	65	18	17

Thus it is obvious that the respondents do not value the advantages of a delivery option based on reception boxes highly enough to be willing to contribute to the financing of the investment, neither through buying nor hiring a box, at least not for the amounts mentioned in the web survey offers.

DISCUSSION

In the consumer study the web customers' attitude towards delivery options with differing service content, different types of delivery points and delivery options based on unattended home delivery were investigated. The results clearly indicate that e-grocery shopping is strongly associated with home delivery, and the preferred delivery option for the majority of the respondents is attended home delivery.

Based on the results from the three studies presented in this chapter, attended home delivery is considered to be the most realistic e-grocery delivery option. Within the scope of attended home delivery there exist possibilities of creating forced delivery stop density as described above. However, the consumer study shows that a significant reduction in delivery fee is required in order to get the customers to accept the restriction in freedom of choice that follows with forced delivery stop density. In any case, an increase in delivery stop density is a prerequisite for covering the costs in distribution activities associated with attended home delivery, given the volume of daily demand and delivery fee in 2001/2002. One might think that a reasonable solution for increasing delivery stop density could be cooperation between several e-grocers in the same market area. However, interviews with the leading Swedish e-grocers[6] (in the year 2000) revealed that cooperation among competing e-grocers is not seen as a possible solution due to fierce competition (Karlsson and Rosén 2002).

One delivery option that many have set great hopes on is unattended home delivery. The consumer study shows that a relatively high share of the respondents in principle would accept unattended home delivery provided that they did not have to contribute to financing the reception facility. Probably, this unwillingness hampers the introduction of delivery options based on reception boxes in the Swedish market in the near future, since the costs associated with investments in reception boxes are higher than estimated savings from unattended home delivery options. The remaining option then, is unattended home delivery based on delivery boxes, since they lead to a lower investment cost than reception boxes, while creating the same improved conditions for efficient routing and scheduling. In order for unattended home delivery based on delivery boxes to become a realistic delivery option, however, an efficient reverse flow for collecting empty boxes has to be developed.

Only one respondent in every ten would unconditionally consider choosing a system with delivery points as an alternative to attended home delivery, given equal delivery fees for both options. The principal condition for considering choosing a system with delivery points as an alternative to attended home delivery is that the delivery point is located near the house. By fulfilling this condition, a large portion of the potential for improved efficiency in routing and scheduling disappears, since a large number of delivery points would be required in order to satisfy the customers' condition of closeness to their homes. Possibly, the special cases of delivery points at place of work and pre-school or similar, have a potential for being realistic delivery options, since they were valued higher than delivery points in general by the web survey respondents.

Finally, a comment on to what extent the results in this chapter can be transferred to other markets and countries. Like studies on the Finnish market for e-grocery (Tanskanen 2000; Kämäräinen 2001a), the results from the evaluation process show the importance of high delivery stop density. However, it should be mentioned that parameter values of input data differ, hence direct comparisons are difficult to make. With reference to the results from the consumer study, no similar studies (with a clear focus on the attitudes and preferences towards different delivery options) have been found. Therefore no parallels are drawn to other countries. Furthermore, when it comes to whether the results are transferable to other markets, the results from the focus group study (Karlsson and Rosén 2002) clearly state that attitudes and preferences regarding delivery options differ between groceries and other types of products (e.g. books, clothes, electronics, etc.). There is a considerably stronger connection between e-grocery and home delivery than between other types of products and home delivery. Collection points seem to be a good or acceptable delivery option for other types of products. Thus it is not likely that the results can be transferred to e-retailing for other products.

CONCLUSIONS

This chapter presents the different e-grocery delivery options that are dealt with in theory and practice. These delivery options are home delivery on the one hand, and collection points and delivery points on the other hand. In answer to the question 'What profitability potential have e-grocery delivery options put into practice in Sweden up to now?' the results from the evaluation study show that these delivery options (i.e. attended home delivery with unrestricted freedom of choice regarding day of delivery and delivery time window) have a good chance to become profitable provided there is daily demand of approximately 400 orders and given that the charge for providing this service stays at about €9–11. From the results of the consumer study it can be concluded that e-grocery is strongly connected with home delivery and that the most preferred delivery option is attended home delivery.

The primary value of this research lies in the identification of realistic delivery options for e-grocery given the conditions on the Swedish market, which has been done through investigation and consideration of the conditions for the retailers and logistics service providers as well as the attitudes and preferences of the customers. The realistic e-grocery delivery options are above all attended home delivery with imposed restrictions regarding freedom of choice but possibly also unattended home delivery based on delivery boxes.

Further research will evolve in several directions. First of all, the identified realistic delivery options will be evaluated by means of a routing and scheduling tool in order to capture the cost structure and critical volume for each option. Moreover, since unattended home delivery seems a promising alternative for e-grocery, the Swedish households' readiness and attitudes, as well as the option's physical and technical conditions, need to be investigated further. Finally, it would also be interesting to conduct cross-cultural research on the topic to find out to what extent these results are country-specific or can be translated into other countries.

NOTES

1. Svensk Handel (The Swedish Federation of Trade) ceased to perform measurements of e-commerce's share of total retail sales in 2002.
2. As Figure 10.1 above revealed, all but one of the central e-grocery initiatives have been terminated, which is the reason why this chapter is based on data collected in 2001/2002 and not on more recent data.
3. Developed by DPS International (http://www.dps-int.com/)
4. In October 2004 the only remaining centralized e-grocery store in Sweden, www.netxtra.se, charged between €8.25 and €10 for attended home delivery, depending on distance between delivery address and picking facility. In addition to the delivery fee, a picking fee of €5.5 was charged. NetXtra also offered collection points as a delivery option and for this only the picking fee was charged.
5. Since this offer signifies that the households use the same reception box, they cannot receive goods on the same day.
6. www.expressfood.kf.se, www.spar.se, and www.willys.nu.

REFERENCES

Bloor, Michael, Jane Frankland et al. (2001), *Focus groups in social research*, London, UK and Thousand Oaks, US: Sage Publications.

Delden, Peter, Anders Hansson et al. (2001), *E-handel i Sverige – En explorativ studie*, Stockholm: Konkurrensverket.

Englund, Björn (2004), 'Suget efter nätmat ökar', <http://www.dagenshandel.se/otw/archive.nsf/0/5F053755E863ADDFC1256F1E003763AD?open>, downloaded 23 September 2004.

Forsebäck, Lennart (2001), *Cybershoppare, intermediärer & digitala handelsmän – Elektronisk handel i ett hushållsperspektiv*, Stockholm: KFB & Teldok.

Frostling-Henningsson, Maria (2002). *What is wrong with the net grocery store?*, Stockholm: School of Business, Stockholm University.

<http://www.peapod.com/corpinfo/GW_index.jhtml>, downloaded 31 October 2004.

<http://www.svenskhandel.se> (1999-2002), 'Internetindikatorn', Stockholm: Svensk Handel.

Jansson, David (2000), 'Stort intresse för att handla mat på nätet', *Supermarket* (1–2), 9.

Karlsson, Elisabeth and Peter Rosén (2002), *Leveransalternativ för e-handel med dagligvaror*, Göteborg: School of Economics and Commercial Law, Göteborg University.

Karlsson, Elisabeth and Peter Rosén (2002), *Distributionsalternativ för e-handel med dagligvaror*, Stockholm: VINNOVA.

Kämäräinen, Vesa (2000), *Supply Chain for e-commerce and home delivery in the food industry*, Helsinki: Helsinki University of Technology.

Kämäräinen, Vesa (2001a), 'New approach to retailing in the digital economy', in Gunnar Stefansson and Bernhard Tilanus (eds), *Collaboration in Logistics*, proceedings of the 13th Annual Nordic Conference on Logistics Research NOFOMA 14 – 15 June in Reykjavik, Göteborg: Chalmers University of Technology.

Kämäräinen, Vesa (2001b), 'The reception box impact on home delivery efficiency in the e-grocery business', *International Journal of Physical Distribution & Logistics Management*, 31 (6), 414–426.

Kämäräinen, Vesa, Johanna Småros et al. (2001), 'Cost-effectiveness in the e-grocery business', *International Journal of Retail & Distribution Management*, 29 (1), 41–48.

Moore, Kelley, Celena Kingson and Kelly Sherman (2004), *Final e-strategy report*, Austin, TX: Whole Foods Market.

Morgan, David L. (1997), *Focus groups as qualitative research*, London, UK and Thousand Oaks, US: Sage Publications.

OECD (2002), *Measuring the information economy*, Paris: OECD Publications.

Punakivi, Mikko and Juha Saranen (2001) 'Identifying the success factors in e-grocery home delivery', *International Journal of Retail & Distribution Management*, 29 (4), 156–163.

Punakivi, Mikko and Kari Tanskanen (2002), 'Increasing the cost efficiency of e-fulfilment using shared reception boxes', *International Journal of Retail & Distribution Management*, 30 (10), 498–507.

Punakivi, Mikko, Hannu Yrjölä and Jan Holmström (2001), 'Solving the last mile issue: reception box or delivery box?', *International Journal of Physical Distribution & Logistics Management*, 31 (6), 427–439.

Tanskanen, Kari (2000), *Logistical strategies for electronic grocery shopping*, Helsinki: Helsinki University of Technology.

Yrjölä, Hannu (2001), 'Physical distribution considerations for electronic grocery shopping', *International Journal of Physical Distribution & Logistics Management*, 31 (10), 746–761.

11. Packaging Trends for E-Commerce Shipments in the United States: A Focus on Perishables!

S. Paul Singh

INTRODUCTION

This decade has shown a tremendous increase in the use of small parcel direct shipments of products from manufacturers to consumers. The increase in *e-shopping* (buying and selling products through the Internet) has become very popular. As a result small parcel delivery companies such as United Parcel Service (UPS), Federal Express (FedEx), United States Postal Service (USPS), Roadway Packaging Services (RPS), Airborne Express, etc. have grown significantly over the past decade. This trend of shipping manufactured goods, is now also being used by growers of premium fresh produce to sell their products directly to the consumer over the Internet.

A significant development in the last decade is the increasing complexity of the types of products that are being shipped in this environment. This complexity is associated with the increased weight and size of packages that the single parcel delivery companies can handle. In addition they have greatly expanded their distribution networks for both domestic and international shipments. There have been several previous studies conducted by the author and other researchers that have measured and analyzed the parcel environment for these types of distribution environments (Singh and Cheema 1996; Singh and Voss 1992; Singh, Newsham, and Pierce 1999; Marcondes 1998; Pierce 1999; Singh and Hays 2000; Buechner 2000;Welby and McGregor 1997 and Burgess 1999). It is important to quantify the environment that these packages face in order to develop laboratory test methods to better design and evaluate packages for shipment.

Based on a survey cited by Business Week [1], the number of consumer e-commerce sites had multiplied tenfold during the last ten months of 1999. An estimated 26 million Americans shopped on-line between Thanksgiving and New Year (1999), and total on-line sales grew over $5 billion in 1999.

However the dot-com bubble burst of 2000 led to several companies that filed for bankruptcy. However, despite the loss of business, several companies emerged stronger after this period. A lot of their success was attributed to factors such as order-fulfillment, package improvements, improved delivery, tracking, and customer satisfaction. The on-line retail sales continued to grow in the United States and were estimated to exceed 40 billion in 2001. In 2002 Amazon the largest US based retailer showed its annual sales exceed $1 billion. The same year WalMart the biggest retailer also became the biggest US company in sales exceeding $230 billion. This clearly shows that while consumers continue looking for cost savings for a majority of retail goods, the e-commerce business has also grown to serve a select few based on direct delivery and for the higher value and time-sensitive products.

A majority of products that were initially launched and sold by various e-commerce companies directly to consumers included books, videos, compact discs, toys, and apparel products. These products are generally very rugged and do not require significant package protection. Leaders in direct consumer sales including amazon.com, columbiahouse.com, toysrus.com, etc., clearly identified that for a majority of these products, order fulfillment was the most critical thing. It is important for such companies to align themselves with manufacturers and suppliers that can provide quick replenishment[2]. The big winners in e-commerce retail sales are companies that know how to warehouse merchandise and pick, pack, and ship customer orders in a timely manner while maintaining product integrity.

During early introductions of e-commerce packages, there was a lot of concern on over-packaging both by shippers and customers. It is important to realize that the challenges and demands for protection for single parcel shipments (e-tailer sold packages) are much higher than those required for shipping palletized loads of product to traditional store based retailers. As a result most e-commerce designed packaging may represent as much as 100-400% in addition to the product by weight or volume. These results have been shown for various packages that are sensitive to physical damage[3]. Another way to describe this is:

The inherent weakness of products is overcome by using optimum packaging to meet the challenges of the shipping and handling environment.

The single parcel shipping environment is significantly more severe in terms of physical and climatic changes, when compared to conventional retail distribution methods where products are palletized and handled in temperature controlled transportation environments. The amount of packaging required for the same products is therefore significantly different.

This paper focuses on the various parameters that are critical in the development of optimum packaging for fresh produce to be sold using e-commerce directly to the consumer. Fruits, vegetables, and fresh flowers, are all live and respiring products and therefore have a limited life after being harvested. They require protection from adverse conditions of temperature, humidity, physical abuse, control of respiration gases, and microbial activity. This paper identifies these various parameters and provides a reference source of materials that can be used to develop custom packaging. Direct consumer sales of fresh produce, meats, and seafood generally involve a high value product, and require a high degree of customer satisfaction.

Produce Protection Requirements

Most fresh produce (fruits, vegetables, and flowers) that are harvested to be shipped directly to customers by e-commerce companies face some severe challenges in the shipping environment. Most of these companies often use one or more of single parcel delivery companies to deliver these packages. The environment varies significantly depending on the type of service, which depends on delivery time (next-day, second day, 3-7 days, etc.) for both domestic and overseas shipments. Fresh produce is extremely sensitive to the following elements of the shipping environment.

Temperature and Humidity

Since fresh produce continues to respire after being harvested, this causes an intake of oxygen and release of carbon-di-oxide. The respiration rate of fruits, vegetables, and flowers is dependent on temperature. An increase in package storage temperature results in an exponential increase in respiration rate that shortens the shelf life of the produce, resulting in eventual decay. The United States Department of Agriculture has documented this information on recommended storage temperature, relative humidity, and approximate shelf life for various fresh produce (Welby and McGregor1997). Also since most fresh produce have high moisture content it is important to maintain a high humidity environment during the transportation environment, so as to reduce any moisture loss that would result in drying of the produce. USDA recommends a high humidity environment (80-95% Relative Humidity) for most fresh produce.

In order to maintain these storage conditions in the package, various studies have been conducted by the School of Packaging, Michigan State University, that assist in the design of insulating packages (Burgess 1999). Most of the packages studied range in size from 0.5 to 5 cu. ft. and vary in construction from ordinary expanded polystyrene to various liner-in-box arrangements with and without aluminum foil surfaces. This study allows users to measure the package R-value[4], and therefore determine if additional refrigerant (regular ice, dry ice, gel packs) is required for a given produce based on temperature levels and delivery times.

Temperature and Humidity are often the most critical parameters that affect the quality of fresh produce. Certain single parcel shipping companies are offering customers the choice of insulated packages with or without refrigerants for such shipments[5].

Shock, Vibration, and Compression

The presence of various dynamic and static forces that occur during storage, shipping and handling can have a severe impact on the quality of fresh produce. Vibration and impact forces can lead to bruising and cutting in fruits and vegetables. This accelerates the respiration rate and also could result in microbial activity due to contact with other materials. It is important to provide a degree of shock and vibration isolation to produce items inside the package. Often packaging materials that provide this protection (bubble wrap, extruded plank foams) offer both physical and insulating properties and therefore can be ideal for these applications.

Presence of Gases

Due to the respiration process, fresh produce absorbs oxygen and releases carbon dioxide. The concentration levels of O_2 and CO_2 can affect the shelf life of fresh produce. These factors would be critical if modified atmosphere packaging concepts are used where the produce is contained in a sealed pouch or container. Lower concentration of O_2 levels will slow down the respiration rate thereby prolonging the shelf life.

Microbial Activity

In the case of modified atmosphere packages it may be critical to inhibit any microbial spoilage due to fungal activity. This can be achieved by introducing various types of gases in the headspace of the package. Carbon monoxide, which is a colorless, odorless, and tasteless is an effective microbial inhibitor. It can inhibit the growth of many bacteria, yeasts and molds when used in small concentrations of about 1%. However due to its high toxicity and explosive nature at higher concentrations CO should be handled with extreme care. Sulfur dioxide has also been used as a microbial inhibitor for a wide range of fresh produce, seafood, and meat products. In aqueous solutions it forms sulfite compounds, which inhibit bacteria. However in recent years, use of SO_2 has come under regulatory scrutiny (Kader, Zagory, and Kerbel 1988).

Presence of Volatile Gases

The presence of ethylene gas, which is a plant hormone, can induce rapid ripening and senescence in many types of produce. It may be important to reduce concentrations of ethylene in the package to enhance shelf life. Also various other volatile gases may be responsible for off odors in fruits and vegetables. Various types of absorbers are available to absorb ethylene and other off odor volatiles.

E-Commerce Packaging Trends

In an ongoing research project at Michigan State University, packages of fresh produce are ordered every year and evaluated for void fill, insulation materials, use of gel or dry ice, package integrity and customer appeal graphics. Results show that most catalog based companies like Harry and David who transformed into an e-commerce business show very good choices of packaging while new comers have struggled trying to optimize the produce quantity, with appropriate amount of coolant and insulation from packaging materials. Also the post-harvest handling of fresh produce and flowers is critical in e-commerce package shipments.

Comparison of Good and Poor Packaging Concepts

In the section at the end of this chapter are pictures of packaging representing various perishables shipments. Sometimes a company may introduce a package that is perceived to be better based on the choice of materials and internal components. An example is the first package introduced by Proflowers and used in 2000. As seen in the pictures strips of expanded polystyrene (EPS) foam that is a good insulating material are laminated to the inside of the corrugated box. However due to the presence of scores in the box material (region between folds), the EPS does not fully seal the inside contents of the box but continues to allow cold air to leak in the edges and corners. In fact even the use of insulated gel products as seen in these early pictures did not offer any significant protection to the product in maintaining a low temperature control. As a result of studies conducted at Michigan State University, it was determined that there is no advantage of using laminated foam or gel packs. It is more critical to do a better job with post-harvest treatment of flowers before they are shipped and guarantee an early morning delivery. As a result the new package and components shown in the Proflowers example from 2003 demonstrates this.

Another example is a comparison of thermally insulated containers and internal refrigerants used for meat products. The samples from Harris Farms contain gel packs and the insulated EPS foam container is a commercially available package. The temperature control of the meat products in these packages was limited when compared to similar products in packaging developed by Omaha Steaks. The Omaha Steak EPS containers are custom developed with a 1.5 inch wall thickness (compared to 1 inch for Harris Farms) and have an internal groove for a sealed tight fit. The containers are also shrink-wrapped so that the lids never get loose in the harsh shipping single parcel shipping environment. Furthermore Omaha Steak uses dry ice as a refrigerant, which has an increasingly superior cooling performance as compared to wet ice that is used by Harris Farms.

In terms of shipping live plants, shipments of bonsai trees (a small size, but high value perishable) were compared between Bonsai Boy of New York and Harry and David. The design of Bonsai Boy of New York package is low in cost and easy to fulfill. It consists of a top loaded corrugated box where the potted plant is placed in the box and then top loaded with loose fill cushioning. Since parcel carriers have very little control of the shipping orientation, the boxes most likely travel on their sides (most stable configuration) thereby resulting in damage to leaves, fruit and branches during transport. On the contrary the Harry and David pace design is more complex. It uses a die cut corrugated box with insert and locking tabs that restrict the free movement of the potted plant inside the shipping container even when shipped on its side.

Similarly various fruit packages are shown with different internal packaging ranging from plastic wraps to natural fiber based straw cushions. Again while the straw cushions may be perceived to be protective, these materials are highly abrasive and can result in surface bruising of high value fruit. It may therefore have to be wrapped, which on the contrary may result in quicker ripening.

CONCLUSIONS

In conclusion it is critical to understand the interaction of the various elements of the shipping environment for the single parcel environment and their affect on fresh produce shipments to the consumer. The choice of packaging system in most cases is customized to types of fresh produce and their respiration and biological activity during shipping.

Examples Of E-Commerce Perishables Package Shipments

The various pictures shown below describe examples of e-commerce package shipments by various companies in the United States in 2002 and 2003. These include fruits, vegetables, meats, seafood, fresh flowers and plants [12].

2002 SHIPMENTS

Diamondorganics.com

HarryandDavid.com

Halegroves.com

HarryandDavid.com

Proflowers.com

Omahasteak.com

HarryandDavid.com

Harrisfarms.com   **Proflowers.com**

Proflowers.com

2003 SHIPMENTS

Harry and David

Bonsai Boy of New York

Gotfruit.com

Harry and David

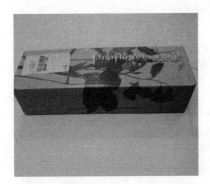 

Proflowers

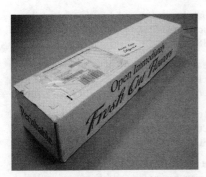 

Rosesonline.com

NOTES

1. Buechner, M. M. (2000), How'd They (E-Companies) Do?, Business Week, January 24,.
2. Se note 1
3. Singh, S. P."Packaging for E-Commerce", Consortium of Distribution Packaging Annual Report, School of Packaging, Michigan State University, USA. 2000-2003
4. R-Value is a measure of the thermal resistance of an insulated container. A higher R-Value indicates a better insulating packaging system.
5. www.dhl-usa.com/thermobox, April 19, 2000.

REFERENCES

Burgess, G.(1999), *"Practical Thermal Resistance and Ice Requirement Calculations for Insulating Packages"*, Packaging Technology and Science, John Wiley & Sons, Vol. 12, 75-80.

Kader, A., D. Zagory, and E. Kerbel (1988), *"Modified Atmosphere Packaging of Fruits and Vegetables"*, CRC Critical Rev. Food Sci. Nut., Vol. 28(1), 1-30.

Marcondes, J. M.(1998), *"MADE Study Update"*, Proceedings of the ISTACON'98, International Safe Transit Association, East Lansing, MI, April.

Pierce, S. (1999), *"Environmental Research: The Latest Transport Data"*,

Proceedings of the ISTACON'99, International Safe Transit Association, East Lansing, MI, April.

Singh, S. P. and T. Voss (1992), *"Drop Heights Encountered in the United Parcel Service Small Parcel Environment in the United States"*, Journal of Testing and Evaluation, ASTM, Vol 20, No. 5, 382-387.

Singh, S. P., and A. Cheema (1996)., "Measurement and Analysis of the Overnight Small Package Shipping Environment for Federal Express and United Parcel Service", *Journal of Testing and Evaluation*, ASTM, Vol. 24, No. 4, 205-211, July.

Singh, S. P., and Z. Hays (2000), "Measurement and Analysis of the United Parcel Service Ground Shipping Environment for Large and Heavy Packages", *ISTACON 2000 Proceedings*, Orlando, FL.

Singh, S. P., M. D. Newsham, and S. Pierce (1999), "Distribution, Parcel Labels Pose Challenges for Drop Orientation", *Packaging Technology and Engineering*, Vol. 8, No. 4.

Welby, E. and B. McGregor (1997), Agricultural Export *Transportation Handbook, USDA.*

12. First-Movers in the E-Grocery Sector – A Framework for Analysis

Mads Vangkilde

INTRODUCTION

Common sense would dictate that in an industry with fierce competition, any new means of offsetting the balance and gaining new customers, higher margins or greater market shares would be exhausted. Of course, new means of competing always involve an element of risk and uncertainty, but once something new has presented itself, it cannot be taken back. So what determines when a new path of competition should be initiated? What determines the dynamics of active initiation or waiting for others to develop a market? In effect, what needs to be uncovered are the motivations and inhibitors of initiating a new idea. This tool is provided via the concept of *First-Mover Advantage* (FMA). The concept of FMA helps to unveil the depth of the situation – from looking at gains and losses to strategic implications and competitive dynamics.

The grocery industry is a prime object of analysis to explore these exact dynamics; that is, for analysis of the grocery industry and its collective response to the opportunity of establishing e-commerce solutions. In Denmark, a few attempts at breaking into this new market have been made, mostly with devastating results. Notably, none have involved the major actors in the industry. A number of reasons explain this lack of success. Most prominent among the different reasons is a lack of attention to operational handling and the implications hereof for overall business success (Kornum et al. 1999; Johnsson and Kornum 2001; Kornum 2002). It seems that the dazzling new possibilities blinded the need for old-fashioned business understanding and handling of materials. Calibrating operational set-up, service level and customer potential have proven lethal to most attempts at establishing e-commerce solutions in this industry – foreign and domestic. The most common answer as to why there has been no renewed interest in entering this new market channel is lack of profitability. Does lack of potential profit really account for the lack of attempts to enter the e-commerce channel? There is little doubt that operational set-up and the ensuing profitability are significant factors regarding the lack of e-commerce solutions.

In this chapter, I propose the concept of FMA as a tool to dissect the complexity of understanding the extent of e-grocery existence. In doing so, I outline the concept of FMA as it has evolved over time. A specific issue that appears pivotal in connection with FMA generally, and with e-grocery initiation specifically is that of durability of advantages. Any given company may or may not be able to harvest advantages from being first. Crucial to understanding why a company would refrain from seeking such advantages in the first place is 'durability'. Durability in connection with competitive advantages is a much-discussed subject. It can be considered both in a context where it is eroded by time and/or money, but also as having a more intangible nature where money and/or time have less of an effect. An advantage should be sustained long enough for a company to break even or earn rents. Given the importance of durability of advantages from an FMA perspective, how does the concept treat this factor? Although accounting for many and very different possible sources of first-mover advantages, the FMA literature contributes very little to understanding concerning the durability of those advantages. I will therefore examine the extent of focus on durability[1] of advantages within the FMA framework.

When dealing with the subject of competitive advantages, two main approaches are favoured. First, the structural or positioning view based on Porter's work (Porter 1980). Here, the foundation of above normal returns originates from a company's position within an industry with lucrative structural characteristics. The industry is the level of analysis, thus implying that relations between actors are critical. Secondly, competitive advantages can be explained via the theoretical perspective: the resource-based view of the firm (RBV). Here, firm resources are assumed to be heterogeneous. Acquiring resources that are valuable, rare and difficult to imitate yields above normal returns for firms (Wernerfelt 1984; Peteraf 1993; Barney 1997). This view focuses on the firm as an isolated entity, leaving the relational aspect unattended. I will argue that the external relationship oriented views as well as the internal resource-based views are right – and both are justified in such a discussion.

To supplement the framework of Porter (1980) dealing primarily with bargaining power and substitutability, I suggest resource dependence theory (Emerson 1962; Pfeffer and Salancik 1978) as the operational tool for the analysis. Ultimately, I suggest a model for understanding the impact of durability in connection with FMA via a combination of the theories of RBV and resource dependence. Hereby, I utilise both a firm specific perspective as well as the relational perspective of competitive advantages. By elaborating on the concept of FMA using a model to evaluate durability of advantages, a powerful tool for the forthcoming analysis of e-grocery existence will emerge.

At this stage, there are no empirical findings to publish, and my contribution will rely on the presentation of the suggested framework. In sum, the aim of this chapter is to:

- Unveil the concept of FMA and its applicability in my PhD dissertation.
- Uncover the extent to which durability of advantages is explored within the literature about FMA.
- Suggest a model for incorporating the element of durability of advantages into the concept of FMA.

FIRST – WHO AND WITH WHAT?

The advantage of being the first to utilise a new business model was derived from theoretical reasoning in which the empirical confirmation proved more difficult to obtain than assumed (Carow et al. 2004). That advantages can be derived from being first would appear to be easily demonstrated via, for example, the actions of the legendary CEO of Sony, Akio Morita. Against all surveys and advice, he chose to pursue the opportunity of introducing a portable cassette player. The success of the Walkman as a product in its own right, and for Sony in general cannot be disputed (Ohmae 1998). The problem in demonstrating the existence of first-mover advantages in general relates to the definition of being first. Is it relevant to differentiate between being the first to have the idea, the first to produce a working model and the first to market it? In practice, these need not be one and the same company. Another problem with defining first-mover advantages concerns the degree of novelty of a new product. With a radically new product such as the Walkman at the time, there can be little doubt. However, most new ideas only result in incremental changes to existing offerings. How big a change is required for a new idea to be considered part of the research in FMA?

Defining a First-Mover

In the context of scientific research, the importance of a definition of first-mover advantages is very significant. However, does this importance transfer to the world of business managers? As there is a close relationship between the profitability of a new business model and the intended market, the answer must be yes. In other words, when one seeks to realise a new business idea, one should consider whether it is realistic to pursue the idea as far as to the introduction into the market. Alternatively, one could look for others to carry the idea into the marketplace. Logically, the first to market an idea is the first-mover. Kerin et al. (1992) describe this very broad perspective as follows:

> A firm can achieve first-mover status in numerous ways. For example, the first firm to (1) produce a new product, (2) use a new process, or (3) enter a new market can claim this distinction. (Kerin et al. 1992, p. 33)

It is difficult to argue with such logic, but as a definition, it is too broad to add further understanding to the matter. For this purpose, it is useful to incorporate the element of profitability:

> First-mover advantages exist when the pioneering firm earns positive present value of profits as the consequence of its early entry (i.e. positive profits net those attributable to more general types of firm proficiency). (Lieberman and Montgomery 1988, p. 51)

This definition effectively captures everything that contributes to making profit from an idea. Earnings from specific endeavours are rarely communicated to broad audiences, and the measure of first-mover advantages is often market share or survival itself. By definition, a pioneer will hold a relatively great share of the market – initially, for no other reason than because the pioneer is creating the particular market. Using market share as a measure for first-mover advantage therefore represents a bias. Attributing the long-term survival of a company to its original first-mover advantages is also difficult as these initial advantages have most likely been supplemented and expanded. Being first is not in itself a guarantee of financial success:

> a head start alone is not sufficient to achieve cost or differentiation advantages over rivals that result in dominant and enduring market shares and abnormal economic returns. (Kerin et al. 1992, p. 34)

In order to gain further understanding, it is beneficial to examine the literature on innovation. Golder and Tellis differentiate between three types of pioneers:

> *Inventor* – the firm(s) that develop(s) patens or important technologies in a new product category.[2]
> *Product pioneer* – the first firm to develop a working model or sample in a new product category.
> *Market pioneer* – the first firm to sell in a new product category. (1993, p. 159)

The term 'market pioneer' coincides with the general perception of what a first-mover is. From the perspective of timing and entrepreneurship, it is important to take into consideration the difference between being dependent on critical new technologies that are prerequisites for your own idea and being the keeper of such radical new innovations, but not having the resources to develop a prototype. Thus the success of a new business idea can be dependent on developments by others, when the ownership over the technology becomes decisive for the market introduction. Considering this perspective, the working definition in this chapter for first-mover advantages relies on the ability of the pioneer to make a profit from the invention – this is in alignment with the definition by Lieberman and Montgomery (1988).

Degrees of Novelty

In 1997, 25,261 new products were launched according to Market Intelligence Service (Fellman 1998). Not all of the producers of the new products were able to claim first-mover advantages, just as they most certainly were not all radical new innovations. In order to understand the significance of radical innovations, it is relevant to look at the matter of change. Cooper (2000) offers some definitions to this effect:

> Alpha Change is a variation measured on a fixed scale. In this context, this kind of change amounts to repositioning a brand in an existing framework, such as a perceptual map. The dimension do not change, nor is there any implied change in what people value. Rather, the attempt is to realign the brand image to capture existing values better.

> Beta Change is a variation on a changing scale. A beta change occurs when values change with a corresponding change in ideal points in a product map. For example, when children finally leave home, parents can indulge their desire for sportier cars. Without any change in brand positioning (i.e. alpha change), sportier cars are preferred because the consumer's values have changed.

> Gamma Change is a variation that can be measured only by adding new perceived dimension to product positioning that redefines the products and ideal points in a perceptual map of a market. If General Motors introduces an electric vehicle, consumers must consider recharging stations; rethink carpooling notions; and reset reliability. These factors change the dimensions of the problem, which is the defining characteristics of gamma change. (2000, p. 2)

Radical change is the equivalent of Gamma Change. Another, and to some degree more simplistic, way of defining novelty is via a typology of only two entities. Denoting incremental change as *continuous innovation*[3] and radical change as *discontinuous innovation*[4] is also far more common in the distinction of innovations. Continuous innovations represent normal upgrading of products that does not require change in the behaviour of the buyer. Discontinuous innovations, on the other hand, require buyers to change behaviour or modify other products/services they rely on (Moore 1998).

The important factor here is the characteristics and definitions that help us understand the nature of terms such as radical or incremental change. Coupling these with the references from the FMA literature provides a complete picture and deeper understanding of the mechanisms involved.

THE HISTORY OF FIRST-MOVER ADVANTAGE

The concept of FMA has been a research matter for some time now, but attention has most often been focused on first-mover advantages as a function of a specific event or as the result of an isolated mechanism. Bain (1956) argued that pioneering brands could build advantages through publicity and preference. Because of the pioneering state of the incumbents' brands, other competitors are unable to compete without massive investments in marketing or drastic reductions in costs. This work by Bain (1956) is not a conceptualisation of first-mover advantages, but rather an example of using FMA as a tool for understanding situations or events. Such an approach to FMA is very common, but leaves a fragmented picture of what first-mover advantages really are. Early on the contributions to the discussion on FMA were dominated by researchers of the *industrial organisation economics* school of thought, in which the principle of FMA relies on the creation of temporal barriers (Demsetz 1982).

Other origins of first-mover advantages may stem from economies of scale. For example, constructing the first plant in a growing market is dependent on correct timing within a duopoly (Rao and Rutenberg 1979). Mansfield et al. (1981) investigate imitation costs versus innovation costs as a source of deterrence for later entrants. Mansfield (1985) elaborates on his early work with a study on technological diffusion. It was found that innovations are often imitated rapidly after introduction, and that the rate of diffusion of technology information is not directly related to the inter-industry ease of imitation of innovations. Rather the concentration of a given industry impacts the costs of imitation of innovations.

Lippman and Mamer (1993) demonstrate the case of extreme first-mover advantages as a result of pre-emptive innovation rendering the market unattractive for competitors. Lippman and Rumelt (1982) introduce the term *uncertain imitability* to allow analytical treatment of causal ambiguity. In applying this term, they demonstrate how models of free-entry industry equilibrium are built. Conrad (1983) studies the price advantage of pioneers over later entrants as a consequence of imperfect information by buyers. This work indicated that price advantages exist for pioneers primarily for products where the purchase frequency is low or where there are high costs associated with product failure. Smiley and Ravid (1983) also investigate prices. This is done in relationship learning. Price in this study could also be expressed as costs – the incumbent is able to reduce his price via learning amassed in the production process and ensuing lower costs.

Schmalensee (1982) attributes first-mover advantages to the uncertainty of buyers towards the products of later competitors. Customers build a preference towards the product of the incumbent because they already know what they get. Urban et al. (1986) demonstrate that in the consumer product category, the order of entry by a brand is inversely related to market share – in favour of the incumbent. Robinson and Fornell (1985) and Robinson (1988) investigate the effect of pioneering advantages in the consumer goods industry and the industrial goods industry respectively. Both these studies propose advantages through switching costs, relative to marketing mix and relative to direct costs. Robinson and Fornell (1985) find a significant advantage by pioneers in the consumer goods industry, as does Robinson (1988) in the industrial goods industry. Robinson and Min (2002) specifically investigate the difference between first- and early movers in the industrial goods industry – confirming the results of the early work stating that pioneers do hold an advantage, even over early entrants. Kardes and Kalyanaram (1992) examine the advantages of pioneering brands specifically in the context of consumer memory and judgement. This study is remarkable for the proposition that pioneering advantages not only exist, but increase over time.

Yet other researchers approach the subject from a game-theoretical perspective. Gal-Or (1985) establishes a model where identical players moving sequentially find that higher profits are bestowed on the first-mover (Stackleberg leader). This work is broadened to investigate the disadvantages of the Stackleberg leader in the presence of incomplete information (Gal-Or 1987). Carpenter and Nakamoto (1990) investigate the persistence of dominant brands when challenged by new competition and find that preference asymmetry affect timing strategies.

Schnaars (1986), Lambkin (1988), Mahajan et al. (1993), Bowman and Gatignon (1996), Shamsie et al. (2004) and Carow et al. (2004) investigate the correlation between order of entry and performance (performance of sales and/or market share). Lambkin (1988) sets out to verify the assumption by managers and academics alike that first-mover advantages exist via an analysis of behaviour and performance by three categories of firms:

pioneers, early followers and late entrants. The study supports two main conclusions – that order of entry is systematically related to competitive performance and that variation in the structures and strategies of the businesses in different entrant categories will moderate this. The study supported the notion of advantages for pioneers in a market.

In 1988, Lieberman and Montgomery published the first article treating FMA on a conceptual level, providing a framework for understanding the components and dynamics of FMA. The origins of first-mover advantages were categorised into three main groups: technological leadership, pre-emption of assets and buyers' switching costs and uncertainty (Lieberman and Montgomery 1988). Kerin et al. (1992) provide a new model for a conceptual understanding of FMA encompassing both the strategic choices of first-movers and later entrants, and later entrants' advantages, as well as identifying four factors of FMA: economic, pre-emptive, technological and behavioural. Also in 1993, Patterson addressed the strategic nature of FMA, building on the preservation of advantages via the creation of strategic barriers. Here, a taxonomy of strategic emulation barriers supporting first-mover strategy is provided. Gilbert and Birnbaum-More (1996) elaborate on the notion of strategic application of timing strategies. This work yields a model to evaluate the advantages of being first or second to enter a new market.

From the late 1990s and into the new millennium, first-mover advantages are considered in the context of new ideas and concepts. Mueller (1997) links FMA to the notion of path dependence, while Makadok (1998) investigates first-mover advantages specifically in the context of an industry with low entry barriers. López and Roberts (2002) examine product innovation and first-mover advantages in regimes of weak appropriability – logically, such advantages would not exist or be eroded quickly. The study found a negative relationship between order entry onto the market and long-term market share. The implication was that early-mover advantages are present, as the 10th entrant would only capture 11% of the market share of the pioneer, on average. Clark and Montgomery (1998) examine how competitive reputation and multi-market competition can deter entry of competitors to an incumbent actor, finding that aggressiveness proved a valuable indicator for market attractiveness and perceived risk. Michael (2003) seeks to explain how first-mover advantages can occur as a result of franchising. Coeurderoy and Durand (2004) investigate the existence of first-mover advantages in 1042 French manufacturing companies, specifically linking the results to proprietary technology versus cost leadership.

Most of the research on FMA has been performed in the USA via the PIMS and ASSESSOR databases. These databases are heavily debated and have given varying results. The reason for this reflects the discussion on defining the term first-mover. First, these databases contain no data from companies that have ceased to exist (closed, merged, bankruptcy, etc.). Secondly, the data are self-reported input from individuals on their own status as a first-mover. Finally, the working definition of a first-mover in the PIMS database is not the same as that used by researchers and can therefore only be used to demonstrate the success of early entrants. Because the database does not specifically differentiate pioneers from early entrants, further conclusions on first-mover advantages are difficult (Golder and Tellis 1993). It needs to be stressed that a number of studies *do* confirm the existence of first-mover advantages for pioneers (Golder and Tellis 1993, Carow et al. 2004, Patterson 1993, Urban et al. 1986, Robinson and Fornell 1985, Robinson 1988, Lambkin 1988 and Makadok 1998). Please refer to Appendix A, where a table of all the contributions can be found, listing them in order of publication date.

Durability in the context of FMA is dealt with implicitly. The entire concept is built on the balance of exploiting first-mover advantages and avoiding the pitfalls of competitors harvesting second-mover advantages. Essentially, this balance concerns durability of advantages. The problem with this approach in relation to durability is the lack of means of assessing durability. We are given a frame of reference and a terminology to describe durability, but no real means of assessing it, and therefore no means of understanding why firms would or would not embark on a new business venture. This applies to both the conceptual work of Lieberman and Montgomery (1988) and the application oriented (decision support) work of Gilbert and Birnbaum-More (1996).

1988 – Conceptualising a Framework

In 1988, Lieberman and Montgomery published a seminal article on the subject of FMA. The article separates itself from earlier works, because it treats FMA on a conceptual level, discussing the prerequisites of first-mover advantages. Other attempts to conceptualise the knowledge on FMA have been carried out (Kerin et al. 1992 and Patterson 1993), however they did not receive such broad recognition as the article by Lieberman and Montgomery. *Strategic Management Journal* rewarded the 1988 piece with the title of best article of the decade.

The generation of first-mover advantages builds on the existence of asymmetry enabling a company to exploit a new opportunity. A company cannot simply choose to follow a pioneering strategy – the opportunity to exploit first-mover advantages arises from a combination of luck and the proficiency to act on changes in the environment. The example with the Walkman supports this causality. Akio Morita's foresight (luck and proficiency) combined with the expertise of the Sony Corporation to develop a Walkman (proficiency) and the acceptance by the market of this new product (luck) resulted in the exploitation of first-mover advantages (Sanderson and Uzumeri 1995). The exploitation of first-mover advantages may stem from pure luck or proficiency alone. As demonstrated in the literature review, there are numerous sources of first-mover advantages. Within all these sources, there are a number of overlaps and correlations. Lieberman and Montgomery (1988) sort the different sources into three main categories: technological leadership, pre-emption of scarce assets and switching costs, and buyers' choice under uncertainty.

There are two underlying mechanisms for achieving first-mover advantages via technological leadership: progression on the learning or experience curves leading to reductions in costs of increased production output, and via successful R&D yielding advances in product or process technology. As a consequence of being first in a given market, a company can drive unit costs down at increased levels of output through experience. To the extent that the pioneer is able to maintain the leading position on learning, it is possible to maintain a sustained cost advantage and thus leverage greater market share. If the market proves profitable, new competitors are forced to sell below production costs in order to reduce the experience advantage of the incumbent (Lieberman and Montgomery 1988). Pioneers can also seek to protect the output of their R&D efforts via patents. The purpose is protection as well as discouraging competitors from embarking into the same competitive arena as the incumbent. Patents have proven to provide only slight protection. In many industries, competitors simply invent around the existing patents. Studies by Mansfield et al. (1981) show that competitors were able to imitate patented innovations for around 65% of the costs incurred by the incumbent to develop the same output.

By acting first in a new business venture, a company can acquire important and scarce resources and thereby pre-empt competitors from exploring these. This involves the exploitation of existing assets rather than assets created via technological developments. If a first-mover possesses critical knowledge, then this knowledge can be used to acquire assets at market price. The price of these assets will be lower than the price level that will dominate at a later stage. This can include input factors or prime locations for retailers and production facilities, and so on. See Rhim et al (2003) for further insights. Assets such as employees, suppliers and distributors are also found in this category. Pioneering a new market entails the opportunity to seize the most attractive niches whence competitors can be repelled. Pre-empting such positions can signal to competitors that only less desirable positions are available, ultimately avoiding new entries. Wal-Mart has deliberately and successfully applied a strategy of occupying desirable physical locations. Their strategy has been to acquire locations that do not appear attractive and combining this with the very efficient logistical operations of Wal-Mart, thus turning unwanted locations into strategically desirable positions. Having transformed the locations into desirable strategic positions then allows the company to charge premium margins, thus securing the position. Continuous investments in plant and equipment also send a clear signal that a position will be defended against competitors through increased volumes (Lieberman and Montgomery 1988).

In the event of switching costs, a first-mover will always hold an advantage, as competitors need to invest extra resources to lure customers away from the incumbent. Switching costs increase the value of market shares attained at early stages of the market's development. Having a large market share does not always translate into high profit margins for the pioneer, as these may have been won under harsh competition. Gaining large market shares at an early stage can result in negligence by the first-mover towards incoming competitors. The initial high profit rates the first-mover has been able to demand come under pressure from new entrants and unawareness or negligence towards low cost/low price new competitors can erode pioneering advantages.

Different types of switching costs exist. First, there are initial transaction costs or investments from the customer in adaptations to the seller's product. Examples of these kinds of switching costs include efforts in qualifying a new supplier, cost of dependence on ancillary products and training of employees (time spent, disruption from normal routines and financial inputs). These switching costs are associated with the initial stage of switching suppliers. Secondly, supplier specific learning by the customer is a type of switching cost. As customers become knowledgeable and comfortable with the product characteristics of the first-mover's product, switching costs are associated with changing brands. These switching costs occur when customers have established preferences. Thirdly, explicit and deliberate costs, that is, contractually determined switching costs, could be applied. In a situation where the customer is uncertain about the market and the quality of suppliers, the choice of purchase will often be placed with the supplier that first satisfied the demand of this buyer. Regardless of whether competitors can accommodate the needs of this customer to a greater degree.

Establishing a presence early is therefore pivotal. This type of brand loyalty is particularly found among low-involvement consumer goods. Being first yields a disproportionate degree of recognition in the mind of the buyer, which forces competitors to noticeably outperform the incumbent firm or invest in campaigns to establish a position. As volumes are greater in a Business-to-Business (B2B) context, there is a bigger incentive for buyers to seek out new suppliers and the effect is therefore lesser here than in a Business-to-Consumer (B2C) context (Lieberman and Montgomery 1988).

Whereas advantages can be achieved from being the first to service a new market, these are countered by a number of elements working to the advantage of second-movers that minimise or completely erode the first-mover's advantage. A realistic analysis of a new business model should include an assessment of these elements as they directly affect the durability of advantages sought from pioneering. Thus the assessment should indicate if the threats are so severe that the idea must be abandoned, if alternatives should be investigated or even if a second-mover strategy should be applied. The disadvantages of being first include competitors benefiting from the work and efforts of the first-mover, technological or market uncertainties being resolved, shifts occurring in technology or customer needs, and finally the incumbent firm succumbing to inertia. Figure 12.1 depicts these elements.

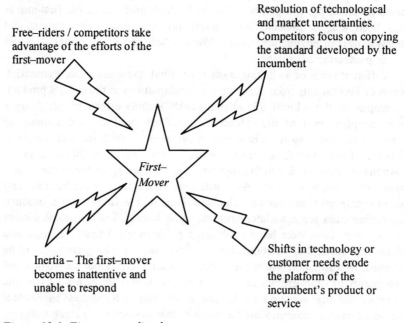

Figure 12.1 First-mover disadvantages

THE DURABILITY OF FIRST-MOVER ADVANTAGES

The concept of competitive advantages is by no means a new one; neither is the question of why some firms perform better economically than others.

The answer, however, is far more complex. There have been many and very different attempts to describe the creation of competitive advantages and only a few have succeeded in gaining widespread acceptance in the academic world. The industry structure view and RBV are two such theoretical contributions that have received general acceptance in explaining the occurrence of competitive advantages. More recently, the relationship view or network perspective has gained increasing attention. This has come about because existing theory struggled to explain how some firms outside desirable industries and without specialised resources managed to earn positive returns. Studies indicated that this situation was the result of business relations within a network of companies.

The problem of addressing the nature of advantages within a concept like FMA is that most academics subscribe to one theoretical direction. While investigating the literature of the FMA concept, sources of first-mover advantages that are introduced could be attributed to the industry structure view, RBV or the network perspective alike. Alternatively, when trying to describe competitive advantages, why not strive to develop a framework comprising, if possible, all three perspectives? Instead of stringently subscribing to one approach, one should realise that there are no right or wrong theories – only theories that are more or less applicable. In the following sections, I describe the three theoretical directions and how their contributions are applicable to the discussion of how durability of advantages can be explored.

Resource-Based View

What a firm wants is to create a situation where its own resource position directly or indirectly makes it more difficult for others to catch up. (Wernerfelt 1984, p. 173)

Margaret Peteraf (1993) presents a model operating with four elements describing the cornerstones of competitive advantage: heterogeneity, ex post limits to competition, imperfect mobility and ex ante limits to competition within RBV.

Heterogeneity of resources is assumed within RBV and implies that firms with varying capabilities can at least break even, firms that own only marginal resources can achieve no more than break-even and firms with superior resources are able to earn profits. Different types of rents can be earned: Ricardian rents, fixed rents, quasi-fixed rents and monopoly rents (Peteraf 1993). Entry barriers (Rumelt 1984) or mobility barriers (Caves and Porter 1977) explain how *ex post limits to competition* are dependent on imperfect imitability and imperfect substitutability in order to preserve the rent generation. The contribution by Dierickx and Cool (1989) further helps us understand how non-tradable assets are created in a company and hereby elaborates on the notion of imperfect mobility.

Non-tradable assets are a result of *imperfect mobility*. Firm-specialised resources, whose value is higher to the firm employing them than to other companies, are imperfectly mobile resources. This notion can be expanded to *co-specialised* assets. In such a scenario, investments would become sunk costs if waived by either party. At the same time, cooperation between companies (investment valuable only in the interplay between the two firms) in a network can yield advantages. Imperfect mobility is a key element in preserving sustained competitive advantages as it prevents erosion of rents and imitation of resources (Peteraf, 1993). For any company to take on the endeavour of a new business area, there must be *ex ante limits to competition* (Peteraf, 1993). This pertains to the cost of implementing a strategy – there must be limited competition for the position sought. Although a position is unfilled, it is necessary to observe competitors likely to compete for the same position. Within the FMA concept, this notion is denoted second mover-advantages – how fast can competitors close the gap to a first-mover and erode the rents generated from being first.

While the work by Peteraf (1993) describes the foundation of competitive advantages within RBV the VRIO framework by Barney (1997) is utilised to measure the durability of advantages. This analysis is intended to be performed on all resources, capabilities, and competences in a company. Barney (1997) does not differentiate between resources, capabilities and competences. Not to confuse the situation, I adopt this view and in this chapter disregard substantial discussion of the subject at this time. The logic behind the framework is a step-by-step process determining first the value, rareness, imitability and lastly the degree to which it is organised to be exploited, thus determining the competitive implication and the ensuing economic performance. If a given resource is progressively positive to these questions, the economic performance hereof increases. Please refer to Barney (1997) for a detailed account of the model. The implication of the VRIO analysis is that a given company would be able to recognise the sources of the value offered to partners and customers.

While RBV filled a much-needed gap in the discussion on competitive advantages[5] by addressing the matter of resource heterogeneity, it implicitly excludes the environment of the firm. Developing competitive advantages via cooperation or acknowledging the importance of external influences is left unattended.

Industry Structure View

The industry structure view is most commonly associated with Michael E. Porter and his groundbreaking work from 1980. In this approach, there are two determinants of the profitability of a firm (competitive advantage) – the overall attractiveness of the industry and the relative position of a firm within the industry (Porter 1985). Industry attractiveness comprises five components found in the oft-quoted Five-Forces model. These components are: bargaining power of suppliers, bargaining power of buyers, threat of new entrants, threat from substitutes, and industry rivalry determinants. The second element of competitive advantage is determined via the position of the individual firm within the industry.

According to Porter (1985), there are two basic types of competitive advantages a firm can possess compared to competitors – lower costs or differentiation. This is not to be confused with the well-known generic strategies that are the function of these competitive advantages and the competitive scope. The three generic strategies that Porter (1985) defines are (1) cost leadership, (2) differentiation and (3) focus.

> The fundamental basis of above-average performance in the long run is sustainable competitive advantage. Though a firm can have a myriad of strengths and weaknesses vis-à-vis its competitors, there are two basic types of competitive advantage a firm can posses: low cost or differentiation. The significance of any strength or weakness a firm possesses is ultimately a function of its impact on relative cost or differentiation. Cost advantages and differentiation in turn stem from industry structure. They result from a firm's ability to cope with the five forces better than its rivals. The two types of competitive advantage combined with the scope of activities for which a firm seeks to achieve them lead to three generic strategies for achieving above-average performance in an industry: Cost leadership, Differentiation, and Focus. (1985, p. 11)

From the above quote, it can be deduced that competitive advantages are manifested via the generic strategies. Sustainability is also discussed in the context of these strategies. It is important to note that these are mentioned as functions of how well a firm exploits the five forces. Ultimately, we need to address the determinants of the five forces to understand how Porter treats the matter of durability of advantages.

The work of Porter is pivotal and the insights it offers are crucial. Performing an analysis on competitive advantages is somewhat cumbersome because of the multitude of variables. Also, when dealing with an industry level analysis, firm resources are assumed to be homogeneous. Strategies are formulated to navigate the industry forces of competition, while internal resources are completely mobile and therefore not included in this aspect.

See Barney (1991) for further input on this discussion. The strength of this work is obviously the understanding of the interconnectedness of all these elements and the importance of the industry level for competitive advantages.

The Network Perspective

The Uppsala school in Sweden launched the concept of a network perspective (Håkansson 1987; Håkansson and Johanson 1992; Håkansson and Snehota 1995), but the subject matter has also been explored in the marketing channel/distribution literature (Hultman 1993; Wilkinson 1973; Stern et al. 1996), applying a relationship denotation, as well as by Porter. Porter (1998) applies the terminology of clusters and looks explicitly at company groupings working in close physical proximity. The other directions have not assumed close physical proximity. The interest in this aspect originates from the occurrence of company success stories. Their success could not be easily explained using existing theory, and thus new approaches had to be developed. The ARA model (Actors, Resources, Activities) provides a model for understanding and explaining the complexity of the environment within which a given firm operates. This is achieved via an examination of the bonds between actors in the network, the ties between resources controlled by different actors and how the activities of the different actors link together.

Although many different schools of research explore the phenomenon of network-based economics, little work has been done to explore the connection between competitive advantages and network-based economics. The basis for this is often borrowed from Transaction Cost Economics (Williamson 1975, 1979, 1981, 1991). The most prominent attempts to explain the strategic applicability come from Reve (1990) and Dyer and Singh (1998). The terminology of these explorations is inspired by the industrial organisational view or RBV. This is quite natural, as this perspective in essence is an elaboration of both. This new network-inspired terminology thus applies the external view of Porter and couples it with the understanding of resources from RBV. The most obvious shortcoming here is the reliance on the RBV terminology to explain the creation of competitive advantages. The tools themselves are solid enough, but they fail to incorporate the external connectivities of a network/relationship.

Inside AND out

When revisiting the statement of not having right or wrong theories – but only theories that are more or less applicable – I am left with a view on industry factors that yields many variables that are thereby difficult to apply in order to measure durability, a network perspective that offers no real answers and a formidable tool to observe only the firm internal elements via RBV. The problem with using only the RBV approach is that it assumes a firm will have complete insights into the competitive performance of its resources, thus implying that an objective analysis of the root causes of performance is possible. As demonstrated through the concept of causal ambiguity, this cannot always be carried out. Solely applying an outside performance perspective and judging competitive advantages from this perspective is just as flawed; or just as dangerous, because the effects on the market may be reasonably determined and not realising the internal production leading to such advantages leaves a firm vulnerable to imitation. As the FMA concept investigates both firm internal and external sources of competitive advantages, it would be insufficient to only choose one approach. It is necessary to look both at the internal functions of a firm and the external products in the market to observe the overall competitive advantage.

Within the marketing channel literature – because of its specific attention to relationships – the valuation of cooperation has been calculated via resource dependence theory. The origins of this theory come from Emerson (1962) and Pfeffer and Salancik (1978). A precondition of gaining competitive advantages from any kind of network or relationship is power. Mutual dependence and power in a cooperative relationship are determined via the control over resources (Weber 2002; Gelderman and van Weele 1999). Applying this approach to the subject of evaluating the durability of advantages in a firm *external* perspective provides the tool necessary to supplement the VRIO analysis for the firm *internal* perspective. Gelderman and van Weele (1999) present a model on the situation of dependence, where the relative dependence between two actors determines their relative power. As both parties in a relationship must be assumed to draw a benefit, a mutual dependence must exist. This dependence is described as the net dependence of each actor.

Pfeffer and Salancik (1978) and Emerson (1962) propose that the relative power position between two actors is determined via three variables – importance of resources, scarcity of resources, and discretion over resource allocation and use. These variables have a striking resemblance to those presented in the VRIO framework (allowing for semantic differences). There is indeed a significant overlap and one very important distinction. The resources mentioned in these three variables are not the objective capabilities as in RBV. Rather, they are the product of the *perceived* value of resources of one actor by the other. The distinction on perception is vital. We move away from the 'objective' evaluation of resources and examine – not the resources as valued by others – the perceived value of the offering that a firm's resources produces. This can be the perceived value by partners, competitors and customers alike. Including perception is crucial in this context. There is no objective truth about the value of a resource in a relationship, but there is a perceived value by the recipient or user of this resource.

According to Pfeffer and Salancik (1978), the *importance* of resources offered by other actors is influenced by two elements – relative magnitude of the resources and the criticality of these resources. Criticality in the sense that it is used here refers to the question of whether a firm is able to continue functioning. That is, if this resource were to be taken away, could the receiving firm continue operations or would the market disappear. Criticality addresses the proportion of total output an exchange generates (turnover, etc.). As firms strive to acquire resources that will be favoured in the market place, a supplementary means of assessing the value of a resource is the firm's own perception of the resource's importance to others. *Scarcity* is related to concentration. In other words, it is important whether many or few actors possess the resources that are perceived as being valuable. It becomes pivotal whether the focal firm has access to this resource. Sanctions become an issue here, as the relative number of alternative firms, and their size and importance in the industry influence the scarcity of resources. Freely opting to source a resource from an alternative firm can be restricted, because of these factors. Fear of retaliation by a powerful actor can lock other firms into a relationship (Pfeffer and Salancik 1978). Possession of resources, access to resources and use of external resources are the three elements comprising the factor of *discretion over resource allocation and use*. Possession in this context means ownership; directly or via rights of ownership. Access, on the other hand, means control over a resource, without actually possessing it. The final element is closely related to this. Again, it involves use of resources – that are directly owned by others (Pfeffer and Salancik 1978).

Table 12.1 Assessing perceived value of resources

Importance of resources	Scarcity of resources	Discretion over resource allocation and use
Measured on:	*Measured on:*	*Measured on:*
Relative magnitude of resource	Concentration of resources	Ownership
Criticality of the resource	Relative number of alternatives	Access
		External use

Source: Own illustration after Pfeffer and Salancik (1978).

As the notion of using resource dependence theory in this context stems from the relationship/network perspective, it is relevant to look at how it addresses the industry structure view. Resource dependence theory directly addresses the issues of bargaining power – regardless of perspective, whether buyers' or suppliers'. Porter's (1980) contribution lies in an overall understanding of the structural importance of industry on competition, and resource dependence directly addresses these issues. Threats from substitutes are also covered via the functions of importance and scarcity of resources. Entry barriers and rivalry are both a mix of internal and external components, so elements will be covered via the VRIO internal framework. Resource dependence arguably addresses these factors, as it looks at the perceived value of the resources gained externally. Entry barriers and rivalry are high if the relative power position of a newcomer is low, and vice versa.

A NEW FRAMEWORK

Or rather, a way of using known frameworks in a new setting and using new combinations.

There are now two frameworks for assessing the durability or sustainability of competitive advantages. One applies to the internal resources and combination of resources to produce goods and services found via the VRIO framework: here, the answer to how fast/easily competitors will be able to imitate the processes and internal productions. For the external assessment of the perceived value of a firm's 'offering'[6] a tool is given via resource dependence theory and the three factors; importance, scarcity and discretion of resources (ISD framework). Applying the ISD framework to buyers and suppliers determines the threat of substitutes as well as potential competitors and industry rivalry – to the extent that this is a question, which can be answered without looking at firm specific resources. The VRIO framework fills this gap.

The practical applicability of these models in a coherent fashion would involve the differentiation of resources and offerings. As suggested by Barney (1997), resources are applied in an analytical sense to encompass resources, competences, capabilities, and so on. This includes all firm inputs, tangible and intangible, used to produce goods or services. In this context resources denote all of these terms as suggested by Barney (1997). Analytically, this is applied to the firm's internal analysis. Offerings on the other hand would be the term applied in an external setting. When dealing with the perceived value of a product/service, it is difficult to maintain the term resource. It represents a means to another party, which contains a certain amount of perceived value. Offerings need to be assessed on the basis of their perceived value in connection with the focal firm's external environment. An illustration of this process is shown in Figure 12.2.

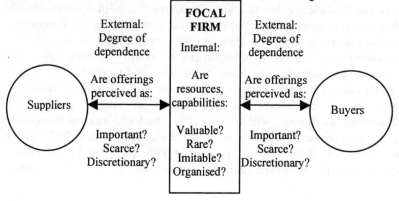

Source: Own Illustration

Figure 12.2 The conceptual framework

This conceptual framework needs to be modelled for the analytical context of first-mover advantages in the grocery industry. Adapting this model to the context of FMA would result in the situation shown in Figure 12.3.

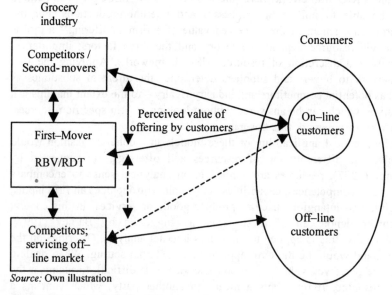

Source: Own illustration

Figure 12.3 The analytical framework

The first-mover is the equivalent of the focal company in Figure 12.3. Competitors (second-movers) are those firms that compete directly on an Internet platform serving the same customer segment. The last group of competitors are those servicing off-line customers. This group has a potential impact on the consumer segmentation, as these firms may be able to broaden the number of on-line consumers. If more firms move into this business area, there is a chance that the on-line market will gain credibility or simply have consumers follow the new on-line grocers into this segment. A very important aspect here is that of perceived value. A critical element of the e-grocery business as we know it today is that it has not – generally speaking – been able to provide sufficient added value for consumers. They will therefore most likely judge the value of internet-based grocery shopping as an extension or a supplement to existing channels. The off-line market is therefore an important piece in this competitive puzzle.

Specifically applying this model to the Danish industry could include Aarstiderne.com at the centre as the focal firm. Other firms attempted e-grocery in Denmark, but none have survived that constitutes a significant actor in the industry. Second-movers are to date populated by actors similar to Aarstiderne.com – smaller, regional or specialised, e.g. Skagenfood and DenFranskeKasse. Interestingly, Coop has initiated on-line sales. To date, this solution does not offer home deliveries. Coop is therefore difficult to fit into the model. For the sake of this analysis, Coop will be placed in the 'off-line competitors' segment. A full-scale adaptation of e-commerce by Coop could have effects for the entire on-line customer segment as via their reputation and assortment they could attract new customers to this group.

Customers' reaction to firms' offerings is not within the scope of this chapter though. Therefore the model includes the analysis of customers' perceived value of offerings. Aarstiderne.com do appear to have an advantage here (Friese et al. 2003 and Kornum 2005). Customers perceive the offerings not only as the most complete access to organic products, but also as belonging to a group and thus creating more value from the perspective of customers than the physical goods and the accompanying service. All grocers venturing onto the electronic scene must take into account the aspect of what is offered – apart from the actual groceries themselves.

Moving from the conceptual model to the analytical model implies the elimination of the 'supplier' factor. As mentioned previously, this element has less of an empirical importance to the existence of e-grocery solutions. Suppliers do affect the situation, but special, cognitive and timing limits prevent the full-scale transformation of the conceptual model. And having a less significant impact, the element of 'suppliers' is therefore excluded in the analytical model.

CONCLUSION

The concept of first-mover advantages has been explored in many different connections. However, much of this work has been dedicated to confirming that first-mover advantages exist. Although difficult to prove and affected by discussions on definition and methodological approach (PIMS database), empirical evidence of FMA has been presented. In this context, it is important to note that although these advantages are proven, they are not automatic rewards for entrepreneurial action. The creation and exploitation of first-mover advantages require both luck and skill. More importantly, for a sustainable business to emerge, supplements and continued work are prerequisites. The element of sustainability or durability of advantages is one area the FMA literature has not yet explored in depth. The abundance of potential sources for FMA does not provide qualitative confirmation. Are some advantages more sustainable than others? Naturally, but how can this be incorporated?

Many contributions have been made to the study of FMA and many of these represent milestones. So far, none has been able to measure up to the work of Lieberman and Montgomery (1988) who managed to describe the concept of first-mover advantages rather than just the occurrence of FMA as a function of a single event. This work captured all the different sources of FMA and organised them into three main groupings; technological leadership, pre-emption of scarce assets, and switching costs and buyers' choice under uncertainty. In doing so, the elements for each of these factors were accounted for and, moreover, the disadvantage of being first was also described.

The literature on FMA, in particular the more conceptual contributions such as Lieberman and Montgomery (1988), highlights the aspects needed to unveil the complexity of a very simple question: what type of advantages do grocers stand to gain by pioneering e-commerce solutions? The FMA concept provides a tool to understand the competitive aspect, the potential gains and pitfalls of launching a new business. Apart from operational issues of making e-grocery profitable, the elements such as being imitated and having profits eroded by competitors are key in understanding this situation. The element of durability must therefore be included into the FMA framework to encompass the entire spectrum of understanding.

The discussion on sustainability and indeed that of how firms gain competitive advantages is primarily performed within two theoretical frameworks: RBV and the industry structure view. More recently, a new perspective (network-based economics) has gained attention because of the existing theories' difficulties in explaining the occurrence of relationship-based advantages. My discussion was carried out on the premise that all three directions have validity and yet all three are missing a component covered by the others. The normal approach in this situation is to subscribe to one and try to argue for the shortcomings of the others. As first-mover advantages can occur on the basis of constructs that could be subscribed to different views, I set out to describe the common grounds for them. I would argue this represents not only the most thorough approach, but also the most appropriate. Stating the advantages and shortcomings of each theoretical view is fairly straightforward. Constructing a view allowing for all three to work together, however, is not.

The RBV perspective on sustainability of advantages represents the easiest applicable model for an empirical analysis. The VRIO framework from Barney (1997), offers an optimal tool for assessing the durability of advantages – from a firm internal perspective. However, it does not tell us whether the offering has any staying power in the market itself. To answer this question, a combination of the network perspective and the industry structure view was proposed via resource dependence theory by Emerson (1962) and Pfeffer and Salancik (1978). Neither the network perspective nor the industry structure view provides a tool for understanding the sustainability of advantages derived from firm activities. Applying resource dependence theory in the context of relationships (external environment) has been suggested in the marketing channel literature.

By looking at the relative power position between actors, dependence can be deduced. The power position is dependent on the perceived importance of a firm's own resources compared to those of the other actor. This perceived importance is measured via the importance, scarcity and discretion of the combined resources. It is crucial to include the element of perception when adopting a relational view. Instead of having to analyse all components of a company (traditional VRIO approach), the input from the dependence analysis will indicate where the value of a firm's offerings lie. Thus a connection between external (perceived) value of a firm and its internal resource base is established. This approach helps determine what is valued and what lies behind the value proposition of a firm for its external environment, consisting of competitors, customers, suppliers, and so on. A perceived value is in essence the net sum of what others offer – competitors and suppliers are hereby implicitly included.

The idea behind the proposed framework is to analyse the relative value of e-grocer offerings from the perspective of a single actor in relation to the external environment. If sustainable advantages can be detected in the external environment, then the durability of the internal processes and input is evaluated via the VRIO framework. Sustainability in this approach is not judged on internal resources alone (if the market changes or an offering is surpassed by innovation, then the value in the market is decreasing) or solely on external factors (if a highly profitable offering is easily duplicated, then the sustainability is low). Taking both aspects into account will yield a comprehensive framework for understanding the advantages that firms stand to gain from venturing onto the e-grocery scene; and just as important, an understanding of what firms potentially stand to lose.

NOTES

1. In the management literature, durability is referred to as 'sustainability'.
2. The authors define 'product category' as: *a group of close substitutes such that consumers consider the products substitutable and distinct from those in another product category* (p. 159).
3. In the marketing literature also referred to as *dynamically continuous innovations* and in the technology management literature as *sustained innovations* (Cooper 2000).
4. Also known as *disruptive innovations* (Cooper 2000).
5. And opposite previous work treating the firm not as a black-box.
6. In the literature, the term resource is applied to minimize confusion and call attention to the fact that – external resources are actually the perceived value of the product yielded by the combination of internal resources. In essence, this constitutes an offering rather than a resource. Recipients may not even acknowledge these offerings as resources.

REFERENCES

Bain, Joe S. (1956), *Barriers to New Competition*. Cambridge, MA: Harvard University Press.

Barney, Jay B. (1991), 'Firm resources and sustained competitive advantage'. *Journal of Management*. 17(1), 99–120.

Barney, Jay B. (1997), *Gaining and Sustaining Competitive Advantage*. Ontario: Addison-Wesley Publishing.

Bowman, Douglas and Hubert Gatignon (1996), 'Order of entry as a moderator of the effect of the marketing mix on market share'. *Marketing Science*. 15(3), 222–242.

Carow, Kenneth, Randall Heron and Todd Saxton (2004), 'Do early birds get the returns? An empirical investigation of early-mover advantages in acquisitions'. *Strategic Management Journal*. 25(6), 563–585.

Carpenter, Gregory S. and Kent Nakamoto (1990), 'Competitive strategies for late entry into a market with a dominant brand'. *Management Science*. 36(10), 1268–1278.

Caves, Richard E. and Michael E. Porter (1977), 'From entry barriers to mobility barriers: Conjectural decisions and contrived deterrence to new competition'. *Quarterly Journal of Economics*. 91(2), 241–262.

Clark, Bruce H. and David B. Montgomery (1998), 'Competitive reputations, multimarket competition and entry deterrence'. *Journal of Strategic Marketing*. 6(2), 81–96.

Coeurderoy, Regis and Rodolphe Durand (2004), 'Leveraging the advantage of early entry: Proprietary technologies versus cost leadership'. *Journal of Business Research*. 57(6), 583–590.

Conrad, Cecilia A. (1983), 'The advantage of being first and competition between firms'. *International Journal of Industrial Organization*. 1(4), 353–364.

Cooper, Lee G. (2000), 'Strategic marketing planning for radical new products'. *Journal of Marketing*, 64(1), 1–16.

Demsetz, Harold (1982), 'Barriers to entry'. *The American Economic Review*. 72(1), 47–57.

Dierickx, Ingemar and Karel Cool (1989), 'Asset stock accumulation and sustainability of competitive advantage'. *Management Science*. 35(12), 1504–1511.

Dyer, Jeffrey H. and Harbir Singh (1998), 'The relational view: Cooperative strategy and sources of interorganizational competitive advantage'. *Academy of Management Review*. 23(4), 660–679.

Emerson, Richard M. (1962), 'Power-dependence relations'. *American Sociological Review*. 27(1), 31–41.

Fellman, Michelle W. (1998), 'Forecast: New products storm subsides'. *Marketing News*. 32(7), 1–2.

Friese, Susanne, Mogens Bjerre, Torben Hansen, Niels Kornum and Christine Sestoft (2003), *E-Bizz Øresund Report – Barriers and Motivators of Online Grocers Shopping in Denmark, Research Report January 2003*. Copenhagen: Copenhagen Business School – Department of Marketing.

Gal-Or, Ester (1985), 'First mover and second mover advantages'. *International Economic Review*. 26(3), 649–653.

Gal-Or, Ester (1987), 'First mover disadvantages with private information'. *Review of Economic Studies*. 54(178), 279–292.

Gelderman, Kees and Arjan van Weele (1999), '*New perspectives on Kraljic's purchasing portfolio approach*'. Paper presented at the 9th International Annual IPSERA Conference.

Gilbert, Joseph and Philip H. Birnbaum-More (1996), 'Innovation timing advantages: From economic theory to strategic application'. *Journal of Engineering and Technology Management*. 12(4), 245–266.

Golder, Peter N. and Gerard J. Tellis (1993), 'Pioneering advantage: Marketing logic or marketing legend?'. *Journal of Marketing Research.* 30(2), 158–170.

Hultman, Claes (1993), *Managing Relations in Marketing Channels for Industrial Goods: An Analysis of Producer-Distributor dyads.* Linkoping: Linkoping University – Department of Management & Economics.

Håkansson, Håkan (1987), *Industrial Technological Development – A Network Approach.* London: Routledge.

Håkansson, Håkan and J. Johanson (1992), 'A model of industrial networks', in B. Axelsson and G. Eaton (eds), *Industrial Networks: A New View of Reality.* London: Routledge, pp. 28–34.

Håkansson, Håkan and Ivan Snehota (1995), *Developing Relationships in Business Networks.* London: Routledge.

Johnsson, Mats and Niels Kornum (2001), '*Designing Distribution Systems for Consumer Related E-Commerce*'. Paper presented at the 13th NOFOMA Conference, Iceland.

Kardes, Frank R. and Gurumurthy Kalyanaram (1992), 'Order-of-entry effects on consumer memory and judgment: An information integration perspective'. *Journal of Marketing Research.* 29(3), 343–357.

Kerin, Roger A., P. Rajan Varadarajan and Robert A. Peterson (1992), 'First-mover advantage: A synthesis, conceptual framework, and research proposition'. *Journal of Marketing.* 56(4), 33–52.

Kornum, Niels (2002), '*Characteristics and development of store based – and specialty e-grocer.* Paper presented at the 14th NOFOMA Conference, Trondheim.

Kornum, Niels (2005), 'Resource dependence theory in an e-grocery BTC context – the case of specialty e-grocer X', in D. Sharma and J. Johansson (eds), *Managing Customer Relationships with IT and Internet,* Pergamon: Elsevier Science Ltd (Forthcoming).

Kornum, Niels, Mogens Bjerre and Robert Langberg (1999), *Elektronisk handel – udfordringer for logistik og distribution. [E-commerce – Challenges for Logistics and Distribution].* København: Forskningsministeriet og Foreningen af Dansk Internet Handel.

Lambkin, Mary (1988), 'Order entry and performance in new markets'. *Strategic Management Journal.* 9(Special Issue: Strategy Content Research), 127–140.

Lieberman, Marvin B. and David B. Montgomery (1988), 'First-Mover Advantages'. *Strategic Management Journal.* 9(Special Issue: Strategy Content Research), 41–58.

Lippman, Steven A. and John W. Mamer (1993), 'Preemptive innovation'. *Journal of Economic Theory.* 61(1), 104–119.

Lippman, Steven A. and Richard P. Rumelt (1982), 'Uncertain imitability: An analysis of interfirm differences in efficiency under competition'. *Bell Journal of Economics*. 13(2), 111–118.

López, Luis E. and Edward B. Roberts (2002), 'First-mover advantages in regimes of weak appropriability: The case of financial services innovations'. *Journal of Business Research*. 55(12), 997–1005.

Mahajan, Vijay, Subhash Sharma and Robert D. Buzzell (1993), 'Assessing the impact of competitive entry on market expansion and incumbent sales'. *Journal of Marketing*. 57(3), 39–52.

Makadok, Richard. (1998), 'Can first-mover and early-mover advantages be sustained in an industry with low barriers to entry/imitation?'. *Strategic Management Journal*. 19(7), 683–696.

Mansfield, Edwin, Mark Schwartz and Samuel Wagner (1981), 'Imitation costs and patents: An empirical study'. *Economic Journal*. 91(364), 907–918.

Mansfield, Edwin (1985), 'How rapidly does new industrial technology leak out?'. *Journal of Industrial Economics*. 34(2), 217–223.

Michael, Steven C. (2003), 'First mover advantage through franchising'. *Journal of Business Venturing*. 18(1), 61–80.

Moore, Geoffrey A. (1998), *Crossing the Chasm: Marketing and Selling Technology Products to Mainstream Customers, 2nd edn.* Chichester: Capstone Publishing Limited.

Mueller, Dennis C. (1997), 'First-mover advantage and path dependence'. *International Journal of Industrial Organization*. 15(6), 827–850.

Ohmae, Kenichi (1998), 'Guru of gadgets'. *Time South Pacific*. 12/07/98(49), 143–145.

Patterson, William C. (1993), 'First-mover advantage: The opportunity curve'. *Journal of Management Studies*. 30(5), 759–777.

Peteraf, Margerat A. (1993), 'The cornerstones of competitive advantage: A resource-based view'. *Strategic Management Journal*. 14(3), 179–191.

Pfeffer, Jeffrey and Gerald R. Salancik (1978), *External Control of Organizations. A Resource Dependence Perspective*. London: Harper & Row Publishers.

Porter, Michael E. (1980), *Competitive Strategy: Techniques for Analyzing Industries and Competitors*. New York: Free Press.

Porter, Michael E. (1985), *Competitive Advantage: Creating and Sustaining Superior Performance*. New York: Free Press.

Porter, Michael E. (1998), 'Clusters and the new economics of competition'. *Harvard Business Review*. 76(6), 77–99.

Rao, Ram C. and David P. Rutenberg (1979), 'Preempting an alert rival: Strategic timing of the first plant by analysis of sophisticated rivalry'. *Bell Journal of Economics.* 10(2), 421–428.

Reve, Torger (1990), 'The firm as a nexus of internal and external contracts', in M. Aoki, B. Gustafsson and O. Williamson (eds), *The Firm as a Nexus of Treaties.* London: Sage Publications.

Rhim, Hosun, Teck H. Ho and Uday S. Karmarkar (2003), 'Competitive location, production, and market selection'. *European Journal of Operational Research.* 149(1), 211–229.

Robinson, William T. (1988), 'Sources of market pioneer advantages: The case of industrial goods industries'. *Journal of Marketing Research.* 25(1), 87–94.

Robinson, William T. and Claes Fornell (1985), 'Sources of market pioneer advantages in consumer goods industries'. *Journal of Marketing Research.* 22(3), 305–317.

Robinson, William T. and Sungwook Min (2002), 'Is the first to market the first to fail? Empirical evidence for industrial goods businesses'. *Journal of Marketing Research.* 39(1), 120–128.

Rumelt, Richard P. (1984), 'Toward a strategic theory of the firm', in R. Lamb (ed.), *Competitive Strategic Management.* Englewood Cliffs, NJ: Prentice Hall.

Sanderson, Susan Walsh and Mustafa Uzumeri (1995), *Managing Product Families.* Chicago: Irwin Professional Publishing.

Schmalensee, Richard (1982), 'Product differentiation advantages of pioneering brands'. *American Economic Review.* 72(3), 349–365.

Schnaars, Steven P. (1986), 'When entering growth markets, are pioneers better than poachers?'. *Business Horizons.* 29(2), 27–36.

Shamsie, Jamal, Corey Phelps and Jerome Kuperman (2004), 'Better late than never: A study of late entrants in household electrical equipment'. *Strategic Management Journal.* 25(1), 69–84.

Smiley, Robert H. and S. Abraham Ravid (1983), 'The importance of being first: Learning price and strategy'. *The Quarterly Journal of Economics.* 98(2), 353–362.

Stern, Louis W., Adel I. El-Ansary and Anne T. Coughlan (1996), *Marketing Channels, 5th ed.* New Jersey: Prentice Hall International.

Urban, Glen L., Theresa Carter, Steven Gaskin and Zofia Mucha (1986), 'Market share rewards to pioneering brands: An empirical analysis and strategic implications'. *Management Science.* 32(6), 645–659.

Weber, Oliver Jacob (2002), *'Resource dependency as barrier or driving force for grocery BtC e-commerce and subsequent changes in the supply chain'.* Paper presented at the 14th NOFOMA Conference, Trondheim.

Wernerfelt, Birger (1984), 'A resource-based view of the firm'. *Strategic Management Journal.* 5(2), 171–180.

Wilkinson, Ian F. (1973), 'Power and influence structure in distribution channels'. *European Journal of Marketing.* 7(2), 119–129.

Williamson, Oliver E. (1975), *Markets and Hierarchies.* New York: Free Press.

Williamson, Oliver E. (1979), 'Transaction-cost economics: The governance of contractual relations'. *Journal of Law and Economics.* 22(2), 233–261.

Williamson, Oliver E. (1981), 'The economics of organization: The transaction cost approach'. *American Journal of Sociology.* 87(3), 548–577.

Williamson, Oliver E. (1991), 'Strategizing, economizing, and economic organization'. *Strategic Management Journal.* 12(8), 75–94.

APPENDIX A

Study	Context	Sources of FMA	Mechanisms	FMA disadvantage	Sample size
Bain (1956)	Competitive theory	• Customer awareness	• Publicity • Preference		20 Industries
Rao & Rutenberg (1979)	Strategy / competition	• Economies of scale	• Nash equilibrium	• N/A	N/A
Mansfield et al (1981)	Cost of imitation	• Patents	• Time/cost trade-off	• Imitation costs	48 products
Lippman & Rumelt (1982)	Pre-emptive innovation	• Causal ambiguity	• Nash equilibrium • R&D	• N/A	N/A
Schmalensee (1982)	Product differentiation	• Buyer uncertainty • Preference asymmetry	• Entry time	• N/A	N/A
Conrad (1983)	Pioneering advantages	• Pricing advantages • Market share	• Imperfect information	• N/A	N/A
Smiley & Ravid (1983)	Pioneering advantages	• Learning advantages	• Cost advantages • Pricing • Demand elasticity	• N/A	N/A
Mansfield (1985)	Technology diffusion	• Imitation costs • Ease/time of imitation	• Time • Costs	• N/A	100
Robinson & Fornell (1985)	Pioneering advantages	• Relative consumer information • Marketing mix • Relative direct costs	• Relative product • Relative distribution • Advertising • Relative price • Absolute cost advantages • Scale advantages • Imperfect information	• N/A	371
Gal-Or (1985)	Pioneering advantages	• Game theory	• Stackleberg leadership – consequence of competitors moving sequentially	• N/A	N/A
Urban et al (1986)	Pioneering brands	• Market share distribution and entry timing	• Order of entry • Market positioning • Advertising expenditures • Time lags between entries	• N/A	82 brands across 24 product categories
Schnaars (1986)	Growth markets and entry timing	• Entry timing effect on market share	• Image and reputation are important • Experience effects • Brand loyalty to pioneer • Cost advantages • Entry barriers erected	• Learning from pioneer's mistakes • Early uncertainty • Product enhancement • Low cost production	7 pro FMA 5 con FMA
Gal-Or	Pioneering	• Game theory	• Effect of incomplete	• N/A	N/A

(1987)	advantages		information on demand		
Robinson (1988)	Pioneering advantages	• Switching costs • Marketing mix • Direct costs	• Quality • Broader product lines • Sales force expenditures as percentage of sales increase • Lower prices • Absolute cost • Scale economics • Customized products and service importance • Product's purchase increases and purchase frequency decreases • Value added as a percentage of sales increase	• New product sales as a percentage of total sales increase • Deterioration of pioneering product quality and breadth + increase in price and costs	1209
Lambkin (1988)	Entry timing	• Relationship to parent • Entry strategy • Competitive strategy	• Parent size • Parent diversity • Percentage sales internal • Percentage purchased internal • Shared facilities • Shared distribution • Shared marketing • Patent protection • Breadth product line • Scale market entry • Capacity/ market • Relative marketing • Relative product quality • Relative customer service • Relative price • Relative direct costs	• N/A	129 start-ups 187 adolescent
Lieberman & Montgomery (1988)	First-Mover Advantages Conceptual model	• Technological leadership • Pre-emption of scarce assets • Switching costs and buyer uncertainty	• Learning/experience curve • Success in patens and R&D • Pre-emption of input factors • Pre-emption of locations in geographic and product characteristic space ▪ Pre-emptive investment in plant and equipment • Adoption to seller's products	• Free-riders • Resolution of technological and market uncertainties • Shift in technology and customer needs • Inertia	Literature review

			• Suppliers specific learning by buyers • Contractual switching costs • Buyer choice under uncertainty		
Carpenter & Nakamoto (1990)	Strategy and entry timing	• Preference asymmetry	• Positioning • Advertising • Pricing	• N/A	N/A
Kardes & Kalyanaram (1992)	Order entry effect on consumers	• Consumer memory • Consumer judgement	• Greater recollection – shared features • Greater recollection – unique features • Differential learning – more extreme evaluation of pioneering brand • Differential learning – greater confidence in evaluations of pioneering brand • Effects 1 and 2 more pronounced with greater exposure	• N/A	Sample 1: 46 Sample 2: 40
Lippman & Mamer (1993)	Innovation	• Pre-emptive innovation	• R&D • Nash equilibrium	• N/A	N/A
Mahajan et al (1993)	Entry timing	• Market shares and entry timing	• Brand • Product life cycle	• N/A	
Kerin et al (1992)	First-Mover Advantages Conceptual model	• Economic • Pre-emptive • Technological • Behavioural	• Demand uncertainty • Entry scale • Efficient scale-to-market size • Advertising intensity • Response time • Scope economics • Pre-emptive investments • Product characteristics • Technological innovation characteristics • Technological change and discontinuity • Nature of good • Market type • Market evolution • Buyers' investment in co-specialised assets	• Imitation costs • Free-rider effects • Scope economics • Learning from pioneer's mistakes	13 studies referred
Patterson (1993)	First-Mover Advantages and strategy	• Temporal strategic barriers	• Learning • Pre-emption • Uncertain imitability • Uniqueness • Developmental	• N/A	• Auto 26 • Chemical 23 • Computer 37

			seniority		• Insurance 21 • Oil 27 • Retail 17
Golder & Tellis (1993)	Pioneering advantages	• Consumer based • Product based	• Knowledge of first brand • Pioneer stand determining for followers • Positioning of brand • Switching costs • Economies of scale • Economies of learning • Technological leadership • Pre-emption of scarce assets • Continuous improvements to product • Lock-in of suppliers	• Free-riders • Resolution of technological and market uncertainties • Shift in technology and customer needs • Inertia • Improper positioning • Changing resource requirements • Insufficient investments • Information diffusion • Standard not established	50 product categories
Bowman & Gatignon (1996)	Entry timing	• Marketing mix	• Memory and learning • Categorisation • Price • Product quality • Advertising effectiveness • Distribution	• N/A	
Gilbert & Birnbaum-More (1996)	Timing strategies	• Technological leadership • Pre-emption of scarce assets • Switching costs and buyer uncertainty	• Degree of fragmentation in industry • Industry velocity • Rate of innovation diffusion in industry • Firm strategy – cost leader • Firm strategy – differentiation • Core competences of firms • Connection to technological infrastructure • Degree of novelty of good • Difficulty of production • Customer resources invested	• Free-riding on first-mover investments • Resolution of market, technology or regulatory uncertainties • Changes in technology or customer needs	Literature review
Mueller (1997)	Path dependence	• Demand related, inertia advantage • Supply related,	• Set-up and switching costs • Network externalities • Buyer inertia (uncertainty over	• Choosing second best design • Difficulties processing information	N/A

		efficiency advantages	quality) • Buyer inertia (habit formation) • Set-up and sunk costs • Network externalities and economies • Scale economies • Learning-by-doing cost reductions	• Inertia	
Makadok (1998)	Timing advantages	• Low barriers	• Market shares • Higher price • Time – increasing market shares over time • Price – over time command a higher price	• Market share lower as a function of total number of competitors • Price advantage lower as a function of total number of competitors	132 MMMF
Clark & Montgomery (1998)	Entry deterrence	• Reputation • Multi-market competition • Attractiveness / risk	• Aggressiveness (competitor) • Intelligence (buyer) • Reputation for aggressiveness and multimarket contracts high	• Aggressiveness (buyer) • Intelligence (competitor) • Reputation for intelligence and multimarket contracts high	Sample 1: 122 Sample 2: 96
López & Roberts (2002)	Regimes of weak appro-priability	• Market share • Entry time	• Time	• N/A	
Robinson & Min (2002)	Entry timing	• Time	• Time	• N/A	167 first-entrants 267 early followers
Michael (2003)	Franchising	• Resource scarcity	• Higher outlet share • Higher market shares from outlet shares	• N/A	Sample 1: 100 Sample 2: 137 Sample 3: 72
Shamsie et al. (2004)	Entry timing	• Market shares • Survival rate	• N/A	• Enter when still sufficient market opportunity • Enter with considerable resources • Strong position: quality, price and innovation	165
Carow et al. (2004)	Entry timing	• Combined (target and acquirer)	• Acquisitions early in an acquisition wave • Cash paid, growth	• N/A	520

		stock returns • Acquirer stock returns	industry conducted and related business acquisition		
Coeurderoy & Durand (2004)	Proprietary techno-logy	• Early entry and market share • Early entry and technological resources • Early entry and cost leadership	• Time • Owning proprietary technology	• Cost leadership as strategy	1042

13. Innovative Opportunities and Strategies for Online Transactions

Peder Inge Furseth

INTRODUCTION

This chapter reviews the innovative opportunities available to retailers and banks that sell goods or services online as well as offline. The retailing industry is in a dilemma because companies are afraid of missing an epochal opportunity (Christensen and Tedlow 2000: 42). In this chapter the topic is pursued by interviewing experienced managers about the factors they believe to be critical for generating profitability in terms of the online channel. Based on such interviews with managers, this chapter presents unique data about managers' perceptions of factors that have a bearing on the integration of online and offline channels. With reference to the same companies that employ the managers, consumers are interviewed about various issues such as online spending and satisfaction with online solutions.[1]

There are different views about what the Internet is. Basically, it is a channel for taking orders, for marketing and for searching for information about products and services. That interpretation underpins this chapter. Channels other than the Internet can perform the same functions, for example stores, telephones, faxes, mobile solutions, direct marketing, and interactive TV. Unlike the store channel, however, the Internet channel is available only through a set of technologies.

Some people see the Internet as a technology. The Internet is typically defined as a world-wide network that provides electronic connections between computers, enabling them to communicate with each other using software such as electronic mail, telnet, Gopher, www browsers (e.g. Mosaic or Netscape) and so on. The Internet is in this respect not a single network, but a collection of interconnected networks.

Finally, some people consider the Internet to be a business model for guiding the decisions of companies that are seeking profit. Elliot (2002: 9) presents various types of B2B and B2C business models and classifies them along two dimensions: by degree of innovation and level of functional integration. The e-shop, which bears the greatest resemblance to the kinds of companies in the current study, is classified as having a low degree of innovation and few functions. In my opinion, this categorisation is rather misleading for people who are trying to develop Internet strategies for e-shops. Appropriate strategies for these companies seem to be much more complicated than an overview of business models would lead us to believe.

PHASES OF BUSINESS DEVELOPMENT

It is the Internet channel as such and not the business done there that is new. However, new strategies need to be developed for the channel. For example, online auctions are not really new. There have always been marketplaces like the stock market and other places where auctions have been held.

This chapter departs from the theoretical perspectives that present the various phases of business development with a view to electronic commerce. There is not much available on this topic. In fact, the concept of multi-channel business that figures in the media rather often does not have any accepted definition in the literature.[2]

Michael Earl (2000) pointed out that becoming an e-business is an evolutionary journey for most firms. He described the six-stage journey companies are likely to experience. The first two phases are external and internal communication, stage three is e-commerce, and stage four is e-business. The final two phases are called e-enterprise, and transformation. While these steps are stylistic, they present companies in terms of their progress in the work that needs to be done to get a presence online, but they do not give any hard advice to managers about what challenges they will face or how to handle them.

The benefits of e-commerce arise from the way in which tasks and activities are performed in the retail channel (Burt and Sparks 2003: 284). Burt and Sparks also point out that consumer reactions are not fully understood. In a study of phases of multi-channel retailing, it is therefore important to consider consumers' actions in the light of the way the strategies among companies with transactional websites develop. I will try to move a step in that direction in this chapter.

In a recent article, Aldin et al. (2004: 55) pointed to three phases of business development within electronic commerce: Companies initially started with changes on an activity level, followed later by changes in more holistic, business and chain or channel-wide restructuring in an effort to reap the full benefits of electric commerce applications. In the first phase, activities are refined to promote internal efficiency. In the second phase, companies change processes to increase integration and reduce time and costs, enabling service improvements and promoting interplay between the two. In the third phase, companies reshape structures and penetrate new segments and markets. These stepwise refinements are appealing, but they seem too compact in the sense that there are too many factors in each phase, making it impossible for companies to identify appropriate steps in the direction of an online channel. In our opinion, business integration between offline and online channels is a question of degrees. This view is presented in Figure 13.1.

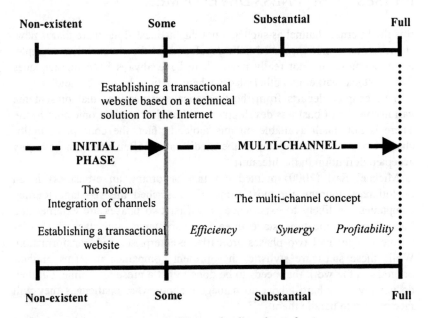

Figure 13.1 The two phases of multi-channel retailing

Some degree of integration should be taken to mean that a company that has a physical outlet also sells goods or services online. This is the degree of integration found in most companies with an online channel, and this is the degree experienced by the companies in this study. However, although there are stronger degrees of integration, I will not focus on them here.

First of all, companies need to establish a website. Websites are generally used for information, marketing or transactional purposes. Companies then need to align their IT strategy with their company strategy. The companies included in this study have launched transactional websites. Although websites for information and marketing are also important and represent challenges, such challenges cannot be avoided for companies that have transactional websites. Accordingly, this chapter will focus on the challenges facing companies with transactional websites.

Once a company has established a channel for selling goods or services online, the multi-channel strategy starts. Multi-channel goals include making the online channel more efficient, developing synergies between offline and online channels, and achieving profitability in all channels. To reach the multi-channel stage, companies need to take advantage of certain innovative opportunities that are addressed in the current chapter.

METHOD

Eleven retail chains and banks in Norway were selected for the purpose of interviewing managers as well as consumers. These companies represent a microcosm of the retailing and banking sectors. A total of 11 of the 13 companies in the research project had transactional websites, five of which were traditional retailers: books, electronics, wine, flowers, and sport equipment. There were four banks or banking service companies among the 11 companies as well as one airline and one cruise line with transactional websites. The 13 included just two companies with websites for information purposes.

Personal interviews of the managers in these companies were carried out in October 2003. The insights from the interviews were presented to all the managers at two different meetings, giving them an opportunity to discuss all the insights and to try to arrive at the content of the eight factors. The chapter subsequently reports the insights that are common among the managers. These insights were implemented in the managers' own companies, although to somewhat different degrees. Key figures such as online sales and conversion rates were collected from the companies on a monthly basis from December 2002 until October 2004. That facilitated a comparison of online sales and conversion rates before and after the personal interviews were conducted with the managers. Finally, about 300 customers in each of the retail chains and banks were surveyed in June 2004, receiving a response comprising some 3155 questionnaires.

In the event these customers were to buy more about a year after the managers decided on the success factors, I would be inclined to believe that the success factors the managers pointed out may be a relevant source for explaining an increase in online sales. Please note that there is no causal relationship between the success factors and consumers' actions. However, as managers were interviewed in a number of industries, their insights may have a bearing on other industries in retailing and banking than those named above. For example, one of the companies sells flowers. They are fresh products like milk and bread, so the insights of the flower company represent some of the same challenges facing online grocers.

WHY IT IS INTERESTING TO STUDY E-COMMERCE IN NORWAY

Norwegian consumers are innovative and adopt new technologies faster than consumers in almost any other country. Twenty-five per cent of Norwegian Internet users have ordered a product and/or service online during the past 30 days. This is one of the highest percentages in Europe. Furthermore, Norwegian customers plan to order a lot more on the Internet. Fifty-four per cent of Norwegian Internet users will shop online in the next 12 months. Most customers who shop online spend NOK 1000 to 5000 per month. Customers expect well-known retailers to offer a website with information as a minimum, and a large group of customers even expect retailers to offer a transactional website. Figures from Gallup indicate that 20 per cent of Norwegian customers use the Internet prior to a purchase in a physical store (*Gallup Interbuss* 2003). About 75 per cent of all Norwegian companies have a website and a little over 30 per cent of them have a transactional website (e-Business Watch 2004: 38). These are among the highest percentages in Europe, where only Denmark has higher figures than Norway.

EIGHT SOURCES OF INNOVATIVE OPPORTUNITIES

This chapter will present eight sources of innovative opportunities, or success factors, that managers indicated were of key importance when establishing a transactional website. Each factor presents a choice that companies need to make.[3] There are two ways to increase a company's competitive advantage, that is positioning and operational effectiveness (Porter 2001), and those eight factors are related to this.

The managers suggested eight innovative opportunities. It appears to me that the first four factors seem to be linked to positioning while the others are linked to operational effectiveness. Some factors are specific and concrete while others are intangible. They are listed here in increasing order of reliability and predictability. The first factors are the ones managers know the least about so special consideration is given to them in this chapter. This became apparent during our interviews with the managers.

The first four factors refer to positioning, or to doing something better than competitors do. These are:

- business culture; my or our customers. In many cases people in stores and banks have personal relationships with customers, but Internet channels make these relationships more distant.
- internal organisation; should there be a separate Internet department? If so, how high up in the organisation should the Internet initiative be located?
- assortment; should assortment in the online channel be the same as in the physical channel. If not, should it be wider or narrower?
- price; should a company charge the same price for identical articles sold online and in stores, or should prices differ?

The second set of factors for innovative opportunities refer to operational effectiveness, or to doing different things than competitors do. There are four factors here as well:

- logistics; should a company have a central distribution centre or should it ship goods from stores?
- customer history; how best to make use of customer data.
- IT/ERP; should a company use its original system or should it invest in a new system aimed at taking online orders?
- marketing; should customers see the company as one across various channels, or should the company conduct its marketing in different ways in different channels.

For some of these eight factors, the lines will be blurred and there will be considerable overlap. This will become apparent when the factors are presented in more detail later. Each factor has its own characteristics and therefore requires separate analysis.

FOUR INNOVATIVE OPPORTUNITIES RELATED TO STRATEGIC POSITIONING

Although each of the eight factors presents new challenges, the interviews with the managers indicate that the following four factors need careful consideration when managers identify Internet strategies. During the interviews, when presenting these insights to the managers, it became apparent that these factors were harder to handle than the other four.

The first innovative opportunity is *business culture.* Companies seek a situation where the employees feel ownership in respect of the Internet channel as well as other channels. Companies also want to get divisions and employees to move away from a situation with my customer and over to our customer. This is typical for retailers and banks. For example, when an item is sold online in an area where the retail chain has a store, the manager of that retail store believes the online sale represents a loss for the store. Management therefore believes it is crucial to have employees understand the benefit of shopping on the Internet, as the consumer sees it, and to indicate that the Internet channel represents a synergy and does not represent a conflict between channels.

One manager of a retail company said:

> I would have used a lot more time on each employee in the stores when we launched the Internet channel. That is very important, because you cannot succeed with transactions online if the storekeepers and other employees don't support the online channel and present it to customers in a favourable way.

A manager in another retail company said:

> We tell our employees that customers who shop in more than one of our channels visit us more often, spend a higher amount and are more loyal to our retail chain.

Launching an Internet channel therefore represents cultural challenges to a great degree. Apparently, no matter how well a company solves problems of a technical nature, it cannot succeed with online sales unless their store employees have accepted the channel and support it.

Company management believes customers should perceive the company's contact points as one integrated company. However, in the early phase after the launch of the Internet channel, there are typically various opinions inside each company about whether the Internet channel should be an information channel or be for transactional purposes. Companies have experienced that the level of channel conflicts has become lower, but they also realise it takes time to get acceptance for the Internet as a channel in the companies.

As regards *internal organisation,* companies build their organisation around the Internet channel in various ways, but it seems clear that the Internet division has gained a more distinct role in companies over the past few months. A number of companies will also establish service centres in connection with increased internal focus on online sales. The evaluation underlying these choices is that companies are organising to meet customers' needs as well as possible. The availability of customer service for the consumer is a key issue. Experience with these considerations varies among the companies. A growing number of people in the Internet division allow latitude for conflicts, but the experience of the managers in this dataset indicates that the division has also contributed to positive results.

As far as *assortment* is concerned, the companies have different strategies. One company has 20 per cent of its stock keeping units (SKUs) for sales online (in the sporting goods business), other companies have the same assortment both online and offline, while yet other companies have more items online than offline (books for example). Most companies take account of customers' wishes when choosing their online assortment strategy. At the same time, the assortment online is influenced by costs and internal resources. One manager says that: 'It is neither practical nor feasible to sell all products in all channels'. Another manager points to the fact that some products are easier to handle through online transactions. This represents a risk, however: 'If you choose to have fewer SKUs online than offline, you at the same time choose to turn a great number of customers away from the stores'.

The companies say they will continue being market-oriented as regards what part of the assortment will be available online. Customer feedback is considered useful for determining which products should be sold online.

The fourth innovative opportunity that the managers pointed to was *price*. The majority of the companies initially use lower prices online than offline in an attempt to draw customers to the online channel. This is typical for retailers and travel companies as well as banks. One retail manager says that:

> To drive traffic to the website, with the increase in rivalry among competitors, it seemed obvious to us we needed to introduce lower prices online.

A representative from a bank says that:

> The most important technique to motivate consumers to visit the website is a lower price online that offline. For example, we charge NOK 1 when a consumer pays a bill online, but NOK 20 when he or she pays a bill in the branch office.

Generally speaking, companies that set different prices online and offline do so to attract sales online, and to meet the strong competition from online players. They believe online sales cost less than offline sales.

However, most other companies are convinced that having similar prices online and offline is an important part of their strategy. They fear that consumers may get into the habit of expecting lower product prices online, and that in the long run this would undermine the business model of the company.

The companies that use similar prices in both channels do so partly to boost efficiency and partly owing to a desire not to cannibalise the various channels.

FOUR INNOVATIVE OPPORTUNITIES RELATED TO IMPROVING OPERATIONAL EFFECTIVENESS

I now turn to the innovative opportunities related to improving operational effectiveness. The first factor here is *logistics,* which is a challenge for retailers in particular. Companies state that the integration of systems and the automation of processes are important. Furthermore, managers believe that customers should be given a larger number of delivery options when ordering online. What lies behind these strategic considerations is the fact that logistics is an area where the companies have identified huge potential economic gains. However, several of them have experienced problems realising these potential gains. Their experience is that establishing real-time in-stock databases and an automated flow of products is perceived as a large and challenging process. However, the managers believe that success in this area entails a huge potential for increasing profits.

When it comes to *customer history* it is apparent that most of the companies collect information. Banks in particular practise this, since customers give a lot more information to banks than they do to retailers. Most companies have customer database systems and CRM systems. Companies also want to merge databases for traditional stores and online stores. Yet the companies in our sample used this information to a very small degree, if at all. Very few companies have the IT systems required to accomplish this kind of integration since they have old systems, but they realise that such databases are necessary for creating loyalty and sales across channels.

As far as *IT/ERP* is concerned, companies believe these systems should be built with a focus on the new distribution channels and the Internet in particular. Most companies develop systems based on internal resources and competence, while one of 11 companies said that it relies on vendors because it has plans to change its whole IT system. One reason most companies use their own resources to alter their IT systems is that they want to maintain control. The companies realise, however, that their current IT systems often complicate the multi-channel process. The companies realise that upgrading their IT systems is a more time-consuming process than they originally believed.

Finally, as regards *marketing,* many believe that companies need integrated marketing across the various channels. They see a considerable potential for making use of the Internet channel to build company and product knowledge in the market. Most companies want to be perceived as a single brand and a single voice in the market, even if they have channels in addition to the store. The rationale behind this is that companies want consumers to have the possibility to shop through multiple channels. It is believed that customers who shop in more than one channel are more profitable. Most companies report good results from placing strong emphasis on the Internet as a sales channel. This has led to an increased number of visits as well as sales online. Companies have also identified a tendency towards a larger degree of selling across the channels. That being said, efforts to become a multi-channel retailer are clearly perceived as being demanding.

In summary, based on personal interviews and two meetings at which the managers discussed their insights, companies tended to select the following strategies for each of the eight factors presented in Table 13.1.

According to the interviews, companies can be positioned better first by making sure that each employee feels a customer is our customer and not his or her personal customer, regardless of the channel in which a transaction takes place. This is an important element in changing company culture for the better once the Internet is launched as a channel for that particular company. It is also important to link the management of the Internet channel to the company's executive management. Most managers point out that a company should present all its products on the online channel as well, then explain it to customers if all items are not sold online.

Finally, as an important element in doing things differently from most companies, prices should be similar online and offline. Most of the companies that participated in the study implemented these strategies. At the beginning of the data collection period, in December 2002, some of the companies had lower prices online than offline, but that was not the case at the end of the period. The implementation of this strategy means companies have completed the first phase referred to in Figure 13.1 when it comes to factors that will engender a strategic advantage by positioning them better. In fact, some of the companies penetrated the multi-channel phase slightly, finding that the same prices online and offline increased efficiency.

Table 13.1 Strategy suggestions based on the innovative opportunities

Eight innovative opportunities	Suggested strategies for creating a strategic advantage by positioning the company better
Business culture	Make sure each employee feels a customer is ours and not mine regardless of the channel in which a transaction takes place
Internal organisation	Link the management of the Internet channel to executive management of the company
Assortment	Present all items in the stores in the online channel, and include an explanation if all items are not available online
Price	Similar prices online as well as offline
	Suggested strategies for creating a strategic advantage by improving operational effectiveness
Logistics	Give customers as many delivery options as possible
Customer history	Have moderate ambitions regarding the integration of customer databases with CRM systems
IT/ERP	Buy a new IT system sooner rather than later
Marketing	Project your company as representing one voice and one brand no matter which channels the customer meets

There was greater consensus among the managers in this project about factors that would create a strategic advantage by improving operational effectiveness. It is important to give the customers as many delivery options as possible to facilitate convenient delivery for them. Most companies should keep their ambitions for integrating customer databases with CRM systems at a moderate level. In fact, most companies realised that they were in great need of a whole new IT/ERP system rather than building more solutions on top of their original systems. Finally, a company should be presented as having one voice and one brand regardless of the channel in which customers meet the company. The managers pointed out that these decisions belong in the initial phase of the two phases of multi-channel retailing. For companies to be able to develop synergies, which is one of the three goals in the second phase, the marketing strategy entailing one brand

and one voice needs to be in place. In fact, some of the companies adopted such a marketing strategy after the interviews had been carried out. Nonetheless, the companies had barely begun to enter the second phase. I can therefore conclude this section by saying that in the current study, these companies are in transition between the first and second phase of the multi-channel process. The opportunities and strategies presented in Table 13.1 indicate what companies need to do to penetrate further into the multi-channel process.

CONSUMERS' RESPONSE

Until now the innovative opportunities available to the managers and what they chose to do in terms of each of them have been presented. The next question is what results were achieved about a year after these innovative opportunities were identified. Did consumers buy more from these companies and did they express a higher level of customer satisfaction, or was there no change? Figures 13.2 and 13.3 present key figures from six of the companies participating in the study; the retailers and the cruise line. These figures refer to online sales and conversion rates from December 2002 through October 2004. They enable us to compare month-by-month trends for the two indicators.

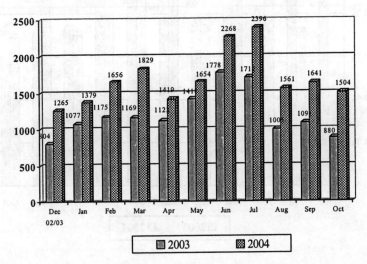

Figure 13.2 The number of online orders among the companies in 2003 compared with 2004

Figure 13.2 indicates that the number of online orders the companies received increased during the period in question. There was an increase in the average figures from 2003 to 2004. Furthermore, there was an increase in the number of online orders from each month in 2003 to the corresponding month in 2004.

The managers were interviewed in October 2003, and they also shared their insights among themselves at two meetings held right after the interviews. During the period prior to the personal interviews, there was an average of 1203 online orders per month. That figure increased to an average of 1524 online orders per month in the period after the interviews. This represents a 26.7 per cent increase in the number of online orders. The fact that these insights were established does not, however, necessarily explain the increase since there are other variables not accounted for in this study which could influence the number of online orders and conversion rates, for example, the positive e-commerce trend and the fact that consumers are becoming more mature in their use of the Internet.

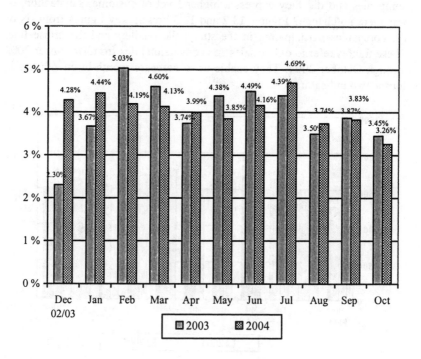

Figure 13.3 Conversion rate among the companies in 2003 compared with 2004

Figure 13.3 presents some results related to the conversion rate, that is, the percentage of website visitors who buy something online. The chart indicates an average conversion rate of 4.5 per cent. In other words, for every 100 people who visit the website, 4.5 people make a purchase there. There was an increase in the conversion rates for half the months in 2003 compared with the corresponding months in 2004, but there was generally little difference from one month in 2003 to the same month in 2004.

Even though the conversion rate remained more or less the same throughout the entire period of data collection, it should be pointed out that the number of unique visits doubled. This means that although the conversion rate remained the same, the number of orders doubled compared with Figure 13.2.

Figures 13.4 and 13.5 refer to a different dataset collected in June 2004. These data were derived from interviews of shoppers or consumers in the companies covered by the current study. Here the amounts of these consumers' spending online as well as figures that indicate customers' level of satisfaction with the transactional websites of the companies in the current study are presented.

Figure 13.4 compares the amounts customers spent online for retailing and travel with the companies in the current project. The data indicate the amounts of consumers' purchases each time they buy something online. Almost 43 per cent of consumers spend between NOK 200 and 500 each time they buy something from a retailer online, while 23 per cent spend between NOK 500 and 1000 each time. About 20 per cent of consumers spend more than NOK 1000 each time they buy something online from a retailer. Only 3 per cent spend more than NOK 5000.

Consumers spend more online with companies in the travel sector. In fact, 21 per cent of the online customers in the travel sector spend more than NOK 5000. More than 50 per cent of online customers in this sector spend more than NOK 1000. Of the consumers who took part in the survey, on average 33 per cent spent between NOK 1000 and NOK 5000 every time they bought something online.

Products and services typically cost more in the travel sector than in the retail sector. The logistics are often easier for products sold in the travel sector; no matter how much a ticket costs, it can easily be slipped into an envelope, while retailers usually have more logistical problems with the products they sell.

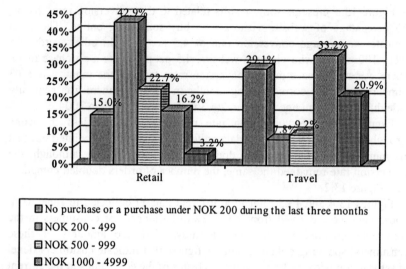

Figure 13.4 Comparison of amounts of consumer purchases for online retailing and travel in Norwegian kroner (NOK). The figures are average amounts each time a consumer buys something online from April through June 2004 (n = 1231)

The next chart examines customer satisfaction when buying online from the companies that took part in this study. The retail, travel, and banking sectors are compared.

Generally speaking, across three sectors consumers are typically either satisfied or very satisfied when they buy something online from the companies participating in the study. As many as 80 per cent of customers in each of these sectors are either satisfied or very satisfied when buying online.

Customers in the banking sector appear to be the most satisfied when the three sectors are compared. More than 87 per cent are either satisfied or very satisfied when buying online. The banking sector has spent more time and resources in developing multi-channel solutions than the other sectors. It is interesting though to find that consumers are nearly as satisfied with the multi-channel solutions in the retail and travel sectors as with the banking sector.

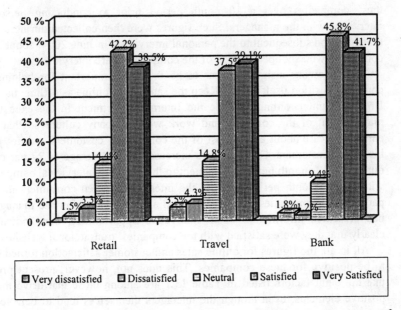

Figure 13.5 Customer satisfaction when buying online: a comparison of three industries (n = 1797)

The numbers presented in the Figures 13.2-13.5 indicate that, generally speaking, the strategies identified by the managers of these 11 companies, as presented in Table 13.1, should not be rejected. Figures 13.4 and 13.5 indicate that consumer spending in these companies is quite high, and that consumers are satisfied with the transactional websites of the companies. It is not possible to determine which of these eight strategies work for increasing orders online and which, if any, do not. Accordingly, they are presented as a set of strategies that should work together.

CONCLUSION

Table 13.1 presents eight innovative opportunities and strategies companies can follow when establishing transactional websites. The opportunities were collected and identified through personal interviews conducted in October 2003 with 11 managers who were responsible for developing e-commerce in each of their companies. These managers also shared their insights among themselves, arriving at agreement on which factors are most important and how to use each factor when establishing a transactional website. Key figures relating to online orders and conversion rates were collected from these companies over a 10-month period prior to conducting personal interviews with the managers. Such figures were then collected during a 12-month period subsequent to the personal interviews. In June 2004, about 300 consumers who shopped in each of the companies were interviewed.

The following insights appear to be the most important for helping a company position itself online. Keep the same price online as offline; have a large assortment online; include the Internet department in the executive management of the company and work with company culture so that all employees care about all or most of the companies' customers and not just his or her customers. Online orders increased by an average of 27 per cent during the 12-month period subsequent to the personal interviews, compared with the 10-month period prior to the interviews. When consumers in the participating companies were interviewed almost a year after the managers had presented information about innovative opportunities, they indicated clearly that they were satisfied with the companies' transactional websites.

All in all, the figures for online sales and customer satisfaction turned out to be positive for these companies. This does not, however, present proof that the eight factors listed in Table 13.1 are among those that drive these positive elements, even though the managers themselves tend to believe in these factors. It is hard to establish these eight factors as the cause of the positive developments or even as *a* cause of these developments. There may be other explanatory factors, such as the positive development in consumers' buying behaviour online and consumers' maturation in terms of online shopping.

However, I would argue that companies should view the eight factors as a set of factors that should be implemented, if possible, at the *same* time. The results regarding consumer satisfaction online and the number of orders indicate that the managers have been successful in developing e-commerce. At any rate, I would claim that the strategies presented in Table 13.1 should be considered by managers interested in boosting online sales.

NOTES

1. This research was supported by the PULS program in the Norwegian Research Council, project number 149937. I am grateful also to my interviewees.
2. See for example Coelho and Easingwood (2004: 2).
3. We start out with a broad view of the company, and suggest departing from factors that are either political, economical, social, or technical, as presented in the PEST- analysis. The Internet as a new channel towards consumers influences the company in a wide variety of ways.

REFERENCES

Aldin, Niklas, Per-Olof Brehmer and Anders Johansson (2004), 'Business Development with Electronic Commerce: Refinement and Repositioning'. *Business Process Management Journal* 10 (1), 44-62.

Burt, Steve and Leigh Sparks (2003), 'E-commerce and the Retail Process: A Review', *Journal of Retail and Consumer Services* 10 (5), 275-286.

Christensen, Clayton M. and Richard S. Tedlow (2000), 'Patterns of Disruption in Retailing', *Harvard Business Review* 78 (January February), 42-45.

Coelho, Felipe J. and Chris Easingwood (2004). 'Multiple Channel Systems in Services: Pros, Cons and Issues', *The Service Industries Journal* 24 (5), 1-29.

Earl, Michael J. (2000), 'Evolving the E-Business', *Business Strategy Review* 11 (2), 33-38.

E-Business Watch (2004), *Electronic Business in the Retail Sector. The Quantitative Picture: Diffusion of ICT and e-business in 2003/2004* Sector Report No. 6 (1). Available in electronic format only: http://www.ebusiness-watch.org/menu/Sector_Impact_Studies_2003%1004/

Elliot, S. (ed.) (2002), *Electronic Commerce: B2C Strategies and Models* Chichester: John Wiley & Sons.

Gallup InterBuss (2003), Number 4. Oslo: Norsk Gallup Institutt AS.

Porter, Michael E. (2001), 'Strategy and the Internet', *Harvard Business Review* 79 (March), 63-78.

14. The Future of Grocery E-Commerce – Will Business be Able to Meet Customer Needs and How?

Niels Kornum and Mogens Bjerre

INTRODUCTION

As already indicated elsewhere in this book, grocery e-commerce is facing serious challenges in its attempt to become profitable. Finding new business configurations in the grocery industry is difficult, as it operates at relatively low margins and sells low value high density products. Furthermore, customers seem fairly disloyal and value discounts. Clearly the business configuration must both be sufficiently efficient to gain profit and offer a service that the customer values to a degree that ensures customer retention and hopefully long-term loyalty.

Consequently, the e-grocery business needs to know what offerings customers value and can relate to emotionally, but must bear in mind that these offerings should be provided in a strategically consistent framework supported by operationally efficient configurations. Thus the first two sections of Chapter 14 summarise results from the consumer behaviour research presented in this book, although it is supplemented by other significant contributions. Focal questions are which preferences and attitudes guide purchase decisions of consumers when they choose between offline and online grocery channels, and how are such decisions embedded in a wider cultural context of values, roles and lifestyles? Developing a more detailed insight into the preferences and values of the consumer is a necessary, but not sufficient undertaking, as business cannot fulfil all the preferences expressed by consumers and accordingly must transform customer demands into viable business strategies. Providing consumers with what they think they want is not always profitable, as the experiences of Webvan[1] and many others have proven. The individual company must find a balance between what customers express as needs, what they can do to make an efficient and profitable business, and what the actions and reactions of competitors may be. These issues are addressed in the third section of this chapter, which presents results primarily from this book relating to the operational economics of the e-grocer, distribution and strategic issues such as first-mover advantages. These results are then compared to consumer/customer attitudes and demands, leading to a concluding discussion on how customer demand and business strategy and profitability can meet. The fourth section proposes themes for further research.

THE PREFERENCES, ATTITUDES AND VALUES OF CONSUMERS

Buying groceries differs from buying other types of consumer goods in a number of aspects. First of all, we need to buy groceries continually in order to survive and do so with relatively high frequency. This means that most adults have at least some experience shopping for groceries and do so more or less in a routine way or perhaps nearly as an automated process. Furthermore, it has been shown that many consumers, perhaps as many as 30 - 40% actually like to shop for groceries and perceive it as a positive experience. In this case, some of the obstacles facing e-grocers are already evident. Traditions and routines are obviously difficult to change, and if people like to grocery shop, why and how could this be changed?

Thus the first part of this section addresses the question as to why or why not consumers choose to buy groceries online. The second part of this section presents how customers or consumers choose between different product or service elements, such as attended or unattended delivery.

Why or Why Not Purchase Online?

The decision to buy or not to buy online can be evaluated by revealing consumer perceptions and experiences in the purchasing process in online and offline grocery services, for example in terms of the relative advantages of each of these channels. Explanations may also stem, however, from examinations of how the decision to purchase online is embedded in a wider context of consumer values and culture.

Focusing on the former, making choices in the purchasing process, consumers are confronted with both benefits and sacrifices whether they choose offline, online or both. With reference to Rogers (1983), Hansen (2002) and Chapter 4, three important concepts can be identified in order to understand consumers adopting the innovation of the Internet. First, there is the perception of relative advantages or disadvantages, compatibility and complexity. Relative advantages and disadvantages refers to the extent that consumers perceive online grocery shopping to be inferior/superior compared to brick-and-mortar grocery shopping. Second, important to the adoption rate may be the extent to which consumers find the online channel compatible with their values, experiences with traditional brick-and-mortar shopping and past behaviour. Finally, if consumers evaluate the channel to be complex, it may impede their motivation to use it.

Results from surveys undertaken in Sweden and Denmark (Hansen 2003) confirm the experiences reported by pioneers in the business that online grocery consumers experience two main *advantages* associated with the Internet: electronic grocery shopping saves much time (Boyer and Hult 2005) and online shopping is favourable as it makes the respondents less dependent on opening hours. The main *disadvantages* perceived by the respondents is that online grocery shopping is less exciting when compared to offline grocery shopping. Moreover, electronic shopping can be complicated because of limited opportunities to see and touch the specific products under consideration. However, consumers who have already purchased online subscribe less to these disadvantages compared to consumers who have not purchased online. Online grocery respondents perceive a high degree of *compatibility* of online grocery shopping with other daily activities, whereas consumers who have not yet purchased online state the opposite view. Thus those with online experience are significantly *more* positive than non-online grocery respondents concerning the compatibility of the online channel. Both off- and online shoppers find the online channel *complex* because of the lack of opportunity online to touch and see the products in full physical appearance (Friese et al. 2003 and Frostling-Henningsson 2003). However, comparing prices, evaluating quality, ease of ordering and finding products was found to be easy. Furthermore, shopping online in general was not found to be complex. Another reported disadvantage in relation to online shopping is problems with web page functionality and missing information, leading to an increase in time spent while ordering, eroding the amount of time saved, which was reported above as an advantage (Chapter 7; Friese et al. 2003; and Frostling-Henningsson 2003).

In general, *consumers who have already purchased groceries online* have a more *positive attitude* towards this new channel, as compared to non-users. Thus those who have adopted online grocery shopping attach higher compatibility, greater relative advantages, more positive social norms, lower risk, and lower complexity to Internet grocery shopping compared to consumers who have not yet bought groceries online. It is surprising that online and offline consumers differ in *all* these dimensions (Hansen 2003). Furthermore, this is valid when those who have adopted online grocery shopping are compared *both* to consumers who have never bought anything on the Internet and to consumers who have purchased goods/services on the Internet other than groceries (see Chapters 4 and 6). In a recent study, the level of customer experience is also found to have a strong impact on their perception of the positive effects of online grocery shopping (Boyer and Hult 2005). What are measured here are the effects of DC based picking versus store based picking. The study relates to the three aspects: better quality, timesavings and behavioural attributes like loyalty. However, experienced customers develop their skills quickly and also tend to become more demanding and less tolerant of shortcomings in product quality and service (Frostling-Henningsson 2003).

Clearly, functional or utilitarian aspects of the consumer buying process guide the decision to buy or not to buy groceries online. However, the decision to purchase groceries online may indeed involve deeper levels that relate to the personal and emotional values of consumers as well as cultural contexts, for example, a desire for health improvements, maintaining an existing lifestyle, a new moral outlook, being more life-giving to the members of the household and sharing the experiences of the day while gathered for a meal. Regarding these aspects, e-grocers are reported to be able to link emotionally to their customers (Chapter 7 and Frostling-Henningsson 2003). A longitudinal study also reveals that the motivation to buy groceries online may be specifically related to one's life situation. Family dynamics change and new children are born, children move away from home, people divorce, participate in new leisure activities, and so on, all of which may influence the possibility of experiencing home-shopping as an advantage (Frostling-Henningsson 2003). The same longitudinal study also reveals that in the beginning customers buy all types of groceries online, but later some switch to buying basic groceries online and specialty products offline, while still others completely give up online shopping for groceries.

Customer Choices Between Different Online Configurations and Options

It is important to identify customer preferences in relation to different online configurations and options when e-grocers configure the product and service palette to be offered. In Chapter 2, consumer preferences for different configurations of product/service offerings are examined and contrasted between off and online shoppers, that is, *customer preference for selected online grocery attributes*. The findings of this research show that a low degree of time usage for ordering the groceries and high product quality are the highest priority attributes for both online and offline shoppers, but offline shoppers attach higher priority to these attributes than online buyers do. Other attributes, however, prove to differ more between these two groups.

For example, delivery time reliability remains a concern for online shoppers, while offline shoppers are still focusing on the content of their shopping basket, finding the possibility of substitutes to be important. Furthermore, identifying five segments with similar preferences reveals significant differences in prioritising attributes between the segments, which indicates that an aggregated model may be less reliable as the basis for acquiring or retaining customers.

In contradiction to industry experience (Ramaswamy and Dikalov 2001), consumer *assortment requirements* with regard to fresh produce seem surprisingly low and can, based on the present results, hardly be regarded as a major obstacle for firms considering launching an online grocery store (Hansen 2003).

An argument often used in favour of online grocery shopping is that the direct channel from producer to customer, without the extra link of the shop, results in fresher foods. Boyer and Hult (2005), who focus upon this issue and address it in their main thesis, ask whether DC based picking and delivery direct to customers results in fresher foods and better quality and range due to the shortened supply chain as compared to store-based picking. The results show that picking from a distribution centre can provide better product quality because of a shorter channel. It may, however, take customers a while to realise the advantages because of their concern about dealing with a far off DC that they cannot physically see or touch. In Chapter 5 this perspective is supplemented with a study that examines service and product quality as perceived by in-store versus online customers. The results reveal that online customers view all aspects of service quality better handled online than offline. Furthermore, in-store customers rate product quality higher than online customers and consequently, there is room for improvements in the product quality of the e-grocers, although DC based picking is doing better than in-store picking (ibid.). Finally, the findings of Chapter 5 indicate that online shoppers do more of their shopping with their e-grocer than the in-store shoppers do with their grocers; a finding also reported in relation to Tesco.com (Ramaswamy and Dikalow 2001).

Another important issue regarding the service offered by e-grocers is the *method of delivery* that is chosen, for example, home delivery, delivery at work or traditional shopping. According to Chapter 4, a large proportion of consumers value, not surprisingly, traditional shopping, delivery of groceries at work is not attractive, whereas one third of consumers prefer home delivery. Respondents who value home delivery as compared to those who primarily value traditional shopping, differ primarily with respect to Internet experience and the number of household members. With regard to delivery on specific weekdays, consumers prefer midweek with delivery occurring between 4 pm and 10 pm, which, with respect to the latter, is not surprising.

Chapter 10 confirms that consumers prefer home delivery as compared to delivery at work or other delivery points such as schools. Consumers prefer attended home delivery with as few choice restrictions as possible and they expect a reduction in the delivery charge before accepting choice restrictions. Unattended delivery using delivery boxes is also valued by consumers, however they are unwilling to pay the costs related to the investment.

Delivery fees are an important part of delivery options and involve such aspects as consumer willingness to pay these fees, feasibility of fee size and how big an order would need to be to obtain delivery free of charge. On average, most Danish and Swedish respondents find it reasonable that an order costing below €80 should have free packing and delivery. Only a few Danish and Swedish respondents find that the limit for free packing and delivery should be more than €80. In addition, on average, the higher the outlay considered reasonable in order to get free packing and delivery, the more respondents are willing to pay (in delivery fee) for orders less than this limit. Very few respondents are willing to pay a delivery fee of any substantial size: in Denmark only 3% are willing to pay a delivery fee exceeding €8, whereas the percentage (11%) is remarkably higher in Sweden (Hansen 2003). US consumers are apparently not more inclined to pay delivery fees of any significant size (Kornum and Singh 2005). In Chapter 3, this lack of willingness to pay a delivery fee is confirmed based on Austrian cases where habits regarding more frequent shopping or larger perceived distance to the shop are reported not to influence the willingness to pay a delivery fee. In addition, Chapter 2 seems to indicate that the UK offline shoppers studied are more sensitive to delivery costs than online shoppers.

The results confirm Nordic, and to some degree, US industry experience; however, Tesco.com and others have managed to convince UK consumers to pay a delivery fee. The reason for this has not been looked at specifically, but may be due to UK specific socio-demographic circumstances such as urban structure and congestion, as mentioned in Chapter 1.

The results can be summarised as follows:

- The major advantage of grocery e-commerce is considered to be time saving and the possibility of ordering whenever you like. This is not surprising. However, this evaluation is influenced negatively by the time spent on ordering and/or waiting for the delivery to arrive. Thus the perception of saving time may erode if, for example, ordering and other online functions are too time consuming. Another reported advantage is that fresh produce delivered directly from a DC is perceived to be fresher than produce packed and delivered from the physical shop.

- The major disadvantages of online grocery shopping are reported to be the restricted possibility of seeing or touching the product prior to purchase and the lack of potential for being inspired in the physical shop. Furthermore, slow and badly designed websites are also mentioned as disadvantages, which also relates to the importance of being able to order quickly.

- Prior experience from online grocery shopping has a significant positive impact on the consumer perception of all aspects of online shopping. The perception of the experienced consumer, however, may change in the long run. Yet if changes in online offerings do not correspond to changes in customer perception, this may lead to reduced sales.

- Online grocery shopping is viewed both as a utilitarian driven process and as a process invoking deeper values within consumers. Some e-grocers are able to present offerings and experiences that make consumers link emotionally to the home delivery service offered.

- The prioritisation of valued attributes relating to online shopping varies between different segments identified in a population of both off- and online shoppers. It is therefore important to disaggregate customers into proper segments and specify strategies for, for example, service and product offerings accordingly.

- Consumers demand home delivery without restrictions, for example, narrow time windows, short lead times, a small or no delivery fee and attended or unattended delivery if the e-grocer pays for the delivery box.

HOW CAN BUSINESS MEET THE CHALLENGE?

Short-term Survival – Making a Profit from Offering Services to E-Grocery Customers

Ordinary grocery retailing is increasingly becoming an international business operating on a large scale, for example regarding distribution systems and store formats. The characteristics of this business model are, on average, low margins and selling low value products in large volumes. These characteristics are also heavily influencing the e-grocery business. Previously, for example in relation to Andersen Consulting's Smarte Store (Stahre 1998), cost reductions due to bypassing shops were thought to outweigh the extra cost of call centres and packaging and transportation, and result in larger average profits than the ordinary grocery business ($.01 for shop channel and $.06 for online channel). This, however, is probably not the case; at least not for DC based picking and sales in smaller volumes.

Thus, concerning *DC based picking and delivery* recent research presented in Chapters 8 and 9 shows that profits in the e-grocery business are much harder to obtain. Being profitable is only possible under certain conditions, such as charging a delivery fee or achieving certain levels of turnover. Both Chapters 8 and 9 investigate the cost structure of a home delivery system that includes picking and packing in a DC (as opposed to store-based picking) and direct deliveries from that DC. Figure 8.1 shows that the total operating costs of the DC are estimated to be between 25% and 32% of sales when sales are approximately €2 million, reduced respectively to 11% and 14% when sales are approximately €7 million. It is not possible from the text to determine whether total operating costs are total logistics costs or whether they also include fixed costs for call centres, IT&C, administrative functions, and so on. If the estimates only include logistics costs, the cost structure resembles the estimates in Chapter 9. In Chapter 9, it can be derived from Figure 9.4 that the total logistics costs are reduced from approximately 18% to 10% when sales rise from €3 to €70 million. But if administrative costs (fixed costs) are included, then the share of costs will rise to 38% and 15% respectively in the span of sales between €3 to €70 million. Thus if the estimates in Chapter 8 only include total logistics costs, then the cost structure follows a similar pattern, but if it too includes fixed costs, then further comparative research is needed in order to show the cause of this difference.

Chapter 9 presents a DC based solution that resembles Streamline's system, with weekly deliveries and an average order size of €106, unattended delivery[2] and delivery free of charge. Such a system needs a turnover of €67 million to breakeven and the e-grocer will accumulate a debt of around €15.8 million if this turnover is generated over a period of five years. If delivery fees are introduced from the start (turnover €2.65 million), a delivery fee of €22.9 per order is necessary if the system is to breakeven and the need for a delivery fee is gradually reduced to zero when the turnover reaches €67 million. The prospects for this DC based e-grocery system do not seem overwhelmingly positive. Nevertheless, DC based solutions do occur in this second phase of introducing grocery e-commerce, for example Sainsbury, Peapod and Ocado. Ocado.com is a London based e-grocer partly owned by the English grocery retailer Waitrose and financed by a €67 million[3] investment (Boyer et al. 2005). They offer a one-hour delivery time window and require a minimum order of €36. For orders from €36 to €109, they charge a delivery fee of €7.25 per order; anything above €109 has free delivery. With a volume of 10,000 orders a week (ibid.) and if the average order size is €109 (see Chapter 9) and the number of weeks is set to 50 this generates a turnover of €54.5 million. When or if they reach this limit, they are close to a turnover size estimated to break even and, furthermore, some of the initial losses may be covered by the large initial investment. However, Ocado.com is offering a one-hour time window and attended deliveries (see Chapter 8), as compared to the unattended deliveries on fixed weekdays used in the estimates in Chapter 9. According to Chapter 8, a one-hour time window and attended delivery service is 170% more time consuming than an unattended service on fixed weekdays. Although not yet calculated, an increase of that size in transport/delivery costs in the model presented in Chapter 9 will probably cause this scenario never to break even. Nevertheless, one of the factors that may improve Ocado's possibilities for becoming profitable has to do with a large proportion of orders perhaps falling below the €109 limit for delivery free of charge, consequently covering a significant part of the picking and transport costs. Furthermore, customers in certain areas of Central London are charged an extra €7.25 delivery fee irrespective of the order size. The significance of this can of course not be verified. Another factor could be lower wages for warehouse workers and drivers in the UK as compared to the scenario in Chapter 9 that is based on data from Denmark. Wages for drivers and warehouse clerks, however, seem only slightly (about 9%) lower in the UK[4] (Ramaswamy and Dikalov 2001). Ocado.com operates its own warehouse and own fleet of vehicles.[5] Based on secondary sources, it is possible to estimate the picking and transport costs per order that Ocado.com generates and compare this with the fees charged. Drivers, who cost €17.40 per hour (Ramaswamy and Dikalov 2001), can handle two orders per hour based on the one-hour time window (Boyer et al. 2005, p. 97). The vehicle costs are €1.16 per order (Ramaswamy and Dikalov 2001), and according to Chapter 9, the costs of picking and packing orders in the warehouse is estimated to range from €7.14 to €7.16 per order per hour, which is related to a warehouse clerks salary of €11.6 per hour (Ramaswamy and Dikalov 2001). This causes the total delivery cost per order to range from €10.59 to €11.48. Compared to the delivery fee of €7.25 it is clear that not all costs would be covered even if every order was below the €109 limit. Ocado.com does not seem to be able to gain profit from this business in any easy way. There are, however, a number of reasons why they may succeed after all. According to Boyer et al. (2005)[6] they had a carefully planned and phased rollout of the service and, as already mentioned, initial investments were substantial. In addition, London has a significant number of potential customers who are more time sensitive than price sensitive and located with high density and, as mentioned elsewhere, congestion may cause UK consumers to be more willing to pay delivery fees. In addition, competition from major players such as Tesco, Sainsbury and Asda may increase Waitrose's motivation to support the initiative until it is self-sustaining and profitable. Both the competitive environment and the customer base are quite different than, for example, in Denmark, causing large retailers here to largely posit a wait and see attitude with respect to home delivery. Thus depending on socio-demography and competitive environments, the DC based solution is likely to progress at very dissimilar paces.

Store based picking and delivery are represented by the biggest player in the market, Tesco.com, but also by significant retailers such as Albertson's, Sainsbury and Peapod. The store based approach has a number of known advantages, such as small initial investments and access to a large assortment in the shops, but also a number of disadvantages, such as inefficient picking systems. See, for example, Chapter 8. What, however, is the short-term profitability of this approach? It is obvious that a number of fixed costs are hidden in the overall costs of the specific shop, or as administrative costs at the retailer headquarters' level, including website development and maintenance costs. However, the costs directly associated with home delivery should be covered by a delivery fee, because the shop is more or less obliged not to give visible discounts to home delivery customers if they do not offer similar discounts to the rest of its customer base. Nevertheless, if a retailer wants to rapidly increase home delivery by offering free delivery above a certain order limit like Ocado's, then customers in the physical shop should perhaps also be offered a discount when buying in large quantities. Notwithstanding, the overall strategy of most e-grocers has been to cover the direct costs by a delivery fee, which Tesco's success shows is possible. The more exact features of these operational costs are explained in estimations from secondary sources. Thus, in the case of Tesco, the delivery costs are only €1.6 higher than the delivery fee, but since the average order size is 3½ times larger than in the shop, the net margin is higher than for the shop-based sales (Ramaswamy and Dikalov 2001). Based on US data, a similar type of reasoning is proposed by Boyer et al. (2005, p. 99). The cost difference between delivery fee and delivery costs is calculated at €1.56, a difference balanced precisely by larger orders (basket sizes), generating higher net margins. Profitability is then likely because this segment tends to buy higher margin products.

The overall conclusion on short-term profitability of grocery home delivery solutions is that the losses in the initial phase, before a possible break-even somewhere around €70 million in sales for a DC based solution, either should be paid by a patient investor or by a delivery fee per order. And, as the former, for example grocery industry external investors, have been in short supply since 2000, the question is what then should be the strategy of the retailing industry? A paradoxical vicious circle of initiating grocery home delivery seems liable to develop. For example, the Nordic countries have one of the highest Internet penetration rates in the world and reasonable online sales in categories other than groceries (Hansen 2003). Despite this, sales of grocery home delivery services are marginal, for example, they are estimated to be 0.3% of the total grocery market in Denmark.[7] As already noted, consumers are not willing to pay a delivery fee of any substantial size, which retailers of course know. On their part, large retailers are unwilling to pay the initial investment because they are afraid of second mover advantages because of earlier experiences in, for instance, the introduction of organic products. They find that the cannibalisation of their own shop sales is important, because the total market is not expanding. The possible long-term advantage of creating a substantially closer bond with consumers is not considered to balance the short-term disadvantages (Kornum et al. 1999). The general resistance towards paying delivery fees is also reported in surveys done in the Chicago area and on the East Coast of the USA, where only 9% of respondents were willing to pay above €5.46 (Kornum and Singh 2005). Nevertheless, home delivery services are operating in these areas, their success seeming to depend on the specific socio-demographic circumstance that consist of a metropolis with a large customer base that is not price sensitive and consequently pays the delivery fee with a smile. Thus the 9% are probably located in sufficient density to form a base that is willing to pay delivery fees, so covering the initial costs of developing a home delivery service. So, in the UK the short-term prospects of grocery home delivery are that this new market has already been created and is gaining momentum with a significant market share (see Chapter 2). In Chicago and on the East and West Coasts of the USA, the market is in the process of being created, but elsewhere, for instance, in the Nordic countries, the creation of this market is in a process that includes first and foremost niche and specialty companies, causing low growth and a marginal share of the total grocery market. Accordingly, specific socio-demographic circumstances may play a major role in the penetration of home delivery systems. Still, the long-term strategies of retailers involved also differ. Tesco, Ocado and Albertson's seem to have had a long-term strategy that guided the short-term decisions concerning e-commerce set-up, whereas the long-term strategy of most Nordic retailers seems to have been wait and see or we have already tried it and it did not work. Coop Denmark, Nettorvet.dk is one of the few exceptions, but they primarily sell non-food and customers must collect their orders at Coop's shops. This naturally leads us to consider the long-terms prospects of grocery e-commerce.

Long-term Prospects and Strategies

Many of the existing players like Tesco and Albertson's have developed home delivery systems as an extra channel that supplements their shops. Consequently, the online channel is likely to recall the same brand association in customers' minds. But is it better to differentiate the home delivery brand from the shop brand? The investigations of consumer behaviour and socio-cultural contexts indicate that this may be a good idea. For the more mature markets like those in the UK, this could be a strategy for differentiation, while for more immature markets like those in the Nordic countries, this may be the key to an entry strategy. Some of the results from consumer research relate primarily to functional and utilitarian aspects of a home delivery service, whereas other results focus on how the service is experienced as a brand and how customers relate emotionally to this and how well the service corresponds to the basic values and life circumstances of its customers.

Concerning functional and utilitarian aspects, consumer studies reveal two major areas of concern: one is the fact that many consumers do not plan their meals in advance, not even a week or a day ahead of time. Second, consumers seemingly have inexhaustible demands concerning service flexibility and frequency, but their willingness to pay, for example, separate fees is not overwhelming.

If we discuss the second issue first, a theme touched upon in several sources is the importance of a smoothly functioning website. *New customers* are very sensitive to website functionality and give up completely if it does not function well. Bear in mind that research has shown that consumers without prior e-grocery experience have significantly less positive attitudes towards this service. Dysfunctions in basic online infrastructure simply are not tolerated any more. This further emphasises the importance of giving extra attention to first-time customers in order to secure (as far as possible) a positive first impression.[8] Otherwise, these customers may never return. The *experienced customer*, on the other hand, may develop new demands and investigations have shown that it is important to reduce ordering time as much as possible. Some underlying themes, however, have no straightforward answers, such as the balance between the number and size of pictures and speed of website transactions. For a more detailed discussion of this theme as a whole, refer to, for example, Boyer et al. (2005, pp. 205 - 230).

Customer demands concerning *service offerings and service flexibility*, such as delivery time windows, frequency, attended vs. unattended delivery, and so on seem inexhaustible. Thus most research indicates that customers want the best service without paying extra. A very important lesson learned from the first phase of grocery home delivery is that is very badly received, changing the delivery conditions for the worse, for example charging a delivery fee instead of free delivery or changing time windows from one to two hours. Matomera, a Swedish firm (Carlheim-Gyllenskjold and Rangefeld 2002 and Chapter 10), and the former Danish e-grocer, ISO.dk, experienced that many customers left the service when such changes were made. Accordingly, it is much better to start with lower levels of delivery service and then improve when the financial situation permits. Aarstiderne.com is an example of a niche player who has combined high-profile specialty products with low service flexibilty: weekly deliveries on fixed weekdays with unattended delivery.

Customers, who seem to have accepted this type of delivery have probably done so because they see the process as being more or less automated. The customer subscribes to receiving a number of fruit and vegetable boxes, often once a week. The firm decides the exact content, payment is monthly and transferred automatically. Delivery is unattended, but the firm substitutes with the same or a similar box if a box disappears or is stolen. From the perspective of the customer, they experience receiving fresh premium produce by doing absolutely nothing, except paying, and this is the value creating aspect of this set-up, not the time windows or other delivery features as such. The surprise element of the boxes, which also include recipes, appears partly to replace the role of the shop as inspiration when composing a meal for the family.

And this guides us directly to the first question mentioned in the beginning of this section, namely that many consumers do *not plan in advance what they expect to serve as a meal*. This is a major obstacle, but customers may like being relieved of some these decisions by being offered the choice between several boxes containing all the necessary ingredients specified by the recipe. This makes the planning decision simpler, reducing the time spent ordering and thereby opening up the possibility of weekly deliveries and larger order quantities. Furthermore, this set-up differentiates the home delivery service from the offerings of ordinary supermarkets, opening the path for a quite new brand, reducing logistics costs, and perhaps first and foremost, making price comparisons more difficult.

A differentiation of the home delivery service as compared to ordinary supermarket offerings shifts the focus from a service system selling products to a corporate brand that is capable of attracting customers that link emotionally. Behind the surface of boring routine, grocery shopping evokes a set of emotions that are embedded in the fundamental value systems of the family. As already mentioned in this chapter, grocery shopping is part of a story which tells of assisting families to live healthy lives, reducing the environmental and social impact of producing, for example, child labour.

Grocery shopping normally leads to meals that are the symbolic centre of social interaction and communication in the family.

Being able to unravel and identify these sets of emotions and fundamental value systems relates to the most fundamental and durable level of a long-term strategy for a grocery home delivery service. An example is Ocado.com: Our mission is to make grocery shopping a highlight of the week for every Ocado customer. We have sought to create an exciting new grocery experience in which our actions speak louder than our words. Our people are encouraged and trusted to exceed their own and customers expectations. Together we will deliver an unrivalled personal service that surprises and delights customers everytime, everywhere. Every touch counts.[9] As Director Robertson, Ocado.com expresses it: We are working to change the habits of a lifetime (Boyer et al. 2005, p. 120). And Ocado's customers seem to find that they get slightly better products and much better service than in ordinary shops (ibid., pp. 122 - 125).

Another example is Aarstiderne.com, who sell fresh organic produce, primarily vegetables and fruit in pre-selected boxes via a subscription service. Their philosophy is: Aarstiderne delivers organic food products directly to the kitchen door of the customer, who values quality, variety and taste – and thereby creates economic freedom for the development of the company and its employees. And their mission is: Aarstiderne recreates the close connection between the cultivation of the soil and joy in meals that are full of good raw materials, health, taste and presence. This last example illustrates the described story telling of families gathered around the dinner table, enabling health, taste and presence. Aarstiderne.com is realising profits and has attracted 30,000 customers in the four years since its launch and apparently has loyal customers (Baagø and Andersen 2001).

Thus, as also mentioned in Chapter 7, the online grocery business needs to focus much more on its practices and values. It has to strategically rethink itself as a new type of businesses concerned with the total welfare of consumers, attentive to consumer values. If online business wants a strategic advantage it needs to focus more on what it can do better than traditional supermarkets and at the same time on solving problems in the daily lives of its customers.

These general strategic reflections are specified below in relation to three main formats that have developed within grocery home delivery (Kornum 2002): a) shop based home delivery, b) DC based home delivery and c) DC based specialty home delivery.

a) Shop based home delivery
The strategic situation for this format is different in more *mature markets* such as the UK and markets that have barely emerged, consisting of few and

small players, such as in Denmark. In more mature markets consumers have more available offerings to choose from instead of just accepting an e-grocer because there are few or no alternatives. Likewise, Chapter 2 mentions that as a market matures, e-grocers should pay attention to the creation of a variety of online offerings for different customer acquisition and retention purposes. If the e-grocer wishes to increase customer retention, it is possibly more efficient to select one or two segments from among online shoppers and focus resources on their most important preferences rather than looking at the online shopppers as a whole.

Besides focusing on narrower ranges of customer segments, identifying how to differentiate from emerging competitors may be a challenge. Some of the emerging competitors of, for instance, Tesco.com are DC based solutions like Ocado.com. According to Boyer and Hult (2005), customers perceive DC based grocery offerings to be of better freshness, quality and range. Thus shop based home delivery must evaluate to what extent the offerings of competitors are better regarding aspects that are crucial to their customers' value systems. For example, if Ocado.com and similar systems prove better and eventually erode Tesco's customer base, then this combined with logistics and assortment considerations may lead them to re-evaluate using a DC based solution instead of a shop based system.

The possibility of competitors eroding the customer base of, for example Tesco.com, reveals another important theme relating to more mature markets, namely the possibility of the first-mover sustaining its competitive advantage. Accordingly, Chapter 12 suggests that if the e-grocer possesses resources that are valuable, rare and difficult to imitate, this may prove to generate sustainable competitive advantages. As e-grocers normally do not develop new technologies or possess patents, how can they build resources and capabilities that are not easily imitated? First of all, customers must perceive the offerings of the first-mover e-grocer as more valuable and rare compared to competitors' offerings. Second, these offerings and the internal organisation that develops and maintains them must be difficult to imitate. One study of a specialty e-grocer (Kornum 2005) reveals that customers may value the premium and specialised assortment of home delivery and the sense of being a member of a club (brand). This specialty assortment is available in ordinary supermarkets, but only if the customer searches several shops. Home delivery is available, but immediate competitors do not have as large an assortment as the focal e-grocer, and if assortment, home delivery and brand are evaluated as a whole, the synergy effect adds to the rareness of the valued offerings. How difficult is it for competitors to imitate the offerings? The combination of a large home delivery system and a specialised assortment is of course possible to imitate, but it demands a considerable effort in resources and would be very risky. If implemented gradually, it takes a significant amount of time to build, during which the first-mover may already have developed new offerings. The feelings toward the brand and of belonging to a club may be rooted in capabilities containing tacit and ambiguous elements, making it difficult to imitate at all. The organisation that created the brand is a unique combination of founders and other staff that have evolved together and the delicate balance that has evolved in this network is very difficult to imitate. Moreover, if external sources intervene, for instance by acquisition, this balance may be completely destroyed. In summary, mature markets give new challenges to the first-mover e-grocer. As a result, it is probably worthwhile to investigate to what degree the competitive advantage of the e-grocer is sustainable or durable as competitive pressure intensifies.

The situation of the pioneering firm undertaking shop based home delivery in an *immature market* is different. As discussed earlier, this format has covered the direct costs of the home delivery system by charging a delivery fee. In many markets, including the Danish one, delivery fees seem to be the primary reason why these home delivery systems did not expand faster. Hence, a number of the pioneering retailers experienced that home delivery sales stayed marginal and therefore decided to close this channel. What then should motivate these grocery retailers to re-establish a home delivery channel? First, there are a number of reasons that support a decision to keep the channel closed. A considerable part of what consumers buy in a supermarket was not planned in advance and retailers are reluctant to lose these spontaneous purchases. Another problem is cannibalisation, which is more likely to occur for large retailers in their own physical shops than for smaller retailers also offering an online channel. Yet it is not a given that the introduction of home delivery will influence shop sales negatively. When the regional Danish retailer ISO established home delivery, the intensified PR that this gave had the effect that sales in ordinary shops grew and 70% of home delivery customers were estimated to be new (Juul 2001). In addition, it is reported that 25% of Tesco home delivery customers are new and 25% are existing customers, however Tesco has higher sales as a consequence of home shopping (Ramaswamy and Dikalov 2001). Hence, instead of cannibalisation and lost spontaneous purchases, the home delivery method may instead lead to new customers both off- and online. The differences in market configuration, of course, need to be considered.

How then should shop based home delivery be able to expand? The delivery fee is the most obvious parameter to examine closely. As already mentioned, free delivery may be proposed for orders somewhere around €110 and if this proves problematic for store customers, then giving them a similar discount should be considered as well.[10] Such a strategy is more costly in the initial phases, but has a much greater chance of leading to faster expansion. Despite an initial marginal volume, home delivery needs total commitment and attention from the entire organisation, with regard to both planning and launching, if it is to succeed. The shop-based formats have, at least in Denmark, generated many complaints from their customers involving, for example, website and service organisation, which were reported to be partly dysfunctional and inconsistent in appearance (Friese et al. 2003). Consequently, total commitment, attention to detail and a consistent appearance are important factors when introducing home delivery in relation to the specific set-up of the store based format. Although risky, the long-term prospect is acquiring new and perhaps also more profitable customers in a non-expanding market, thereby invoking new value and flexibility in the retailer organisation.

b) DC based home delivery

Initiating home delivery as a DC based solution has the advantage of potentially creating a new profile with no reference to ordinary supermarkets, allowing closer contact with the value systems of customers. Ocado.com express this point: If you were going to create a revolutionary online grocery business, how would you go about it? In short, you'd create Supermarket shopping, the way it should be. At Ocado, that's exactly what we've done. We have literally built a new online grocery service from a blank sheet of paper to address the needs of busy people. Thus this delivery format gives the freedom to design a brand and a service package from scratch, but also allows for more direct and fresher deliveries, a more dedicated service staff and system, and so on.

In addition, this format invites management to re-think the grocery business, embedding groceries in a much larger and potentially more profitable context. A long-term mission for a DC based home delivery service might instead of just groceries expand to be: *The Preferred Convenience Partner of the Household*. Stahre (1998, p. 1) summarises how the former Streamline perceived their relationship to customers:

> Streamline wants to own a horizontal relationship with the consumer being a convenience partner. Streamline sees themselves in the lifestyle solution business. They don't see themselves in the food or grocery business. Streamline hopes to show families that it can improve the quality of their lives by taking on the burden of a significant number of household responsibilities, [e.g.] not only groceries ..., but also rental videos, Postage Stamps and UPS package pick-up, dry cleaning and collecting films for development.

As already noted several times in this book, the grocery business is low margin, selling low value high density products, causing logistics costs to be a significant share as compared to sales. Including a broader assortment and defining the business as convenience & lifestyle gives a much better basis for configuring the service package, making the total concept difficult to compare with ordinary supermarket grocery shopping, including the crucial parameter of price. Another important point is that home delivery develops a unique infrastructure suitable for the delivery of any kind of product or service offering that coincides with the corporate brand of the firm. In general, groceries may account for as much as 95% of the total volume of consumer goods that are sold to households (Kornum et al. 1999) and groceries are purchased more frequent than other types of consumer goods. Consequently, if this infrastructure has been built in the first instance, then it is much easier and less costly to add on extra products to the portfolio. A recent example is Aarstiderne.com, who in four years has developed a distribution system that covers 80–90% of all Danish households. Another Danish online company, oeltorvet.dk, who sells domestic and imported specialty and quality beer, has contracted with Aarstiderne.com and is now using their distribution system to implement home delivery to their customers. A paradoxical long-term consequence of such a development may be that certain home delivery services may gradually compete with parcel distributors, at least on a regional level and in smaller countries like Denmark.

A longitudinal study done in Sweden (Frostling-Henningsson 2003) shows that consumers, after having used a home delivery service for some time, tend to use the service primarily for basics or dry groceries. Accordingly, it would be interesting to take a closer look at a DC based home delivery that could perhaps be entitled: Dry Grocery Direct. Such a service has earlier been proposed by the industry as a likely format that could become successful (Kornum et al. 1999). To our knowledge, home delivery with such a focus has not yet been introduced; still the question remains open whether some existing services are heading in that direction. For instance, Peapod's customers generally have an average outlay of €112 and shop twice a month. This indicates that customers use the service for buying infrequently and in relatively large quantities, which can be viewed as a strategy for minimising the delivery fee burden and its effect on the average sales price. Nonetheless, Peapod offers a broad range of products online and their homepage does not show the average assortment configuration of the baskets.[11]

A Dry Grocery Direct service should also be based on infrequent deliveries in relatively large quantities using one centrally located warehouse with highly automated picking systems. Such a service should also use general parcel distributors in order to reach large areas of the population in the start-up phase in order to break even quickly. There are some drawbacks to such a solution. Dry groceries represent the part of the grocery assortment with the lowest margins and the parcel distributors, at least in some countries and regions, normally have neither late afternoon deliveries nor evening time windows. It is not impossible, however, that such problems could be solved in collaboration with the parcel distributors. The most challenging issue is that the service will compete directly with the discount-oriented side of the grocery business, which in many countries suffers very intense competition. Therefore an existing large player with grocery retailing and discount retailing experience seems to be the most likely investor. However, the known obstacles of spontaneous purchase and cannibalisation still exist for such a service.

A final issue related to DC based home delivery also originates from the above-mentioned Swedish study (Frostling-Henningsson 2003). Consumers who have used an online service for some time tend to evaluate the physical shop from a new perspective. They value the positive aspects, for example getting inspiration by visiting the actual shop, more than they did before using the online service. In the long run, this may be advantageous for brick-and-mortar firms that have branded the firm as a dual channel option. Notwithstanding, only the future development of the business can tell whether these trends will materialise and influence players that offer systems dedicated to the online channel.

c) DC based specialty home delivery

This format generally makes a business by offering a specialty assortment with premium products, for example Omahasteak.com (US), HarryandDavid.com (US), Harrisfarms.com (US), GotFruit.com (US), and/or products that are not easily available in ordinary shops; at least not with as wide an assortment, for example Diamondorganics.com (US), Rivernene.co.uk (UK), Riverford.co.uk (UK), Aarstiderne.com (DK) and Arstiderna.com (SE). The specialty assortment in general seems to provide higher margins and higher value density than groceries on average. Furthermore, many of these services offer pre-packed boxes, which reduces picking and packing costs. Some companies such as Diamondorganics.com and Aarstiderne.com do unattended home deliveries, which also reduces transport costs significantly. This format therefore tends to become profitable at lower levels of sales than the DC based grocery home delivery service. The specialty e-grocer also seems to have better possibilities for designing a brand that the customer can link with emotionally because it corresponds well with the value system of the family, thereby generating more satisfaction (Friese et al. 2003) and generate loyal customers. See Kornum (2002) for a detailed discussion of the features of this format.

Thus the focus on a narrow assortment has some obvious advantages, but depending on domestic market size, expansion beyond a relatively narrow customer base may prove to be a challenge. Expansion can follow at least three different strategies:

1. Differentiation of the niche position by adding more services or deepening the assortment within the specialised field,
2. Gaining economies of scale and thereby cost reductions within their specialised field by expanding in existing or into new markets,
3. 'Diversifying' by adding more grocery products to their assortment, moving from a niche to a mega player position.

The first strategy is the least resource demanding strategy to implement, but also has the smallest effect on expansion, because existing customers are not likely to be able consume much more within the specialised assortment than they already do. Products in a broader price spectrum (wider assortment) may increase sales. Attracting new customers may also be possible by, for example delivery service improvements. Concerning strategy two, expansion in existing markets may be difficult because the service attracts primarily a niche segment. Expansions into other markets are normally difficult because of cultural, legal and other constraints. The third strategy also contains some obstacles. First, the specialty e-grocer must be very careful not to just add new products adhoc without any clear analysis of whether specific product categories may erode the brand. Second, some product categories of groceries are traffic builders with a very low or negative margin, for instance fresh milk in some markets, and other voluminous products with low value density. Thus expanding the assortment should be initiated primarily with high margin and high value density products while products at the other end of the scale should wait as long as possible to be introduced as home delivery. In this situation, the consumer and the home delivery service obviously have opposing interests, because bulky or voluminous items represent products that consumers would prefer not to have to carry home from the shop. The willingness to pay extra is, however, not overwhelming, as already mentioned many times. A more detailed strategy should include the specific market contexts in order to prioritise between the different elements of the three strategies.

FURTHER RESEARCH

Based on the status of research within the topic of grocery e-commerce, this section suggests areas where further research would be fruitful. The following themes are proposed specifically within *consumer behaviour and customer relationship research*:

- A more precise picture as to why or why not, and how consumers plan their grocery shopping would be helpful, especially the planning relating to composing meals. General consumer behaviour literature should be reviewed with a focus on the planning process involved in composing a meal, and meal planning in relation to the online channel as well as the dual channel interaction of planning should be examined in new studies.

- In close connection, further studies of what assortments are needed to prepare a meal are suggested. According to Hansen (2003), consumers did not prioritise fresh produce such as vegetables, fruit, sliced meat, cheese, milk, and so on, very high. This is astonishing because in relation to Tesco.com, for example, it is reported that fresh produce (Ramaswamy and Dikalov 2001) makes up a larger proportion than in shops, indicating that further research on, for example how consumers prioritise between different types of shopping baskets is recommended. In general, studies of the patterns or clusters in the configuration of the shopping basket content should be encouraged. A Danish study showed that only 20% of the orders (shopping baskets) from a home delivery service could be organised in clusters that include orders of at least some similarity (Rusbjerg 2005). This is confirmed by industry experience, causing Tesco.com to maintain store based picking because of access to a larger assortment (Child 2002). In keeping with this, cross-country studies of off- and online orders would be interesting.

- In most industrialised countries the household sizes are reduced. This potentially causes the outlay size in grocery shopping to decrease, reducing the size of the segments interested in grocery home delivery in the long run because the households using these services primarily are dual income multi-child families. Other aspects of this change relate to changes in activity patterns, where the families are more outwardly oriented, perhaps causing household members to meet less often for the evening meal. In this respect, there are significant cultural differences, for example, between Sweden and Denmark, where Swedes frequently eat a hot meal at work, school, and so on, whereas the hot meal is more often eaten at home in Denmark, which gives widely different consumer segments from which a specialty grocery like Aarstiderne.com can attract customers. International studies of these mega trends in family structure and activity and consumption patterns should be combined with a focus on the online channel or in combination with the offline channel.

- As part of international studies, how consumers perceive delivery fees as part of the total cost-benefit structure of a service offering should be examined. One specific question that also needs to be addressed is to what extent are UK consumers more willing to pay delivery fees compared to consumers in other countries? And if they are, why is that the case?

In addition, the following themes are proposed in relation to *business strategy and distribution research*:

- As mentioned the specialty e-grocer could consider widening and deepen its assortment as part of an expansion strategy. However, adding a number of products not only has implications for brand and assortment mix considerations, but also affects the delivery service and thereby the cost structure. Consequently, quantitative modelling and analysis of the relation between assortment breadth (and depth), level of delivery service and the related costs is probably of immediate interest for the business.
- In connection with this, economic modelling of different formats of grocery home delivery should be refined, in particular the shop based and the DC specialty e-grocer need to be modelled and compared to the DC based grocery home delivery system (Chapters 8 and 9 and Boyer et al. 2005). As part of this, two further issues could be of interest. First, more studies are needed to make cost comparisons across national borders more precise and informative. Second, additional data from the retailing industry relating to how the share of turnover of different cost categories is reduced as compared to increasing turnover (scale factor) need to be collected and examined. The models presented in Chapters 8 and 9 estimate these scale factors, but experience from other types of online industry and offline retailing specifying how different cost categories interrelate when the total sales increase will support a refinement of the model, making it more robust.
- When the initial problems involved in developing the industry to make it profitable have been addressed, then the next issue is how the first-mover can sustain the competitive advantages potentially arising from its position. Similar to the discussion in Chapter 12 and earlier in this chapter, international research on how the first-mover in more mature markets can sustain its advantages is

relevant. One aspect involves understanding when and why channel conflict (as a consequence of resource dependence between the involved parties) occurs and what strategies will prove to be important. A part of this is to begin analysing the potentially stronger tie between the e-grocer and its customers, which the direct home delivery connection may develop. In Kornum (2005), some initial conceptual considerations exemplified by the case of a specialty e-grocer have been presented. This line of thought can be supported by further research that incorporates and combines theoretical constructs from consumer behaviour theory, service marketing theory and resource-based theory.

- Finally, ergonomic changes occurring as a consequence of introducing home delivery directly from DC to the home need further examination. The ergonomic issues relate to the warehouse clerk and to the driver of the van from the DC to the household. The work of the warehouse clerk is similar to the work of clerks in ordinary grocery DCs, but the size of items is smaller, thus more items are handled. Whether this in ergonomic terms is more problematic depends on a number of factors in the total layout and set-up of the specific warehouse and needs to be clarified in specific studies in this context. If the process from DC to the household is compared between the two channels, the shop personnel in the shop based channel and the customer both take part in filling and emptying the shelves, whereas in the online system the driver carries the load all the way to the doorstep. In the offline system, carrying the load is undertaken by shop personnel and the customer and this task is only part of their daily physical activity, whereas the driver uses much of the day doing this task. This change should therefore be investigated from an ergonomic perspective, seeking the best system-wide solution. In addition, the environmental effect of driving directly from the DC or shop to the household has been studied and the results point to both positive (Orremo and Wallin 1999) and negative effects (PLS Consult and DMU 1996). Nevertheless, international comparative studies in this field need to be promoted. For example, we do not know whether the time potentially saved by the household when home shopping is instead used on activities that generate more transport kilometres compared to shopping in a brick-and-mortar shop.

NOTES

1. Rufat-Latre, What killed Webvan was bricks, not clicks. *Chicago Tribune.* 18/07/2001
2. Streamline operated unattended deliveries, however, including the costly Streamline (reception) box (Stahre 1998). Today unattended delivery without reception box is operating at e.g. Peapod.com that offers unattended delivery in most markets http://www.peapod.com/corpinfo/peapodFacts.pdf and Aarstiderne.com , a Danish specialty e-grocer.
3. One pound is calculated as € 1.45
4. In the US , however, it is nearly 60% lower based on data from Boyer, Frohlich and Hult (2005, p. 97) and chapter 9.
5. Se this website: http://corporate.ocado.com/ourcompany/dedicatedtohomedelivery.html
6. One dollar is calculated as € 0.78
7. Estimations presented by Niels Kornum on the Ebizz Øresund conference 18th November 2004, Copenhagen.
8. See also Chapter 2.
9. From the website: http://corporate.ocado.com/ourcompany/
10. This may cause the customer to shop less frequently, which then may reduce the share of spontaneous purchase?
11. http://www.peapod.com/corpinfo/GW_index.jhtml

REFERENCES

Baagø, Marie C and Andersen, Pernille (2001), *Aarstiderne - en økologisk virksomhed på vej mod Brand Religion* [Aarstiderne – an organic company heading towards Brand Religion]. Masters Thesis. Syddansk Universitet

Boyer, Kenneth K., Frohlich, Markham T. and Hult, Thomas. M. (2005), *Extending the Supply Chain*, AMACON, New York.

Boyer, Kenneth K. and Hult, Tomas. M. (2005), *Predicting Customer Loyalty for Online Purchases: An Examination of Pick Method and Customer Experience Level*, Michigan State University Working Paper

Carlheim-Gyllenskjold, Rutger and Rangefeld, Jens (2002), *Matomera*, Masters Thesis, Division of Packaging Logistics, Department of Design Sciences, Lund University.

Child, Peter N. (2002), 'Taking Tesco global'. *McKinsey Quarterly.* 3(7106143), 135 - 144.

Friese, S., Bjerre, M., Hansen, T., Kornum, N. and Sestoft, C. (2003), *E-bizz Øresund report. Barriers and Motivators of Online Grocery Shopping in Denmark,*

Research Report, No. 2003-09 January, Department of Marketing, Copenhagen Business School.

Frostling-Henningsson, Maria (2003), *Internet Grocery Shopping. A Necessity, A Pleasurable Adventure or an Act of Love*, Research Report No. 2003: 8, Stockholm University, School of Business.

Hansen, Torben (2002), *Forbrugeren og Internettet - en litteraturgennemgang og forslag til yderligere forskning* [The Consumer and the Internet - review and proposals for further research], Working Paper, Copenhagen Business School, Department of Marketing.

Hansen, Torben (2003), *Ebizz Øresund - The Online Consumer: Results from Two Scandinavian Surveys; Research Report January 2003*, Copenhagen: Copenhagen Business School.

Juul, Carsten (2001), *(Al magt til supermarkederne)*, [All power to the supermarkets] An interview concerning ISO.dk with Director Peter Midtgaard, ISO.

Kornum, Niels (2002), *Characteristics and Development of Store Based - and Specialty E-Grocer*. NOFOMA conference, Trondheim.

Kornum, Niels (2005), *Resource Dependence Theory in an E-grocery BTC Context - the Case of Specialty E-grocer X* in Deo Sharma and Jan Johansson (eds), Managing Customer Relationships with IT and Internet, Pergamon, Elsevier Science Ltd (Forthcoming)

Kornum, Niels, Bjerre, Mogens and Langberg, Robert (1999), *Elektronisk handel - udfordringer for logistik og distribution.* [E-commerce - Challenges for logistics and distribution], København: Forskningsministeriet og Foreningen af Dansk Internet Handel.

Kornum, Niels and Singh, Paul (2005), *Grocery E-commerce - Consumer Preferences in Three Countries* . Working Paper (Forthcoming).

Orremo, Frederik and Wallin, Claes (1999) *IT, mat och miljö - en miljökonsekvensanalys av elektronisk handel och dagligvaror,* [IT&C, Foods and the Environment - an investigation of the environmental effects of e-commerce and groceries] Publ no. ISRN LUTMDN/TMTP—5418—SE, Förpackningslogistik, Lunds Universitet.

PLS Consult A/S & DMU (1996) *Transportkonsekvenser af distancearbejde og teleindkøb* [Transport Effects from Work at Home and Homeshopping] Rapport for Transportrådet, December.

Ramaswamy, Kannan and Dikalov, Gennady (2001), *Tesco, PLC: From Mouse To House in Online Grocery Retailing*. Case, Thunderbird - The American Graduate School of International Management. A07-01-0011. 1-13.

Rogers, E.M. (1983), *Diffusion of Innovations*, 3rd ed., The Free Press, New York.

Rusbjerg, Jane (2005), *E-Grocers-Order Picking for BTC Customers*. Masters Thesis, Selection of non-confidential sections (in Danish)(Forthcoming).

Stahre, Fredrik (1998): *Streamline.* Working Paper, Linköping University

Yrjölä, Hannu (2003), *Supply Chain Considerations for Electronic Grocery Shopping*, PhD Dissertation, Helsinki.

Index

Aarstiderne.com 150-151, 155-156, 183,
    195, 199, 218, 261, 306-307,
    311-312, 314, 317
administrative costs, *see also* fixed costs
    195-197, 301, 303
advantages 2, 66, 90, 102-103, 117, 128,
    139, 142-145, 167, 183-184, 188,
    191, 198, 208, 224, 242-260,
    262-268, 295-296, 298, 300,
    303-304, 308, 312, 315
Albertson's 190, 203, 303-305
Amazon.com 11, 36, 161, 231
Argos.co.uk 10
Arstiderna.com 312
Asda.co.uk 13, 302
Assortment 1, 43, 54, 91, 184, 199, 204-
    205, 218, 261, 281, 283, 286, 292,
    303, 308, 313-314, 316-317, 320
attended delivery 5, 163, 172, 174,
    176-177, 209-212, 219-220,
    224-230, 298, 303, 308, 310-315

Barnes & Noble [barnesandnoble.com]
    11
basic groceries
    297
Billhalls.se 205
books 10, 76-77, 136, 158, 226, 231
Borders [borders.co.uk,
    bordersstores.co.uk] 11
Break-even / break even 1, 5, 162, 169,
    185, 187, 197-198, 217, 242, 253,
    302, 311

call centre *see also* help line 4, 300-301
cannibalisation 304, 309, 312
CD's 10
channel conflict 282, 316

compatibility, perceived 97, 99-100,
    106-110, 112-113, 115-116
complexity, perceived 99-102,
    107-110, 112-113, 116
consumer culture theory 127-128,
    130-131, 134, 157, 158
consumer preference 3, 6, 18, 34,
    137, 297, 318
consumer subject 123, 126-127, 132,
    134-138, 140-141, 144-145,
    147, 149-150, 152, 154
consumer values 122, 124-126, 129-
    133, 135-138, 142, 145-152
Coop / Coop Nettorvet 261, 264-265,
    304
cultural context 2, 4, 294, 297, 305
culture 122, 125-132, 134, 137, 140,
    144-145, 149, 153, 155-159,
    281-282, 285-286, 292
culture theory 127, 129, 131
customer acquisition 85, 95, 166, 308
customer relationship 169, 266, 319,
    323
customer retention 23, 26, 28-29,
    294, 308

DC-based picking 191
delivery at work 3, 65-66, 69-71,
    298-299
delivery charge / delivery fee 1-3, 21,
    40, 66, 82, 122, 150, 162-163,
    183-184, 197-199, 216,
    221-223, 225-227, 299-304,
    306, 309, 311, 315
delivery time 12, 14, 18-21, 23,
    25-29, 61, 162-163, 172-173,
    206-210, 212-214, 216-218,
    220-224, 226, 298, 301

Diamondorganics.com 236, 312
disadvantages, perceived relative 90
dry groceries 311

emotional 11, 294, 297, 300, 305-306,
312
expressfood.kf.se 205-206, 227

first-mover advantages 13, 241-254, 260-
263, 266-267, 295, 308-309, 315
first-time customers 305
fixed costs, *see also* administrative costs
47, 171, 173, 185, 187, 189, 301,
303

GotFruit.com 238, 312
grocery market 13, 122, 197, 203, 304

Harrisfarms.com 235, 237, 312
HarryandDavid.com 239-240, 317
helpline *see also* call centre 14, 17-19, 27
hemkop.se 205
home page, *see also* web page and web
site 197

ica.se 205
immature market 305, 309
in store picking, *see also* store based
picking 298
Internet experience 298
ISO.dk 155, 306, 309, 318
IT&C 188, 192, 194, 301, 318

Latent Class analysis 13, 23-24, 30, 33
Lifestyle 2, 127, 130, 140, 142, 145-146,
152, 156, 294, 297, 310-311
Loyalty 10, 12, 15, 83, 85, 89, 91, 93,
168, 170, 179, 254, 297, 317

Matomera.se 205-206
mature market 305, 307-309, 315
meal 297, 305-307, 314
multi channel 9, 12

Netxtra.se 205-206, 227

Ocado.com 182, 301-304, 307-308,
310, 317
Omahasteak.com 235-236, 312
ordering time 14, 18-22, 25-29, 164,
305
organic 138, 145, 183, 199, 218, 261,
303-304, 307, 312, 317

parcel distributor 311-312
Peapod.com 58, 160-161, 163, 167,
182, 206, 228, 317
political consumer 132-133, 149, 159
price premium 11, 91
product quality 3, 80-81, 84-85, 89,
91, 93, 297-298

quality 3, 14, 17-21, 23, 25-29, 59,
60-63, 67, 77, 297-298,
307-308, 310-311

recipes 168, 306
resource dependence 242, 257, 259,
263, 266-268, 316, 318
retail brand 10-11
Riverford.co.uk 312
Rivernene.co.uk 29

Sainsbury 13, 300-303
Segment 4, 13, 23-29, 31-32, 59, 65,
77, 80, 98-106, 109-117, 120,
127, 135, 198-199, 298, 300,
303, 308, 313, 314
service marketing 76, 316
service offering 297, 305, 311, 315
service quality 59, 63-64, 78, 82-83,
85, 89-90, 93-97, 158, 298
shopping basket 21, 26, 28-29, 40, 42,
46, 48, 51, 161-164, 170, 175,
180, 298, 314
specialty assortment 308, 312
specialty e-grocer 6, 199, 202, 266,
308, 310, 312, 315-318

specialty grocer 314
store based picking, *see also* in store
    picking 297, 303, 314
story telling 307
Streamline.com 59, 160, 168-170,
    172-173, 183, 185, 190, 193, 205,
    301, 310, 317, 319
subscribe, *see also* subscription
    144, 146, 180, 253, 263, 296, 306
subscription, *see also* subscribe
    69, 144, 151, 307
substitute – substitution 14, 18-21, 25-26,
    28, 30, 62, 165, 204, 255, 259,
    264, 298, 306
surprise 7, 47, 49, 145, 306-307
sustainable competitive advantage 92,
    255, 308-309

Tesco.com 1-3, 7, 11-13, 29, 35, 54, 56,
    58, 76, 160-161, 163, 167,
    173-174, 177, 181-184, 190,
    199-200, 202, 298-299, 302-305,
    308-309, 314, 317-318

time saving 84, 87, 166, 304
time window 5, 12, 164, 169, 174,
    176-177, 208, 212, 214-216,
    218-221, 223-227, 230, 305,
    307, 311, 317

unattended delivery 5, 172, 174,
    176-177, 190, 210-212, 295,
    299-301, 305-306, 317
utilitarian 149, 217, 300, 305

value density 312-313
value system 306-308, 310, 312
virtual warehouse 13

Waitrose 13, 161, 301-302
web page – web site *see also* home
    page 7, 9, 12-13, 20, 23, 29,
    86-87, 97, 103, 296, 301
Webvan 1, 6, 39, 160-163, 170, 173,
    183, 190, 193, 200, 202-203,
    205, 294, 317
willys.nu 205, 227